SQL Queries
2012 Joes 2 Pros®
Volume 3

Advanced Query Tools and Techniques for SQL Server 2012

(SQL Exam Prep Series 70-461 Volume 3 of 5)

By

Rick A. Morelan
MCDBA, MCTS, MCITP, MCAD, MOE, MCSE, MCSE+I

Pinal Dave
Founder of SQLAuthority.com

EAN: 978-1-939666-02-4

Rick A. Morelan
Info@Joes2Pros.com

Table of Contents

Chapter 7.   Creating Indexes **239**

Chapter 8.   Creating Indexes with Code **273**

Chapter 9.   Index Analysis

About the Authors

We write each book in this series to help anyone seeking knowledge about SQL Server – whether an intermediate looking to fill gaps in their knowledge, an expert looking for new features in the 2012 version of SQL Server, or even a developer picking up SQL Server as their second or third programming language. At the heart of the mission as an educator remains the dedication to helping people with the power of SQL Server. The goal of education is action.

Rick Morelan

In 1994, you could find Rick Morelan braving the frigid waters of the Bering Sea as an Alaskan commercial fisherman. His computer skills were non-existent at the time, so you might figure such beginnings seemed unlikely to lead him down the path to SQL Server expertise at Microsoft. However, every computer expert in the world today woke up at some point in their life knowing nothing about computers.

Making the change from fisherman seemed scary and took daily schooling at Catapult Software Training Institute. Rick got his lucky break in August of 1995, working his first database job at Microsoft. Since that time, Rick has worked more than 10 years at Microsoft and has attained over 30 Microsoft technical certifications in applications, networking, databases and .NET development.

His books are used the world over by individuals and educators to help people with little experience learn these technical topics and gain the ability to earn a Microsoft certification or have the confidence to do well in a job interview with their new found knowledge.

Rick's speaking engagements have included SQL PASS, SQL Saturdays and SQL Server Intelligence Conferences. In addition to these speaking engagements Rick gives back to the community by personally teaching students at both Bellevue College and MoreTechnology in Redmond, WA.

Pinal Dave

Pinal Dave is a technology enthusiast and avid blogger. Prior to joining Microsoft, his outstanding community service helped to earn several awards, including the Microsoft Most Valuable Professional in SQL Server Technology (3 continuous years) and the Community Impact Award as an Individual Contributor for 2010.

Playing an active role in the IT industry for over eight years, his career has taken him across the world working in both India and the US, primarily with SQL

Server Technology, from version 6.5 to its latest form. His early work experience includes being a Technology Evangelist with Microsoft and a Sr. Consultant with SolidQ, and he continues to work on performance tuning and optimization projects for high transactional systems.

Pinal's higher education degrees include a Master of Science from the University of Southern California, and a Bachelor of Engineering from Gujarat University. In addition to his degrees, Pinal holds multiple Microsoft certificates and helps to spread his knowledge as a regular speaker for many international events like TechEd, SQL PASS, MSDN, TechNet and countless user groups.

At the time of this writing, Pinal has co-authored three SQL Server books:

- o SQL Server Programming
- o SQL Wait Stats
- o SQL Server Interview Questions and Answers

Pinal's passion for the community drives him to share his training and knowledge and frequently writes on his blog http://blog.SQLAuthority.com covering various subjects related to SQL Server technology and Business Intelligence. As a very active member of the social media community it is easy to connect with him using one of these services:

- o Twitter: http://twitter.com/pinaldave
- o Facebook: http://facebook.com/SQLAuth

When he is not in front of a computer, he is usually travelling to explore hidden treasures in nature with his lovely daughter, Shaivi, and very supportive wife, Nupur.

Acknowledgements from Rick Morelan

As a book with a supporting web site, illustrations, media content and software scripts, it takes more than the usual author, illustrator and editor to put everything together into a great learning experience. Since my publisher has the more traditional contributor list available, I'd like to recognize the core team members:

Editor: Lori Stow
Technical Editor: Richard Stockhoff
Technical Review: Tony Smithlin
User Acceptance Testing: Sandra Howard

Thank you to all the teachers at Catapult Software Training Institute in the mid-1990s. What a great start to open my eyes. It landed me my first job at Microsoft by August of that year. A giant second wind came from Koenig-Solutions, which gives twice the training and attention for half the price of most other schools. Mr. Rohit Aggarwal is the visionary founder of this company based in New Delhi, India. Rohit's business model sits students down one-on-one with experts. Each expert dedicates weeks to help each new IT student succeed. The numerous twelve-hour flights I took to India to attend those classes were pivotal to my success. Whenever a new generation of software was released, I got years ahead of the learning curve by spending one or two months at Koenig.

Dr. James D. McCaffrey at Volt Technical Resources in Bellevue, Wash., taught me how to improve my own learning by teaching others. You'll frequently see me in his classroom because he makes learning fun. McCaffrey's unique style boosts the self-confidence of his students, and his tutelage has been essential to my own professional development. His philosophy inspires the *Joes 2 Pros* curriculum.

A giant second wind came from Koenig-Solutions, which gives twice the training and attention for half the price of most other schools. Mr. Rohit Aggarwal is the visionary founder of this company based in New Delhi, India. Rohit's business model sits students down one-on-one with experts. Each expert dedicates weeks to help each new IT student succeed. The numerous twelve-hour flights I took to India to attend those classes were pivotal to my success. Whenever a new generation of software was released, I got years ahead of the learning curve by spending one or two months at Koenig.

Dr. James D. McCaffrey at Volt Technical Resources in Bellevue, Wash., taught me how to improve my own learning by teaching others. You'll frequently see me in his classroom because he makes learning fun. McCaffrey's unique style boosts the self-confidence of his students, and his tutelage has been essential to my own professional development. His philosophy inspires the *Joes 2 Pros* curriculum.

Introduction

Sure I wrote great queries and was always able to deliver precisely the data that everyone wanted. But a "wake up call" occasion on December 26, 2006 forced me to get better acquainted with the internals of SQL Server. That challenge was a turning point for me and my knowledge of SQL Server performance and architecture. Almost everyone from the workplace was out of town or taking time off for the holidays, and I was in the office for what I expected would be a very quiet day. I received a call that a query which had been working fine for years was suddenly crippling the system. The request was not for me to write one of my brilliant queries but to troubleshoot the existing query and get it back to running well. Until that moment, I hadn't spent any time tuning SQL Server – that was always done by another team member. To me, tuning seemed like a "black box" feat accomplished by unknown formulas that I would never understand. On my own on that Boxing Day, I learned the mysteries behind tuning SQL Server. In truth, it's really just like driving a car. By simply turning the key and becoming acquainted with a few levers and buttons, you can drive anywhere you want. With SQL Server, there are just a few key rules and tools which will put you in control of how things run on your system.

Skills Needed for this Book

If you have no SQL coding knowledge, then I recommend trying out one of these excellent books that are written specifically to help you get off on the right foot:

- o The gateway to first get into the groove of coding is…
  - *Beginning SQL 2008 Joes 2 Pros* (ISBN 978-1-4392-5317-5) or
  - *SQL Queries 2012 Joes 2 Pros Volume1*

- o To get really good at writing more advanced queries, then a great starting point before tackling the architecture and programming topics are….
  - *SQL Queries Joes 2 Pros* (ISBN 978-1-4392-5318-2) or
  - *SQL Queries Joes 2 Pros 2012 Volume2*

About this Book

As companies grow and do more business, the data they store in databases similarly grows. If you want to be a go-to person on the inner workings of SQL Server, then this book will be your partner in achieving that goal. If you have completed the *SQL Queries 2012 Joes 2 Pros Volume 2* book, you already have written some advanced queries. This book builds on that knowledge and will show you more about the parts of SQL Server at work behind the scenes when you are running queries and creating new database objects. Most importantly, you will learn how to make the essential queries for your business run most efficiently and at the fastest speed possible.

It is time for books and schools to compete on quality and effectiveness and not a mass marketing push. The more this book succeeds, the more we will get their attention about what people really need and are demanding. To put it simply, there is a recipe for success – you are empowered to choose your own ingredients. Just learn the lesson, do the lab, study the Points to Ponder, and play the review game at the end of each Chapter.

Most of the exercises in this book are designed around proper database practices in the workplace. The workplace also offers common challenges and process changes over time. For example, it is good practice to use numeric data for IDs. If you have ever seen a Canadian postal code (zip code), you see the need for character data in relational information. You will occasionally see an off-the-beaten-path strategy demonstrated so you know how to approach a topic in a job interview or workplace assignment.

I'm often asked about the Points to Ponder feature, which is popular with both beginners and experienced developers. Some have asked why I don't simply call it a "Summary Page". While it's true that the Points to Ponder page generally captures key points from each section, I frequently include options or technical insights not contained in the Chapter. Often these are points which I or my students have found helpful and which I believe will enhance your understanding of SQL Server.

The *Joes 2 Pros* series began in the summer of 2006. The project started as a few easy-to-view labs to transform the old, dry text reading into easier and fun lessons for the classroom. The labs grew into stories. The stories grew into Chapters. In 2008, many people whose lives and careers had been improved through my classes convinced me to write a book to reach out to more people. In 2009 the first book began in full gear until its completion (*Beginning SQL Joes 2 Pros*, ISBN 978-1-4392-5317-5).

How to Use the Downloadable Labs

Clear content and high-resolution multimedia videos, coupled with code samples and lab work will help you during this journey. To give you all this and save printing costs, all supporting files are available with a free download from www.Joes2Pros.com. A breakdown for these supporting files is listed below:

Training videos: To get you started, the first three Chapters of video format are available to download for free. The videos demonstrate concepts, review the Points to Ponder, and show Labs along with tips from the appendix. Ranging from 3-15 minutes in length, they use special effects to highlight key points. A setup video demonstrating how to download and use all other files is included with the free download. A big benefit of each video is that you can go at your own pace and pause or replay within lessons as needed.

Answer Key files: Written as T-SQL scripts, these files allow you to verify your completed work has performed correctly. Another helpful use for independent students is that these scripts are available for peeking at if you get really stuck.

Resource files: These files hold the few non-SQL script files needed for some specific labs. You will be prompted by the text each time you need to download and utilize a resource file from this folder.

Lab Setup files: SQL Server is a database engine and we need to practice on a database. The primary sample database used in this series is for a fictitious travel booking company named Joes 2 Pros. The name of the database, JProCo, is a shortened version of the company name. Multiple setup scripts to prepare the JProCo database as you advance through each chapter and Skill Check are available in this folder.

Bug Catcher files: Ready to take your new skills out for a test drive? This folder has slides for the ever popular Bug Catcher game, an interactive approach to review the skills you have learned during each Chapter.

AdventureWorks2012: While JProCo is the primary database used with this book, another database, AdventureWorks2012, is required to be installed in order to do some of the lessons. Download the AdventureWorks2012 sample database and follow the installation instructions available at Microsoft's CodePlex website http://msftdbprodsamples.codeplex.com/releases/view/55330.

What this Book is Not

This is not a memorization book. Rather, this is a skills book to make preparing for the certification test a familiarization process. This book prepares you to apply what you've learned to answer SQL questions in the job setting. The highest hopes are that your progress and level of SQL knowledge will soon have business managers seeking your expertise to provide the reporting and information vital to their decision making. It's a good feeling to achieve and to help at the same time. Many students comment that the training method used in *Joes 2 Pros* was what finally helped them achieve their goal of certification and career advancement.

When you go through the *Joes 2 Pros* series and really know this material, you deserve a fair shot at SQL certification. Use only authentic testing engines to measure your skill. Show you know it for real. At the time of this writing, MeasureUp® at http://www.measureup.com provides a good test preparation simulator. The company's test pass guarantee makes it a very appealing option.

Chapter 1.   Table Data Actions

In this book, tables are the SQL Server objects most frequently seen supplying data to our queries. Other objects inside SQL Server, such as stored procedures, views, and functions can also return data to a query window.

When joining a table to one of these objects, a regular join may not always work. It is possible to join a table to a view, but with other objects we may need an alternate solution. In this chapter we will explore two solutions first introduced with the release of SQL Server 2005, CROSS APPLY and OUTER APPLY. Another focus for this chapter will be in distinguishing between the similarities and differences when using DELETE and TRUNCATE and their effects upon table data.

The term truncating, is often used interchangeably in conversation with deleting. Sometimes we also hear the terms depopulating or un-populating in reference to deleting. The latter two terms are not SQL Server keywords. These terms all relate to the idea of emptying data from a table, however, SQL Server professionals need to be clear on what these distinctions are and when to use them effectively.

To populate, is a generic geek speak term for entering data into a container, such as a table, field, form, or variable. Back in *SQL Queries 2012 Joes 2 Pros Volume 2* and in Chapter 1 of this book, we often describe creating a table (using the DDL statement CREATE TABLE) and then populating it. Unpopulated, is another geek speak term usually describing a new container where no data has been entered yet. Depopulating describes the process of generically removing data from a container.

This chapter will add new tools to our SQL Server toolbox and will increase a growing understanding of effectively manipulating and handling table data.

READER NOTE: *Please run the SQLQueries2012Vol3Chapter1.0Setup.sql script in order to follow along with the examples in the first section of Chapter 1. All scripts mentioned in this chapter may be found at www.Joes2Pros.com. Also, on our site there is a selection of free videos to watch to help you get started. Our entire video instruction library is available via online subscription and DVD.*

Deleting, Updating and Truncating

What is the difference between evacuating a building and imploding a building? In either case there are no people in the building. In the case of evacuating the building it's still standing there, even though it is unpopulated. When imploding a building the structure will no longer exist. Sometimes we want to empty a table and sometimes we want the entire table gone and want to replace it with a new one of the same name.

Deleting vs. Truncating

Since our code in this section involves the destruction of tables, we will use a new JProCo table created specifically for these examples. Go ahead and run the setup script for this chapter, SQLQueriesChapter1.0Setup.sql, and this table will appear in the Object Explorer for the JProCo database.

Using the Object Explorer window, locate the Contractor table within the JProCo database, which was created using the following code:

```
USE JProCo
GO

CREATE TABLE Contractor (
ctrID INT IDENTITY PRIMARY KEY,
LastName VARCHAR(30) NOT NULL,
FirstName VARCHAR(30) NOT NULL,
HireDate DATETIME NOT NULL,
LocationID INT NULL)
GO

INSERT INTO Contractor VALUES
('Disarray','Major','01/02/2008', 1),
('Morelan','Rick','02/27/2008', 1),
('Plummer','Joe','01/13/2008', 2),
('Kim','Gene','01/13/2008', 1)
```

The Contractor table has one auto-populating identity field (ctrID) and four other fields. We can delete, insert, and update records in this table all we like.

We've already worked quite a bit with DELETE. Recall DELETE is a DML statement, meaning that it removes data but not structure.

READER NOTE: *To remove structure, use the DDL statement DROP (i.e., DROP TABLE, DROP DATABASE, DROP VIEW, etc.).*

We can perform the following actions with the DELETE statement:

- o DELETE all records in a table:

```
--Removes all records: Table is empty but intact
DELETE FROM TableName
```

- o DELETE specific records in a table (filtering with a WHERE clause):

```
--Removes records with LocationID 2, or greater
DELETE FROM TableName
WHERE LocationID > 1
```

READER NOTE: *Recall the FROM keyword is optional with a DELETE statement. However, it is recommended to use it by first writing the query as a SELECT statement to safely preview what the impact will be on the table before running the actual DELETE statement.*

Now that we've recapped what we know about DELETE, let's run some examples using the new practice table, Contractor.

```
SELECT * FROM Contractor
```

	ctrID	LastName	FirstName	Hiredate	LocationID
1	1	Disarray	Major	2008-01-02 00:00:00.000	1
2	2	Morelan	Rick	2008-02-27 00:00:00.000	1
3	3	Plummer	Joe	2008-01-13 00:00:00.000	2
4	4	Kim	Gene	2008-01-13 00:00:00.000	1

4 rows

Figure 1.1 The Contractor table has one auto-populating field (ctrID) and four other fields.

What happens when we run this DELETE? All records and data are removed.

```
DELETE FROM Contractor
```

Pretty straightforward – the structure is intact, but the table is empty.

```
SELECT * FROM Contractor
```

ctrID	LastName	FirstName	Hiredate	LocationID

0 rows

Figure 1.2 The Contractor table is empty, but the structure is intact.

Chapter 1. Table Data Actions

Now what happens when we INSERT records back into the table? Will the identity field (ctrID) still show Major Disarray having a ctrID of 1? Check the results of the query in Figure 1.3.

```
INSERT INTO Contractor VALUES
('Disarray','Major','01/02/2008', 1),
('Morelan','Rick','02/27/2008', 1),
('Plummer','Joe','01/13/2008', 2),
('Kim','Gene','01/13/2008', 1)

SELECT * FROM Contractor
```

	ctrID	LastName	FirstName	hiredate	LocationID
1	5	Disarray	Major	2008-01-02 00:00:00.000	1
2	6	Morelan	Rick	2008-02-27 00:00:00.000	1
3	7	Plummer	Joe	2008-01-13 00:00:00.000	2
4	8	Kim	Gene	2008-01-13 00:00:00.000	1
					4 rows

Figure 1.3 The identity field kept right on counting after the DELETE.

No, Major Disarray does not show as ctrID 1. He now shows as ctrID 5. When running a DELETE statement and re-inserting records into a table, the identity field does not reset back to its initial value. Instead, it resumes right where the last count left off before the DELETE statement was executed (Figure 1.3).

Now let's use TRUNCATE to remove all records from the Contractor table.

```
TRUNCATE TABLE Contractor
```

Notice the TRUNCATE confirmation message didn't supply a count of affected rows. It simply wiped out all the data in the table regardless of how many rows there were.

READER NOTE: *TRUNCATE is a DDL statement, and its messages are similar to the other DDL statements (CREATE, ALTER, and DROP).*

Now run the SELECT statement and notice there is no data remaining.

```
SELECT *
FROM Contractor
```

ctrID	LastName	FirstName	hiredate	LocationID
				0 rows

Figure 1.4 No data remains in Contractor following the TRUNCATE TABLE statement.

18
www.Joes2Pros.com

Now run the insert statement to insert the four rows:

```
INSERT INTO Contractor VALUES
('Disarray','Major','01/02/2008', 1),
('Morelan','Rick','02/27/2008', 1),
('Plummer','Joe','01/13/2008', 2),
('Kim','Gene','01/13/2008', 1)
```

TRUNCATE caused the counter field to reset and start the count all over.

```
SELECT * FROM Contractor
```

	ctrID	LastName	FirstName	hiredate	LocationID
1	1	Disarray	Major	2008-01-02 00:00:00.000	1
2	2	Morelan	Rick	2008-02-27 00:00:00.000	1
3	3	Plummer	Joe	2008-01-13 00:00:00.000	2
4	4	Kim	Gene	2008-01-13 00:00:00.000	1

4 rows

Figure 1.5 TRUNCATE caused the identity field to reset the count back to its seed value (1).

All rows in the Contractor table are intact and back in their original state. Let's attempt to have TRUNCATE remove only some rows (Figure 1.6).

```
TRUNCATE TABLE Contractor
WHERE LocationID > 1
```

Messages
Msg 156, Level 15, State 1, Line 2
Incorrect syntax near the keyword 'WHERE'.

0 rows

Figure 1.6 TRUNCATE TABLE cannot be used with criteria.

We get an error, because TRUNCATE cannot use criteria, as it is designed to destroy all of the data in a table, not just parts of it.

DELETE works with criteria and removes only the rows you specify.

```
DELETE FROM Contractor
WHERE LocationID > 1
```

Messages
(1 row(s) affected)

0 rows

Figure 1.7 DELETE works with criteria and removes only the rows you specify.

So far we've seen that DELETE and TRUNCATE can both remove all data from a table while leaving the structure intact. Neither DELETE nor TRUNCATE changes table structure or permissions.

TRUNCATE is a DDL statement, which means it pertains to table structure. When running TRUNCATE with other statements, it is necessary to end the TRUNCATE statement with a GO to signal the end of the batch. DELETE is a DML statement, which means it pertains to data manipulation – not structure. It behaves like the other DML statements, SELECT, INSERT, and UPDATE.

With respect to data, TRUNCATE is more of a blunt instrument and simply wipes out all the data in one move. It doesn't keep track of the number of rows it removes. DELETE, however, is careful with data because it is a DML statement. It tracks and logs all the changes it makes, which is why the counter of the identity field kept on counting (i.e., it did not reset) when we deleted and then re-inserted rows into the Contractor table.

This hints at a significant difference between DELETE and TRUNCATE. Behind the scenes, TRUNCATE runs a lot faster than DELETE. The impact is less noticeable in the small-scale examples we demonstrated in this chapter, however with large tables the impact can be quite dramatic. This is because TRUNCATE doesn't log the activity as a transaction. It simply wipes out all the data as if the table was dropped and re-created while still preserving all existing permissions.

This means that for tables where the transaction log is important, the use of TRUNCATE TABLE may not be advisable.

Table 1.1 A summary of DELETE versus TRUNCATE TABLE statements.

DELETE	TRUNCATE TABLE
DML statement	DDL statement
Can use WHERE clause criteria to delete only certain records	Can only remove all records from the table
Logs each transaction (slower)	Only page deallocation is logged (faster)
Easier to rollback	Cannot be rolled back; Can only be restored from backup
Does not reset identity field counter	Resets the identity counter to seed value
Can be used with triggers	Cannot be used if triggers are present
Can be used with tables involved in replication and log shipping	Cannot use on a table that is set up for replication or log shipping
Can delete records with foreign key (FK) constraints	Cannot truncate a table containing foreign key (FK) constraints

READER NOTE: *In Volume 2, Chapter 14 of SQL Queries 2012 Joes 2 Pros, we saw another capability of the DELETE statement. When used in conjunction with the OUTPUT clause, the DELETE statement can show a copy of the deleted records. This ability allows these records to be simply reviewed and discarded or a copy can be retained for tracking purposes.*

Lab 1.1: Deleting, Updating and Truncating

Lab Prep: Each lab has one or more Skill Checks. Start with Skill Check 1 and proceed until reaching the Points to Ponder section.

Before beginning this lab, verify that SQL Server 2012 is properly installed and operating. Before running the lab setup script for resetting the database (SQLQueries2012Vol3Chapter1.1Setup.sql), please make sure to close all query windows within SSMS. An open query window pointing to a database context can lock that database preventing it from updating when the script is executing. A simple way to assure all query windows are closed, is to exit out of SSMS, then open a new instance of SSMS, and lastly run the setup script.

Since this is the first lab, please watch the first few videos relating to this book by visiting the www.Joes2Pros.com website.

Skill Check 1: Write a SQL statement to remove records from the Contractor table where the LocationID is not 1. When done, the results should resemble Figure 1.8.

```
SELECT * FROM Contractor
```

	ctrID	LastName	LastName	Hiredate	LocationID
1	1	Disarray	Major	2008-01-02 00:00:00.000	1
2	2	Morelan	Rick	2008-02-27 00:00:00.000	1
3	4	Kim	Gene	2008-01-13 00:00:00.000	1
					3 rows

Figure 1.8 Remove all LocationID except for LocationID 1.

Skill Check 2: Remove all records from the Contractor table in the fastest possible manner so that all identity fields will reset back to the seed value (1). Insert a new Contractor named Bill Barker for LocationID 1, with today's date. Bill will receive a ctrID of 1 after the insert. When done, the results should resemble Figure 1.9.

```
SELECT * FROM Contractor
```

	ctrID	LastName	LastName	Hiredate	LocationID
1	1	Barker	Bill	2012-05-13 14:20:51.500	1
					1 rows

Figure 1.9 Remove all data and then insert the new Contractor Bill Barker in Location 1.

Answer Code: The T-SQL code to this lab can be found in the downloadable files in a file named Lab1.1_TruncatingData.sql.

Points to Ponder - Deleting, Updating and Truncating

1. There are two ways to empty records from a table: DELETE and TRUNCATE TABLE.

2. TRUNCATE TABLE is similar to DELETE but there are significant differences between the two.

3. DELETE is a DML statement. TRUNCATE is a DDL statement.

4. DELETE can use a WHERE clause to apply criteria and remove only the specified rows. TRUNCATE cannot be used with criteria.

5. DELETE does not reset the counters, whereas TRUNCATE will reset all counters.

6. TRUNCATE TABLE statements cannot be used for tables involved in replication or log shipping, since both depend on the transaction log to keep databases consistent. DELETE can be used on these tables and is slower because it must log every transaction (Note: Replication and log shipping are beyond the scope of this book).

7. TRUNCATE TABLE statements cannot be used for tables containing foreign key (FK) constraints.

8. TRUNCATE TABLE statements cannot be used on tables impacted by triggers.

9. With larger tables, TRUNCATE is much faster than DELETE.

Cross Apply

As we learned earlier, other objects (beside tables), such as stored procedures, views, and functions can return data to a query window in SQL Server.

When joining a table to one of these objects, a regular join may not always work, and some objects may need an alternate method. In this chapter we will explore two of those alternative ways, CROSS APPLY and OUTER APPLY.

Let's begin with some familiar tables to build a path to the non-table object we will need. We'll first get all records and all fields from the SalesInvoice table.

```
SELECT * FROM SalesInvoice
```

	InvoiceID	OrderDate	PaidDate	CustomerID	Comment
1	1	2009-01-03...	2009-01-11...	472	NULL
2	2	2009-01-04...	2009-02-01...	388	NULL
3	3	2009-01-04...	2009-02-14...	279	NULL
4	4	2009-01-04...	2009-02-08...	309	NULL
5	5	2009-01-05...	2009-02-10...	757	NULL

1885 rows

Figure 1.10 We are unable to see purchase details in the SalesInvoice table.

Looking at the first invoice from Customer 472, there is very little detail. We can't see how many items or quantities they bought. For this level of detail, we need to join it to the SalesInvoiceDetail table (Figure 1.11).

```
SELECT * FROM SalesInvoice AS si
INNER JOIN SalesInvoiceDetail AS sd
ON si.InvoiceID = sd.InvoiceID
```

	InvoiceID	OrderDate	PaidDate	CustomerID	Comment	InvoiceDetailID	InvoiceID	ProductID	Quantity	UnitDiscount
1	1	2009-01-03 00:00:00.000	2009-01-11 03:22:44.587	472	NULL	1	1	76	2	0.00
2	1	2009-01-03 00:00:00.000	2009-01-11 03:22:44.587	472	NULL	2	1	77	3	0.00
3	1	2009-01-03 00:00:00.000	2009-01-11 03:22:44.587	472	NULL	3	1	78	6	0.00
4	1	2009-01-03 00:00:00.000	2009-01-11 03:22:44.587	472	NULL	4	1	71	5	0.00
5	1	2009-01-03 00:00:00.000	2009-01-11 03:22:44.587	472	NULL	5	1	72	4	0.00
6	2	2009-01-04 02:22:41.473	2009-02-01 04:15:34.590	388	NULL	6	2	73	2	0.00
7	3	2009-01-04 05:33:01.150	2009-02-14 13:45:02.580	279	NULL	7	3	74	3	0.00
8	4	2009-01-04 22:06:58.657	2009-02-08 22:06:14.247	309	NULL	8	4	14	3	0.00

Figure 1.11 Join the SalesInvoice table to the SalesInvoiceDetail table to bring in more detail.

As we can see, InvoiceID 1 contained quite a few products on it (ProductID 76 ordered twice, several of ProductID 77, etc.). InvoiceID 2 contained just one product ordered, as did InvoiceID 3.

It would be nice to see the natural table order to see how much the InvoiceID 1 order amounted to. We've got the ProductID but not the price. So we need a join to the CurrentProducts table.

```
SELECT * FROM SalesInvoice AS si
INNER JOIN SalesInvoiceDetail AS sd
ON si.InvoiceID = sd.InvoiceID
INNER JOIN CurrentProducts AS cp
ON cp.ProductID = sd.ProductID
```

	InvoiceID	OrderDate	PaidDate	CustomerID	Comment	InvoiceDetailID	InvoiceID	ProductID	Quantity	UnitDiscount
1	1	2009-01-03 00:00:00.000	2009-01-11 03:22:44.587	472	NULL	1	1	76	2	0.00
2	1	2009-01-03 00:00:00.000	2009-01-11 03:22:44.587	472	NULL	2	1	77	3	0.00
3	1	2009-01-03 00:00:00.000	2009-01-11 03:22:44.587	472	NULL	3	1	78	6	0.00
4	1	2009-01-03 00:00:00.000	2009-01-11 03:22:44.587	472	NULL	4	1	71	5	0.00
5	1	2009-01-03 00:00:00.000	2009-01-11 03:22:44.587	472	NULL	5	1	72	4	0.00
6	2	2009-01-04 02:22:41.473	2009-02-01 04:15:34.590	388	NULL	6	2	73	2	0.00
7	3	2009-01-04 05:33:01.150	2009-02-14 13:45:02.580	279	NULL	7	3	74	3	0.00
8	4	2009-01-04 22:06:58.657	2009-02-08 22:06:14.247	309	NULL	8	4	14	3	0.00

Figure 1.12 Join the CurrentProducts table to the query in order to see pricing.

Now we see some pricing data, but we are also getting every field from every table, which is a lot to look at. The natural sort of this query is on ProductID, although we need the records to appear in order of InvoiceID, so we can see the InvoiceID 1 items together. We will ORDER BY InvoiceID and narrow the fields to show only the InvoiceID, OrderDate, ProductID, Quantity, ProductName and RetailPrice.

```
SELECT si.InvoiceID, si.CustomerID, si.OrderDate,
sd.ProductID, sd.Quantity, cp.ProductName, cp.RetailPrice
FROM SalesInvoice AS si
INNER JOIN SalesInvoiceDetail AS sd
ON si.InvoiceID = sd.InvoiceID
INNER JOIN CurrentProducts AS cp
ON cp.ProductID = sd.ProductID
ORDER BY si.InvoiceID
```

	InvoiceID	CustomerID	OrderDate	ProductID	RetailPrice
1	1	472	2009-01-03 00:00:00.000	71	309.30
2	1	472	2009-01-03 00:00:00.000	72	556.74
3	1	472	2009-01-03 00:00:00.000	76	130.404
4	1	472	2009-01-03 00:00:00.000	77	163.005
5	1	472	2009-01-03 00:00:00.000	78	293.409
6	2	388	2009-01-04 02:22:41.473	73	32.601

6960 rows

Figure 1.13 Narrow the field selection and use ORDER BY InvoiceID to organize the results.

We can see exactly when things were ordered, how many were ordered, and individual line item prices. There isn't a total price column, so we'll manually add the individual retail prices to get a total amount for InvoiceID 1 ($1452.858).

Detailed reports like this are often built to narrow down the focus to one particular customer. Let's take a look at a report for CustomerID 4.

```
SELECT si.InvoiceID, si.CustomerID, si.OrderDate,
sd.ProductID, sd.Quantity, cp.ProductName, cp.RetailPrice
FROM SalesInvoice AS si
INNER JOIN SalesInvoiceDetail AS sd
ON si.InvoiceID = sd.InvoiceID
INNER JOIN CurrentProducts AS cp
ON cp.ProductID = sd.ProductID
WHERE si.CustomerID = 4
```

	InvoiceID	CustomerID	OrderDate	ProductID	Quantity	ProductName	RetailPrice
1	811	4	2010-10-30 20:52:58.477	53	2	History Tour 1 Week Canada	566.435
2	1509	4	2012-04-24 19:02:28.210	50	5	History Tour 2 Days Canada	203.9166

Figure 1.14 Narrow down the results to show just invoice activity for CustomerID 4.

It looks like CustomerID 4 has ordered on two different invoices. Now that's a pretty nifty report. By simply changing the filter on this query, we can see invoice details for CustomerID 1, CustomerID 2, CustomerID 3, and so forth.

Another way to view this handy report is by creating a table function. The combination of tables we just worked with are contained in the table function **fn_GetCustomerOrders()**. This table function was created when running the chapter reset script and now appears in our Object Explorer (Figure 1.15). We can navigate to it by using this path:

Object Explorer > Databases > JProCo > Programmability > Functions > Table-valued Functions > choose dbo.fn_GetCustomerOrders and press F7 to open the Object Explorer Details tab > double-click the parameters folder to view what parameters are required.

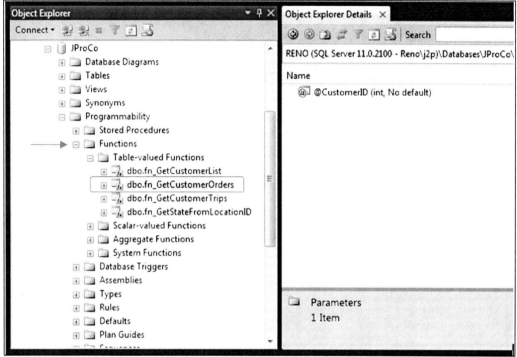

Figure 1.15 Path to locate the dbo.fn_GetCustomerOrders()function using Object Explorer.

User defined functions were first introduced in SQL Server 200 *(Functions will be covered in depth in a subsequent book in the Joes2Pros series)* Within the Functions folder of the JProCo database, it is possible to navigate to several table-valued functions, including dbo.fn_GetCustomerOrders().

READER NOTE: *To peek at the code used to create this function, right-click dbo.fn_GetCustomerOrders(), and then SELECT the following: **Script Function As > Create To > New Query Editor Window**.*

This table-valued function will produce a detailed report of all the invoices and all the products on those invoices and the amounts for any given customer passed into the function. Not only that, it also calculates the total spent on that invoice.

Let's pass the value 3 into the function and see the report for CustomerID 3.

```
SELECT * FROM fn_GetCustomerOrders(3)
```

	InvoiceID	CustomerID	OrderDate	ProductID	Product Name	Quantity	Retail Price	Total Invoice
1	443	3	2010-01-03 21:06:28.120	29	Underwater Tour 1 Week Scandinavia	2	580.59	1161.18
2	443	3	2010-01-03 21:06:28.120	61	Ocean Cruise Tour 1 Day West Coast	4	122.441	489.764
3	443	3	2010-01-03 21:06:28.120	49	History Tour 1 Day Canada	3	113.287	339.861
4	443	3	2010-01-03 21:06:28.120	25	Underwater Tour 1 Day Scandinavia	4	116.118	464.472
5	828	3	2010-11-11 16:26:37.253	69	Ocean Cruise Tour 3 Days East Coast	2	185.58	371.16
6	828	3	2010-11-11 16:26:37.253	30	Underwater Tour 2 Weeks Scandinavia	2	1045.062	2090.124
7	949	3	2011-02-11 16:51:09.897	49	History Tour 1 Day Canada	3	113.287	339.861

Figure 1.16 Pass the value 3 into the function to see the report for Customer 3.

Likewise, entering a value of 2 will provide results for CustomerID 2. While it would be nice to see the customer name, it does not appear that the function provides this info for us.

```
SELECT * FROM fn_GetCustomerOrders(2)
```

	InvoiceID	CustomerID	OrderDate	ProductID	Product Name	Quantity	Retail Price	Total Invoice
1	943	2	2011-02-07 02:45:03.840	72	Ocean Cruise Tour 2 Weeks East Coast	4	556.74	2226.96

Figure 1.17 The function fn_GetCustomerOrders() doesn't contain the customer name.

We can take a look directly at the Customer table and figure out what the name is for CustomerID 2.

```
SELECT * FROM Customer
WHERE CustomerID = 2
```

	CustomerID	CustomerType	FirstName	LastName	CompanyName
1	2	Consumer	Lee	Young	NULL
					1 rows

Figure 1.18 Run just the Customer query to see the name of CustomerID 2 (Lee Young).

CustomerID 2 is Lee Young. So the question is, how can we join a table to a function? Let's begin by trying a regular join (Figure 1.19).

```
SELECT * FROM Customer AS cu
INNER JOIN dbo.fn_GetCustomerOrders(2) AS fn
ON cu.CustomerID = fn.CustomerID
```

	CustomerID	CustomerType	FirstName	LastName	CompanyName	InvoiceID
1	2	Consumer	Lee	Young	NULL	943
						1 rows

Figure 1.19 A regular INNER JOIN works, but only one value may be included as a parameter.

If we want all the records from both result sets what do we join them on? We might be tempted to try connecting them using cu.CustomerID, but that won't work, not with an INNER JOIN (Figure 1.20).

READER NOTE: *Functions do not support passing a value through an ON clause.*

```
SELECT * FROM Customer AS cu
INNER JOIN dbo.fn_GetCustomerOrders(cu.CustomerID) AS fn
ON cu.CustomerID = fn.CustomerID
```

Messages
Msg 4104, Level 16, State 1, Line 3
The multi-part identifier "cu.CustomerID" could not be bound.

0 rows

Figure 1.20 An attempt to join the Customer table and function by passing a value fails.

Now change the INNER JOIN to a CROSS APPLY. This will take all the CustomerIDs and pass them into the function (Figure 1.21).

```
SELECT * FROM Customer AS cu
CROSS APPLY dbo.fn_GetCustomerOrders(cu.CustomerID)
```

	CustomerID	CustomerType	FirstName	LastName	CompanyName	InvoiceID
1	597	Consumer	Thomas	Anderson	NULL	9
2	736	Consumer	William	Carter	NULL	10
3	47	Consumer	Sarah	Campbell	NULL	15
4	251	Consumer	Deborah	Moore	NULL	19
5	529	Consumer	Carol	Smith	NULL	20
6	151	Consumer	Carol	Young	NULL	22

6959 rows

Figure 1.21 CROSS APPLY successfully joins the Customer table to the function.

Success! The table is now joined to the function. **CROSS APPLY is like an INNER JOIN between a table and a function.** Let's add an ORDER BY, since the natural sort of this function appears to be on ProductID (Figure 1.22).

```
SELECT * FROM Customer AS cu
CROSS APPLY dbo.fn_GetCustomerOrders(cu.CustomerID)
ORDER BY cu.CustomerID, InvoiceID
```

	CustomerID	CustomerType	FirstName	LastName	CompanyName	InvoiceID
1	1	Consumer	Mark	Williams	NULL	824
2	1	Consumer	Mark	Williams	NULL	1027
3	1	Consumer	Mark	Williams	NULL	1401
						6959 rows

Figure 1.22 Adding an ORDER BY clause to order results by cu.CustomerID and InvoiceID.

CustomerID 1, Mark Williams, had quite a bit of invoice activity, so the first 19 lines of our results contain his invoices and order totals. Let's take a look at the next few customers on the list (Figure 1.23).

```
SELECT * FROM Customer AS cu
CROSS APPLY dbo.fn_GetCustomerOrders(cu.CustomerID)
WHERE cu.CustomerID IN (2,3,4)
ORDER BY cu.CustomerID, InvoiceID
```

	CustomerID	CustomerType	FirstName	LastName	InvoiceID	TotalInvoice
1	2	Consumer	Lee	Young	943	2226.96
2	3	Consumer	Patricia	Martin	443	1161.18
3	3	Consumer	Patricia	Martin	443	489.764
4	3	Consumer	Patricia	Martin	443	339.861
5	3	Consumer	Patricia	Martin	443	464.472
6	3	Consumer	Patricia	Martin	828	371.16
7	3	Consumer	Patricia	Martin	828	2090.124
8	3	Consumer	Patricia	Martin	949	339.861
9	4	Consumer	Mary	Lopez	811	1132.87
10	4	Consumer	Mary	Lopez	1509	1019.583
						10 rows

Figure 1.23 The CROSS APPLY results for CustomerID 2, CustomerID 3 and CustomerID 4.

We see CustomerID 2, Lee Young has ordered one item, so he appears only once along with his total. CustomerID 3, Patricia Martin, ordered several items on three invoices. As we saw before, CustomerID 4, Mary Lopez, ordered two products, each on a different invoice. Her result is similar to that from the original query in Figure 1.14, except we also have a total amount for each invoice (Figure 1.23).

CROSS APPLY finds matching records between a table and a table-valued function the same way an INNER JOIN finds the matching records between two tables. The distinction is that CROSS APPLY passes the match criteria directly into the function rather than needing to use an ON clause required by join statements.

Lab 1.2: Cross Apply

Lab Prep: Each lab has one or more Skill Checks. Start with Skill Check 1 and proceed until reaching the Points to Ponder section.

Before beginning this lab, verify that SQL Server 2012 is properly installed and operating. Before running the lab setup script for resetting the database (SQLQueries2012Vol3Chapter1.2Setup.sql), please make sure to close all query windows within SSMS. An open query window pointing to a database context can lock that database preventing it from updating when the script is executing. A simple way to assure all query windows are closed, is to exit out of SSMS, then open a new instance of SSMS, and lastly run the setup script.

Skill Check 1: The function dbo.fn_GetStateFromLocationID() returns fields from the StateList table for each JProCo LocationID. This function is shown in the Object Explorer (Figure 1.15).

Show the 12 employees who currently work in a JProCo location. Part of the query is shown. Be sure to sort the results by LastName and FirstName.

HINT: *John Marshbank should not appear.*

When finished, the result set should resemble Figure 1.24.

```
SELECT em.FirstName, em.LastName,
gsfl.StateName, gsfl.RegionName
FROM Employee AS em
--Remaining code goes here
```

	FirstName	LastName	StateName	RegionName
1	Alex	Adams	Washington	USA-Continental
2	Eric	Bender	Washington	USA-Continental
3	Barry	Brown	Washington	USA-Continental
4	Lisa	Kendall	Washington	USA-Continental
5	David	Kennson	Washington	USA-Continental
6	Alex	Adams	Washington	USA-Continental

12 rows

Figure 1.24 Skill Check 1 applies the Employee table to dbo.fn_GetStateFromLocationID().

Skill Check 2: The function dbo.fn_GetCustomerTrips() accepts a CustomerID and shows one record for the unique combination of each CustomerID + InvoiceID + ProductID purchased. For example, the following code shown returns the five fields for the purchases of CustomerID 4.

```
SELECT *
FROM dbo.fn_GetCustomerTrips(4)
```

	ProductID	ProductName	InvoiceID	Quantity	CustomerID
1	50	History Tour 2 Days Canada	1509	5	4
2	53	History Tour 1 Week Canada	811	2	4

2 rows

Figure 1.25 The dbo.fn_GetCustomerTrips() function shows the trip list for each CustomerID.

CROSS APPLY the Customer table with the function dbo.fn_GetCustomerTrips() to show the customer FirstName and LastName with the trip list. Alias the Customer table as cu and dbo.fn_GetCustomerTrips() function as gct. Sort results first by CustomerID, then by InvoiceID. When done, the result set will resemble Figure 1.26.

	FirstName	LastName	ProductID	ProductName	InvoiceID	Quantity	CustomerID
1	Mark	Williams	61	Ocean Cruise Tour 1 Day West Coast	824	4	1
2	Mark	Williams	49	History Tour 1 Day Canada	1027	4	1
3	Mark	Williams	15	Underwater Tour 3 Days Mexico	1401	2	1
4	Mark	Williams	49	History Tour 1 Day Canada	1401	5	1
5	Mark	Williams	50	History Tour 2 Days Canada	1401	5	1
6	Mark	Williams	51	History Tour 3 Days Canada	1401	5	1
7	Mark	Williams	53	History Tour 1 Week Canada	1401	4	1
8	Mark	Williams	55	History Tour 1 Day Scandinavia	1401	4	1
9	Mark	Williams	57	History Tour 3 Days Scandinavia	1401	1	1
10	Mark	Williams	60	History Tour 2 Weeks Scandinavia	1401	5	1

Figure 1.26 Use CROSS APPLY to join Customer table to dbo.fn_GetCustomerTrips().

Skill Check 3: The function dbo.fn_GetCustomerList() accepts a ProductID and shows the list of customers who have purchased the product.

```
SELECT *
FROM dbo.fn_GetCustomerList(27)
```

	ProductID	InvoiceID	Quantity	CustomerID	FirstName	LastName
1	27	625	4	185	Sanjay	Garcia
2	27	873	5	181	Daniel	Young
3	27	1105	1	561	Rick	Evans
4	27	1110	1	416	Elizabeth	Baker

4 rows

Figure 1.27 The function dbo.fn_GetCustomerList() shows the customer list for each ProductID.

CROSS APPLY the CurrentProducts table with the dbo.fn_GetCustomerList() function to show the ProductName. Alias the CurrentProducts table as cp and dbo.fn_GetCustomerList() function as gcl. Sort results by CustomerID and InvoiceID in ascending order. When done, the result set should resemble those shown in Figure 1.28.

	Product Name	ProductID	InvoiceID	Quantity	CustomerID	First Name	Last Name
1	Ocean Cruise Tour 1 Day West Coast	61	824	4	1	Mark	Williams
2	History Tour 1 Day Canada	49	1027	4	1	Mark	Williams
3	History Tour 1 Day Canada	49	1401	5	1	Mark	Williams
4	History Tour 2 Days Canada	50	1401	5	1	Mark	Williams
5	History Tour 3 Days Canada	51	1401	5	1	Mark	Williams
6	History Tour 2 Weeks Scandinavia	60	1401	5	1	Mark	Williams
7	History Tour 1 Week Canada	53	1401	4	1	Mark	Williams
8	History Tour 1 Day Scandinavia	55	1401	4	1	Mark	Williams
9	History Tour 3 Days Scandinavia	57	1401	1	1	Mark	Williams
10	Underwater Tour 3 Days Mexico	15	1401	2	1	Mark	Williams

Figure 1.28 CROSS APPLY the CurrentProducts table with dbo.fn_GetCustomerList().

Answer Code: The T-SQL code to this lab can be found in the downloadable files in a file named Lab1.2_CrossApply.sql.

Points to Ponder - Cross Apply

1. CROSS APPLY acts like an INNER JOIN between a table and a table-valued function.

2. The table must appear first in the CROSS APPLY statement.

3. CROSS APPLY only returns records where the data passed into the function matches a record found from the values passed in by the table.

4. CROSS APPLY will not work with scalar functions. Note: Scalar valued functions only return 1 value.

Outer Apply

Now that we are getting the hang of CROSS APPLY after completing the last lab, working with OUTER APPLY will be a breeze!

Recall that we learned CROSS APPLY works much like an INNER JOIN and finds the matching records between a table and a table-valued function. An OUTER APPLY works much like an OUTER JOIN, specifically a LEFT OUTER JOIN which favors all records from the table.

To lead us into OUTER APPLY, we'll need to be very familiar with the matched and unmatched records between the Customer table and the results obtained from the fn_GetCustomerOrders() function. Let's look closely at the purchases of the first seven customers in the Customer table as our test cases.

```
SELECT * FROM Customer
WHERE CustomerID IN (1,2)

SELECT * FROM fn_GetCustomerOrders(1)

SELECT * FROM fn_GetCustomerOrders(2)
```

	CustomerID	CustomerType	FirstName	LastName	CompanyName
1	1	Consumer	Mark	Williams	NULL
2	2	Consumer	Lee	Young	NULL

	InvoiceID	CustomerID	OrderDate	ProductID	ProductName	Quantity	RetailPrice	TotalInvoice
1	824	1	2010-11-09 11:23:51.043	61	Ocean Cruise Tour 1 Day West Coast	4	122.441	489.764
2	1027	1	2011-04-17 16:13:59.480	49	History Tour 1 Day Canada	4	113.287	453.148
3	1401	1	2012-01-31 07:21:03.997	69	Ocean Cruise Tour 3 Days East Coast	1	185.58	185.58
4	1401	1	2012-01-31 07:21:03.997	60	History Tour 2 Weeks Scandinavia	5	1005.615	5028.075
5	1401	1	2012-01-31 07:21:03.997	15	Underwater Tour 3 Days Mexico	2	315.177	630.354
6	1401	1	2012-01-31 07:21:03.997	53	History Tour 1 Week Canada	4	566.435	2265.74
7	1401	1	2012-01-31 07:21:03.997	63	Ocean Cruise Tour 3 Days West Coast	4	367.323	1469.292
8	1401	1	2012-01-31 07:21:03.997	70	Ocean Cruise Tour 5 Days East Coast	5	247.44	1237.20

	InvoiceID	CustomerID	OrderDate	ProductID	ProductName	Quantity	RetailPrice	TotalInvoice
1	943	2	2011-02-07 02:45:03.840	72	Ocean Cruise Tour 2 Weeks East Coast	4	556.74	2226.96

Figure 1.29 CustomerID 1 and 2 have both purchased items on JProCo invoices.

```
SELECT * FROM Customer
WHERE CustomerID = 3

SELECT * FROM fn_GetCustomerOrders(3)
```

	CustomerID	CustomerType	FirstName	LastName	CompanyName				
1	3	Consumer	Patricia	Martin	NULL				

	InvoiceID	CustomerID	OrderDate	ProductID	ProductName	Quantity	RetailPrice	TotalInvoice
1	443	3	2010-01-03 21:06:28.120	29	Underwater Tour 1 Week Scandinavia	2	580.59	1161.18
2	443	3	2010-01-03 21:06:28.120	61	Ocean Cruise Tour 1 Day West Coast	4	122.441	489.764
3	443	3	2010-01-03 21:06:28.120	49	History Tour 1 Day Canada	3	113.287	339.861
4	443	3	2010-01-03 21:06:28.120	25	Underwater Tour 1 Day Scandinavia	4	116.118	464.472
5	828	3	2010-11-11 16:26:37.253	69	Ocean Cruise Tour 3 Days East Coast	2	185.58	371.16
6	828	3	2010-11-11 16:26:37.253	30	Underwater Tour 2 Weeks Scandinavia	2	1045.062	2090.124
7	949	3	2011-02-11 16:51:09.897	49	History Tour 1 Day Canada	3	113.287	339.861

Figure 1.30 Patricia Martin has purchased seven different items across three separate invoices.

Now let's see the next customer by changing both values to 4 (Figure 1.31).

```
SELECT * FROM Customer
WHERE CustomerID = 4

SELECT * FROM fn_GetCustomerOrders(4)
```

	CustomerID	CustomerType	FirstName	LastName	CompanyName
1	4	Consumer	Mary	Lopez	NULL

	InvoiceID	CustomerID	OrderDate	ProductID	ProductName	Quantity	RetailPrice	TotalInvoice
1	811	4	2010-10-30 20:52:58.477	53	History Tour 1 Week Canada	2	566.435	1132.87
2	1509	4	2012-04-24 19:02:28.210	50	History Tour 2 Days Canada	5	203.9166	1019.583

Figure 1.31 Mary Lopez has two invoices, one item on each invoice.

Mary Lopez has ordered an item on each of her invoices. Two invoices, one item on each invoice. How about CustomerID 5 and 6? (Figure 1.32)

```
SELECT * FROM Customer
WHERE CustomerID IN (5,6)

SELECT * FROM fn_GetCustomerOrders(5)
SELECT * FROM fn_GetCustomerOrders(6)
```

	CustomerID	CustomerType	FirstName	LastName	CompanyName
1	5	Business	NULL	NULL	MoreTechnology.com
2	6	Consumer	Ruth	Clark	NULL

InvoiceID	CustomerID	OrderDate	ProductID	ProductName	Quantity	RetailPrice	TotalInvoice

InvoiceID	CustomerID	OrderDate	ProductID	ProductName	Quantity	RetailPrice	TotalInvoice

Figure 1.32 CustomerID 5 and CustomerID 6 have not placed orders yet.

CustomerID 5 is a business called MoreTechnology.com, which has ordered nothing yet. CustomerID 6 is Ruth Clark, another customer who has not yet placed an order. How about CustomerID 7? (Figure 1.33)

```
SELECT * FROM Customer
WHERE CustomerID = 7

SELECT * FROM fn_GetCustomerOrders(7)
```

	CustomerID	CustomerType	FirstName	LastName	CompanyName			
1	7	Consumer	Tessa	Wright	NULL			

	InvoiceID	CustomerID	OrderDate		ProductID	ProductName	Quantity	RetailPrice	TotalInvoice
1	508	7	2010-02-24 04:31:02.877		68	Ocean Cruise Tour 2 Days East Coast	2	111.348	222.696

Figure 1.33 CustomerID 7 is Tessa Wright, and she has ordered using one invoice.

CustomerID 7 is Tessa Wright, and she has ordered using one invoice. So of our first seven customers, five of them have placed at least one invoice order. The only two who have not placed orders yet are CustomerID 5 and CustomerID 6.

Let's review how CROSS APPLY took the result sets from the table and the function and combined them into one record set. Copy both these queries into a new query window. Put the Customer table and the fn_GetCustomerOrders() function in the same FROM clause. We will be placing some code where the underline is located shortly.

```
SELECT *
FROM Customer AS cu
_____ fn_GetCustomerOrders(cu.CustomerID)
```

Drop in CROSS APPLY where the underline is located and see all the matched records showing for CustomerID 1 through 7. CustomerID 1, 2, 3, 4, and 7 are the matched records, so they are all present. The invoice data appears in the same row alongside the data from the Customer table.

Notice that the unmatched records we discovered earlier, CustomerID 5 and 6, do not appear in the results for our CROSS APPLY query (Figure 1.34).

```
SELECT *
FROM Customer AS cu
CROSS APPLY fn_GetCustomerOrders(cu.CustomerID)
ORDER BY cu.CustomerID, InvoiceID
```

	CustomerID	CustomerType	FirstName	LastName	CompanyName	InvoiceID	CustomerID	OrderDate	ProductID
19	1	Consumer	Mark	Williams	NULL	1401	1	2012-01-31 07:21:03.997	70
20	2	Consumer	Lee	Young	NULL	943	2	2011-02-07 02:45:03.840	72
21	3	Consumer	Patricia	Martin	NULL	443	3	2010-01-03 21:06:28.120	25
22	3	Consumer	Patricia	Martin	NULL	443	3	2010-01-03 21:06:28.120	29
23	3	Consumer	Patricia	Martin	NULL	443	3	2010-01-03 21:06:28.120	49
24	3	Consumer	Patricia	Martin	NULL	443	3	2010-01-03 21:06:28.120	61
25	3	Consumer	Patricia	Martin	NULL	828	3	2010-11-11 16:26:37.253	30
26	3	Consumer	Patricia	Martin	NULL	828	3	2010-11-11 16:26:37.253	69
27	3	Consumer	Patricia	Martin	NULL	949	3	2011-02-11 16:51:09.897	49
28	4	Consumer	Mary	Lopez	NULL	811	4	2010-10-30 20:52:58.477	53
29	4	Consumer	Mary	Lopez	NULL	1509	4	2012-04-24 19:02:28.210	50
30	7	Consumer	Tessa	Wright	NULL	508	7	2010-02-24 04:31:02.877	68

Figure 1.34 A partial result shows the matched records for CustomerID 1, 2, 3, 4, and 7.

READER NOTE: *Only a partial result shows here. We've scrolled down to Row 19 in order to show the portion of the result set that includes CustomerID 1 through 7.*

We know CustomerID 5 and 6 both appear in the Customer table, (Figure 1.32) but the function does not produce any records for them because they haven't yet purchased. To see CustomerID 5 and 6, we need a report that shows all customers regardless of whether they've placed orders.

Now let's change the CROSS APPLY query to an **OUTER APPLY** query.

```
SELECT *
FROM Customer AS cu
OUTER APPLY fn_GetCustomerOrders(cu.CustomerID)
ORDER BY cu.CustomerID, InvoiceID
```

	CustomerID	CustomerType	FirstName	LastName	CompanyName	InvoiceID	CustomerID	OrderDate	ProductID
19	1	Consumer	Mark	Williams	NULL	1401	1	2012-01-31 07:21:03.997	51
20	2	Consumer	Lee	Young	NULL	943	2	2011-02-07 02:45:03.840	72
21	3	Consumer	Patricia	Martin	NULL	443	3	2010-01-03 21:06:28.120	29
22	3	Consumer	Patricia	Martin	NULL	443	3	2010-01-03 21:06:28.120	61
23	3	Consumer	Patricia	Martin	NULL	443	3	2010-01-03 21:06:28.120	49
24	3	Consumer	Patricia	Martin	NULL	443	3	2010-01-03 21:06:28.120	25
25	3	Consumer	Patricia	Martin	NULL	828	3	2010-11-11 16:26:37.253	69
26	3	Consumer	Patricia	Martin	NULL	828	3	2010-11-11 16:26:37.253	30
27	3	Consumer	Patricia	Martin	NULL	949	3	2011-02-11 16:51:09.897	49
28	4	Consumer	Mary	Lopez	NULL	811	4	2010-10-30 20:52:58.477	53
29	4	Consumer	Mary	Lopez	NULL	1509	4	2012-04-24 19:02:28.210	50
30	5	Business	NULL	NULL	More Technol...	NULL	NULL	NULL	NULL
31	6	Consumer	Ruth	Clark	NULL	NULL	NULL	NULL	NULL
32	7	Consumer	Tessa	Wright	NULL	508	7	2010-02-24 04:31:02.877	68

Figure 1.35 The unmatched records are now included in the results, thanks to OUTER APPLY.

When we run the OUTER APPLY, we see all seven customers. However, CustomerID 5 and 6 have NULLs next to their names. Notice we get CustomerID 5, MoreTechnology.com, who has made no purchases. The same is true for CustomerID 6, Ruth Clark. She has made no purchases, so there are no invoices. But she appears in the OUTER APPLY result set.

All records from the Customer table (the left table) appear alongside the matched and unmatched records of the fn_GetCustomerOrders() function.

Now modify the query to show only the unmatched records. These 64 customers have not yet made a purchase from JProCo (Figure 1.36).

```
SELECT * FROM Customer AS cu
OUTER APPLY fn_GetCustomerOrders(cu.CustomerID)
WHERE InvoiceID IS NULL
ORDER BY cu.CustomerID
```

	CustomerID	CustomerType	FirstName	LastName	CompanyName	InvoiceID	CustomerID	OrderDate	ProductID
1	5	Business	NULL	NULL	MoreTechnology.com	NULL	NULL	NULL	NULL
2	6	Consumer	Ruth	Clark	NULL	NULL	NULL	NULL	NULL
3	18	Consumer	Donald	Walker	NULL	NULL	NULL	NULL	NULL
4	23	Consumer	Daniel	Gonzalez	NULL	NULL	NULL	NULL	NULL
5	61	Consumer	Lisa	Hall	NULL	NULL	NULL	NULL	NULL
6	70	Consumer	Sarah	Smith	NULL	NULL	NULL	NULL	NULL
7	93	Consumer	Joseph	Lee	NULL	NULL	NULL	NULL	NULL
8	110	Consumer	John	Adams	NULL	NULL	NULL	NULL	NULL
9	115	Consumer	Mark	Davis	NULL	NULL	NULL	NULL	NULL
10	117	Business	NULL	NULL	Puma Consulting	NULL	NULL	NULL	NULL

Figure 1.36 There are 64 customers who have not yet made a purchase from JProCo.

Lab 1.3: Outer Apply

Lab Prep: Each lab has one or more Skill Checks. Start with Skill Check 1 and proceed until reaching the Points to Ponder section.

Before beginning this lab, verify that SQL Server 2012 is properly installed and operating. Before running the lab setup script for resetting the database (SQLQueries2012Vol3Chapter1.3Setup.sql), please make sure to close all query windows within SSMS. An open query window pointing to a database context can lock that database preventing it from updating when the script is executing. A simple way to assure all query windows are closed, is to exit out of SSMS, then open a new instance of SSMS, and lastly run the setup script.

Skill Check 1: The fn_GetStateFromLocationID() function returns fields from the StateList table for each JProCo LocationID.

Use this function to list the FirstName, LastName, StateName, and RegionName. Show all employees, even if the employee does not have a location. Sort the result by LastName and FirstName. When done, the results should resemble those shown in Figure 1.37.

	FirstName	LastName	StateName	RegionName
1	Alex	Adams	Washington	USA-Continental
2	Eric	Bender	Washington	USA-Continental
3	Barry	Brown	Washington	USA-Continental
4	Lisa	Kendall	Washington	USA-Continental
5	David	Kennson	Washington	USA-Continental
6	David	Lonning	Washington	USA-Continental
7	John	Marshbank	NULL	NULL
8	James	Newton	Massachusetts	USA-Continental

13 rows

Figure 1.37 Skill Check 1 uses the fn_GetStateFromLocationID() function introduced in Lab 1.2.

Skill Check 2: JProCo's marketing team is running a promotion to encourage repeat purchases. The team needs a full listing of individual customers in JProCo's customer list, along with all their invoices and products they've ordered to date.

Requirement: *Consumer is the only eligible CustomerType; the two Business customers are ineligible and must be excluded.*

All 773 registered customers will be entered into a drawing for a year's worth of free unlimited trips. Customers who haven't yet purchased are eligible. However, customers can increase their odds of winning by making multiple purchases.

HINT: *There should be NULL values for the results of customers who have not yet purchased.*

The team will run their print merge directly from this list, so for each line item appearing in the list, the customer's information will print onto a card for the drawing. The order data will be supplied by the fn_GetCustomerTrips() function (Its five fields are shown in Figure 1.38).

	ProductID	ProductName	InvoiceID	Quantity	CustomerID
1	61	Ocean Cruise Tour 1 Day West Coast	824	4	1
2	49	History Tour 1 Day Canada	1027	4	1
3	15	Underwater Tour 3 Days Mexico	1401	2	1
4	49	History Tour 1 Day Canada	1401	5	1
5	50	History Tour 2 Days Canada	1401	5	1
6	51	History Tour 3 Days Canada	1401	5	1
7	53	History Tour 1 Week Canada	1401	4	1
8	55	History Tour 1 Day Scandinavia	1401	4	1

19 rows

Figure 1.38 Skill Check 2 uses the fn_GetCustomerTrips() function introduced earlier.

Because this function does not include the name of the Customer, we must bring in FirstName and LastName by applying the Customer table to the function. Sort the output by CustomerID. When done, the results should resemble Figure 1.39.

	FirstName	LastName	ProductID	ProductName	InvoiceID	Quantity	CustomerID
19	Mark	Williams	70	Ocean Cruise Tour 5 Days East Coast	1401	5	1
20	Lee	Young	72	Ocean Cruise Tour 2 Weeks East Coast	943	4	2
21	Patricia	Martin	25	Underwater Tour 1 Day Scandinavia	443	4	3
22	Patricia	Martin	29	Underwater Tour 1 Week Scandinavia	443	2	3
23	Patricia	Martin	30	Underwater Tour 2 Weeks Scandinavia	828	2	3
24	Patricia	Martin	49	History Tour 1 Day Canada	443	3	3
25	Patricia	Martin	49	History Tour 1 Day Canada	949	3	3
26	Patricia	Martin	61	Ocean Cruise Tour 1 Day West Coast	443	4	3
27	Patricia	Martin	69	Ocean Cruise Tour 3 Days East Coast	828	2	3
28	Mary	Lopez	50	History Tour 2 Days Canada	1509	5	4

Figure 1.39 Skill Check 2 applies the Customer table to dbo.fn_GetCustomerTrips() (7017 rows).

Skill Check 3: Modify our final query from Skill Check 2 to show the 62 customers who will be entered into the drawing but have not yet purchased. This query will be identical to our previous result, except a second criterion will be added to the WHERE clause. The final results should resemble Figure 1.40.

HINT: *in the Customer table, each of these customers has a CustomerID, but in the OUTER APPLY one of the CustomerID fields is NULL.*

	First Name	Last Name	Product ID	Product Name	Invoice ID	Quantity	Customer ID
1	Ruth	Clark	NULL	NULL	NULL	NULL	NULL
2	Donald	Walker	NULL	NULL	NULL	NULL	NULL
3	Daniel	Gonzalez	NULL	NULL	NULL	NULL	NULL
4	Lisa	Hall	NULL	NULL	NULL	NULL	NULL
5	Sarah	Smith	NULL	NULL	NULL	NULL	NULL
6	Joseph	Lee	NULL	NULL	NULL	NULL	NULL
7	John	Adams	NULL	NULL	NULL	NULL	NULL
8	Mark	Davis	NULL	NULL	NULL	NULL	NULL
9	Pedro	Brown	NULL	NULL	NULL	NULL	NULL
10	Ruth	Carter	NULL	NULL	NULL	NULL	NULL

Figure 1.40 Skill Check 3 applies the Customer table to function fn_GetCustomerTrips() (62 rows).

Answer Code: The T-SQL code to this lab can be found in the downloadable files in a file named Lab1.3_OuterApply.sql.

Points to Ponder - Outer Apply

1. The OUTER APPLY acts like an OUTER JOIN between a table and a table-valued function.

2. CROSS APPLY only returns all records from the table and any matching records found from the values passed in by the table.

3. The only difference between CROSS APPLY and OUTER APPLY is that CROSS APPLY acts like an INNER JOIN, whereas OUTER APPLY acts like a LEFT OUTER JOIN favoring all records from the table.

4. The table must appear first in the OUTER APPLY statement.

Chapter Glossary

CROSS APPLY: Acts like an INNER JOIN between a table and a table-valued function and returns records where the data passed into the function matches a record from the values passed in by the table.

DELETE: Removes records from a table, but does not remove the table from the database.

Depopulating: The process of generically removing data from a container.

OUTER APPLY: Will act like an OUTER JOIN between a table and a function and finds the matching records between the two.

Transaction: A group of actions treated as a single unit to ensure data integrity.

Transaction Log: A record of all transactions on a table.

TRUNCATE: A DDL statement that can only remove all records from a table but resets the identity counter to seed value.

Unpopulated: A new container empty of data.

Review Quiz - Chapter One

1.) A test table, SalesOrderDetail, containing >100,000 records will soon be deployed to production. The first field is called SalesOrderDetailID and is an identity field.

You are required to empty the entire table and ensure that the identity field starts over at its initial value. What T-SQL code will achieve this result?

O a. `RESET SalesOrderDetail`

O b. `DROP TABLE SalesOrderDetail`

O c. `DELETE SalesOrderDetail`

O d. `TRUNCATE TABLE SalesOrderDetail`

2.) DELETE is considered to be a DML statement. DROP is a DDL statement. What family of statements does TRUNCATE belong to?

O a. DML

O b. DDL

O c. DCL

O d. TCL

O e. None of the above.

3.) What are two statements that can remove all records from a table without removing the table itself? (choose two)

☐ a. DELETE

☐ b. TRUNCATE

☐ c. DROP

☐ d. REMOVE

☐ e. DUMP

4.) Which two apply statements can show the combined result set from a table and a table-valued function? (choose two)

☐ a. OUTER APPLY

☐ b. LEFT APPLY

☐ c. INNER APPLY

☐ d. CROSS APPLY

5.) What is the only difference between CROSS APPLY and OUTER APPLY?

O a. CROSS APPLY shows all records from the table and OUTER APPLY only shows matching records from the table and the function.

O b. OUTER APPLY shows all records from the table and CROSS APPLY only shows matching records from the table and the function.

6.) There are 50 records in the dbo.Employee table and anywhere from zero to 12 records returned from the dbo.fn_GetEmployeeActivity() function based on the EmployeeID integer passed into it.

The following code returns 12 records:
```
SELECT * FROM dbo.fn_GetEmployeeActivity(3)
```
Running the following code returns zero records:
```
SELECT * FROM dbo.fn_GetEmployeeActivity(44)
```
After testing each employee ID from 1 to 50, we notice that 7 records produce an empty result set. How many distinct employee records will be returned when using a CROSS APPLY between the dbo.fn_GetEmployeeActivity() function and the dbo.Employee table?

O a. 1
O b. 3
O c. 12
O d. 43
O e. 44
O f. 50

7.) There are 90 records in the dbo.Location table and anywhere from 0 to 3 records returned from the dbo.fn_GetLocationAwards() function based on any given LocationID.

The following code results in one record:

```
SELECT * FROM dbo.fn_GetLocationAwards(1)
```

Running the following code results in zero records:

```
SELECT * FROM dbo.fn_GetLocationAwards(88)
```

After testing each Location ID from 1 to 90 you find that 33 records produce an empty result set. How many distinct LocationID records will be returned when using an OUTER APPLY between the dbo.fn_GetLocationAwards() function and the dbo.Location table?

O a. 1
O b. 3
O c. 33
O d. 57
O e. 88
O f. 90

8.) There is a table-valued function named dbo.fn_GetEmployeeLocHistory() that will show all the locations where an employee has worked. Calling on the function using the following code displays these results for E_ID 52.

```
SELECT * FROM dbo.fn_GetEmployeeLocHistory(52)
```

E_ID	City	State
52	Bismarck	ND
52	Norfolk	VA
52	Tampa	FL
52	Kellogg	ID

Querying the Employee table shows that E_ID 52, is the record for Kevin Huerter. You want to produce a report showing the FirstName and LastName fields from the dbo.Employee table and all records that result from using the dbo.fn_GetEmployeeLocHistory() function.

Which code will achieve this goal?

O a.
```
SELECT em.FirstName, em.LastName, ge.*
FROM dbo.Employee AS em
INNER JOIN dbo.fn_GetEmployeeLocHistory(em.E_ID) AS ge
ON em.E_ID = ge.E_ID
```

O b.
```
SELECT em.FirstName, em.LastName, ge.*
FROM dbo.Employee AS em
CROSS APPLY dbo.fn_GetEmployeeLocHistory(em.E_ID) AS ge
ON em.E_ID = ge.E_ID
```

O c.
```
SELECT em.FirstName, em.LastName, ge.*
FROM dbo.Employee AS em
CROSS APPLY dbo.fn_GetEmployeeLocHistory(em.E_ID) AS ge
```

Answer Key

1.) Since 'RESET SalesOrderDetail' will result in an error (a) is not correct. Because DROP will completely remove the table, and the data stored within the database (b) is also a wrong answer. DELETE will only remove the records from the table without resetting anything, so (c) is also incorrect. Because TRUNCATE will empty the table of data and reset any identity fields (d) is the correct answer.

2.) Because TRUNCATE belongs to the DDL family (a), (c) and (d) are all wrong answers. Because TRUNCATE pertains to table structure, it belongs to the DDL family, making (b) the correct answer.

3.) DROP will completely remove the table, and the data stored within the database, so (c) is incorrect. REMOVE and DUMP have no special meaning when it comes to database tables, so (d) and (e) are incorrect. DELETE and TRUNCATE can both be used to remove all records from a table without removing the table itself, so (a) and (b) are both correct.

4.) LEFT and INNER do not work with APPLY, so (b) and (c) are incorrect. CROSS APPLY works like an INNER JOIN between a table and a table-valued function, while OUTER APPLY works like an OUTER JOIN between a table and a table-valued functions, so (a) and (d) are both correct.

5.) OUTER APPLY will show every record from the table while the CROSS APPLY only displays matches making (a) incorrect. OUTER APPLY will show all records from the table while CROSS APPLY returns only matching records from the table and the function, so (b) is the correct answer.

6.) Since 50 minus 7 always equals 43 (a), (b), (c) and (f) are all incorrect. There are 50 employees and only 7 of them produce an empty result set from the table-valued function, so a CROSS APPLY will return records for 43 distinct customers, making (d) the correct answer.

7.) An OUTER APPLY will always return every row in the table, so there will always be at least 90 rows returned with a table holding 90 Locations making (a), (b), (c), (d) and (e) all wrong answers. Since there are 90 records in the Location table, and an OUTER APPLY will return every row from this table, (f) is the correct answer.

8.) Because INNER JOIN only works between two tabular results (like a table or a view) it will only give exact matches, so it is possible to not get all the employees, making (a) incorrect. Since CROSS APPLY does not use the ON clause, (b) is wrong too. Since CROSS APPLY is used properly to find the matching records between the table and the function, (c) is correct.

Bug Catcher Game

To play the Bug Catcher game, run the SQLQueries2012Vol3BugCatcher01.pps file from the BugCatcher folder of the companion files. These files can be obtained from the www.Joes2Pros.com website.

[THIS PAGE INTENTIONALLY LEFT BLANK.]

Chapter 2.   Database Schemas and Synonyms

Back in 2005, I heard there was some fancy invention called schemas coming later that year in the new SQL Server 2005 release. My initial reaction was, "Yikes, I'm already too busy and schemas must mean some fancy code design that will take many hours of serious late night studying to get a handle on". *As it turned out, schemas weren't difficult at all!* In fact, SQL Server's use of schemas resembles a simple categorization and naming convention used from prehistoric times when humans began organizing themselves into clans. And centuries later, names progressed to the system we have now where we each have our individual name (like Bob or Paul) along with our family name (like Paul *Johnson*). If we were SQL Server objects, our two-part naming convention would be *FamilyName.FirstName*. Our two-part name ensures easier identification and also classification. Paul *Johnson* and Krista *Johnson* are more likely to be in the same immediate family than *Paul* Johnson and *Paul* Kriegel.

In .NET programming languages, the names Johnson and Kriegel would be called namespaces. In SQL Server we might create two tables called Employee and PayRates which belong to the HR department. We can refer to them as HR.Employee and HR.PayRates if we first set up the HR schema. All HR tables would then be created in the HR schema. A schema is used as SQL Server's answer to a namespace used in the .NET languages.

READER NOTE: *Please run the SQLQueries2012Vol3Chapter2.0Setup.sql script in order to follow along with the examples in the first section of Chapter 2. All scripts mentioned in this chapter may be found at* www.Joes2Pros.com.

Schemas

We know that data contained and tracked in SQL Server most likely relates to an organization. The database we frequently use in the *Joes 2 Pros* series is JProCo, which contains all the data for this small fictitious company. No matter how small an organization, certain tables will be more important to one group than to others. For example, even in JProCo, employee and pay data would be controlled by a Human Resources group. Customer data usually is managed by the Sales and Marketing team, whether that team consists of five or 15,000 people.

Shown here is the list of JProCo's tables. Notice that all tables show the default 'dbo' ('database owner') prefix. There are no categories to help indicate whether a table is managed by the Sales team or by HR.

	schema	name	object_id	type_desc	create_date
1	dbo	PayRates	245575913	USER_TABLE	2012-07-24
2	dbo	MgmtTraining	277576027	USER_TABLE	2012-07-24
3	dbo	CurrentProducts	309576141	USER_TABLE	2012-07-24
4	dbo	Employee	341576255	USER_TABLE	2012-07-24
5	dbo	Location	373576369	USER_TABLE	2012-07-24
6	dbo	Grant	405576483	USER_TABLE	2012-07-24
7	dbo	Customer	453576654	USER_TABLE	2012-07-24
8	dbo	SalesInvoice	549576996	USER_TABLE	2012-07-24
9	dbo	SalesInvoiceDetail	581577110	USER_TABLE	2012-07-24
10	dbo	StateList	613577224	USER_TABLE	2012-07-24
11	dbo	RetiredProducts	725577623	USER_TABLE	2012-07-24
12	dbo	Supplier	757577737	USER_TABLE	2012-07-24
13	dbo	Contractor	789577851	USER_TABLE	2012-07-24

13 rows

Figure 2.1 All tables in the JProCo database.

Prior to SQL Server 2005, the syntax for fully qualified names in SQL Server was [server].[database].[owner].[object name], and the idea of 'dbo' pertained to [owner], or whichever database the user created and/or was allowed to access the object. In SQL Server 2005, a new capability was introduced called **schemas**. The introduction of schemas *(SchemaName.ObjectName)* has provided more freedom for Developers and DBAs to use meaningful names to categorize tables and other objects inside a database.

Let's look at a few of the tables in the AdventureWorks2012 database to see how schemas can help organize objects within databases: *dbo, HumanResources, Person, Production and Sales (Purchasing is not shown here).*

	schema	name	object_id	type_desc	create_date
1	Person	Address	373576369	USER_TABLE	2012-03-14
2	Person	AddressType	421576540	USER_TABLE	2012-03-14
3	Dbo	AWBuildVersion	469576711	USER_TABLE	2012-03-14
4	Production	BillOfMaterials	501576825	USER_TABLE	2012-03-14
5	Person	BusinessEntity	629577281	USER_TABLE	2012-03-14
6	Person	BusinessEntityAddress	677577452	USER_TABLE	2012-03-14
7	Person	BusinessEntityContact	725577623	USER_TABLE	2012-03-14
8	Person	ContactType	773577794	USER_TABLE	2012-03-14
9	Person	CountryRegion	837578022	USER_TABLE	2012-03-14
10	Sales	CountryRegionCurrency	805577908	USER_TABLE	2012-03-14
11	Sales	CreditCard	869578136	USER_TABLE	2012-03-14
12	Production	Culture	901578250	USER_TABLE	2012-03-14
13	Sales	Currency	933578364	USER_TABLE	2012-03-14
14	Sales	CurrencyRate	965578478	USER_TABLE	2012-03-14
15	Sales	Customer	997578592	USER_TABLE	2012-03-14
16	Dbo	DatabaseLog	245575913	USER_TABLE	2012-03-14
17	HumanResources	Department	1045578763	USER_TABLE	2012-03-14
18	Production	Document	1077578877	USER_TABLE	2012-03-14
19	Person	EmailAddress	1189579276	USER_TABLE	2012-03-14
20	HumanResources	Employee	1237579447	USER_TABLE	2012-03-14

71 rows

Figure 2.2 AdventureWorks2012 tables are shown sorted alphabetically by name.

Instead of creating all tables in the general dbo schema, AdventureWorks2012 has defined a separate category for the tables used by each of its key departments (e.g., HumanResources, Sales, Production). We can easily see that the Department and Employee tables belong to the HumanResources group. Likewise, the CreditCard, CurrencyRate and Customer tables all belong to the Sales group.

Previous to SQL Server's 2005 release, it was not uncommon for DBAs to house each department's tables in a separate database. Now DBAs have more choices and can simply manage access to schemas, rather than managing separate databases just to be able to distinguish tables belonging to separate categories. Schemas and principals can also have a "One-to-Many" relationship, meaning that each principal may own many differently named schemas. This eliminates the need for a namespace that is tied to the user who created the object.

In the following example we can see the five custom schemas the AdventureWorks2012 DBA defined to manage each of the five departments' tables (Figure 2.3). Notice the many other system-defined schemas which SQL Server has created for its own management and tracking of the database (db_securityadmin, db_denydatareader, etc.).

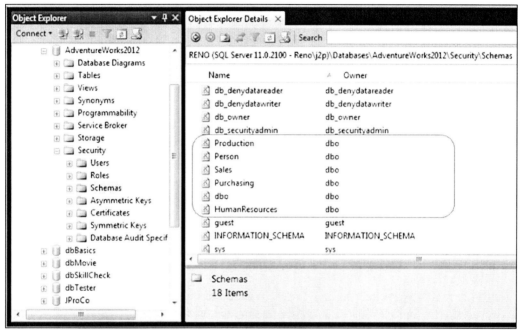

Figure 2.3 The AdventureWorks2012 DBA created five schemas, one for each department.

Creating Schemas With Code

Now we will define several schemas of our own and then create tables using this structure. Later we will add schemas to the JProCo database. First we'll run a few practice examples with the RatisCo database, which currently contains no tables.

Before we make any changes to RatisCo, let's check inside the Object Explorer and confirm what schemas are available by navigating with the following path:

Object Explorer > Databases > RatisCo > Security > Schemas

We can now see all the system-defined schemas for the RatisCo database by looking at the results shown in Figure 2.4

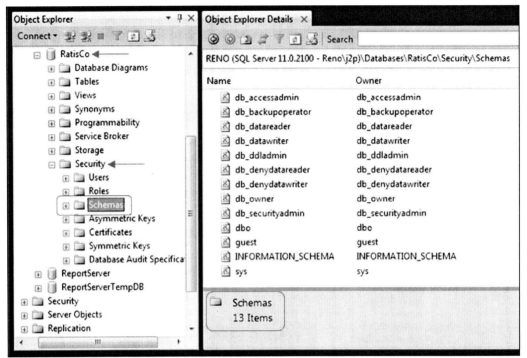

Figure 2.4 RatisCo contains no user-defined schemas. These 13 schemas are all system-defined.

Once the Schemas folder in the RatisCo database is highlighted, we are able to display the Object Explorer Details window, by pressing the F7 key. Alternatively, we are able to use the toolbar and click the following choices:

View > Object Explorer Details

There should be 13 system-defined schemas and no user-defined schemas listed. We are about to create five user-defined schemas for Human Resources, People, Production, Purchases and Sales using both T-SQL code and the SSMS UI.

Make sure we are in the RatisCo database context by doing either of these items:

o   Beginning our code with a "USE RatisCo" statement. Recall that the keyword 'GO' delimits the end of a batch statement and must appear on the line below the last DDL statement.

o   Toggle the dropdown list and select RatisCo (Figure 2.5).

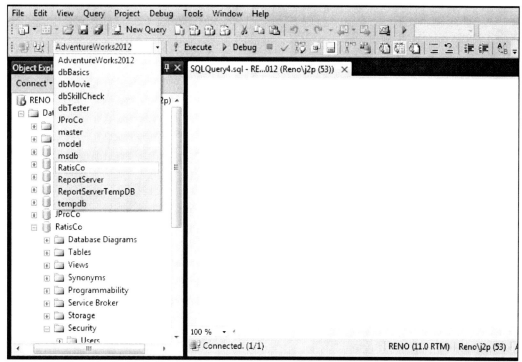

Figure 2.5 Once in the RatisCo database context, we will create the Sales schema and one table.

Now let's run this code to create the Sales schema and the Sales.Customer table.

```
USE RatisCo
GO

CREATE SCHEMA Sales
GO

CREATE TABLE Sales.Customer (
CustomerID INT PRIMARY KEY,
CustomerName VARCHAR(50) NOT NULL,
City VARCHAR(30) NOT NULL)
GO
```

Suppose we ran the code above, but forgot to first check the Object Explorer and see the 13 system-defined schemas by themselves. We would need to drop the Sales schema in order to see just the system-defined schemas. Since the Sales schema has a dependent object (Sales.Customer table), we must drop this table before SQL Server allows us to remove the Sales schema. We can accomplish this by writing the following code:

```
USE RatisCo
GO

DROP TABLE Sales.Customer
GO

DROP SCHEMA Sales
GO
```

READER NOTE: *SQL Server will not allow a schema to be removed if database objects which are dependent on that schema still exist.*

Now let's run the following code to create two additional schemas.

```
USE RatisCo
GO

CREATE SCHEMA HumanResources
GO

CREATE SCHEMA Purchases
GO
```

Re-create the Sales.Customer table:

```
USE RatisCo
GO

CREATE TABLE Sales.Customer (
CustomerID INT PRIMARY KEY,
CustomerName VARCHAR(50) NOT NULL,
City VARCHAR(30) NOT NULL)
GO
```

Now let's check the Schemas folder to see that the newly created schemas are present (HumanResources, and Purchasing). In Figure 2.4, we found 13 system defined schemas. Use the following path to confirm that there is now a total of 15 schemas for the RatisCo database:

Object Explorer > Databases > RatisCo > Security > Schemas

Creating Schemas With Management Studio

Next we will create two more schemas (People and Production) using SQL Server Management Studio's User Interface (SSMS UI):

Object Explorer > Databases > RatisCo > Security > right-click Schemas > New Schema > Schema Name: People > OK

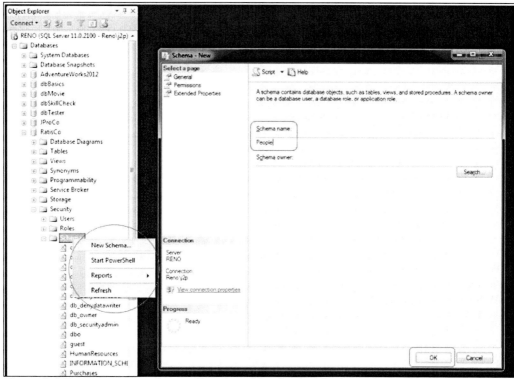

Figure 2.6 Create two new schemas (People and Production) in the RatisCo database.

Figure 2.6 shows the creation steps for the first schema, People. *After creating the People schema, repeat the process and create the **Production** and **Sales** schemas.*

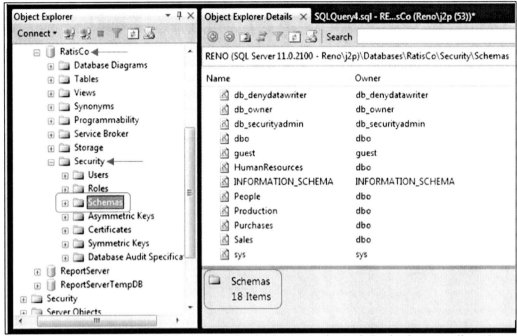

Figure 2.7 We have now added five user-defined schemas to the RatisCo database, totaling 18.

We'll stay with the Management Studio interface to add some records in the Sales.Customer table we created in the last section.

We begin by navigating to this table in Object Explorer:

Object Explorer > Databases > RatisCo > Tables > Sales.Customer

As shown in Figure 2.8, we will right-click the Sales.Customer table which then expands a full menu of options. Choose the 'Edit Top 200 Rows' selection to launch the editing interface in a new tab.

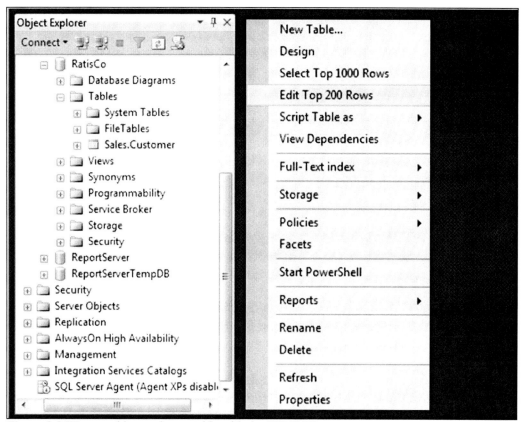

Figure 2.8 We can add records to a table with the SSMS UI.

We can now enter two rows of data as shown in Figure 2.9. By clicking and beginning to type inside the first cell containing *"NULL"*, a new blank row will appear for us to populate. Enter the two records precisely as seen here, as we will continue working with this table later in the Chapter.

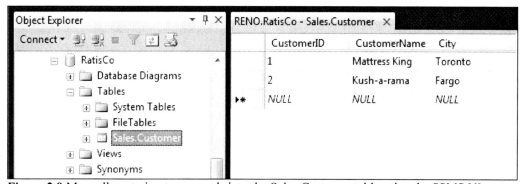

Figure 2.9 Manually entering two records into the Sales.Customer table using the SSMS UI.

This interface is similar to working in Microsoft Access, as there isn't an explicit "OK" or "Enter" button – once the user clicks away from a row, data will be entered into the database. Also, notice the full four-part name in the editing tab *(Server.Database.Schema.ObjectName)*. My server name is RENO, so the fully qualified name of this table object is RENO.RatisCo.Sales.Customer.

Qualified Names Using Schemas

Next we'll query to see the records and confirm they are showing in our Sales.Customer table. If we run the query:

```
SELECT * FROM Customer
```

We will get a SQL Server error (*"Invalid object name 'Customer'."*). Generally speaking, once we create a table within a schema, we must explicitly use the *SchemaName.ObjectName* naming convention whenever we call upon it.

READER NOTE: *In most cases, we explicitly use the two part naming syntax of SchemaName.ObjectName as a best practice for objects created within a specific schema.*

Notice that, when we specify the database, schema, and table name as a three-part name (*DatabaseName.SchemaName.ObjectName*), the query is able to locate our intended table even though the database context is set to a different database (i.e., AdventureWorks2012) .

Running this query will show the two records we entered manually in Figure 2.9.

```
USE AdventureWorks2012
GO

SELECT * FROM RatisCo.Sales.Customer
```

	CustomerID	CustomerName	City
1	1	Mattress King	Toronto
2	2	Kush-a-rama	Fargo

2 rows

Figure 2.10 This query locates the intended table even though the context points to a different db.

When we specify *SchemaName.ObjectName* in our query (SELECT * FROM *SchemaName.ObjectName*), this is known as a qualified query because we are using the qualified name. Qualified queries look in the exact schema for the table.

Unqualified queries such as (SELECT * FROM *ObjectName*) will use the dbo schema as a default and consequently only check within this schema for the object being queried. In other words, SQL Server will actually interpret this simple query:

```
SELECT * FROM ObjectName
```

Unqualified queries such as (SELECT * FROM *SchemaName.ObjectName*) explicitly pick the name of the schema. A two-part table name using the dbo schema is seen in the code sample:

```
SELECT * FROM dbo.ObjectName
```

The four part name (*Server.Database.Schema.ObjectName*) is also referred to as a **fully qualified name**.

Lab 2.1: Schemas

Lab Prep: Each lab has one or more Skill Checks. Start with Skill Check 1 and proceed until reaching the Points to Ponder section.

Before beginning this lab, verify that SQL Server 2012 is properly installed and operating. Before running the lab setup script for resetting the database (SQLQueries2012Vol3Chapter2.1Setup.sql), please make sure to close all query windows within SSMS. An open query window pointing to a database context can lock that database preventing it from updating when the script is executing. A simple way to assure all query windows are closed, is to exit out of SSMS, then open a new instance of SSMS, and lastly run the setup script.

Skill Check 1: In the JProCo database, use T-SQL code to create the following five schemas: **HumanResources, Purchasing, Production, Person,** and **Sales.** Before adding these schemas to JProCo, use Object Explorer and notice that the Owner column has only one schema created for dbo. After adding the five new schemas, the Object Explorer Details window should resemble Figure 2.11.

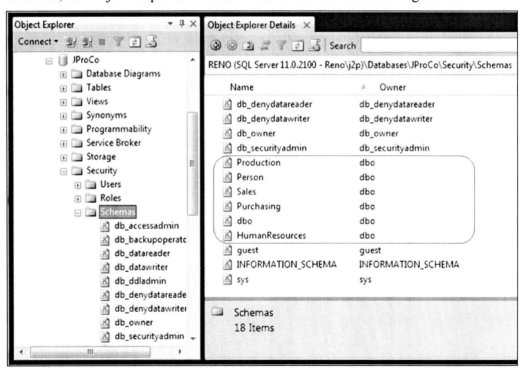

Figure 2.11 Skill Check 1 uses T-SQL code to create five new schemas in JProCo.

Answer Code: The T-SQL code to this lab can be found in the downloadable files in a file named Lab2.1_Schemas.sql.

Points to Ponder – Schemas

1. A schema is a namespace for database objects.

2. In previous versions of SQL Server, database owners and schemas were conceptually the same object. Beginning in SQL Server 2005, owners and schemas are separate, and schemas serve as containers of objects.

3. Objects (tables, stored procedures, views, etc.) are created within a schema inside the database.

4. Objects can be transferred between schemas by using the following code:

    ALTER SCHEMA *SchemaName* TRANSFER *SecurableName* Example:

    ```
    ALTER SCHEMA HumanResources
    TRANSFER Person.Address
    ```

5. Each database has its own schema set.

6. Every object in a database has a fully qualified name, *Server.Database.Schema.ObjectName*. A usage example would be:

    ```
    SELECT * FROM Reno.RatisCo.People.Employee
    ```

7. To use object delimiters with the schema name would be People.Employee.

8. A fully qualified name (FQN) is the complete object identifier. The FQN includes the server name, database name, schema name, and object name.

9. The first three parts (server, database, and schema names) are known as the qualifiers of the object name, as they are used to differentiate the object from any other database object.

10. Partially qualified names omit some of the qualifiers by leaving them out or by replacing them with another period.

    For example, since `Reno.JProCo.Employee` does not list the schema, it is interpreted to be dbo.

11. When using fully qualified names, the object must be explicitly identified.

12. Each object must have a unique fully qualified name. Objects can have the same simple name as long as the fully qualified names are different.

13. With multiple schemas in place, two tables with the same name could exist. For example, two Order tables: `Sales.Order` and `Production.Order`

14. Within a database, the name can be shortened to *SchemaName.ObjectName*.

    Example: `SELECT * FROM People.Employee`

15. A query with a simple name might cause some confusion if multiple schemas have an object with the same name (SELECT * FROM Order).

16. SQL attempts to search schemas for simple object names in this order:

    1) SQL attempts to find simple names from the default schema.

    2) If no default exists, OR if the default does not contain the requested object, it attempts to find simple names from the dbo schema.

17. A default schema can be assigned to a user in two ways.

    1) Using the UI in the properties of a Database user.

    2) Specifying the schema name in the DEFAULT_SCHEMA clause of the CREATE or ALTER user statement.

18. A default schema can be assigned to each database user.

Synonyms

I remember being introduced to a person with a really long name which was hard to repeat back. Fortunately, they told me "Just call me Tex". Now his name is not really Tex, although most everyone he knows calls him by Tex and he gladly answers to that name. In SQL Server, a synonym for an object is equivalent to calling this fellow by the name Tex. Sometimes tables in SQL Server can have really long names or really long qualified names. It is possible to create a synonym for tables, or other database objects, using a shorter name that is easier to reference when coding. Synonyms were introduced in SQL Server 2005 and have been in every version of SQL Server since that time.

Qualified Names Review

We can usually use three-part names with the appropriate access to a server. Sometimes using four-part names is necessary for servers with permissions set for that type of interconnection.

```
--Single-part Name (Simple)
[ObjectName]

--Two-part qualified Name
[SchemaName].[ObjectName]

--Three-part qualified Name
[database].[SchemaName].[ObjectName]

--Four-part fully qualified Name
[server].[database].[SchemaName].[ObjectName]
```

By using synonyms we can replace these long qualified names with a simple to use single-part name of our choosing.

Creating Synonyms

If we are in the JProCo database and select all the records from the MgmtTraining table, we get all the records. Since there is no MgmtTraining table in dbBasics we get the error message shown in Figure 2.12.

```
USE dbBasics
GO

SELECT * FROM MgmtTraining
```

```
Messages
Msg 208, Level 16, State 1, Line 1
Invalid object name 'MgmtTraining'.
                                                    0 rows
```

Figure 2.12 The dbBasics database can't query the JProCo.dbo.MgmtTraining table by a simple name.

If we need to stay in the dbBasics database context and query the MgmtTraining table of JProCo, one option is to use the fully qualified name. An example of how to do this is shown in the following code:

```
SELECT * FROM JProCo.dbo.MgmtTraining
```

There is another way to refer to the JProCo.dbo.MgmtTraining table without using the longer qualified name. We can create a synonym in dbBasics that refers to the JProCo.dbo.MgmtTraining object (Table). We can accomplish this by using the DDL statement CREATE SYNONYM. Now let's use the synonym in a query.

```
USE dbBasics
GO

CREATE SYNONYM Classes
FOR JProCo.dbo.MgmtTraining
GO

SELECT * FROM Classes
```

Notice that our code is using the dbBasics context, and a synonym called Classes was created for the JProCo.dbo.MgmtTraining table. The query against the Classes synonym is actually returning all records for the JProCo.dbo.MgmtTraining table.

	ClassID	ClassName	ClassDurationHours	ApprovedDate
1	1	Embracing Diversity	12	2007-01-01 00:00:00.000
2	2	Interviewing	6	2007-01-15 00:00:00.000
3	3	Difficult Negotiations	30	2008-02-12 00:00:00.000
4	4	Empowering Others	18	2012-07-24 10:34:04.340
				4 rows

Figure 2.13 Query the Classes synonym in dbBasics for records from JProCo.dbo.MgmtTraining.

The syntax for creating synonyms is the CREATE SYNONYM statement. The *ObjectName* is the original fully qualified name of the table, or object, and the *synonym name* is the new name we choose for the object. Synonyms can reference views, tables, stored procedures, or functions. If we don't specify a schema for the synonym, then SQL Server uses the current user's default schema.

So far, we have created a synonym in one database that refers to an object in another database. Our next example will create a synonym in the JProCo database that points to an object in the same JProCo database. This is useful because we sometimes need the same table to be called by different names.

For example: If one company bought out another company they eventually would not want to have two employee tables. Let's say CompanyA has a table called Employees and CompanyB keeps track of its employees in a table called Workers. Eventually they want all the data to be located in the Employees table. However, there are many automated systems using the name Workers and changing all of them at once to use the unified Employees table would be difficult.

This is a workplace situation where existing clients are using the Workers table name and they cannot all be switched at the same time to the new table name of Employees. A synonym using the old name can remain in place until all clients are using the new table name. This makes synonyms a great migration solution for database objects.

Some of our JProCo client processes are trying to query the Classes table instead of the dbo.MgmtTraining table. We want the dbo.MgmtTraining table and all its records to be accessible by the following query:

```
SELECT * FROM Classes
```

The following code uses a two-part name of dbo.MgmtTraining instead of the three-part name of JProCo.dbo.MgmtTraining, since we're already in the JProCo database context:

```
USE JProCo
GO

CREATE SYNONYM Classes
FOR dbo.MgmtTraining
GO

SELECT * FROM Classes
```

Removing Synonyms

What if we no longer need this synonym name anymore? Perhaps the last legacy client has switched over so all clients are now using the new table name. It is apparent that this synonym is no longer being used by our client's processes and it's time to remove any reference to this object in the dbBasics database.

When we no longer need a synonym, we are required to use the following syntax DROP SYNONYM *SynonymName* to accomplish this task. Let's look at this in action by using the following code:

```
USE dbBasics
GO

DROP SYNONYM Classes
GO
```

We can keep our database context in dbBasics and then query all the records from the JProCo.dbo.MgmtTraining table using the synonym Classes to verify it no longer exists (Figure 2.14).

```
SELECT * FROM Classes
```

Messages
Msg 208, Level 16, State 1, Line 1
Invalid object name 'Classes'.
0 rows

Figure 2.14 Query the Classes table to verify it no longer exists (Results: invalid object message).

Notice that when we run the query to find all records in the Classes table again, we receive an error message indicating the object 'Classes' is invalid. This proves the Classes object has been successfully removed from the dbBasics database.

Synonyms Uses and Limitations

Like any feature there are benefits and drawbacks. The benefit of the synonym is very evident, as we get to use a shorter name. There are other benefits, as well as a few rules about using synonyms to remember.

Late Binding

Last year my younger brother and his wife had their first baby. Like any expectant couple they were trying to come up with the perfect name long before the baby was actually born. Some couples even decide on baby names before pregnancy. This is considered good planning, as the name is ready and set aside for use when needed. After the baby is born the hospital will ask "What name did you choose for your new baby?" At this point the name is finally bound to the baby, months later than the day the name was actually chosen for the baby.

We can bind the synonym today to a table that will be created later. This is known as late binding and is not the norm for most SQL Server objects. For instance, SQL Server will not allow us to create a table name with no fields and then add in the design at a later date. Unlike synonyms, tables are unable to be created via late binding techniques. Tables are created with run-time binding, as the design must be specified at the same time the table name is chosen.

In other words the ObjectName for an object doesn't even need to exist before we can create the synonym for the object. Some of the objects that can be referenced by a synonym include: Tables, Views, Stored Procedures and Functions.

Let's say that based on our database design, we know that someday there will be a table named dbo.Region. We can decide today to create a synonym for this table called SalesArea, even though the table itself doesn't currently exist. We can see how to do this with the following code:

```
USE JProCo
GO

CREATE SYNONYM SalesArea
FOR dbo.Region
GO
```

We now have a SalesArea synonym with a table that does not exist yet. So, when we try to query the SalesArea synonym we encounter an error, because the database object it references (the dbo.Region table) is invalid (Figure 2.15).

```
SELECT * FROM SalesArea
```

Messages
Msg 5313, Level 16, State 1, Line 2
Synonym 'SalesArea' refers to an invalid object.
0 rows

Figure 2.15 Querying the SalesArea synonym before the dbo.Region table exists in JProCo.

Now, the time has finally arrived for us to create the dbo.Region table and begin inserting data into it for use by our synonym and subsequently by the client processes. Let's go ahead and do this by writing the following code:

```
CREATE TABLE dbo.Region (
RegionID INT PRIMARY KEY,
RegionName VARCHAR(50))
GO

INSERT INTO dbo.Region VALUES
(1,'Canada')
```

Great! Now we can query the SalesArea synonym and retrieve the results shown in Figure 2.16.

```
SELECT *
FROM SalesArea
```

	RegionID	RegionName
1	1	Canada
		1 rows

Figure 2.16 Query the SalesArea synonym after inserting records into the dbo.Region table.

DML Only

Can we always use a synonym name in place of a table name to accomplish any task necessary to perform on the table? Based on the statements we have run so far, it appears that the same work can be accomplished by using either a synonym or a table name. However, synonyms can only be used with the following DML statements: *SELECT, UPDATE, INSERT, DELETE, MERGE, and EXECUTE.*

READER NOTE: EXECUTE is not a DML statement. It is the only non- DML statement that works with synonyms.

Let's continue working with the dbo.Region table by first adding a new field called PopulationMil and then updating the first record to include data for this field by running the following code:

```
ALTER TABLE dbo.Region
ADD PopulationMil INT NULL
GO

UPDATE dbo.Region
SET PopulationMil = 32
WHERE RegionID = 1
```

We can now query the SalesArea synonym to confirm the new field and data are in the dbo.Region table.

```
SELECT *
FROM SalesArea
```

	RegionID	RegionName	PopulationMil
1	1	Canada	32
			1 rows

Figure 2.17 Query the SalesArea synonym after adding the PopulationMil field to dbo.Region.

When we try to add another field called CorpDate using the SalesArea synonym it produces the error message shown in Figure 2.18, since this is a DDL statement.

```
ALTER TABLE SalesArea
ADD CorpDate DATETIME NULL
GO
```

```
Messages
Msg 4909, Level 16, State 1, Line 1
Cannot alter 'SalesArea' because it is not a table.
                                                        0 rows
```

Figure 2.18 The error message from attempting to add a field to a table with a synonym.

Let's try using the SalesArea synonym with a different DML statement to insert another row of data into the dbo.Region table with the following code.

```
INSERT INTO SalesArea VALUES
(2,'USA',310)
```

Great! We can see that it is possible to insert rows into a table (DML statement) using a synonym, even though we are unable to alter the table itself (DDL statement) by looking at the results of the following query.

```
SELECT * FROM SalesArea
```

	RegionID	RegionName	PopulationMil
1	1	Canada	32
2	2	USA	310
			2 rows

Figure 2.19 Using a synonym with a DML statement will work to add a row to dbo.Region table.

Changing a Synonym

Often times I have worked on testing systems that will someday be live systems for production. Perhaps the live system will have 100,000 real customers. While testing the system I had only 25 pretend customers in the database. All the processes that were linked to my test system are getting 'pretend' data. One day we will want to work with the real data. This might be as simple as just connecting to a new table name. For example the table dbo.CustomerTest has the mock data and the dbo.Customer table has the real data. If we set up the processes to access the dbo.CustomerTest table then we will need to change all of them. However if we set them to use a synonym, then all we need to do for the change to live data is have the synonym point to the new dbo.Customer table.

If we want to change a synonym we must first use a DROP SYNONYM statement and then a CREATE SYNONYM statement (Using ALTER will produce an error).

```
ALTER SYNONYM SalesArea
FOR dbo.StateList
GO
```

Messages
Msg 102, Level 15, State 1, Line 1
Incorrect syntax near 'SYNONYM'.
0 rows

Figure 2.20 A simple ALTER SYNONYM will produce an error.

We can avoid this error message by first dropping the SalesArea synonym and then creating a new SalesArea synonym pointing to the dbo.StateList table.

```
DROP SYNONYM SalesArea
GO

CREATE SYNONYM SalesArea
FOR dbo.StateList
GO

SELECT *
FROM SalesArea
```

	StateID	StateName	ProvinceName	RegionName	Landmass
1	AK	Alaska	NULL	USA	656425
2	AL	Alabama	NULL	USA-Continental	52423
3	AR	Arkansas	NULL	USA-Continental	53182
4	AZ	Arizona	NULL	USA-Continental	114006
5	CA	California	NULL	USA-Continental	163707
6	CO	Colorado	NULL	USA-Continental	104100
					63 rows

Figure 2.21 The SalesArea synonym is now pointing towards the dbo.StateList table.

The bad news is we can't alter a synonym; we can only drop and re-create it. Synonyms do save us some typing, but more importantly they often provide extra stability when naming objects that frequently change in our database.

Changing the name of a table once a client application has been deployed can cause migration issues. The need to be able to reference another object by its older name can become critical during system migrations and application development.

Lab 2.2: Synonyms

Lab Prep: Each lab has one or more Skill Checks. Start with Skill Check 1 and proceed until reaching the Points to Ponder section.

Before beginning this lab, verify that SQL Server 2012 is properly installed and operating. Before running the lab setup script for resetting the database (SQLQueries2012Vol3Chapter2.2Setup.sql), please make sure to close all query windows within SSMS. An open query window pointing to a database context can lock that database preventing it from updating when the script is executing. A simple way to assure all query windows are closed, is to exit out of SSMS, then open a new instance of SSMS, and lastly run the setup script.

Skill Check 1: Remove the Classes synonym from JProCo.

Skill Check 2: Change the SalesArea synonym to point to the dbo.Region table of JProCo. When done, query the SalesArea synonym and the results should resemble Figure 2.22.

```
SELECT * FROM SalesArea
```

	RegionID	RegionName	PopulationMil
1	1	Canada	32
2	2	USA	310
			2 rows

Figure 2.22 Results for Skill Check 2.

Skill Check 3: Write an INSERT INTO statement to place RegionID 3, Mexico, 120 using the SalesArea synonym. When done, query the SalesArea synonym and have the results resemble Figure 2.23.

```
SELECT * FROM SalesArea
```

	RegionID	RegionName	PopulationMil
1	1	Canada	32
2	2	USA	310
3	3	Mexico	120
			2 rows

Figure 2.23 Results for Skill Check 3.

Answer Code: The T-SQL code to this lab can be found in the downloadable files in a file named Lab2.2_Synonyms.sql.

Points to Ponder - Synonyms

1. The synonym was introduced in SQL Server 2005 and is an alternate name that can replace a two-, three-, or four-part object name in many SQL statements.

2. Client applications can use a single-part name to reference a base object by using a synonym instead of using a two-part, three-part, or four-part name to reference the base object.

3. Synonyms can reference views, tables, stored procedures, or functions.

4. Changing the name of a table once a client application has been deployed can cause migration issues. The need to be able to reference another object by its older name can become critical during system migrations and application development.

5. SYNONYMS can be used with these DML statements: *SELECT, UPDATE, INSERT, DELETE, and MERGE.* It also works with the *EXECUTE* statement.

6. The table or SQL object doesn't need to exist when you create the synonym, because synonyms are late bound: SQL Server only checks the base object when you actually use the synonym.

7. You create a synonym by issuing the CREATE SYNONYM FOR `[database].[SchemaName].[ObjectName]` statement.

8. If you don't specify a schema for the synonym, then SQL Server uses the current user's default schema.

9. Run-Time binding takes place as the code is executing. All objects must already exist, or be instantiated for the code to run correctly.

10. Late binding takes place after the referencing code has already run. The object referenced in the code can be created, or instantiated, at a later point in time.

Chapter Glossary

Fully qualified names: The syntax for fully qualified names in SQL Server is [server].[database].[schema].[object name]. In a fully qualified name the object must be explicitly identified.

Naming convention: The convention used for naming databases and files within a system.

Objects: Tables, stored procedures, views, etc. are SQL database objects.

Partially qualified names: Partially qualified names omit some of the qualifiers by leaving them out or by replacing them with another period.

Qualified query: Qualified queries look in the exact schema for the table.

Schemas: A namespace for database objects.

Script: SQL code saved as a file. A tool used by SQL Server Management Studio that will dynamically generate the underlying code for a database or object.

System-defined schema: The schemas created by SQL Server.

User-defined schema: Schemas created by the user.

Review Quiz - Chapter Two

1.)   What is a schema?

O a. A namespace for database objects.

O b. A namespace for tables only.

O c. A graphical map of the tables in your database.

2.)   You want to transfer the Employee table from the dbo schema to the HumanResources schema. What code will achieve this result?

O a. `ALTER SCHEMA dbo`
       `TRANSFER HumanResources.Employee`

O b. `ALTER SCHEMA HumanResources`
       `TRANSFER dbo.Employee`

O c. `ALTER TABLE dbo.Employee`
       `TRANSFER HumanResources.Employee`

3.)   In the following code using a four part fully qualified name, what is the name of the schema? `SELECT * FROM Reno.RatisCo.People.Employee`

O a. SELECT

O b. FROM

O c. Reno

O d. RatisCo

O e. People

O f. Employee

4.)   You are in the context of the JProCo database and want to write a query that will join the records of the Location table of the dbBasics database to the employee table of JProCo. Both tables are in the dbo schema. What code will achieve this result?

O a. `SELECT * FROM Employee AS em`
       `INNER JOIN dbo.Location AS lo`
       `ON em.LocationID = lo.LocationID`

O b. `SELECT * FROM  Employee AS em`
       `INNER JOIN JProCo.dbo.Location AS lo`
       `ON em.LocationID = lo.LocationID`

O c. `SELECT * FROM Employee AS em`
       `INNER JOIN dbBasics.dbo.Location AS lo`
       `ON em.LocationID = lo.LocationID`

5.)   You are in the JProCo database and have these two queries:

```
SELECT * FROM Employee
SELECT * FROM dbo.Employee
```

Assuming the data in the Employee table never changes what is true about these two queries regarding use of the schemas?

O a. These two queries will always produce the same results.

O b. These two queries will always produce the same results as long as all users have dbo as their default schema.

O c. The one with the simple name will error out.

O d. The one with the 2-part qualified name will access another database and get different results.

6.)   You have a database where everyone is using dbo as the default schema, and want to keep it that way, but you have a consultant named Tom who needs to use the Consultant schema. Which statement below is true?

O a. The default schema is a database setting, so changing it affects all users.

O b. A default schema can be assigned to each database user.

7.)   You want to create a new table named Locations.WorldRegions in the RatisCo database and refer to it as dbo.Areas for the JProCo database. You decide to create this table and create a synonym named dbo.Areas in JProCo. What order should this work be performed to get both tasks done?

O a. You MUST create the RatisCo.Locations.WorldRegions before you create the dbo.Areas synonym.

O b. You MUST create the dbo.Areas synonym before you create the RatisCo.Locations.WorldRegions table.

O c. It does not matter which one you create first.

8.)   You have a C# ado.net client application using a single-part name to reference the Invoice table of JProCo. You are changing the name of the table the client application is still using. This is a critical system migration and for the next 6 months you will not be able to change the client application to point to the new code. You are given a 5 minute window where the client will be shut off and need to complete the work. What should you do?

O a.   Create a synonym for the old table name and rename the new table.

O b.   Rename the new table and then create a synonym named after the old tables' name.

9.)   Which Statement can NOT be used with a synonym?

O a.   SELECT

O b.   UPDATE

O c.   INSERT

O d.   DELETE

O e.   EXECUTE

O f.   ALTER

Answer Key

1.) A schema works on more than just a table, so (b) is incorrect. A schema is a namespace for database objects, making (a) correct.

2.) To move an object, it is necessary to alter the schema making (c) incorrect. The schema being altered must be named before moving the table, making (a) wrong and (b) correct.

3.) A schema cannot be a keyword making (a) and (b) wrong. The database uses a fully qualified name of (*Server.Database.Schema.ObjectName*) making (e) the correct answer.

4.) To write a query across a database context, using a three or four part name is necessary, so (a) is incorrect. The three part name in this question needs to access the dbBasics database (not JProCo), so (c) is the correct answer.

5.) A query with a simple name and a two part name will always run in its own database context, so (d) is incorrect. Simple names use the default schema instead of producing an error, so (c) is wrong. The simple name will use the users default schema which could be dbo or another schema, so (a) is wrong. The correct answer is (b).

6.) The default schema is not a database setting, so (a) is wrong. A default schema can be assigned to each database user, so (b) is correct.

7.) Thanks to the late binding nature of synonyms, (a) and (b) are wrong, as either one can be created first, making (c) correct.

8.) Both answers are pretty good, although it is bad practice to create a synonym with the exact same name as an existing table, making (a) incorrect. Renaming the table and then naming the synonym to use the old name of the table is the more preferred practice, so (b) is correct.

9.) SYNONYMS can only be used with DML statements like: SELECT, UPDATE, INSERT, DELETE, MERGE, and EXECUTE making (a), (b), (c), (d), and (e) all usable comments. None of the DDL statements can be used with a synonym, so (f) is the correct answer.

Bug Catcher Game

To play the Bug Catcher game, run the SQLQueries2012Vol3BugCatcher02.pps file from the BugCatcher folder of the companion files. These files can be obtained from the www.Joes2Pros.com website.

[THIS PAGE INTENTIONALLY LEFT BLANK.]

Chapter 3.   Data Type Usage

While processing power, memory, and disk storage have all become cheaper and more plentiful in the last decade, the tasks of capacity planning and estimating infrastructure requirements are still important to the IT world.

It is also incumbent upon a SQL Pro to become intimately familiar with the data types available to SQL Server and their impacts on performance and storage consumption. The next three Chapters will cover data type options and usage. During our career as a database developer we will use this knowledge in designing and implementing our own database systems, as well as troubleshooting and diagnosing performance issues with existing databases.

Factors that affect the space data consumes are the choice of data types, including fixed versus variable length, and whether or not the data type supports Unicode. The building blocks of database objects are fields, so our storage calculations will be based on the fields contained within a row.

READER NOTE: *Please run the SQLQueries2012Vol3Chapter3.0Setup.sql script in order to follow along with the examples in the first section of Chapter 3. All scripts mentioned in this chapter may be found at www.Joes2Pros.com.*

Data Row Space Usage

Most of a table's space is occupied by records. Indexes and other properties use a relatively small amount of known space. Suppose our company manager lays out the design of the SalesInvoiceDetail table and says, "We expect this table to receive an average of 100,000 records per day during the next two years". Then they ask, *"How much hard drive space should we purchase to handle this expected growth rate?"*

Knowing how many rows will be received in a day and how many days there are in a year is a great start. The unknown in this scenario is the amount of space each row will use. Calculating the amount of space each row needs, helps in answering this resource planning question for the new table.

100,000 rows/day * 365 days = 36,500,000 rows

36,500,000 rows * __ KB/row = _____ KB of storage space needed

Our calculations will similarly focus on data rows. In order to estimate a row's space consumption, we must know the amount of space each field's data will use.

There are three key components which contribute to a field's space consumption:

- The data type.
- Whether the data type is fixed or variable.
- Whether the field is nullable.

READER NOTE: *Nullability is a substantial topic, so we will handle it in the next section. The storage calculations in this section will ignore nullability and will be revised in the nullability section.*

Units of Measurement

The data types and storage measurements in this chapter are denominated in bytes, since the smallest data type in SQL Server uses one byte.

A kilobyte (KB) consists of 1024 bytes. A megabyte (MB) consists of 1024 KB, or over a million bytes (1,048,576 bytes), and a gigabyte (GB) consists of 1024 MB.

Row Header

Every row has a four byte header. It contains two bytes that say what kind of record it is, plus one byte for index records and one for the NULL bitmap. The

NULL bitmap is always present whether or not the columns are nullable. (An exception to this rule of thumb would be tables comprised solely of sparse columns, which are discussed in Chapter 4.)

Common Data Types

The names and storage amounts per field for many commonly used data types are shown here *(An * denotes variable length data types).*

Exact Numeric data types

INT (integer)	4 bytes
BIGINT	8 bytes
SMALLINT	2 bytes
TINYINT	1 byte
MONEY	8 bytes
SMALLMONEY	4 bytes
DECIMAL	5-17 bytes, depending on the number of digits
NUMERIC	5-17 bytes, depending on the number of digits
BIT	1-8 bit fields use 1 byte; 9-16 bit fields use 2 bytes; etc.

Approximate Numeric data types

FLOAT	4 bytes (1-24 digits); 8 bytes (25-53 digits)

Character data types

CHAR (character)	1 byte per character (maximum of 8000 characters)
VARCHAR*	1 byte per character (maximum of 8000 characters)
TEXT	1 byte per character (to a maximum of 2 GB)

Date and Time data types

TIME	5 bytes
DATETIME	8 bytes
SMALLDATETIME	4 bytes
DATE	3 bytes
DATETIME2	6-8 bytes, depending on precision

	Data Type	Sample Output
1	Time	12:44:01.7000000
2	DateTime	2012-07-21 12:44:01.573
3	smalldatetime	2012-07-21 12:44:00
4	Date	2012-07-21
5	datetime2	2012-07-21 12:44:01.5730000

5 rows

Figure 3.1 Sample outputs for date and time data types.

Unicode character data types

NCHAR	2 bytes per character (maximum of 4000 characters)
NVARCHAR*	2 bytes per character (maximum of 4000 characters)
NTEXT	2 bytes per character (maximum of 2GB)

Spatial data types *(new since SQL Server 2008 – see Chapter 5)*

GEOGRAPHY	geodetic
GEOMETRY	planar

Other data types

XML	2GB

Unicode Data

Unicode supports foreign language characters needed for international data (e.g., German umlauts, accents for romance language characters, Japanese characters, etc.).

With Unicode data types (e.g., NCHAR, NVARCHAR, NTEXT), each character occupies 2 bytes. In SQL Server, a Unicode data type is generally denoted by an 'n' or 'N'. When SQL Server generates code involving Unicode data, you see an 'N' accompanying Unicode data throughout the script (Refer to *SQL Queries 2012 Volume 1* Chapter 11 for more information on code generators).

Following the pattern of regular character data (CHAR, VARCHAR), a blank space included in Unicode data (e.g., a space in a name [Joe Smith], or an address [1234 Main Street]) is counted as a character.

Fixed Data

Fixed length data types always occupy the amount of space allotted to them. For example, an INT will always use 4 bytes. A CHAR(3) always takes up 3 bytes, even if the field contains just 1 or 2 characters. Fixed length data is predictable and the easiest type of data for SQL Server to manage. Calculations involving fixed data are straightforward. However, variable length data incurs additional overhead.

Variable Block

Every record containing variable length data includes something called a variable block. Creating a field with a variable length data type (e.g., VARCHAR or

NVARCHAR), a variable block is created. This block tracks the number of variable length data fields within the record and takes up 2 bytes.

The more variable length fields, the bigger the variable block grows. Each variable length field adds another 2 bytes to the block. These 2 bytes keep track of where the data is positioned within the row. For example, if there is one VARCHAR field within a row, the variable block would contain 4 bytes. If there are two VARCHAR fields, the variable block would contain 6 bytes (2 bytes per field plus 2 bytes to initiate the block).

Variable Data

Variable length data types do pretty much what the name implies – they expect the data length to vary from row to row. Fields using variable length data types, such as VARCHAR and NVARCHAR, are typically a name or address field where it is difficult to know how long the data will be.

The advantage these data types offer is that shorter names or addresses can take up less storage space than a fixed data type. For example, if the row contains a CHAR(100) field to allow for long addresses, then that field always uses 100 bytes no matter how long the data actually is. However, if we know that most of our addresses consist of 20 characters, we probably would choose a VARCHAR(100) to use less storage space but retain the flexibility to accept addresses up to 100 characters in length.

In addition to the storage used by the variable block, we must count the actual number of characters in each VARCHAR or NVARCHAR field. This is one difference between fixed and varying length data. With fixed data, we can calculate the storage consumption without needing to look at the actual data. While it is possible to estimate maximum storage requirements for varying length data without looking at the actual data, in order to precisely calculate how much storage a row or table is actually utilizing, we need to examine the length of data in each of the variable data fields.

VARCHAR data consumes 1 byte per character. NVARCHAR data consumes 2 bytes per character, because it is Unicode. For example a VARCHAR(10) field containing the name "Rick" would consume 4 bytes. If it were an NVARCHAR, it would use 8 bytes.

```
SELECT *, LEN(RoomName) AS VarDataLength
FROM JProCo.HumanResources.RoomChart
```

	R_ID	R_Code	RoomName	VarDataLength
1	1	RLT	Renault-Langsford-Tribute	25
2	2	QTX	Quinault-Experience	19
3	3	TQW	TranquilWest	12
4	4	XW	XavierWest	10
5	5	NULL	NULL	NULL

5 rows

Figure 3.2 The LEN() function measures the length of data for each RoomName.

Now let's bring in the design interface for the RoomChart table, which we will use to calculate the actual space consumption for rows in the RoomChart table. We will look at the table design along with our LEN() query result, (Figure 3.2) so we have the length measurements handy for the RoomName field (Figure 3.3).

To see this interface, use SSMS to navigate to the following location:

Object Explorer > Databases > JProCo > Tables > right-click HumanResources.RoomChart > Design

READER NOTE: The image in Figure 3.3 has been altered using special software in order to help visualize the SSMS Design tool interface and the Query Results at the same time. Please do not expect to see, or be able to replicate an exact duplication of the following image, as they are two distinct images stitched together for informational purposes only.

We can now begin working with the SSMS Design tool interface.

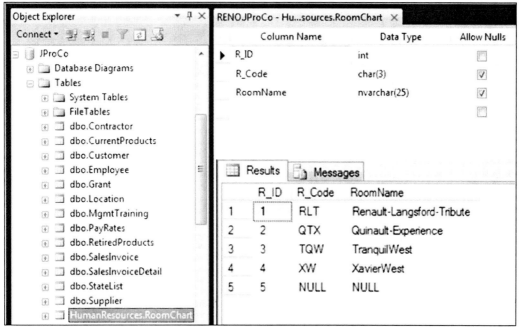

Figure 3.3 The design of the HumanResources.RoomChart table in the JProCo database, with the results from the most recent query added for visual effect (Two images shown as one).

Let's calculate the actual space consumption for Row 1 of the RoomChart table.

We begin with the header, followed by the fixed length data. The header always contains 4 bytes. Each of the four rows have two fixed length fields (R_ID and R_Code). The R_ID field uses 4 bytes and the R_Code field uses 3 bytes. Thus, without looking at the data, we already know each row uses at least 11 bytes.

Header + Fixed Length Fields (R_ID and R_Code fields)

4 bytes + 4 bytes + 3 bytes = **11 bytes**

The final field (RoomName) contains variable length data, so in order to evaluate the space consumption we must first calculate the variable block and then look at the actual data.

Since there is one variable field per row, we must allow 2 bytes for the creation of the variable block. Next, we must multiply the number of variable field(s) in the row by 2 bytes.

Variable Block

2 bytes + (1 field * 2 bytes per field) = **4 bytes**

Actual Data

Renault-Langsford-Tribute has 25 Unicode characters = **50 bytes**

Header 4 | Fixed Data 7 | Variable Block 4 | Variable Data 50 = 65 bytes

The total space used for Row 1 of the RoomChart table is 65 bytes.

Now let's calculate the space used by the second row of this table. Once again, we begin with the header and the fixed length data.

Header + Fixed Length Fields (R_ID and R_Code fields)

4 bytes + 4 bytes + 3 bytes = **11 bytes**

The variable block consumes the same amount of space in each row. We previously calculated Row 1's variable block to be 4 bytes, as will row 2.

Variable Block

2 bytes + (1 field * 2 bytes per field) = **4 bytes**

Actual Data

Quinault-Experience, 19 Unicode characterss = **38 bytes**

Header 4 | Fixed Data 7 | Variable Block 4 | Variable Data 38 = 53 bytes

The total space used for Row 2 of the RoomChart table is 53 bytes.

READER NOTE: *It is recommended to watch the lab video Lab3.1_Data rows.wmv, which recaps the data type guidelines and calculations covered in this section. It also contains additional storage calculation demonstrations. The video shows a helpful interface to reference when checking data type information for columns in each table (Figure 3.4).*

Figure 3.4 shows the Amount field of the Grant table (JProCo.dbo.[Grant]). The storage size of Amount is 4 bytes as shown in the "Size" item on the Column Properties tab of the Design interface.

Object Explorer > Databases > JProCo > Tables > right-click on **dbo.Grant > Design**

We can now begin working with the SSMS Design tool interface.

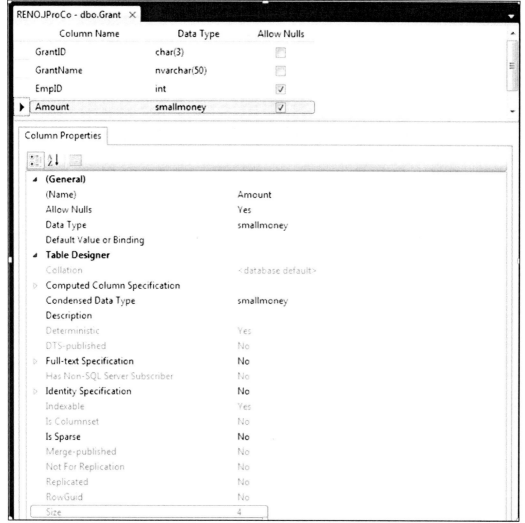

Figure 3.4 The SSMS Design interface shows the table design and detailed column information.

Similar information may also be found in a slightly different user interface (Figure 3.5). Either interface may be used to quickly look up a field's size, which is a helpful reference for how much space a certain data type uses.

The 'Size' property shown above in the Design interface is generally the equivalent of the 'Length' property. With most Unicode types (except NTEXT), the 'Size' column will display the number of bytes, and the 'Length' column will show the number of characters.

Notice that the Column Properties interface, shown in Figure 3.5, includes a description for the behavior of each property.

Object Explorer > Databases > JProCo > Tables > dbo.Grant > Columns >Amount > right-click Properties.

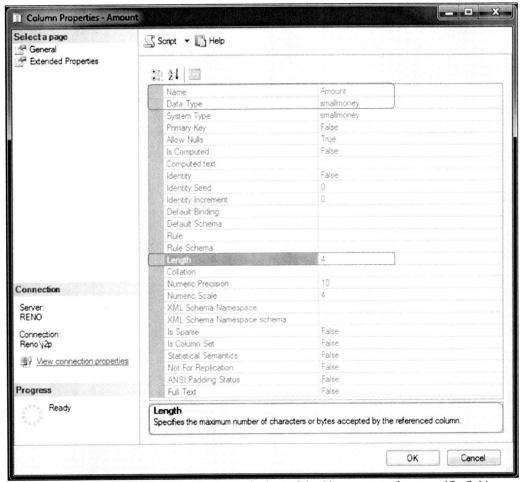

Figure 3.5 "Length" in this interface is the equivalent of the Size property for a specific field.

Lab 3.1: Data Row Space Usage

Lab Prep: Each lab has one or more Skill Checks. Start with Skill Check 1 and proceed until reaching the Points to Ponder section.

Before beginning this lab, verify that SQL Server 2012 is properly installed and operating. Before running the lab setup script for resetting the database (SQLQueries2012Vol3Chapter3.1Setup.sql), please make sure to close all query windows within SSMS. An open query window pointing to a database context can lock that database preventing it from updating when the script is executing. A simple way to assure all query windows are closed, is to exit out of SSMS, then open a new instance of SSMS, and lastly run the setup script.

Skill Check 1: Calculate the space consumption of Rows 3 and 4 according to the table design and data shown in Figure 3.6.

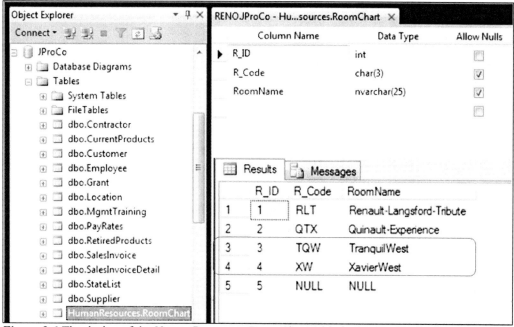

Figure 3.6 The design of the HumanResources.RoomChart table in the JProCo database.

Answer Code: The T-SQL code to this lab can be found in the downloadable files in a file named Lab3.1_DataRows.sql.

Points to Ponder - Data Row Space Usage

1. A data row consists of 1) a row header and 2) a data portion. The row header (positioning header) keeps track of where the row is in the table and the fields it contains.

2. A data row always includes a 4 byte header. The rest of the space is dedicated to holding and supporting the actual data in the data portion.

3. Fixed length data types always occupy the same amount of storage regardless of the number of characters actually present in the field. For example, a CHAR(100) name field will take up 100 bytes in each row whether a name contains NULL, 0, 2, 52, 92, or 100 characters.

4. Fixed length data is easier for SQL Server to manage than variable length data, which incur additional overhead for SQL Server to manage. Where you expect column data to be fairly consistent, it's generally better to use a fixed length data type.

5. If a table includes any variable data types, then each row will contain a variable block. This variable block consists of 1) 2 bytes used to keep track of the number of variable fields in the row; and 2) an additional 2 bytes for each variable data type field.

6. A space in a field is considered a character and consumes the same number of bytes as any other character in the field. For example, the RoomName value 'Blue Room' consists of 9 characters. It would consume 18 bytes in a Unicode field and 9 bytes in a regular (ASCII) field.

7. The manufacturer of SQL Server (Microsoft) has indicated that the data types NTEXT, TEXT, and IMAGE will be removed in a future version of SQL Server (No planned release or date has yet been specified as of the publication date of this book). Since the introduction of the max specification in SQL Server 2005, these data types, known as 'max data types', are the preferred types for handling large values (*The final section of this chapter "Large Values" for more on this topic*).

NULL Data

One important piece of the storage calculation we haven't yet considered is the NULL Block. Somewhat like variable length data fields, each record in a table containing nullable field(s) uses a little extra storage space.

NULL Block

In the last section, we learned that each record begins with a standard 4 byte row header. Right after the row header, the first item in the data portion of the record is the fixed data. SQL Server stores together all of the columns containing fixed width data.

If the table contains nullable data, then a NULL Block follows the fixed data and occupies the third space in the physical structure of the record (*Without the NULL Block, the usual order prevails - #1 Row Header, #2 Fixed Data, #3 Variable Block, and #4 Variable Data payload*).

Row Header	Fixed Data	NULL Block	Variable Block	Variable Data

Figure 3.7 In the data portion of a row, the NULL Block is located immediately after the fixed data.

The NULL Block (also called the *NULL bitmap*) is created at the same time a nullable field is created in a table. The NULL Block in each row begins as 2 bytes but may grow as more fields are added to the table.

Next, we must count the total number of columns in the table. Add an additional byte to the row's NULL Block for the first field and another byte for every 8th field. In other words, if a table has between 1-8 fields (columns), then the NULL Block in each row will be 3 bytes. If the table contains 9-16 fields, then the NULL Block will be 4 bytes per row. If the table contains 17-24 fields, then the NULL Block will be 5 bytes per row, and so forth.

These additional bytes contain an indicator for each column's nullability. In other words, whether the column will allow NULLs (e.g., R_Code, RoomName) or won't allow NULLs (e.g., the R_ID column in the RoomChart table).

NULL Block Storage Allocation

It often surprises people to know that it only takes one nullable field to cause every field in the table to take up 1 bit of extra space in the NULL Block. These additional bits keep track of each column and whether it does or doesn't contain a NULL. The following diagram (Figure 3.8) illustrates two tables: one in which every column is nullable and one containing only a single nullable column.

Table T1

Table T1	Row 1
	Row Data
c1 nullable	1
c2 nullable	2
c3 nullable	3
c4 nullable	4
c5 nullable	5
c6 nullable	6
c7 nullable	7
c8 nullable	8
c9 nullable	9
c10 nullable	10

Null Block

Byte 2								Byte 1							
7	6	5	4	3	2	1	0	7	6	5	4	3	2	1	0
1	1	1	1	1	1	0	0	0	0	0	0	0	0	0	0
Unused						c10	c9	c8	c7	c6	c5	c4	c3	c2	c1

Table T2

Table T2	Row 1
	Row Data
c1 not null	1
c2 not null	2
c3 not null	3
c4 not null	4
c5 not null	5
c6 not null	6
c7 not null	7
c8 not null	8
c9 no nulls	9
c10 nullable	null

Null Block

Byte 2								Byte 1							
7	6	5	4	3	2	1	0	7	6	5	4	3	2	1	0
1	1	1	1	1	1	1	1	0	0	0	0	0	0	0	0
Unused						c10	c9	c8	c7	c6	c5	c4	c3	c2	c1

Figure 3.8 In the data portion of a row, the NULL Block is located immediately after the fixed data.

Each table contains 10 columns, c1 through c10. Since there are 10 columns, and each table contains at least one nullable column, 10 additional bits are needed which means 2 additional bytes are needed. The NULL Block already contains a 2 byte fixed length field, and a variable length bitmap of 1 bit per column. In this case 10 bits (c1 – c10) crosses into the next byte. The variable length bitmap takes up 2 more bytes, bringing the size to 4 bytes for both tables' NULL Blocks.

Notice that in table T1 in Figure 3.8, an INSERT statement placed the integer values 1 through 10 in columns c1 through c10, respectively. Since none of these values is NULL, the NULL Block bitmap contains 0s for columns c1 through c10. On the right half of this figure, we see these bits are located in byte 1 for columns c1 through c8, and byte 2 for columns c9 and c10. The additional 6 bits of byte 2 of the NULL Block bitmap are allocated to the NULL Block not used by any columns. In table T2 we have one NULL value in the last column. An INSERT statement placed the integer values 1 through 9 in columns c1 through c9, and NULL in column c10. Columns c1 through c9 are not NULL, so the NULL Block bitmap contains 0's (zeros) for those columns. Column c10 (lower right half of Figure 3.8) does contain a NULL, so its bit in the NULL Block bitmap reflects a 1.

In a table that contains at least one nullable column, each row will contain a NULL Block whose length depends on the number of columns in the table. If a row of such a table contains a NULL value for a nullable column, its bit in that row's NULL Block bitmap will be set to 1. Columns which are not NULL have their bits in the row's NULL Block bitmap set to 0.

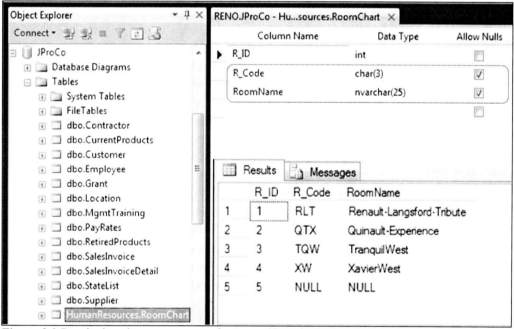

Figure 3.9 Recalculate the storage space for RoomChart, including the two nullable fields.

Recall that we calculated the space consumption for Row 1 as 65 bytes.

Actual Data

Renault-Langsford-Tribute, 25 Unicode chars = **50 bytes**

Header 4 | Fixed Data 7 | Variable Block 4 | Variable Data 50 = 65 bytes

We know a NULL Block is needed, since there are nullable fields in the RoomChart table. The two nullable fields, (R_Code and RoomName) are shown in Figure 3.9.

Creating the NULL Block uses 2 bytes. Then we must count the total number of columns in the table. This table contains 3 columns, so add 1 byte to the NULL Block.

NULL Block

2 bytes + 1 byte (only 3 fields) = **3 bytes**

This means we must add 3 bytes to our original storage calculation for Row 1:

 Header 4 | Fixed 7 | NULL Block 3 | Variable Block 4 | Variable Data 50 = 68 bytes

The full amount of space used by Row 1 of the RoomChart table is 68 bytes.

Now let's recalculate the second row's space usage including the NULL Block. Recall we calculated the space consumption for Row 2 as 53 bytes.

Actual Data

Quinault-Experience, 19 Unicode chars = **38 bytes**

 Header 4 | Fixed Data 7 | Variable Block 4 | Variable Data 38 = 53 bytes

Since the NULL Block for each record in the table will be the same size, we know the NULL Block for Row 2 will be the same as Row 1 (3 bytes).

NULL Block

2 bytes + 1 byte (only 3 fields)] = **3 bytes**

We must add 3 bytes to our original storage calculation for Row 2:

 Header 4 | Fixed 7 | NULL Block 3 | Variable Block 4 | Variable Data 38 = 56 bytes

The full amount of space used by Row 2 of the RoomChart table is 56 bytes.

Some additional tips to keep in mind when calculating variable length data payloads are listed here:

- o Spaces count as characters. Suppose the room in the HumanResources table named "Quinault-Experience" was spelled "Quinault Experience". *Both versions of this name consume 38 bytes.*

o If a variable length field contains a NULL value, then the data payload is 0 bytes.

o A fixed lengh field will always contain the same data payload, even if the field contains a NULL value. For example, a CHAR(20) field will always consume 20 bytes. If that field contains a NULL value, then the data payload for the field is still 20 bytes.

Lab 3.2: NULL Data

Lab Prep: Each lab has one or more Skill Checks. Start with Skill Check 1 and proceed until reaching the Points to Ponder section.

Before beginning this lab, verify that SQL Server 2012 is properly installed and operating. Before running the lab setup script for resetting the database (SQLQueries2012Vol3Chapter3.2Setup.sql), please make sure to close all query windows within SSMS. An open query window pointing to a database context can lock that database preventing it from updating when the script is executing. A simple way to assure all query windows are closed, is to exit out of SSMS, then open a new instance of SSMS, and lastly run the setup script.

READER NOTE: *The video Lab3.2_NullData.wmv recaps the data type guidelines and calculations covered in this section. It also contains additional storage calculation demonstrations from the Grant and Employee tables of the JProCo database.*

Skill Check 1: Calculate the Total storage space used by the Header, Fixed Data, NULL Block, Variable Block, and Variable Data for each row in the table named HumanResources.RoomChart. Use the table design and the data contained in the five rows shown in Figure 3.10 as a reference.

READER NOTE: *Values in some of the records have been changed a bit from the examples used earlier or later in this chapter.*

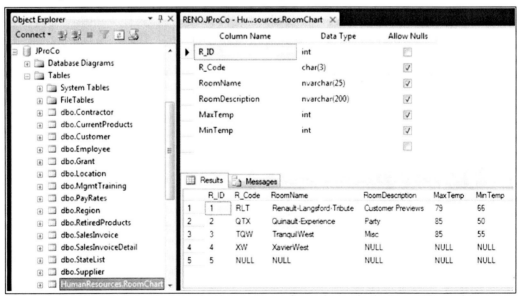

Figure 3.10 Skill Check 1 calculates the storage space for each row in the RoomChart table.

	Header	Fixed Data	Null Block	Variable Block	Variable Data	Total
Row 1						
Row 2						
Row 3						
Row 4						
Row 5						

Answer Code: The T-SQL code to this lab can be found in the downloadable files in a file named Lab3.2_NullData.sql.

Points to Ponder - NULL Data

1. A data row consists of a row header and a data portion. The 4 byte row header contains information about the columns and the data row.

2. The data portion of a row can contain the following elements.
    - Fixed length data
    - NULL Block
    - Variable block
    - Variable length data

3. Data rows can hold up to a total of 8060 bytes per row.

4. Fixed length data (like INT, CHAR, NCHAR etc.) comes right after the row header portion of the record. Fixed length data is always the first section of the data portion of the row space allocation.

5. Variable length data goes at the end of the row data, and takes up varying amounts of space, depending on its content.

6. A 2 byte NULL Block (NULL bitmap) is created to track nullable fields in a table.

7. The NULL Block has one bit per column in the table definition, as long as at least one column in the table is nullable (8 bits make up 1 byte).

8. An additional byte is added to the NULL Block for the first column in the table and every 8th column thereafter. At a minimum the NULL Block adds 3 bytes of storage to each row in the table. *READERNOTE*: only non-sparse columns are included in the one bit per column calculations. In other words, sparse data columns are excluded from the count of columns. The sparse data option is discussed in Chapter 4.

9. A NULL value in a variable length field counts as 0 data payload.

Large Values

Thus far, the data types we've examined carry a maximum of 8000 bytes per field. However, there may be times when it is necessary for a field to hold *large values* – that is to say, values exceeding 8000 bytes.

Every day we see examples of databases containing large items. When a document or an image is uploaded to a SharePoint site, a large value data item is being stored in a database field. Many online shopping outlets use picture and sound files in this way. If a company saves employee photos (e.g., to print onto employee badges), it most likely stores them as VARBINARY files within a database.

Prior to SQL Server 2005, large object (LOB) types were the only way to bypass the 8000 byte limit of typical data types (e.g., CHAR, VARCHAR, VARBINARY, etc.). The three original LOB types were IMAGE, TEXT, *and* NTEXT. We are certain to encounter these LOB types hanging around in legacy systems. However, the use of these types is discouraged since Microsoft plans to eliminate them and the new types introduced with SQL Server 2005 are meant to replace them, as they have better performance and are easier to work with.

Since SQL Server 2005, developers have been praising the new MAX specification used in combination with VARCHAR, NVARCHAR, and VARBINARY to handle large values. In fact, this specification, VARCHAR(MAX), NVARCHAR(MAX), and VARBINARY(MAX) are known as *large-value data types*, which make it easier to include large items with your typical relational database data.

In this section we will explore the difference between programming with regular data types versus large-value data types, as well as SQL Server's behind-the-scenes handling of these data types.

Memory Page

Discussions of large values invariably must consider how SQL Server stores data. A *memory page* is 8 KB (8 kilobytes) of physical space set aside for rapid storage and retrieval of records. This 8 KB actually converts to 8192 bytes, although SQL Server can only utilize 8060 of those 8192 bytes for storage. Therefore data types which limit themselves to 8000 bytes operate very fast and efficiently, because they can fit within the organized pages of memory.

Most data types in SQL Server are known as value types because each value will be 8000 bytes, or less, and thus will fit within an 8 KB page of memory. For example, an NVARCHAR(4000) takes up to 8000 bytes, as does a VARCHAR(8000).

Let's evaluate the HumanResources.RoomChart table with respect to how SQL Server will store data. First we need to calculate how much storage it consumes.

READER NOTE: *The examples shown in this section are taken from the Lab3.3_LargeObjects video. Please watch this video first to better understand the concepts shown in this section*

RENO.JProCo-...rces.RoomChart

Column Name	Data Type	Allow Nulls
ID	int	☐
Code	nchar(3)	☑
RoomName	nvarchar(25)	☑
RoomDescription	nvarchar(200)	☑

Results | Messages

	ID	Code	RoomName	RoomDescription
1	1	RLT	Renault-Langsford-Tribute	This room is designed for Customer Previews
2	2	QTX	Quinault-Experience	Parties and Morale Events get top priority
3	3	TQW	TranquilWest	Misc
4	4	XW	XavierWest	NULL
5	5	NULL	NULL	NULL

Figure 3.11 The RoomChart table as it appears in the Lab3.3_LargeObjects video.

The safest method for performing capacity planning calculations on tables with variable length data is to assume each field will contain the maximum allowable length of data. Now let's calculate the storage requirements for the table.

As always, we will begin with the row header and fixed length data.

Header + Fixed Length Fields (R_ID field and R_Code field)

4 bytes + 4 bytes + 6 bytes = **14 bytes**

The NULL Block consumes the same amount of space in each row. Two (2) bytes for the setup of the NULL Block, one byte for the first column in the table and one byte for every 8th column thereafter.

NULL Block

2 bytes + 1 byte (only 4 fields) = **3 bytes**

The variable block also consumes the same amount of space in each row. The setup of the variable block takes 2 bytes. Add 2 more bytes for each variable length field present (RoomName, RoomDescription).

Variable Block

2 bytes + (2 fields * 2 bytes per field) = **6 bytes**

The variable data can only be calculated after data is placed in the table. A single character in an NVARCHAR(200) it will take up less space than if 200 characters are placed in that field.

Variable Data Fields (estimate the maximum allowable length)

RoomName is set to contain 25 Unicode characters = **50 bytes**
RoomDescription is set to contain 200 Unicode characters = **400 bytes**

Header 4 | Fixed 10 | NULL Block 3 | Variable Block 6 | Variable Data 450 = 473 bytes

Each row of the RoomChart table can use up to 473 bytes.

Rows are meant to fit into a page of data (8060 bytes). Many rows can fit into a page, which is very efficient. For example, since each row of the RoomChart table will use up to 473 bytes, then 17 rows of this size will fit into one 8 KB page.

473 bytes per row * 17 rows = 8041 bytes

A table's rows can become too big, It is most efficient if each field can fit within an 8 KB page. This is why data types which limit themselves to 8000 bytes, or less, operate very fast and very efficiently.

Large Object Types

Suppose we need a field to contain data beyond the typical 8000 byte limit. Example: A request to have a RoomNotes field added to the RoomChart table that is capable of holding lengthy notes for a few of the conference rooms which have historical anecdotes or significance. Perhaps a foreign dignitary visited this room, and we'd like to store that information in the database.

Prior to SQL Server 2005, if a field needed to contain a string greater than 8000 bytes a large object (LOB) type, such as a TEXT or NTEXT would have been needed to accomplish this requirement. These act much like a VARCHAR or an NVARCHAR, but are stored outside of the row's normal memory space.

We will add this field to the table and make the data type NTEXT. We believe the field will likely contain 5000 characters (i.e., 10,000 bytes of Unicode data), and we want our users to be free to include as much data as they wish.

With the NTEXT data type, they will be able to include up to 2 GB of data or over 1 billion Unicode characters (1,073,741,822) . The storage limit for TEXT and IMAGE data is 2,147,483,647 characters which is also 2 GB.

In the design interface, add a RoomNotes column of data type NTEXT (Nullable).

Object Explorer > Databases > JProCo > Tables > right-click **HumanResources.RoomChart > Design**

OR

Object Explorer > Databases > JProCo > Tables > HumanResources.RoomChart > Object Explorer Details > right-click **Columns > New Column**

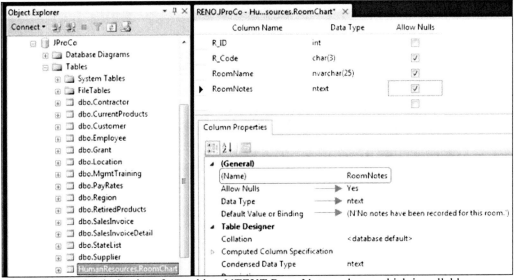

Figure 3.12 In the design interface, add an NTEXT RoomNotes column which is nullable.

Recall that the LOB data is stored outside of the row's normal memory space. LOBs were the first SQL Server data type allowing developers to exceed the 8000 byte constraint. However, they have to be managed by SQL Server in a separate memory space, which costs additional processing time and degrades performance. For each row in a table with a LOB field, SQL Server creates separate memory to pages for that field's data. So, a 100-row table requires separate memory pages be created for every row, even if a row's LOB field is NULL or contains just a small amount of data.

As a database developer or designer, we want to avoid LOBs. Eliminate or convert existing LOBs where possible, and use the newer data types for any new development work. The fact that the LOB is not stored with the rest of the row data automatically increases processing time because SQL Server needs extra I/O (input/output) cycles to access the other data pages – and it must repeat the process for every row in the table. SQL Server logically links the row together when query or update/insert statements are run against the table.

When a LOB field is included in a table, SQL Server stores a pointer to the LOB data in the row along with the regular data. This 16-byte pointer in the data row points to a root structure in another part of memory where the actual LOB data is held.

This 16-byte pointer is indicated by the Size field shown in the Column Properties tab of the Design interface (Figure 3.13).

Object Explorer > Databases > JProCo > Tables > right-click **HumanResources.RoomChart > Design**

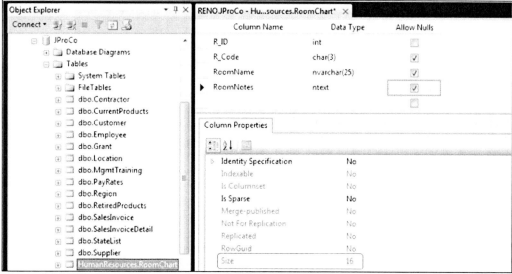

Figure 3.13 SQL Server stores a pointer to LOB data along with regular data in each row.

Next we'll add the RoomNotes field into our storage estimation for the RoomChart table (Refer to the design shown in Figure 3.13).

In a capacity planning report, the net impact of adding the RoomNotes field (NTEXT) is calculated by:

○   An additional 16 bytes in the fixed length portion of the row.

o   Allowing up to 2 GB in the data file (MDF/NDF) for each LOB field. *Since the data payload for LOBs is stored outside the data row, the data payload itself won't be added to the data row.*

Prior to adding the RoomNotes field, recall that we estimated that each row of the RoomChart table would use up to 473 bytes and as many as 17 rows would fit into a single 8 KB page.

Header 4 | Fixed 10 | NULL Block 3 | Variable Block 6 | Variable Data 450 = 473 bytes

473 bytes per row * 17 rows = 8041 bytes

Now we'll add the NTEXT field, RoomNotes, to the row calculation. With LOBs, the 16-byte pointer for each field is stored with the fixed data. The data payload itself is stored outside the data row.

We begin by adding the pointer to the row header and fixed length data calculation.

Header + Fixed Length Fields (R_ID and R_Code fields) + External Row Pointer

4 bytes + 4 bytes + 6 bytes + 16 bytes = **30 bytes**

The RoomNotes field is nullable, although it only increases the number of columns in the table from 4 to 5, so no additional bytes are needed for the NULL Block.

NULL Block

2 bytes + 1 byte (only 5 fields) = **3 bytes**

Variable Block (LOBs never impact the variable block.)

2 bytes + (2 fields * 2 bytes per field) = **6 bytes**

Variable Data Fields (estimate the maximum allowable length)

RoomName is set to contain 25 Unicode characters = **50 bytes**
RoomDescription is set to contain 200 Unicode characters = **400 bytes**

Header 4 | Fixed 26 | NULL Block 3 | Variable Block 6 | Variable Data 450 = 489 bytes

The total for each row of the RoomChart table will now use up to 489 bytes. At 489 bytes per row, one fewer row will now fit within a data page.

489 bytes/row * 17 rows = ~~8313 bytes~~ *(must be below 8060 bytes)*

489 bytes/row * 16 rows = 7824 bytes

We will need to allow for an additional 2GB of RoomNotes data outside of each data row, so an estimate of how many rows are expected is important. The JProCo data file(s) MDF/NDF will need to have that amount of disk storage available, in addition to the 489 bytes for each record in the table.

Also, when we are calculating actual storage for this table, we need to know the length or size of each row's NTEXT field. The actual data payload for each LOB is the amount of storage it uses.

In the next section, we will look at the newer data types which make handling large value data a little easier. ***For large value data, the best practice is to use the newer data types and avoid using LOBs altogether****.* Converting LOB type columns to a max data type is very easy and requires a single ALTER statement:

```
ALTER TABLE HumanResources.RoomChart
ALTER COLUMN RoomNotes NVARCHAR(MAX)
GO
```

However, there may be times when we are forced to work with LOBs (e.g., working with a legacy system containing an **IMAGE** or **TEXT/NTEXT** type and the cost-benefit ratio doesn't favor rebuilding the table(s)). In these cases, there are some mitigation strategies we can attempt.

In our RoomNotes column example, one mitigation strategy is to consider using two separate columns to store notes – e.g., one column called 'RoomNotes' for notes which fit within the limits of a regular data type and another column called 'RoomNotesLrg' to store the notes which exceed 8000 bytes. The LOB data will still be stored separately, and the regular notes will be stored as normal data within the row.

Another strategy is to override the normal behavior of the LOB and force smaller data in the LOB field to be stored in the row along with the regular data types. SQL Server allows for some control over the storage location. SQL Server can be instructed to store data ranging from 24 to 7000 bytes in the regular row. For example, the following code instructs the RoomChart table to store fields containing fewer than 5001 bytes in the regular data row.

```
EXEC sp_tableoption 'HumanResources.RoomChart', 'Text In
Row', 5000
```

When the "Large Value Types Out of Row" property is set to **1** for a table, The large values, like VARCHAR(MAX) or NVARCHAR(MAX), that are normally stored in the row will be stored outside of the row. This setting will have no effect on LOB types like TEXT and NTEXT. When this property is set to **0**, then all values small enough are stored in the row and pointers are only used if the data is too large.

```
EXEC sp_tableoption 'HumanResources.RoomChart', 'Large Value
Types Out of Row', 0
```

When changing this property from 1 (on) to 0 (off), it is necessary to update the column's values in order for the values being stored outside the data row to appear inside the data row.

```
UPDATE HumanResources.RoomChart
SET RoomNotes = RoomNotes
```

Including large data values in the main row can be helpful, if these fields are used frequently in queries and reports. However, if the large data values are seldom queried, then there may be a performance advantage to storing that data outside the main data row. This allows more rows of the table to be stored in the same data page – which means more rows are read with each I/O cycle – thereby improving performance.

READER NOTE: *As with the LOBs, the 'Text In Row' property has been deprecated and will be removed in a future version of SQL Server.*

Large-Value Data Types

The large-value data types VARCHAR(MAX), NVARCHAR(MAX), and VABINARY(MAX) were introduced with SQL Server 2005. These are also known as **max data types** and can contain the maximum amount allowed for a field by SQL Server, which is 2 GB in SQL Server 2005 and newer.

Therefore, a max data type column can hold up to 2 GB (i.e., 2,147,483,647 bytes). In other words, a VARCHAR(MAX) or VARBINARY(MAX) can contain 2,147,483,647 characters and an NVARCHAR(MAX) can contain roughly half that number of characters (1,073,741,822), since Unicode consumes 2 bytes per character.

Suppose that, after populating many records in the HumanResources.RoomChart table, we discover our values in the RoomNotes field rarely exceed 8000 bytes. The large-value data types have the ability to handle our smaller notes in the same way a regular data type would handle them, while the large notes are handled as a LOB type – all within a single column.

This capability is very useful. Essentially, this data type behaves like a regular data type when the field value is ≤8000 bytes, and it stores data in the row page along with the other fields. When the field contains a large value >8000 bytes, then the max data type behaves like a LOB type by storing the data separately and including a 16-byte pointer in the data row.

In our RoomNotes example, where the vast majority of the field values are under the 8000 byte limit, changing to an NVARCHAR(MAX) means we will see a performance gain. At the same time, we won't be limited in cases where a field value causes the row to exceed the 8 KB (8060 byte) limitation.

READER NOTE: *If we want to make this type of a change to an existing table, changing a field from an NTEXT to an NVARCHAR(MAX)), then SQL Server may prompt to drop and re-create the table.*

Because every row in the table has the possibility of being stored either inside or outside the data row based on its size, the Size property for a large value data type field will always display a value of -1 as seen in see Figure 3.14.

Each field exceeding 8000 bytes behaves like a LOB. The data payload is stored outside the data row and a 16-byte pointer is stored in the data row.

Fields containing values of 8000 bytes or fewer, behave like any variable length field. Each row requires a variable block and stores the data payload inside the row.

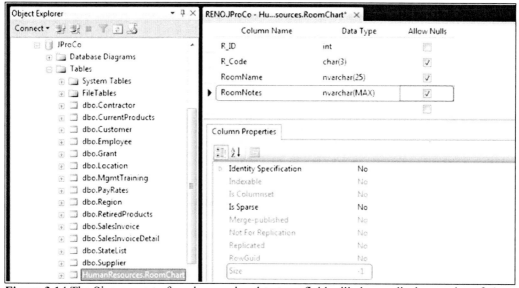

Figure 3.14 The Size property for a large value data type field will always display a value of -1.

The ability of the Large-Value Data Types to automatically handle the placement of data inside or outside the data row is novel and exciting. This is made possible in part, by SQL Server 2005's row-overflow data feature. However, there could be instances where we might want to set the '**Large-Value Types Out of Row'** property to a value of 1 (on) and force all the variable max length fields to be stored outside of the row.

With large value data types, their default setting for that property is "0", so that all values small enough to fit in the row are stored there and pointers are only used if the data is too large.

One reason to consider this unusual step is for a table which is queried frequently and thus performance is a high visibility issue. If the large-value data field(s) is rarely queried, then there may be a performance advantage to storing that data outside the main data row. This would allow more rows in the table to be stored in the same data page – meaning more rows are read with each I/O cycle – and thus should improve performance for the tables the users query frequently.

Finally, let's update our storage estimation for the HumanResources.RoomChart table to show the RoomNotes field as an NVARCHAR(MAX) data type (Refer to the design shown in Figure 3.14).

Recall that, after the addition of the RoomNotes field as an NTEXT, we estimated that each row of the RoomChart table would use up to 489 bytes and as many as 16 rows would fit into one 8 KB page.

Header 4 | Fixed 26 | NULL Block 3 | Variable Block 6 | Variable Data 450 = 489 bytes

489 bytes per row * 16 rows = 7824 bytes

For an actual data calculation, we will need the actual size of each value in the **NVARCHAR(MAX)** column. For each field >8000 bytes, add a 16-byte pointer to the data row and then add the data payload amount to the out of row calculation, which adds to the size of the JProCo data file (MDF/NDF), but doesn't increase the data row. For each field ≤ 8000 bytes, we add 2 bytes to the variable block then add the data payload to the data row, and finally add a 24-byte pointer if the data row exceeds 8060. *We will discuss the 24-byte pointer later.*

However, since we are updating our capacity planning report, we want to estimate the *maximum storage* that should be provided for the HumanResources.RoomChart table. At a high level, we know all rows of the RoomChart table could, at most, consume the same as we calculated for the LOB, which is 489 bytes in each data row and 2 GB stored outside the row (RoomNotes calculated as NTEXT in Figure 3.18).

In the real world some assumptions would have to be made, in order to plan for this table. Ideally, a stakeholder familiar with the underlying business would be able to project how much data the variable length fields would actually receive.

Here we will demonstrate the mechanics for calculating the largest amount each row in the table would consume with the NVARCHAR(MAX) data type for > 8000 bytes and for <= to 8000 bytes (Figure 3.14).

The row header and fixed length data calculation is the same as the LOB estimate for each row with a RoomNote value >8000 bytes.

Header + Fixed Length Fields (R_ID and R_Code fields)

4 bytes + 4 bytes + 6 bytes = **14 bytes**

NULL Block (No change to the NULL Block.)

2 bytes + 1 byte (only 5 fields) = **3 bytes**

Just like LOBs, the >8000 byte values of an NVARCHAR(MAX) do not impact the variable block.

Variable Block

2 bytes + (2 fields * 2 bytes per field) = **6 bytes**

Variable Data Fields (estimate the maximum allowable length) + External Row Pointer (always 16 bytes which is included with the variable data payload)

RoomName is set to contain 25 Unicode characters = **50 bytes**
RoomDescription is set to contain 200 Unicode characters = **400 bytes**
External Row Pointer = **16 bytes**

Header 4 | Fixed 10 | NULL Block 3 | Variable Block 6 | Variable Data 466 = 489 bytes

The total for each row of the table with a RoomChart value >8000 bytes would store its data payload *outside* of the data row and would consume up to 489 bytes in the data row. At 489 bytes per row, 16 rows would fit within a data page.

489 bytes/row * 16 rows = 7824 bytes

Now we will run an estimate for those rows where RoomNotes contains <= 8000 bytes.

There is no need for a 16-byte pointer when the data is stored in row. However, for every data row which exceeds 8060 bytes, the row-overflow data feature will move the largest individual column(s) to a new data page. Each NVARCHAR(MAX) value can be as much as 8000 bytes, row-overflow data will move the RoomNotes column to a different data page. A 24-byte pointer is added to the data row to keep track of that data.

Header + Fixed Length Fields (R_ID and R_Code fields)

4 bytes + 4 bytes + 6 bytes = **14 bytes**

No change to the NULL Block.

NULL Block

2 bytes + 1 byte (only 5 fields) = **3 bytes**

Each NVARCHAR(MAX) value of 8000 bytes will add 2 more bytes to the variable block.

Variable Block

2 bytes + (3 fields * 2 bytes per field) = **8 bytes**

Variable Data Fields (estimate the maximum allowable length) + External Row Pointer (24 bytes)

RoomName is set to contain 25 Unicode characters = **50 bytes**
RoomDescription is set to contain 200 Unicode characters = **400 bytes**
RoomNotes is set to contain 4000 Unicode characters = **8000 bytes**
External Row Pointer = **24 bytes**

 Header 4 | Fixed 10 | NULL Block 3 | Variable Block 8 | Variable 8474 = 8499 bytes

The total for each row of the RoomChart table could use up to 8499 bytes where the NVARCHAR(MAX) field is <= 8000 bytes.

Since row-overflow data will move the 8000 byte field (RoomNotes) to a separate data page, each data row will contain up to 499 bytes. At 499 bytes per row, 16 rows can fit within a data page.

499 bytes/row * 16 rows = 7984 bytes

Be aware of SQL Server references which aren't 100% consistent in their naming convention for large value types. Some resources refer to all the large value types as LOBs (or BLOBs) and call TEXT, NTEXT, and IMAGE types "legacy LOBs".

Lab 3.3: Large Values

Lab Prep: Each lab has one or more Skill Checks. Start with Skill Check 1 and proceed until reaching the Points to Ponder section.

Before beginning this lab, verify that SQL Server 2012 is properly installed and operating. Before running the lab setup script for resetting the database (SQLQueries2012Vol3Chapter3.3Setup.sql), please make sure to close all query windows within SSMS. An open query window pointing to a database context can lock that database preventing it from updating when the script is executing. A simple way to assure all query windows are closed, is to exit out of SSMS, then open a new instance of SSMS, and lastly run the setup script.

Skill Check 1: Calculate the actual amount of storage consumed by the HumanResources.RoomChart table (Design shown in Figure 3.15). Each field length is also shown, as well as each field's size in bytes. For any data which will be stored outside the row, include that in the variable data payload (Variable Data column of the worksheet).

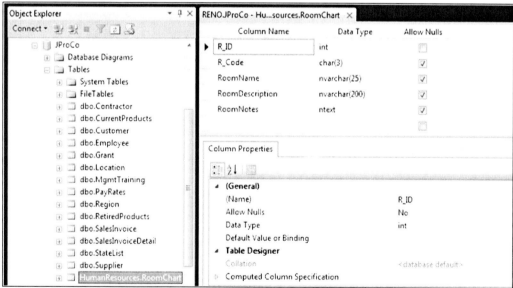

Figure 3.15 The design of the RoomChart table. The data type for RoomNotes is NTEXT.

```
SELECT
LEN(R_ID) AS lenID,
LEN(R_Code) AS lenCode,
LEN(RoomName) AS lenRoomName,
LEN(RoomDescription) AS lenRoomDescription,
DATALENGTH(RoomNotes) AS lenRoomNotes
FROM HumanResources.RoomChart
```

	lenID	lenCode	lenRoomName	lenRoomDescription	lenRoomNotes
1	1	3	25	NULL	NULL
2	1	3	19	NULL	NULL
3	1	3	12	NULL	NULL
4	1	2	10	NULL	NULL
5	1	NULL	NULL	NULL	NULL

5 rows

Figure 3.16 The length of each value in the RoomChart table calculated using the LEN() function. N is the symbol for Unicode data. *Tip: Use the DATALENGTH() function for the RoomNotes field to prevent an error message.*

```
SELECT
DATALENGTH(R_ID) AS ID_bytes,
DATALENGTH(R_Code) AS Code_bytes,
DATALENGTH(RoomName) AS RoomName_bytes,
DATALENGTH(RoomDescription) AS RoomDescription_bytes,
DATALENGTH(RoomNotes) AS RoomNotes_bytes
FROM HumanResources.RoomChart
```

	ID_bytes	Code_bytes	RoomName_bytes	RoomDescription_bytes	RoomNotes_bytes
1	4	3	50	NULL	NULL
2	4	3	38	NULL	NULL
3	4	3	24	NULL	NULL
4	4	3	20	NULL	NULL
5	4	NULL	NULL	NULL	NULL

5 rows

Figure 3.17 The size (bytes) of each value in the RoomChart table is calculated correctly by using the DATALENGTH() function for Unicode data. N is the symbol for Unicode data.

Use the following form to help calculate the total space used in the RoomChart table.

	Header	Fixed Data	NULL Block	Variable Block	Variable Data	Total in Row Storage	Out of Row Storage
Row 1							
Row 2							
Row 3							
Row 4							
Row 5							
Row 6							
Row 7							
Row 8							
Row 9							
Row 10							

Skill Check 2: Calculate the actual amount of storage consumed by the HumanResources.RoomChart table. Both the design of the table and each field's size in bytes are shown in Figure 3.18.

Include any data which will be stored outside the row in the variable data payload (Variable Data column in the worksheet).

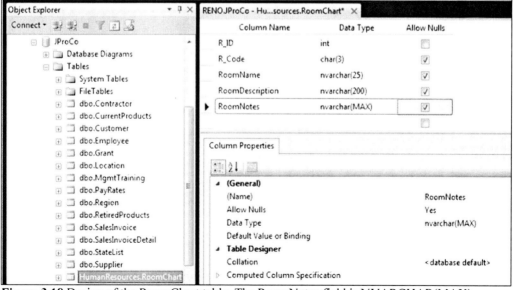

Figure 3.18 Design of the RoomChart table. The RoomNotes field is NVARCHAR(MAX).

	Header	Fixed Data	NULL Block	Variable Block	Variable Data	Total in Row Storage	Out of Row Storage
Row 1							
Row 2							
Row 3							
Row 4							
Row 5							
Row 6							
Row 7							
Row 8							
Row 9							
Row 10							

Answer Code: The T-SQL code to this lab can be found in the downloadable files in a file named Lab3.3_LargeObjects.sql.

Points to Ponder - Large Values

1. Data rows can hold up to a total of 8060 bytes per memory page.

2. If you try to fit more than 8060 bytes in a row, then some data will sit outside that row. A pointer to the location of the data is in the row.

3. A data type can't be larger than a memory page, so LOBs might have to be stored somewhere else and have just a pointer from the row itself.

4. A 16-byte pointer in the data row points to a root structure in another part of memory that holds the actual LOB data. This is why '16' is the size value for **NTEXT**, **TEXT**, and **IMAGE** in the table design.

5. With small to medium sized LOBs, SQL Server provides the option to store values in the row rather than pointing to the data. (Note: the pointer system in SQL Server uses a B-tree structure)

6. When '**Large Value Types Out of Row**' is on (set to 1) the pointer will be used, if off (set to 0) then all values small enough to fit in the row are stored there and pointers are only used if the data is too large.

7. The Max specification was introduced in SQL Server 2005 and is used with the VARCHAR, NVARCHAR, and VARBINARY data types.

8. Max value types are stored in the row if they fit and only moved to another memory space for the rows that go over the limit.

9. Max makes it possible to store values larger than 8060 bytes the same way as a LOB without some of the limitations of TEXT and NTEXT.

10. In SQL Server 2005 and newer, the storage limit for max data types is 2 GB.

11. It is generally considered bad practice to put an index or constraint on any field wider than 900 bytes (Indexes will be covered in Chapters 7-9).

12. Since the introduction of the large-value data types (a.k.a., the max data types) in SQL Server 2005, the manufacturer of SQL Server (Microsoft) has indicated that the data types **NTEXT**, **TEXT**, and **IMAGE** have been deprecated (i.e., will be removed in a future version of SQL Server).

13. These deprecated LOB types (NTEXT, TEXT, and IMAGE) have limited functionality in DML statements. The max data types have much greater functionality and perform more like regular data types (e.g., with queries, subqueries, joins, variables, functions, and triggers).

14. The '**Text In Row**' property has been deprecated and will be removed in a future version of SQL Server.

Chapter Glossary

Data row space usage: The amount of space each row of data will use.

Data portion: A data row consists of the header and the data portion, which is dedicated to holding and supporting the actual data in the data portion.

Fixed data: A block of space occupied in memory based on Fixed Data Length.

Fixed length data types: Fixed length data types always occupy the amount of space allotted to them. Examples of fixed length data types are INT and CHAR(2).

Large Object Types: A data type that is larger than the 8000 byte limit.

Large Value data types: Also known as **max data types,** can contain the maximum amount allowed for a field by SQL Server.

Large Value Types Out of Row: When this is being used the *'Large Value Types Out of Row'* is on (set to 1 or 'ON') the pointer is being used, if off (set to 0 or 'OFF') then all values small enough to fit in the row are stored there and pointers are only used if the data is too large.

MAX data type: These 3 types (VARCHAR(MAX), NVARCHAR(MAX), and VARBINARY(MAX)) introduced in SQL Server 2005, are also known as **max data types** and can contain the max amount allowed for a field by SQL Server.

Memory page: A memory page is 8 KB (8 kilobytes) of physical space set aside for rapid storage and retrieval of records.

NULL Bitmap: Another name for a NULL Block.

NULL Block: This is created to track nullable fields in your table.

Row header: This is a positioning header which keeps track of where the row is placed in the table and which fields the row contains.

Unicode data: Unicode supports foreign language characters needed for international data (e.g., German umlauts, accents for romance language characters, Japanese characters, etc).

Variable block: This block keeps track of the number of variable length data fields within the record and takes up 2 bytes.

Variable data: Data with length that varies from row to row.

Variable length data types: Variable length data types expect the data length to vary from row to row. They include VARCHAR and NVARCHAR data types.

Review Quiz - Chapter Three

1.) If you have two fields in your table, one is an INT and the other is an NCHAR(3), what will be the size of your fixed length data?

O a. 3

O b. 4

O c. 7

O d. 9

O e. 10

2.) You have three variable length data fields. What are the rules that go into the calculation of how large the variable block will be?

☐ a. You will allocate 2 bytes to the creation of the variable block.

☐ b. You will allocate 3 bytes to the creation of the variable block.

☐ c. You will allocate 2 more bytes for each of the three variable fields.

☐ d. You will allocate 1 byte for every eight columns in the table.

3.) All your fields are set to NOT NULL for the dbo.Employee table. What will be the result for your NULL Block?

O a. You will not have a NULL Block for dbo.Employee.

O b. Your NULL Block will be 2 bytes.

O c. Your NULL Block will be 3 bytes.

O d. Your NULL Block will be 2 bytes + Total Fields/8 (rounded up) bytes.

4.) You have one row in a table called dbo.Bonus, which has two fields. The first field is called BonusID and is a NOT NULL SMALLINT. The second field is called BonusAmount set to Money and is nullable. INTs are 2 bytes and Money is 8 bytes. The first record has a BonusID of 1 and a BonusAmount of Null. What is the fixed length data payload?

O a. 2 bytes

O b. 8 bytes

O c. 10 bytes

5.) You have ten fixed length fields in your dbo.Employee table. How much data is dedicated to your header?

O a. 2 bytes

O b. 4 bytes

O c. 6 bytes

6.) Exactly how big is a page of memory in SQL Server?

O a. 8000 Bytes

O b. 8060 bytes

O c. 8192 Bytes

7.) How many bytes of a memory page can SQL Server use for data?

O a. 8000

O b. 8060

O c. 8192

8.) Which of the following are considered Large Object (LOB) types?

☐ a. CHAR

☐ b. VARCHAR(8000)

☐ c. VARCHAR(MAX)

☐ d. TEXT

☐ e. NCHAR

☐ f. NVARCHAR(4000)

☐ g. NVARCHAR(MAX)

☐ h. NTEXT

Answer Key

1.) Because NCHAR is a Unicode data type, each character occupies two bytes, an NCHAR (3) would hold six bytes, since one field is an INT which is four bytes, making (a) (b) (c) and (d) incorrect. The correct answer is (e) ten bytes.

2.) Since a variable block is created the first time you create a field with a variable length data type and takes up two bytes, each variable length field adds another two bytes to the block, making (b) and (d) incorrect. Therefore (a) and (c) are the correct answers.

3.) If none of the fields can be NULL, then a NULL Block is not needed, thus making (b) (c) and (d) incorrect. Therefore (a) is the correct answer.

4.) Fixed length data types always occupy the amount of space allotted to them, so a SMALLINT (2 bytes) and MONEY (8 bytes) makes (c) 10 bytes the correct answer.

5.) Because a row header has four bytes (a) and (c) are incorrect, making (b) the correct answer.

6.) A memory page is 8 KB which converts to 8192 bytes, SQL Server data types limit themselves to 8000 bytes or less and can only use 8060 bytes for storage making (a) and (b) incorrect. This means (c) is the correct answer.

7.) A memory page is 8 kb which converts to 8192 bytes, SQL Server data types limit themselves to 8000 bytes or less and SQL Server can only use 8060 bytes for storage making (a) and (c), incorrect. This means (b) is the correct answer.

8.) A large object type is a field that contains a string larger than 8000 bytes and is a TEXT or NTEXT. A VARCHAR(MAX) and NVARCHAR(MAX) are considered large-value data types but are not LOBs therefore (d) and (h) are the correct answers.

Bug Catcher Game

To play the Bug Catcher game, run the SQLQueries2012Vol3BugCatcher03.pps file from the BugCatcher folder of the companion files. These files can be obtained from the www.Joes2Pros.com website.

[THIS PAGE INTENTIONALLY LEFT BLANK.]

Chapter 4.   Special Data Type Options

At the age of 12, my two main ways of making extra money were delivering papers and mowing lawns. Like most other paperboys with an 80-home coverage area, I wore a double bag. Picture a backpack that is also a "front pack". This contraption held roughly 40 rolled up papers in the front and 40 more in the back. As I began my route, the full packs, with their large loads, made my silhouette look like a pregnant bowling pin. By the end of the route, with both bags empty, it looked like little more than a gray towel loosely hanging over both shoulders. As each paper was delivered, it left more space and my bag contracted. Less room was needed in my bag and the load became smaller.

The infamous Sunday paper was a beast of a job, since each paper weighed approximately three pounds. My father took the time to build a wooden box with two 20-inch wheels from an old bicycle and two long broom handles. You might imagine a wheel barrow but, for steering ease, he crafted a rickshaw. My customers in north Tacoma would sometimes take pictures of the novelty of their paper being delivered by rickshaw. Unlike the double bag I used for weekday deliveries, the rickshaw was no smaller when all the Sunday papers were gone.

So a key question to consider is whether the data type resembles a pack whose size varies according to its payload, or alternatively, whether the data type is more like the hard box shape of the rickshaw, which is the same size at all times. In other words, if a table has 500 integer (4 byte) records and most of them are NULL, do they always have to consume 2000 bytes of space? Many innovative, new data type options have been implemented with SQL Server 2008 and 2012. These new data types also have options to make them work more efficiently. This chapter focuses on the special things that can be accomplished with these exciting new and custom data types.

READER NOTE: *Please run the SQLQueries2012Vol3Chapter4.0Setup.sql script in order to follow along with the examples in the first section of Chapter 4. All scripts mentioned in this chapter may be found at* www.Joes2Pros.com*.*

Sparse Data

The other day, I brought home a gallon of milk from the grocery store and went to the refrigerator to put it away. In my refrigerator, the only shelf tall enough to hold a gallon jug is the top shelf. However, the top shelf was already full. Shorter jars of salsa and mayonnaise were occupying that space, so naturally I moved those to a lower shelf to make space for my tall gallon of milk. I did not want to customize, remodel, or buy a second refrigerator to solve my problem. A quick and easy, innovative solution allowed me to solve a relatively easy dilemma with little expense to my time or existing systems.

From our in depth look at data types in the last Chapter, recall that fields with fixed length data types (e.g., INT, MONEY, CHAR) always consume their allotted space irrespective of how much data the field actually contains. This is true even if the field is populated with a NULL.

Occasionally, we will encounter a column in a database which is rarely used. For example, suppose a field called Violation in the Employee table has very few employees with any violations – perhaps two or three for every 1000 employees. In this case, over 99% of the Violation field values are NULL. This is known as a *sparsely populated field*.

To demonstrate a sparsely populated field, we will create a simple table in the JProCo database. Create the Bonus table by running this code.

```
CREATE TABLE JProCo.dbo.Bonus (
BonusID INT NOT NULL,
BonusRecipient CHAR(2) NULL,
BonusAmount MONEY NULL)
GO
```

Now populate the fields, utilizing row constructors (available in versions of SQL Server 2008 and newer), by using the following code.

```
INSERT INTO JProCo.dbo.Bonus VALUES
(1,'AB',NULL), (2,'CD',NULL), (3,'EF',NULL)
```

When using SQL Server 2005 and older versions the following code will be necessary to insert data into our new table.

```
INSERT INTO JProCo.dbo.Bonus VALUES (1,'AB',NULL)
INSERT INTO JProCo.dbo.Bonus VALUES (2,'CD',NULL)
INSERT INTO JProCo.dbo.Bonus VALUES (3,'EF',NULL)
```

Now look at all the records in the table. Since all fields contain fixed length data types (i.e., INT, CHAR(2), MONEY), we could have accurately calculated the per row consumption before we even added any data to the table. With no variable data types in the table, there is no variable block or variable data payload to calculate.

```
SELECT * FROM JProCo.dbo.Bonus
```

	BonusID	BonusRecipient	BonusAmount
1	1	AB	NULL
2	2	CD	NULL
3	3	EF	NULL
			3 rows

Figure 4.1 At 21 bytes per row, 1000 rows of the Bonus table would require three data pages.

Each row of the Bonus table will consume 21 bytes.

Row Header = 4 bytes

Fixed Data = 14 bytes

BonusID is an INT (4 bytes) and the *BonusAmount* data type is MONEY (8 bytes).

NULL Block (aka NULL Bitmap) = 3 bytes

The table contains 3 non-Sparse Fields (Sparse fields do not contribute to the NULL Block). Creation of the NULL Block (2 bytes) + 3 fields (1 byte/8 non-Sparse Fields) rounded up to the nearest byte.*

As we reviewed earlier, the NULLs in the money field do not change the space consumption – *fixed length data types always use the full amount of space allocated to them.*

At 21 bytes per row, 1000 rows of the Bonus table would require 21,000 bytes and fill up about 3 data pages (1 data page = 8060 bytes).

Analyzing Space Used

When I was about 10, my big brother introduced me to a British comedy group called Monty Python. We had fun listening to their tapes and I'll never forget one sketch in particular. Michael Palin visits a university in Australia and is welcomed by several faculty members. One comic point of the sketch is that there are a lot of Australians named Bruce. "Michael, this is Bruce" was repeated over and over as Michael was introduced to each faculty member. At the time, I remember saying it would have taken a lot less airspace to just say the name Bruce once and point to everyone. Well, what if all your records for a field are NULL? Is it possible to store NULL values once and simply point each field to that sparse data? If so, what are the pros and cons of being able to accomplish this feat?

In the last Chapter, we talked quite a bit about memory pages which physically contain data. Within a database's data files (MDF/NDF), SQL Server organizes data into 8 KB memory pages (Also called *data pages*). SQL Server attempts to fit the greatest number of rows from a table into a single data page, since this enables the fastest and most efficient data retrieval. If rows in a table exceed 8060 bytes, and/or contain a large value (>8000 bytes/field), then SQL Server will move the largest variable length field(s) into a separate data page.

A newly created table consumes no storage space until data is added to it. The table we created at the beginning of this chapter (JProCo.dbo.Bonus) was empty and consumed no space until we began populating the fields. The moment we added a value to the first row, SQL Server reserved space in memory for the rows of JProCo.dbo.Bonus and began filling up the first 8 KB page.

A handy tool for checking the storage amount which an object occupies is **sp_spaceused**. Figure 4.2 shows the results of the Bonus table being passed into this stored procedure. We see the Bonus table contains three rows and its data has not yet exceeded its first 8 KB page *(Note: indexes are ignored for now, as they will be covered in depth by Chapters 7 thru 9).*

```
EXEC sp_spaceused 'Bonus'
```

	name	Rows	reserved	data	index_size	unused
1	Bonus	3	16KB	8KB	8KB	0KB

1 rows

Figure 4.2 With three rows, the Bonus table is still filling its first 8 KB memory page.

If we hadn't passed in the Bonus table as a parameter, this sproc (short for stored procedure) would have shown similar detail for the current database context, which is JProCo.

```
USE JProCo
GO

EXEC sp_spaceused
```

To view the code underlying this system stored procedure, we can utilize the SSMS code generator:

Object Explorer > Databases > JProCo > Programmability > Stored Procedures > System Stored Procedures > right-click **sys.sp_spaceused > Modify**

Since we are still in the process of filling up the first data page for the Bonus table, many more records can be added before the first data page is full.

Let's write some code containing a loop to quickly add 997 more records to the Bonus table. The first record populated will be row 4 with these values:

BonusID = 4, BonusRecipient = NULL, BonusAmount = NULL

Our code increments each subsequent BonusID value by 1, and the loop continues to run as long as the BonusID value is <=1000. Once the row containing a BonusID value of 1000 has been entered into the table, the loop will terminate.

```
DECLARE @ID INT
SET @ID = 4

WHILE @ID <= 1000
BEGIN
   INSERT INTO JProCo.dbo.Bonus
   VALUES (@ID,NULL,NULL)
   SET @ID = @ID + 1
END
```

We can execute the following code to view all records in the Bonus table and verify that our loop worked correctly inserting the additional 997 rows for a new total of 1000 rows.

```
SELECT * FROM JProCo.dbo.Bonus
```

	BonusID	BonusRecipient	BonusAmount
1	1	AB	NULL
2	2	CD	NULL
3	3	EF	NULL
4	4	NULL	NULL
5	5	NULL	NULL
6	6	NULL	NULL
			1000 rows

Figure 4.3 The Bonus table now contains 1000 records.

Since one row occupies 21 bytes, we know these 1000 rows will take up approximately 21 KB of space and should fit within three data pages.

$$21000 \text{ bytes} / (8060 \text{ bytes per page}) = 2.61 \text{ pages}$$

Let's rerun the **sp_spaceused** sproc and confirm the number of data pages.

```
EXEC sp_spaceused 'Bonus'
```

	name	rows	reserved	data	index_size	unused
1	Bonus	1000	32KB	24KB	8KB	0KB

1 row

Figure 4.4 The Bonus table's 1000 rows (21 KB) fit within three data pages.

The information provided by **sp_spaceused** confirms what we expected – the data currently in the Bonus table fits within 24 KB (i.e., three data pages).

Now this seems a little wasteful with respect to storage space usage. NULLs are taking up 8 bytes in the money field, because it's a fixed length data type. *BonusAmount is considered a **sparsely populated field**.*

Using the Sparse Data Option

The sparse data option was a new feature starting with SQL Server 2008 and is designed for fields expected to be predominantly NULL. Using the sparse data option, we can instruct SQL Server to not have NULLs consume space in sparsely populated fields. In this section we will demonstrate the sparse option, including how SQL Server handles the non-NULLs in a Sparse Field.

We're going to delete the Bonus table and then re-create it using the same steps we took previously. The only difference will be that the BonusAmount field will be created using the sparse option, as we expect it to contain very little actual data – most records will be NULL.

First, we need to drop the JProCo.dbo.Bonus table, so that we can rebuild it using the sparse column option on the BonusAmount field.

```
DROP TABLE JProCo.dbo.Bonus
GO
```

We can reuse our code with one small modification. Add the SPARSE option to the BonusAmount column in the CREATE TABLE statement.

```
CREATE TABLE JProCo.dbo.Bonus (
BonusID INT NOT NULL,
BonusRecipient CHAR(2) NULL,
BonusAmount MONEY SPARSE NULL)
GO

INSERT INTO JProCo.dbo.Bonus
VALUES (1,'AB',NULL), (2,'CD',NULL), (3,'EF',NULL)

DECLARE @ID INT
SET @ID = 4

WHILE @ID <= 1000
BEGIN
   INSERT INTO JProCo.dbo.Bonus
   VALUES (@ID,NULL,NULL)
   SET @ID = @ID + 1
END
GO
```

Recall, that we expect the BonusAmount field to contain very little actual data – most records will be NULL. The Bonus table now contains 1000 records and looks the same as it did previously (Figure 4.3). BonusAmount is a Sparse Field, but so far there is no apparent difference when viewing the table or data (Figure 4.5).

```
SELECT * FROM JProCo.dbo.Bonus
```

	BonusID	BonusRecipient	BonusAmount
1	1	AB	NULL
2	2	CD	NULL
3	3	EF	NULL
4	4	NULL	NULL
5	5	NULL	NULL
6	6	NULL	NULL
			1000 rows

Figure 4.5 BonusAmount is now a Sparse Field, but the data and table do not appear differently.

Now let's review how much space the Bonus table is consuming. As originally designed (i.e., before we rebuilt the table with a sparse column), each row of the Bonus table consumed 21 bytes.

Header 4 | Fixed Data 14 | NULL Block 3 = 21 bytes

21 bytes/row * 1000 rows = 21,000 bytes

129

From what we know of the sparse data option, the NULLs in our sparse column (BonusAmount) should not take up any storage space. With BonusAmount as a sparse column, each row of the Bonus table will now consume 13 bytes.

Row Header = 4 bytes

Fixed Data = 6 bytes

READER NOTE: *BonusID is an INT (4 bytes). BonusRecipient is a CHAR(2) of 2 bytes. None of the BonusAmount values will consume storage space, since all values are equal to NULL. Rows in a sparse column consume storage space only when they contain non-NULL values. In our example, the sparse column (BonusAmount) contains only NULL values.*

NULL Block (aka NULL Bitmap) = 3 bytes

*Creation of the NULL Block (2 bytes) + 2 non-Sparse Fields * (1 byte/8 non-Sparse Fields) rounded up to the nearest byte.*

At 13 bytes per row, 1000 rows of the Bonus table would require 13,000 bytes and fill up about 2 data pages (1 data page = 8060 bytes).

Header 4 | Fixed Data 6 | NULL Block 3 = 13 bytes

13 bytes/row * 1000 rows = 13,000 bytes

We can confirm the space saved by using the SPARSE option by executing the **sp_spaceused** stored procedure with 'Bonus' as a parameter.

```
EXEC sp_spaceused 'Bonus'
```

	name	Rows	reserved	data	index_size	unused
1	Bonus	1000	24KB	16KB	8KB	0KB

1 rows

Figure 4.6 The sparse option saved an 8 KB data page -- a significant amount of space.

As predicted – the sparse option saved a significant amount of space. Even though the data in the Bonus table is identical, it now uses two data pages thanks to the sparse option. In large tables, this savings can be quite substantial.

Along with the benefits of the sparse option, we also need to be mindful of the associated tradeoffs or limitations:

o   For any populated rows in a sparse column, the populated data will consume more space than would a regular field.

o   The sparse option cannot be used with certain data types.

In addition to the actual data payload, the sparse option adds 4 bytes to each record when the Sparse Field is non-null. In the case of our Bonus table, any non-NULL value in the BonusAmount field will consume 12 bytes (8 bytes for the SMALLMONEY data payload + 4 bytes for the sparse vector).

Thus, the sparse option should only be used with fields expected to be sparsely populated and primarily containing NULL values. Consider the current state of the Bonus table (Refer to Figure 4.5). The BonusAmount value for each of the 1000 rows is Null. As a non-sparse column, BonusAmount will consume 8000 bytes. As a sparse column, however, BonusAmount consumes 0 bytes.

Suppose some rows of the sparse column, BonusAmount, were populated. If 600 of these 1000 rows contained non-NULL values, they would consume 7200 additional bytes. This is still less than the 8000 bytes that this field would consume, if it were not a sparse column.

The sparse option works with most regular numeric and character data types in SQL Server i.e. INT, DECIMAL, CHAR, VARCHAR, NCHAR, NVARCHAR. However, it cannot be used with several data types, such as CLR data types (e.g., GEOGRAPHY, GEOMETRY) or FILESTREAM, in addition to the old LOB data types of TEXT, NTEXT or IMAGE.

In order to modify an existing column and make it a sparse column, we can either use the following code, or utilize SSMS to open the Design view of the table and toggle the "Is Sparse" column property to Yes.

```
ALTER TABLE JProCo.dbo.Bonus
ALTER COLUMN BonusRecipient
ADD SPARSE
GO
```

Alternatively, we can use T-SQL code or the table's Design view to remove the sparse option from an existing column.

```
ALTER TABLE JProCo.dbo.Bonus
ALTER COLUMN BonusRecipient
DROP SPARSE
GO
```

Since SQL Server's process of adding the sparse option to a column can cause the data row to temporarily exceed the row limit (8060 bytes for tables with no sparse columns, 8018 bytes for tables with a sparse column(s)), be aware that it may be necessary to rebuild a table in order to add the sparse option to an existing column.

Lab 4.1: Sparse Data Option

Lab Prep: Each lab has one or more Skill Checks. Start with Skill Check 1 and proceed until reaching the Points to Ponder section.

Before beginning this lab, verify that SQL Server 2012 is properly installed and operating. Before running the lab setup script for resetting the database (SQLQueries2012Vol3Chapter4.1Setup.sql), please make sure to close all query windows within SSMS (An open query window pointing to a database context can lock that database preventing it from updating when the script is executing). A simple way to assure all query windows are closed, is to exit out of SSMS, then open a new instance of SSMS, and lastly run the setup script.

Skill Check 1: The CompanyName field of the Customer table is a sparsely populated field with 773 of 775 rows containing NULLs. Currently this column takes up 48 KB, which consumes the equivalent of about 6 data pages.

```
SELECT *
FROM JProCo.dbo.Customer
WHERE CompanyName IS NULL
```

	CustomerID	CustomerType	FirstName	LastName	CompanyName
1	1	Consumer	Mark	Williams	NULL
2	2	Consumer	Lee	Young	NULL
3	3	Consumer	Patricia	Martin	NULL
4	4	Consumer	Mary	Lopez	NULL
5	6	Consumer	Ruth	Clark	NULL
					773 rows

Figure 4.7 Skill Check 1 optimizes the CompanyName field, which currently consumes 48 KB.

Use T-SQL code to change the CompanyName field to be optimized for sparsely populated data. When finished, check the Design view of the Customer table and confirm it resembles Figure 4.8.

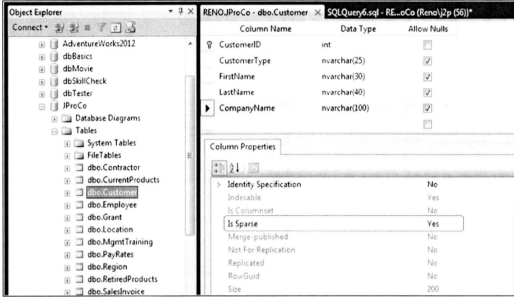

Figure 4.8 After Skill Check 1, the Design view will show CompanyName as a sparse column.

Answer Code: The T-SQL code to this lab can be found in the downloadable files in a file named Lab4.1_SparseDataOption.sql.

Points to Ponder - Sparse Data Option

1. A table operation with a SPARSE column takes a performance hit over a normal column. SPARSE will save space for NULL values at the cost of more overhead to retrieve non-NULL values.

2. A numeric SPARSE column that contains data will take up 4 bytes more space than a non-SPARSE column. For instance, a non-SPARSE INT will take up 4 bytes, whereas a SPARSE INT will take up 8 bytes.

3. SPARSE cannot be used for every data type. For instance, it cannot be used with the old LOB types (TEXT, NTEXT and IMAGE). The SPARSE option cannot be used with CLR (Common Language Runtime) data types, such as GEOGRAPHY or GEOMETRY.

4. For an identical block of data, a column marked as SPARSE will take more space. The SPARSE option will only save space if that column is NULL.

5. SPARSE is best used when expecting a column to predominantly be populated with NULL values and there is a goal to save hard drive space.

6. A SPARSE column cannot be a primary key.

7. A column defined as SPARSE cannot have a default value.

8. When a column is defined as SPARSE and contains only NULL values then that column requires no storage space.

9. SPARSE columns should be considered when the storage savings is at least 20 to 40 percent. A list, consisting of Estimated Savings by Data Type, can be found at http://msdn.microsoft.com/en-us/library/cc280604.aspx.

10. You cannot use the SPARSE option with the FILESTREAM attribute.

Custom Data Types

This spring, one of my brothers wanted to pour 3000 lbs. of new concrete in his basement. This would have been a small and very costly job (several thousand dollars), had he hired a professional crew with a cement truck. He had access to a cement mixer, but hauling buckets full of wet cement downstairs would be taxing on his friends who volunteered a few Saturday hours. He realized that he needed a chute so the mixer upstairs could simply pour cement down the chute to the spreaders located downstairs. How much does a chute cost? Significantly more than the custom contraption my brother devised.

His long, narrow piece of plywood with 2x4s on each side looked a lot like a wooden park slide. It worked brilliantly and things went smoothly. This custom contraption was really made up of a standard wood type you can get at the hardware store. Customized solutions typically begin with standard materials. So, what does it take to create our own custom data type?

Most data types we encounter are supplied directly by the system. However, SQL Server also gives users the option of defining their own types. In this section, we will demonstrate creating, using, and removing these custom types.

Let's take a look at the Location table, which is a fairly simple table consisting of five records and four fields as seen in Figure 4.9.

```
SELECT *
FROM JProCo.dbo.Location
```

	LocationID	Street	City	State
1	1	111 First ST	Seattle	WA
2	2	222 Second AVE	Boston	MA
3	3	333 Third PL	Chicago	IL
4	4	444 Ruby ST	Spokane	WA

4 rows

Figure 4.9 We begin our look at constraints and custom data types with JProCo.dbo.Location.

Let's edit some of the data in the Location table using SSMS UI:

Object Explorer > Databases > JProCo > Tables > right-click **Location > Edit Top 200 Rows.**

Try adding a fifth location by typing the word, Five, instead of the numeral, 5, for the LocationID (Figure 4.10).

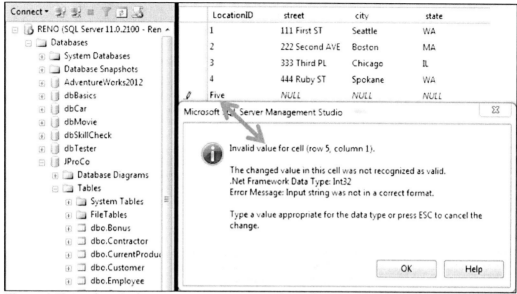

Figure 4.10 A column's data type serves as a constraint and protects the data integrity of the table.

Here we see that a data type can serve as a safety catch, in that it won't allow data to be added which is improper according to the table design. In the database world, this is known as a *constraint*. A constraint restricts data input to values within the limits specified in the design of a table and its fields.

If we attempt another entry which doesn't follow the design of our Location table, we will similarly get an error. Suppose we try to enter Nevada in the [State] field, which is a CHAR(2). We will get a prompt telling us that our data input can't be committed as we've typed it *(Error: "String or binary data would be truncated.")*. Our table design allows only two characters in this field. SQL Server enforces data constraints whether attempting to input values using T-SQL code or via the Design interface (Shown in Figure 4.10).

Now let's look at a *custom data type* (also known as a *user-defined data type*). The data type shown in Figure 4.11, CountryCode, is a custom data type created from a regular value type, in this case a CHAR(2).

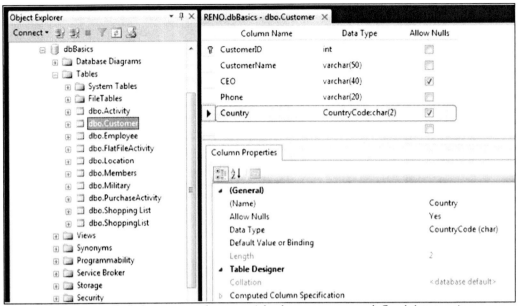

Figure 4.11 CountryCode is a custom data type (also known as a user-defined data type).

READER NOTE: *The two-letter country codes shown here are known as ISO codes. These codes are established and maintained by the International Standards Organization. www.iso.org/iso/english_country_names_and_code_elements*

When a custom data type is created, it may be used as the data type for any field within the same database. Therefore, the custom data type CountryCode is available to every field of every table in the dbBasics database. We can see that, if we add a new field to another table in the dbBasics database, the custom data type appears as an option in the Data Type dropdown list (Figure 4.12).

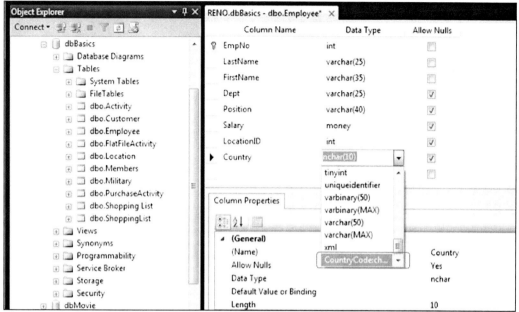

Figure 4.12 The custom data type CountryCode is available to every field in the dbBasics database.

Creating Custom Types

Let's walk through creating a custom data type. First we will demonstrate this using the SSMS UI, and later using T-SQL code to create a custom data type.

We want to create the custom CountryCode data type in the JProCo database. Begin by navigating to this location:

Object Explorer > Databases > JProCo > Programmability > Types > right-click **User-Defined Data Types > New User-Defined Data Type**

In the New User-Defined Data Type dialog, we will make the following selections:

1) Retain the pre-populated **Schema** dbo.

2) Enter '**CountryCode'** in the Name box.

3) Select **CHAR** in the Data type dropdown.

4) Enter a **Length:** of '**2'**.

5) Place a check in the **Allow NULLs** box.

6) Then click **OK** to save the data type and close the dialog (Figure 4.13).

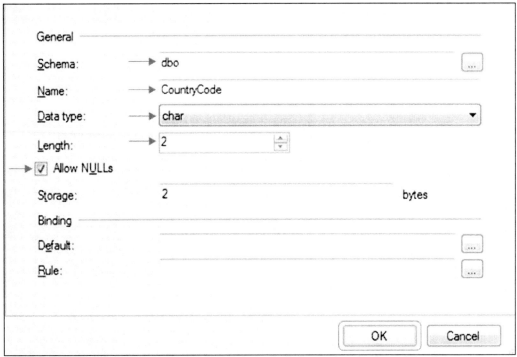

Figure 4.13 Creating the custom data type CountryCode in another database (JProCo).

This data type is now available to every table and field in the JProCo database. For example, if we wanted to add a Country field to the JProCo.dbo.Supplier table or the JProCo.dbo.Location table, we can add the field and use CountryCode as the data type.

READER NOTE: *Make sure to save and close the table design for this example or this data type may not appear as an option. If the data type does not appear, close the design window and then re-open it.*

Now let's create a custom data type running the following T-SQL code.

```
USE dbBasics
GO

CREATE TYPE dbo.EmailType
FROM NVARCHAR(50) NULL
GO
```

In addition to both of these new custom data types being available to every field within their respective databases, these new data types are also visible in the SQL Server Management Studio interface.

**Object Explorer > Databases > dbBasics > Programmability > Types >
User-Defined Data Types > dbo.EmailType**

Using Custom Types

Now let's see a table actually consume this data type. Using either T-SQL code or
the Design view, (Figure 4.13) add a new field named EmailAlias to the
Employee table of the dbBasics database. Use dbo.EmailType as the data type for
this new field.

```
ALTER TABLE dbBasics.dbo.Employee
ADD EmailAlias dbo.EmailType
GO
```

We can also drop the EmailAlias field by running the following code:

```
ALTER TABLE dbBasics.dbo.Employee
DROP COLUMN EmailAlias
GO
```

We have practiced both adding and dropping the EmailAlias field using T-SQL
code. Now let's use the Design interface to accomplish this task and then we will
be able to populate the EmailAlias with actual values.

Object Explorer > Databases > dbBasics > Tables > right-click **dbo.Employee > Design**

Add a field called **EmailAlias** and use the data type EmailType (Last in the
dropdown). Save the change and then close the Design interface (Figure 4.14).

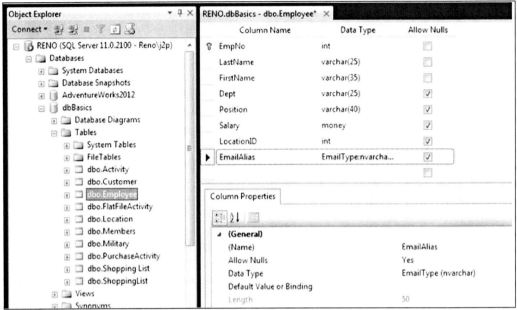

Figure 4.14 Adding an EmailAlias field to the Employee table using the Design interface.

We can also see the EmailAlias field by navigating to the Object Explorer view of the dbBasics.dbo.Employee table:

Object Explorer > Databases > dbBasics > Tables > dbo.Employee > expand Columns > confirm the new EmailAlias column appears in the list.

EmailAlias is a custom data type (EmailType), that we created earlier using T-SQL code. Next we will populate the EmailAlias field and then look at the first few records of the dbBasics.dbo.Employee table.

```
UPDATE dbBasics.dbo.Employee
SET EmailAlias = FirstName + LastName + '@dbBasics.com'
GO

SELECT TOP(3)
EmpNo, LastName, FirstName, LocationID, EmailAlias
FROM dbBasics.dbo.Employee
```

	EmpNo	LastName	FirstName	LocationID	EmailAlias
1	101	Smith	Sarah	2	SarahSmith@dbBasics.com
2	102	Brown	Bill	2	BillBrown@dbBasics.com
3	103	Fry	Fred	1	FredFry@dbBasics.com

3 rows

Figure 4.15 The new EmailAlias field is populated with employee email addresses.

Dropping Custom Types

Suppose we no longer needed the new data type we created (dbo.EmailType in dbBasics). A DROP statement will remove a user-defined data type. However, dependencies on this object must be handled before dropping dbo.EmailType. In other words, any table(s) using this custom data type must first drop the column utilizing dbo.EmailType before it can be dropped as well.

```
DROP TYPE dbo.EmailType
GO
```

```
Messages
Msg 3732, Level 16, State 1, Line 1
Cannot drop type 'dbo.EmailType' because it is being referenced by object
'Employee'. There may be other objects that reference this type.

                                                                    0 rows
```

Figure 4.16 The Employee table is dependent upon dbo.EmailType, and cannot be dropped yet.

When executing the previous code, we receive an error message stating that the Employee table is dependent upon the dbo.EmailType data type (Figure 4.16). We encountered this same situation in Chapter 2, when we had to remove tables, or any other dependent objects, before SQL Server allowed us to delete a schema.

Notice the error message names the Employee table as an object which is currently referencing dbo.EmailType. However, it's possible there are other objects within the dbBasics database which are referencing this custom data type.

SSMS can help us find which table(s) is using this data type by navigating within the Object Explorer pane (Figure 4.17):

Object Explorer > Databases > dbBasics > Programmability > Types > User-Defined Data Types > right-click **dbo.EmailType** > **View Dependencies**

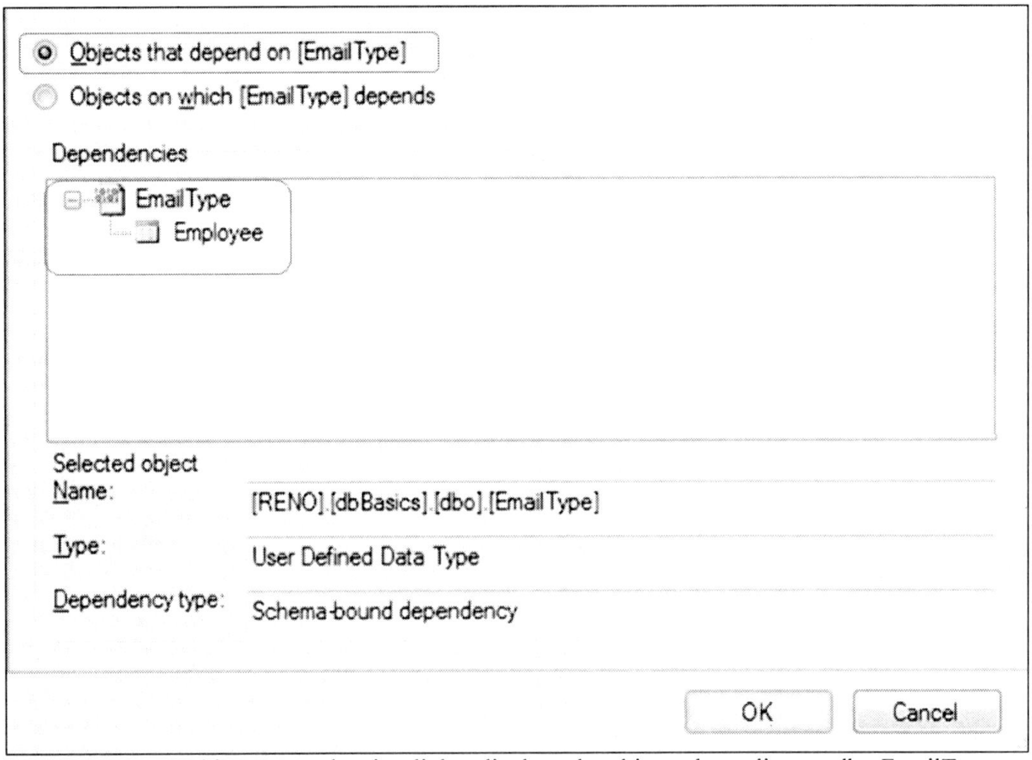

Figure 4.17 The Object Dependencies dialog displays the objects depending on dbo.EmailType.

The Object Dependencies dialog tells us the only object using the dbo.EmailType is the Employee table. To remove this dependency, we will DROP the EmailAlias column by running the T-SQL following code:

```
ALTER TABLE dbBasics.dbo.Employee
DROP COLUMN EmailAlias
GO
```

There are no longer any tables or fields in dbBasics referencing our user-defined data type, dbo.EmailType. This can be confirmed by navigating to the Object Dependencies dialog box.

We are now ready to code the DROP TYPE statement and find that our user defined data type, dbo.EmailType, is removed without any error messages.

```
USE dbBasics
GO

DROP TYPE dbo.EmailType
GO
```

Lab 4.2: Custom Data Types

Lab Prep: Each lab has one or more Skill Checks. Start with Skill Check 1 and proceed until reaching the Points to Ponder section.

Before beginning this lab, verify that SQL Server 2012 is properly installed and operating. Before running the lab setup script for resetting the database (SQLQueries2012Vol3Chapter4.2Setup.sql), please make sure to close all query windows within SSMS. An open query window pointing to a database context can lock that database preventing it from updating when the script is executing. A simple way to assure all query windows are closed, is to exit out of SSMS, then open a new instance of SSMS, and lastly run the setup script.

Skill Check 1: In the JProCo database, use T-SQL code to create a user-defined data type called **dbo.Email**. Use this data type in a new field, EmailAddress, which will be added to the Employee table. When complete, the Employee table design will resemble Figure 4.18.

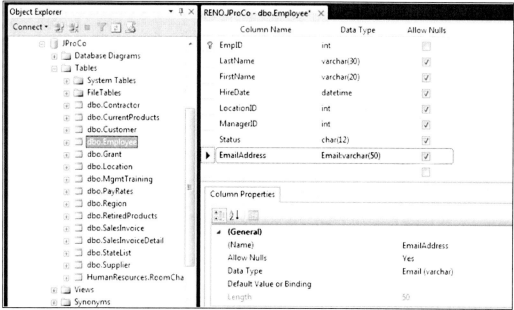

Figure 4.18 Skill Check 1 creates a user-defined data type and uses it in a new column added to the Employee table (JProCo.dbo.Employee).

Skill Check 2: Drop the custom data type, CountryCode, from the JProCo database. If any field(s) is using this data type, then first drop the field(s) from the table. This Skill Check is complete when the following code executes successfully, without any error messages.

```
USE JProCo
GO

DROP TYPE dbo.Employee
GO
```

Answer Code: The T-SQL code to this lab can be found in the downloadable files in a file named Lab4.2_CustomDataTypes.sql.

Points to Ponder - Custom Data Types

1. The data type defines characteristics of the data that is stored in a column.

2. A data type should be chosen based on the information being stored in the field. For example: Using an integer data type for an employee name field would not be a good choice for the information being stored (e.g., non-numeric characters).

3. There are more than 30 system supplied data types such as: CHAR, INT, MONEY, VARCHAR, IMAGE, XML, etc.

4. The data length defines the size of the data string that can be held in the column. The data length is automatically defined for most data types. The length can be defined for these data types: BINARY, CHAR, NCHAR, VARCHAR, VARBINARY, and NVARCHAR.

5. In addition to the system-supplied data types, user-defined data types (also known as an Alias data type) can be created for specific needs.

6. Alias data types are defined in a specific database. If a CountryCode data type is created in the Publishing database it will only be available in that database.

7. When creating a data type in a CREATE TABLE statement, its nullability can be specified by using either the NOT NULL or NULL option.

8. If a custom data type is not nullable then all tables which use this data type must implement it as NOT NULL during table creation.

9. Once created, a data type cannot be changed without first executing a DROP TYPE statement and then using a CREATE TYPE statement to implement the change.

10. A data type cannot be dropped while it is currently being used by a table.

11. To determine which tables are using a User-Defined Data Type, navigate to the Object Dependencies dialog box: **Programmability > Types > User-Defined Data Types >** right-click *[name of the custom data type]* **> View Dependencies**.

12. User-defined data types are located in the database node with the following path: **Programmability** > **Types** > **User-Defined Data Types**.

Date and Time Data Types

Keeping track of date and time data points has always been a critical part of online transactional databases. For example, each sales invoice needs a date-time stamp, as do systems which track quotes and customer contacts regarding sales opportunities.

Think of how many times during the workday we rely on a date-time stamp as helpful metadata to sort or locate the latest information in a report or data source. Global organizations, in particular, have a need for their in-house communication, reporting, and collaboration tools to appropriately convey accurate date and time information in order to keep every part of the organization in sync.

Recap of DateTime Functions

Let's review some common date and time functions. **GETDATE()** returns the current time for our time zone.

```
SELECT GETDATE() AS GetDateFunction
```

GetDateFunction
1   2012-07-28 01:28:30.170
1 rows

Figure 4.19 The GETDATE() function returns the current time for our time zone.

The **GETDATE()** and **SYSDATETIME()** functions both return the current date and time for our time zone. However, the precision for the **GETDATE()** function shows fractional seconds expressed in milliseconds (.123 second), and the precision for the **SYSDATETIME()** function shows fractional seconds expressed in nanoseconds (.1234567 second).

```
SELECT SYSDATETIME() AS SysDateTimeFunction
```

SysDateTimeFunction
1   2012-07-28 01:28:46.4158516
1 rows

Figure 4.20 GETDATE() and SYSDATETIME() return similar results but their precisions differ.

What time is it right now in the UK? We know it's based on UTC, which is Coordinated Universal Time, formerly known as Greenwich Mean Time (GMT), and SQL Server has a function made specifically for this time zone *(UTC is also known by the terms zulu time, world time, and universal time)*.

The **GETUTCDATE()** function will show the current time expressed in terms of UTC. Like GETDATE(), the **GETUTCDATE()** function is expressed in milliseconds and is less precise than the **SYSUTCDATETIME()** function, which is expressed in nanoseconds.

Let's run all four of these statements together, with the two top times in our local time zone and the two bottom times in UTC.

```
SELECT GETDATE() AS GetDateFunction
SELECT SYSDATETIME() AS SysDateTimeFunction
SELECT GETUTCDATE() AS GetUTCDateFunction
SELECT SYSUTCDATETIME() AS SysUTCDateTimeFunction
```

	GetDateFunction
1	2012-07-28 01:55:53.303

	SysDateTimeFunction
1	2012-07-28 01:55:53.3055498

	GetUTCDateFunction
1	2012-07-28 08:55:53.303

	SysUTCDateTimeFunction
1	2012-07-28 08:55:53.3055498

4 rows

Figure 4.21 Local time zone and UTC are expressed in milliseconds and nanoseconds.

Standard Date and Time Data Types

In our dbBasics database, we have a dbo.Activity table which tracks the book(s) a library card number has checked out. We would like to expand the design of this table to include the date-time when each book is checked out and checked in. Let's expand the Design view of our table (dbBasics.dbo.Activity) and add the field CheckOutTime. Lastly, save all changes and then close the Design interface as shown in Figure 4.22.

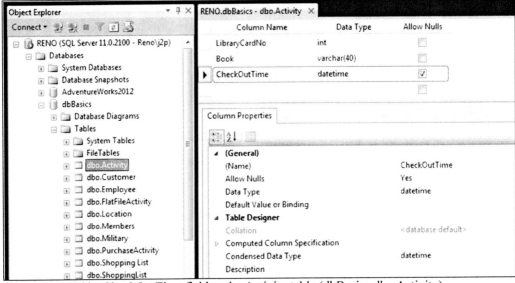

Figure 4.22 Add a CheckOutTime field to the Activity table (dbBasics.dbo.Activity).

```
USE dbBasics
GO

UPDATE dbo.Activity
SET CheckOutTime = GETDATE()
WHERE LibraryCardNo = 1001
GO

UPDATE dbo.Activity
SET CheckOutTime = SYSDATETIME()
WHERE LibraryCardNo = 1003
GO
```

Let's query the results of our UPDATE statements (Figure 4.23).

```
SELECT * FROM dbo.Activity
```

	LibraryCardNo	Book	CheckOutTime
1	1001	Dust Bowl	2012-07-29 02:46:53.030
2	1001	How to Fix Things	2012-07-29 02:46:53.030
3	1003	Yachting for dummies	2012-07-29 02:46:53.027
4	1005	How to marry a millionaire	NULL
5	1005	Spice world	NULL
6	1005	Juice Master tells all	NULL

8 rows

Figure 4.23 The CheckOutTime field has been populated for LibraryCardNo 1001 and 1003.

The **GETDATE()** function captures the CheckOutTime in milliseconds, when we run the UPDATE statement for LibraryCardNo 1001. However, the UPDATE statement for LibraryCardNo 1003 is storing the CheckOutTime in milliseconds, despite the fact that we used **SYSDATETIME()**, which returns nanoseconds. The additional four digits of precision that we know **SYSDATETIME()** returns, have been truncated by the CheckOutTime field. This is because the CheckOutTime field is designed with the **DATETIME** data type, which always stores data in milliseconds, even if more precise data (e.g., nanoseconds) is provided.

The **DATETIME2** data type introduced with SQL Server 2008 is capable of storing nanosecond data (Seven digit precision). Let's add a new field and call it, CheckInTime, to the Activity table utilizing the new **DATETIME2** data type.

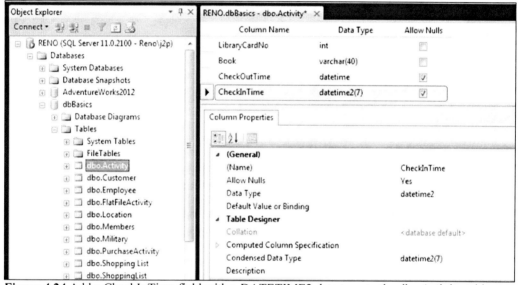

Figure 4.24 Add a CheckInTime field with a DATETIME2 data type to the dbo.Activity table.

We can now run UPDATE statements to populate the CheckInTime field for LibraryCardNo 1001 and 1003.

```
USE dbBasics
GO

UPDATE dbo.Activity
SET CheckInTime = GETDATE()
WHERE LibraryCardNo = 1001
GO
```

```
UPDATE dbo.Activity
SET CheckInTime = SYSDATETIME()
WHERE LibraryCardNo = 1003
GO
```

Thanks to the new **DATETIME2** data type, we will now see all time values for the CheckInTime field displayed in nanoseconds (Figure 4.25).

```
SELECT * FROM dbo.Activity
```

	LibraryCardNo	Book	CheckOutTime	CheckInTime
1	1001	Dust B…	2012-07-29 02:46:53.030	2012-07-29 03:48:04.4630000
2	1001	How to…	2012-07-29 02:46:53.030	2012-07-29 03:48:04.4630000
3	1003	Yachti…	2012-07-29 02:46:53.027	2012-07-29 03:48:04.4694749
4	1005	How to…	NULL	NULL
5	1005	Spice …	NULL	NULL
6	1005	Juice …	NULL	NULL

8 rows

Figure 4.25 Time values for the CheckInTime field are displayed in nanoseconds.

Why are there four extra 0's in the CheckInTime value for LibraryCardNo 1001? Since the **GETDATE()** function provides a time value expressed in milliseconds, the **DATETIME2** data type padded any unused precision spaces with a 0. This allows data in the CheckInTime field to conform with the format of this data type.

Notice that the CheckInTime for LibraryCardNo 1003 is more precise, due to the **SYSDATETIME()** function returning time expressed to the nanosecond.

Date and Time Zone Types

Let's take a trip back to the JProCo database and look at all the records in the CurrentProducts table. Notice the OriginationDate field, which is a **DATETIME** data type. When JProCo originates a product record, this field captures the date and time, although it does not store any time zone information (Figure 4.26).

```
SELECT * FROM JProCo.dbo.CurrentProducts
```

	ProductID	ProductName	RetailPrice	OriginationDate
1	1	Underwater Tour…	61.483	2009-05-07 13:33:09.957
2	2	Underwater Tour…	110.6694	2010-06-29 23:43:22.813
3	3	Underwater Tour…	184.449	2012-02-03 16:07:49.900
4	4	Underwater Tour…	245.932	2008-11-28 04:59:06.600
5	5	Underwater Tour…	307.415	2004-04-13 19:20:11.400

485 rows

Figure 4.26 OriginationDate captures the time we originated the product but not the time zone.

Suppose we needed to know what time it was in the U.K. when Product 2 was originated, or what time it was in India when the record for Product 3 was created. You would need to know what time zone the existing data was stored in, but this date field (OriginationDate) did not store that information.

So what we can do is add the time zone alongside each time value. If we do that, then when we need to move or query our data to adjust for a particular timezone (e.g., the U.K., India, Japan), it becomes an easy process.

We want to alter the CurrentProducts table to add an OriginationOffset field. This field will use a data type created in SQL Server 2008 called **DateTimeOffset**.

```
ALTER TABLE dbo.CurrentProducts
ADD OriginationOffset DateTimeOffset NULL
```

Now we see our original OriginationDate, and we have a new field which is ready to hold the OriginationDate value plus the time zone (Figure 4.27). Next we'll populate the new field with all the values from OriginationDate.

```
SELECT ProductID, ProductName,
OriginationDate, OriginationOffset
FROM dbo.CurrentProducts
```

	ProductID	ProductName	OriginationDate	OriginationOffset
1	1	Underwater Tour…	2009-05-07 13:33:09.957	NULL
2	2	Underwater Tour…	2010-06-29 23:43:22.813	NULL
3	3	Underwater Tour…	2012-02-03 16:07:49.900	NULL
4	4	Underwater Tour…	2008-11-28 04:59:06.600	NULL
5	5	Underwater Tour…	2004-04-13 19:20:11.400	NULL
				485 rows

Figure 4.27 OriginationOffset will hold the original time value and its corresponding time zone.

Populate the new field with the OriginationDate values with the following code:

```
USE JProCo
GO

UPDATE dbo.CurrentProducts
SET OriginationOffset = OriginationDate
GO
```

This helps us, because we now have all the OriginationDate values in the new field. However, our OriginationOffset field needs two pieces of information:

    1) The date and time.   2) The time zone (In single quotes).

Thus, we can't achieve our goal unless we add meaningful time zone information.

The genius of the **DateTimeOffset** data type is that it stores time zone information, which is the next component supplied to our field. Notice that OriginationOffset shows a '+00:00' for the time zone, which indicates either: 1) the UTC time zone or 2) no time zone information has yet been supplied.

```
SELECT ProductID, ProductName,
OriginationDate, OriginationOffset
FROM dbo.CurrentProducts
```

	ProductID	ProductName	OriginationDate	OriginationOffset
1	1	Underwater Tour 1 Day West Coast	2009-05-07 13:33:09.957	2009-05-07 13:33:09.9570000 +00:00
2	2	Underwater Tour 2 Days West Coast	2010-06-29 23:43:22.813	2010-06-29 23:43:22.8130000 +00:00
3	3	Underwater Tour 3 Days West Coast	2012-02-03 16:07:49.900	2012-02-03 16:07:49.9000000 +00:00
4	4	Underwater Tour 5 Days West Coast	2008-11-28 04:59:06.600	2008-11-28 04:59:06.6000000 +00:00
5	5	Underwater Tour 1 Week West Coast	2004-04-13 19:20:11.400	2004-04-13 19:20:11.4000000 +00:00
				485 rows

Figure 4.28 We haven't yet supplied any meaningful time zone information to OriginationOffset.

We can supply the time zone info by modifying our UPDATE statement. Add the function **ToDateTimeOffset()** to indicate which time zone we are in. Since each OriginationDate was recorded in Seattle, which is JProCo's main headquarters, those times all are Pacific Time (Pacific Time is -08:00 of GMT).

```
USE JProCo
GO

UPDATE dbo.CurrentProducts
SET OriginationOffset =
  TODATETIMEOFFSET(OriginationDate,'-08:00')
GO
```

Now let's look at the data again. Notice the offset field now shows the time zone, which is Pacific (-08:00). Also notice that this field is a **DATETIME2** data type with a time zone in it (Figure 4.29).

```
SELECT ProductID, ProductName,
OriginationDate, OriginationOffset
FROM dbo.CurrentProducts
```

	ProductID	ProductName	OriginationDate	OriginationOffset
1	1	Underwater Tour 1 Day West Coast	2009-05-07 13:33:09.957	2009-05-07 13:33:09.9570000 -08:00
2	2	Underwater Tour 2 Days West Coast	2010-06-29 23:43:22.813	2010-06-29 23:43:22.8130000 -08:00
3	3	Underwater Tour 3 Days West Coast	2012-02-03 16:07:49.900	2012-02-03 16:07:49.9000000 -08:00
4	4	Underwater Tour 5 Days West Coast	2008-11-28 04:59:06.600	2008-11-28 04:59:06.6000000 -08:00
5	5	Underwater Tour 1 Week West Coast	2004-04-13 19:20:11.400	2004-04-13 19:20:11.4000000 -08:00

485 rows

Figure 4.29 The offset field now shows the correct time zone for our CurrentProducts data.

Let's think about why this would be a useful tool in our global organization. The **ToDateTimeOffset()** function can be used to translate a list of date-time event values into equivalent values for another time zone. For example, imagine that JProCo is a global organization with its Asia operations headquartered in Hyderabad. Workers at the JProCo corporate headquarters (in Seattle), might want to take Hyderabad's list of weekly conference calls for 2009-2010 and transpose it into a list with Seattle time values. It might even be necessary to provide this list to managers in multiple regions and time zones with the India call schedule. In this case, providing each manager's local time alongside the India time is a useful capability, so each manager knows when to dial in for the call.

Implementing the **ToDateTimeOffset()** function in a query is a handy way to see an equivalent date-time for another time zone. It is common to receive an email thread including colleagues from differing time zones, and then mentally calculating what the local time was for each email by looking at the timestamps on the various responses. Another good use for this function is to cross-reference documents that colleagues have posted on a team sharepoint site, which displays timestamps in their time zone.

Let's see another **ToDateTimeOffset()** example using the CurrentProducts table. Imagine the India regional team handled the setup of all these products, but most of this data was input a few years ago – before we had SQL Server 2008 with the ability of using the nifty **DateTimeOffset** field on the CurrentProducts table to capture the time zone. Until now, all data in CurrentProducts has reflected the time zone of the JProCo corporate headquarters in Seattle. The legal department has asked when ProductID 1 (Underwater Tour 1 Day West Coast) was created, and specifies the information must be expressed in India time. *So when ProductID 1 was originated, what time would it have been in India?* India is UTC +05:30.

In order to answer this question, we'll run a SELECT statement similar to the update statement we ran earlier. Namely, we will add the **ToDateTimeOffset()** function and tell it which time zone we are in. Since each OriginationDate was recorded in Seattle, all those times are Pacific Time. Pacific Time is -08:00 of GMT.

Now we're going to take the OriginationOffset and put a switch on it to show what the time would have been in India (i.e., when OriginationDate was input). Using a **DateTimeOffset** field allows the **SWITCHOFFSET()** function to calculate the equivalent time of another time zone.

```
SELECT ProductID, ProductName, OriginationDate,
SWITCHOFFSET(OriginationOffset, '+05:30') AS IndiaOffset
FROM dbo.CurrentProducts
```

	ProductID	ProductName	OriginationDate	IndiaOffset
1	1	Underwater Tour 1 Day West Coast	2009-05-07 13:33:09.957	2009-05-08 03:03:09.9570000 +05:30
2	2	Underwater Tour 2 Days West Coast	2010-06-29 23:43:22.813	2010-06-30 13:13:22.8130000 +05:30
3	3	Underwater Tour 3 Days West Coast	2012-02-03 16:07:49.900	2012-02-04 05:37:49.9000000 +05:30
4	4	Underwater Tour 5 Days West Coast	2008-11-28 04:59:06.600	2008-11-28 18:29:06.6000000 +05:30
5	5	Underwater Tour 1 Week West Coast	2004-04-13 19:20:11.400	2004-04-14 08:50:11.4000000 +05:30
				485 rows

Figure 4.30 Use the SWITCHOFFSET() function to display times in a different time zone.

Now we can see it was 1:33 p.m., Seattle time, on 07May2009 when ProductID 1 was originated, and at that same moment in India it was 3:03 a.m. on 08May2009. Likewise, ProductID 2 was originated at 11:43 p.m., Seattle time, on 29Jun2010, which corresponds to 1:13 p.m. on 30Jun2010 in India.

Lab 4.3: Date and Time Data Types

Lab Prep: Each lab has one or more Skill Checks. Start with Skill Check 1 and proceed until reaching the Points to Ponder section.

Before beginning this lab, verify that SQL Server 2012 is properly installed and operating. Before running the lab setup script for resetting the database (SQLQueries2012Vol3Chapter4.3Setup.sql), please make sure to close all query windows within SSMS. An open query window pointing to a database context can lock that database preventing it from updating when the script is executing. A simple way to assure all query windows are closed, is to exit out of SSMS, then open a new instance of SSMS, and lastly run the setup script.

Skill Check 1: Add two new fields to the JProCo.dbo.Employee table called HiredOffset and TimeZone. HiredOffset is nullable and is a **DateTimeOffset** data type. TimeZone is nullable and is a CHAR(6) data type.

Populate all Seattle and Spokane employee TimeZone fields with '-08:00'. Populate all Chicago and mobile employees with '-06:00'. Populate all Boston employees with '-05:00'. After these steps, the Employee table should resemble Figure 4.31.

```
SELECT * FROM JProCo.dbo.Employee
```

	EmpID	LastName	FirstName	HireDate	TimeZone
1	1	Adams	Alex	2001-01-01 00:00:00.000	-08:00
2	2	Brown	Barry	2002-08-12 00:00:00.000	-08:00
3	3	Osako	Lee	1999-09-01 00:00:00.000	-05:00
4	4	Kennson	David	1996-03-16 00:00:00.000	-08:00
5	5	Bender	Eric	2007-05-17 00:00:00.000	-08:00
6	6	Kendall	Lisa	2001-11-15 00:00:00.000	-08:00
7	7	Lonning	David	2000-01-01 00:00:00.000	-08:00
8	8	Marshbank	John	2001-11-15 00:00:00.000	-06:00

13 rows

Figure 4.31 Skill Check 1 adds two fields and includes each employee's time zone information.

Skill Check 2: Use the ToDateTimeOffset() function to populate the HiredOffset field based on the HireDate and TimeZone fields. When done, the results should resemble Figure 4.32.

```
SELECT * FROM JProCo.dbo.Employee
```

	EmpID	LastName	FirstName	HireDate	HiredOffset
1	1	Adams	Alex	2001-01-01 00:00:00.000	2001-01-01 00:00:00.0000000 -08:00
2	2	Brown	Barry	2002-08-12 00:00:00.000	2002-08-12 00:00:00.0000000 -08:00
3	3	Osako	Lee	1999-09-01 00:00:00.000	1999-09-01 00:00:00.0000000 -05:00
4	4	Kennson	David	1996-03-16 00:00:00.000	1996-03-16 00:00:00.0000000 -08:00
5	5	Bender	Eric	2007-05-17 00:00:00.000	2007-05-17 00:00:00.0000000 -08:00

13 rows

Figure 4.32 Skill Check 2 populates HiredOffset from the HireDate and TimeZone fields.

Skill Check 3: Add a column to the beginning of the JProCo.dbo.Employee results called AlaskaHireTime that displays the HireDate for all employees using Alaska Time '-09:00'. When done, the results should resemble Figure 4.33.

	AlaskaHireTime	EmpID	LastName	FirstName	HireDate
1	2000-12-31 23:00:00.0000000 -09:00	1	Adams	Alex	2001-01-01 00:00:00.000
2	2002-08-11 23:00:00.0000000 -09:00	2	Brown	Barry	2002-08-12 00:00:00.000
3	1999-08-31 20:00:00.0000000 -09:00	3	Osako	Lee	1999-09-01 00:00:00.000
4	1996-03-15 23:00:00.0000000 -09:00	4	Kennson	David	1996-03-16 00:00:00.000
5	2007-05-16 23:00:00.0000000 -09:00	5	Bender	Eric	2007-05-17 00:00:00.000

13 rows

Figure 4.33 Skill Check 3 expresses each employee's hire date in Alaska Time.

Answer Code: The T-SQL code to this lab can be found in the downloadable files in a file named Lab4.3_DateAndTimeTypes.sql.

Points to Ponder - Date and Time Data Types

1. A DateTimeOffset field can use the SWITCHOFFSET() function to show the equivalent time from another time zone.

2. The **DateTimeOffset** data type requires two pieces of information:
    1) The Date and Time.
    2) The Time Zone (In single quotes).

Chapter Glossary

Alias Data Types: A custom data type based on a system-supplied data type.

CLR Data Types: Common language runtime data types, such as GEOGRAPHY or GEOMETRY.

Constraint: A constraint restricts your data input to values within the limits you specify in the design of your table and its fields.

Custom Data Types: This user defined data type defines the characteristic of the data that is stored in a column.

Data Pages: Another name for memory pages.

DATETIME: This data type only stores data out to milliseconds.

DATETIME2: A data type that is capable of storing nanosecond data.

DATETIMEOFFSET: This data type stores time zone information.

DROP TYPE: Data types cannot be changed. They first have to be dropped via a DROP TYPE statement and then recreated.

GETDATE(): A non-deterministic function which returns a value for the local time zone of the server using a DATETIME data type. The ANSI equivalent to this Microsoft function is CURRENT_TIMESTAMP.

GETUTCDATE(): A non-deterministic function which returns a value for the UTC time zone of the server using a DATETIME data type. The database time zone offset is not included in the returned value.

SPARSE Data: A SQL Server 2008 feature for fields that are expected to be predominantly occupied by NULL values.

Sparsely Populated Field: When the majority of records for a given field contain NULL values, it is considered to be a sparsely populated field.

SPROC: Short for **S**tored **PROC**edure; a set of defined, precompiled SQL statements stored on a SQL Server.

SWITCHOFFSET(): If you have a DATETIMEOFFSET field, you can use the SWITCHOFFSET function to see the equivalent time in another time zone.

SYSDATETIME(): This function returns the current date and time in your time zone and shows fractional seconds expressed in nanoseconds (.3333333 second).

SYSUTCDATETIME(): A UTC function that gets down to the nanoseconds.

TODATETIMEOFFSET(): This function is used to translate a list of date-time event values into equivalent values for another time zone.

Review Quiz - Chapter Four

1.) You have two fields in your Bonus table of INT and MONEY. You have 1000 records and all instances of the money column are NULL. When you set up the money field, you used the SPARSE option. How much space are the 1000 rows of the money field using?

  O a. None

  O b. 4000 bytes

  O c. 8000 bytes

2.) You are expecting to have some sparsely populated data in your table and need to know what types of data can use the SPARSE option. Which of the following can use the SPARSE option? (choose three)

  ☐ a. INT

  ☐ b. CHAR(10)

  ☐ c. TEXT

  ☐ d. MONEY

  ☐ e. GEOMETRY

  ☐ f. NTEXT

  ☐ g. GEOGRAPHY

3.) You have a table with three fields of VARCHAR(MAX), TEXT, and GEOMETRY. Which is the only field that can use the sparse option?

  O a. VARCHAR(MAX)

  O b. TEXT

  O c. GEOMETRY

4.) You have one record in a table called dbo.Bonus, which has two fields. The first field is called BonusID and it is a NOT NULL integer. The second field is BonusAmount, which is set to MONEY and is nullable. Integers are 4 bytes and MONEY is 8 bytes. The first record has an Id of 1 and an amount set to NULL. What is the fixed length data payload?

  O a. 4 bytes

  O b. 8 bytes

  O c. 12 bytes

5.) You have a custom data type called CountryCode and have been instructed by your manager to delete it. What must you do first?

O a. Delete all system-supplied data types which CountryCode is based on.

O b. Remove all fields which are using that CountryCode.

O c. Set all rows to NULL for any field using the CountryCode type.

6.) Which of the following functions will return the date and time in the current time zone to a precision of milliseconds?

O a. GETDATE()

O b. SYSDATETIME()

O c. GETUTCDATE()

O d. SYSUTCDATETIME()

7.) Which of the following functions will return the current time in Coordinated Universal Time format to a precision of nanoseconds?

O a. GETDATE()

O b. SYSDATETIME()

O c. GETUTCDATE()

O d. SYSUTCDATETIME()

8.) You have an enterprise level database storing information from all over the world. You have been using a column to contain the local time and a column to contain the difference between local time and UTC time. You now have SQL Server 2012 and want to store this in one column. Which data type should you use?

O a. TIME

O b. DATE

O c. DATETIME

O d. DATETIME2

O e. DATETIMEOFFSET

9.) You have a DATETIME2 data type and want to turn it into a DateTimeOffset data type for the Alaska Time zone -09:00. What method will achieve this result?

O a. SWITCHOFFSET()

O b. TODATETIMEOFFSET()

10.) You work for an online ordering company that processes web purchases from all over the world. You work at the Headquarters in Vancouver BC. At the exact moment an order is accepted, it is entered as a value into an OrderDate field which uses the DateTimeOffset data type. A user in Hawaii wants to know the exact time of their last order. You recorded the transaction in Vancouver BC time and want to show the results in Hawaii's time. Which function will change the time zone while preserving the UTC stored time?

O a. DATEADD()

O b. DATEDIFF()

O c. TODATETIMEOFFSET()

O d. SWITCHOFFSET()

11.) You have an enterprise level database storing information from all over the world. You have been using a column to contain the local time as a Datetime2 and another column to contain the difference between local time and UTC time. You now have SQL Server 2012 and want to store this in one column. Which function will create a DateTimeOffset from a DATETIME2 if you give it the time zone?

O a. DATEADD()

O b. DATEDIFF()

O c. TODATETIMEOFFSET()

O d. SWITCHOFFSET()

12.) You currently store date information in two columns (SaleTime, SaleZone). SaleTime contains the date in local time and SaleZone contains the difference between local time and Greenwich Mean Time. You need to store this data in a single column. Which data type should you use??

O a. TIME

O b. DATETIME2

O c. DATETIME2(5)

O d. DATETIMEOFFSET

13.) What function can store time in your DateTime2 field down to the exact single millisecond?

   O a. ENDOFMONTH

   O b. GETUTCDATE()

   O c. SYSDATETIME()

   O d. CURRENT_TIMESTAMP

14.) You're a SQL Developer from Portland, OR and have implemented the DATETIMEOFFSET data type using the offset time for Seattle, WA. Your company has an office in Kiev and needs to display the dates and times translated for the Kiev office. Which function will you use to achieve this result?

   O a. CAST()

   O b. DATEADD()

   O c. SWITCHOFFSET()

   O d. TODATETIMEOFFSET()

Answer Key

1.) When the Sparse data option is used, NULLs in a Sparse column will not take up any storage space making (a) the correct answer.

2.) The sparse option cannot be used with the old LOB types TEXT, NTEXT and IMAGE, so (c) and (f) are incorrect. The Sparse option works with most regular numeric and character data types; it cannot be used with several data types such as CLR data types such as GEOGRAPHY and GEOMETRY therefore (e) and (g) are incorrect. The correct answers are (a), (b), and (d).

3.) TEXT is an LOB data type and cannot be used with the Sparse option, so (b) is incorrect. GEOMETRY is a CLR data type and cannot be used with the sparse option, so (c) is incorrect making (a) VARCHAR(MAX) is the correct answer.

4.) Fixed length data types always occupy the amount of space allotted to them, making INT (4 bytes) (a) and MONEY (8 bytes) (b) wrong, and (c) 12 bytes correct.

5.) Deleting any system-supplied data types is not the goal, so (a) is incorrect. Setting the rows to NULL is still using the system data type, so (c) is incorrect. The goal is to remove any dependencies or tables using the customer data type, so (b) is the correct answer.

6.) SYSDATETIME() shows fractional seconds expressed in nanoseconds, so (b) is incorrect. GETUTCDATE() shows the current time in terms of UTC, so (c) is incorrect. SYSUTCDATETIME() also shows time in nanoseconds, so (d) is incorrect. This makes (a) GETDATE() the correct answer.

7.) GETDATE() returns the current time in the server's local time zone and shows fractional seconds expressed in milliseconds, so (a) is incorrect. SYSDATETIME() shows fractional seconds expressed in nanoseconds, so (b) is incorrect. GETUTCDATE() shows the current time in terms of UTC, so (c) is incorrect. SYSUTCDATETIME()shows time in nanoseconds, which means (d) is correct.

8.) The DATETIME data type will only show HH:MM:SS, so (a) is incorrect. The DATE data type will only show YYYY-MM-DD, so (b) is incorrect. The DATETIME data type will only show the date down to the millisecond, so (c) incorrect. The DATETIME2 data type will only show down to nanoseconds, so (d) is incorrect. The DATETIMEOFFSET stores time zone information, making (e) the correct answer.

9.) The SWITCHOFFSET() function shows the equivalent time in another time zone, so (a) is incorrect. The TODATETIMEOFFSET() function turns a regular DATETIME into a DATETIMEOFFSET data type, making (b) the right answer.

10.) Since the data is collected all over the world with the time and time zone already recorded, a DATETIMEOFFSET exists and there is no need to switch to one, making (c) incorrect. Changing the time is not required, so (a) is incorrect. The requirement is to display the actual time of all records listed in Hawaii's time, so SWITCHOFFSET() (d) is the correct answer.

11.) Since the date is stored in UTC time, it has not been stored with a time zone yet and doesn't have a DATETIMEOFFSET data type. SWITCHOFFSET() cannot be run on a DATETIME without a time zone, so (a) is incorrect. The goal is to create a new data type of DATETIMEOFFSET, so (c) using the function TODATETIMEOFFSET() is the correct answer.

12.) Only the DATETIMEOFFSET data type stores the time and the time zone making (d) the correct answer. All other answers do not store the time zone.

13.) Only the SYSDATETIME() function returns data down to the millisecond and nanosecond, making (c) the correct answer.

14.) TODATETIMEOFFSET() is used to create a DateTimeOffset field and this already exists, so (d) is incorrect. If the time is available and the goal is to see it in a new time then use SWITCHOFFSET() making (c) the correct answer.

Bug Catcher Game

To play the Bug Catcher game, run the SQLQueries2012Vol3BugCatcher04.pps file from the BugCatcher folder of the companion files. These files can be obtained from the www.Joes2Pros.com website.

[THIS PAGE INTENTIONALLY LEFT BLANK.]

Chapter 5.   Spatial Data Types

Maps have played an important role for navigators and cultures down the centuries. A map can chart a journey, or it can depict a place on the earth or even an entire country. Maps can also be non-geographical, like the map of all the shops in a mall. All maps have one thing in common: they show how each item in the map relates to the other items in terms of position. Most maps combine several types of items. For example, think of a treasure map where X marks the spot. If this map contains an island with the treasure mark in the middle, then the island is a shape which contains the point indicating the treasure's location.

Ever notice that on our round shaped world, almost every piece of property sold is either a rectangular, or a polygon-shaped lot? Occasionally, we might see a round lawn design but generally, it will still be contained within a rectangular plot having decorative accents (e.g., flower gardens) in each corner.

To represent land, we need to use a flat map. To represent points on the earth we need a spherical, or ball-shaped map. For this reason you have two spatial data types to pick from called GEOGRAPHY or GEOMETRY. One is better for measuring parcels of land, while the other is better for GPS or other global type measures.

Spatial data types in SQL Server 2008 were probably the most anticipated new feature and with good reason. More features were added to these types in SQL 2012. Entire books are now written on the subject and this chapter will show the basics with the new 2012 enhancements in the next Chapter.

READER NOTE: *Please run the SQLQueries2012Vol3Chapter5.0Setup.sql script in order to follow along with the examples in the first section of Chapter 5. All scripts mentioned in this chapter may be found at* www.Joes2Pros.com.

GEOGRAPHY Data Type

The spatial data types are called **GEOGRAPHY** and **GEOMETRY**. The **GEOGRAPHY** data type can store information for areas and points on the earth. It also provides a built-in function to calculate distance and overlaps with other locations. This data type stores and handles calculations based on round-earth (or *ellipsoidal*) data, which relates to coordinate systems, such as GPS and longitude-latitude.

We can see from querying the JProCo.dbo.Location table, there is no information available to support geographic calculations, such as values for latitude and longitude. This type of positional data has been stored in databases for years, so we will need to add columns to store this data before we begin working with the geography data type.

```
SELECT *
FROM dbo.Location
```

	LocationID	Street	City	State
1	1	111 First ST	Seattle	WA
2	2	222 Second AVE	Boston	MA
3	3	333 Third PL	Chicago	IL
4	4	444 Ruby ST	Spokane	WA
5	5	1595 Main	Philadelphia	PA

5 rows

Figure 5.1 The true nature of geographical data could not be stored in the database prior to SQL Server 2008. Developers had to extract the data points into a custom application.

If we wanted to ask this database what the longitude-latitude difference between Seattle and Boston is, it would have no idea. To the database, these are just arbitrary flat data values. In order to turn each pair of numbers into a meaningful geographical point, we would have to extract this data into a custom application outside of SQL Server (e.g., into a C# application) and then run calculations using the customized application.

In other words, the true ellipsoidal nature of this geographical data wasn't stored in the database prior to SQL Server 2008. The database would have been unable to differentiate any longitude-latitude data from any other kind of information in the database. Now, thanks to SQL Server 2008 and 2012, a custom application is no longer necessary, as both of these pieces of data can be stored in one **GEOGRAPHY** field. The **GEOGRAPHY** type also makes available built-in functionality to perform calculations involving round-earth data.

Storing Latitude and Longitude

Prior to SQL Server 2008, two FLOAT or DECIMAL fields would be used to store latitude and longitude values. Now these can be stored, along with other geospatial data, in one **GEOGRAPHY** field.

Let's begin by looking at the design and all the records in the Location table. To see the Design tool interface, use SSMS to navigate to the following location:

Object Explorer > Databases > JProCo > Tables > right-click **dbo.Location** > **Design**

READER NOTE: The image in Figure 5.2 has been altered using special software in order to help visualize the SSMS Design tool interface and the Query Results at the same time. Please do not expect to see, or be able to replicate an exact duplication of the following image, as they are two distinct images stitched together for informational purposes only.

The basic location data is all here, (Street, City, and State) for the five JProCo office locations (Seattle, Spokane, Chicago, Boston, and Philadelphia). We will add fields for latitude and longitude to this table, before combining them into a single field using the **GEOGRAPHY** data type.

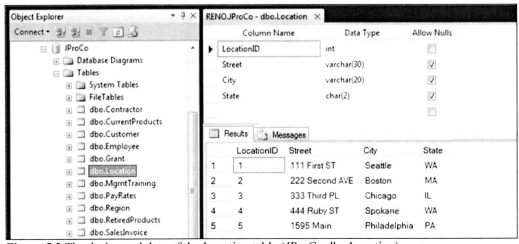

Figure 5.2 The design and data of the Location table (JProCo.dbo.Location).

First, we will add a latitude and longitude field with the following code:

```
--Add a Latitude Field.
ALTER TABLE Location
ADD Latitude FLOAT NULL
GO

--Add a Longitude Field.
ALTER TABLE Location
ADD Longitude FLOAT NULL
GO
```

Next, we will populate these fields using values supplied with the following code:

```
--Seattle
UPDATE Location
SET Latitude = 47.455, Longitude = -122.231
WHERE LocationID = 1
GO

--Boston
UPDATE Location
SET Latitude = 42.372, Longitude = -71.0298
WHERE LocationID = 2
GO

--Chicago
UPDATE Location
SET Latitude = 41.953, Longitude = -87.643
WHERE LocationID = 3
GO

--Spokane
UPDATE Location
SET Latitude = 47.668, Longitude = -117.529
WHERE LocationID = 4
GO

--Philadelphia
UPDATE Location
SET Latitude = 39.888, Longitude = -75.251
WHERE LocationID = 5
GO
```

Now let's take a look at the results of all the UPDATE statements by querying the
dbo.Location table (Figure 5.3).

```
SELECT *
FROM dbo.Location
```

	LocationID	Street	City	State	Latitude	Longitude
1	1	111 First ST	Seattle	WA	47.455	-122.231
2	2	222 Second AVE	Boston	MA	42.372	-71.0298
3	3	333 Third PL	Chicago	IL	41.953	-87.643
4	4	444 Ruby ST	Spokane	WA	47.668	-117.529
5	5	1595 Main	Philadelphia	PA	39.888	-75.251

5 rows

Figure 5.3 One geography field can do more than two latitude/longitude fields.

Creating GEOGRAPHY as a Field in a Table

We're now going to add another field called GeoLoc (short for geographical
location), which will use the new **GEOGRAPHY** data type.

```
ALTER TABLE Location
ADD GeoLoc GEOGRAPHY NULL
```

We now have the latitude and longitude fields populated with values for each
JProCo location and the GeoLoc field has been added to the table.

```
SELECT *
FROM dbo.Location
```

	LocationID	City	State	Latitude	Longitude	GeoLoc
1	1	Seattle	WA	47.455	-122.231	NULL
2	2	Boston	MA	42.372	-71.0298	NULL
3	3	Chicago	IL	41.953	-87.643	NULL
4	4	Spokane	WA	47.668	-117.529	NULL
5	5	Philadelphia	PA	39.888	-75.251	NULL

5 rows

Figure 5.4 The latitude and longitude values and GeoLoc field are now in place.

Populating a GEOGRAPHY Data Type

Based on the two data points, latitude and longitude, we can generate the
geospatial locations for the GeoLoc field. We will use the Point() static function
to pass in three parameters: latitude, longitude, and a Spatial Reference ID (SRID)
value. The most common value for the SRID parameter is 4326.

```
--Seattle
UPDATE Location
SET [GeoLoc] = GEOGRAPHY::Point(47.455, -122.231, 4326)
WHERE LocationID = 1
GO
```

T-SQL code for entering all location values into the GEOGRAPHY field, GeoLoc.

```
--All Locations via data stored in Latitude and Longitude
UPDATE Location
SET [GeoLoc] = GEOGRAPHY::Point(Latitude, Longitude, 4326)
GO
```

Now let's take a look at the results of our UPDATE statements by querying the JProCo.dbo.Location table.

```
SELECT *
FROM dbo.Location
```

LocationID	City	State	Latitude	Longitude	GeoLoc
1	Seattle	WA	47.455	-122.231	0xE6100000010C0AD7A3703DBA4740105839B4C88E5EC0
2	Boston	MA	42.372	-71.0298	0xE6100000010C560E2DB29D2F4540EE5A423EE8C151C0
3	Chicago	IL	41.953	-87.643	0xE6100000010C448B6CE7FBF94440FED478E926E955C0
4	Spokane	WA	47.668	-117.529	0xE6100000010C2FDD240681D5474060E5D022DB615DC0
5	Philadelphia	PA	39.888	-75.251	0xE6100000010C8B6CE7FBA9F14340F2D24D6210D052C0

5 rows

Figure 5.5 We have successfully combined latitude and longitude into GEOGRAPHY data.

The SRID used to format the GEOGRAPHY value identifies which spatial reference system the coordinates belong to. An SRID of 4326 represents WGS 84, which is the most commonly used system and is used by GPS systems.

We can query the ***sys.spatial_reference_systems*** table to view a list of all systems currently supported since the introduction of SQL Server 2008 (Figure 5.6).

```
SELECT *
FROM sys.spatial_reference_systems
```

	spatial_reference_id	authority_name	well_known_text	unit_of_measure
181	4326	EPSG	GEOGCS["WGS 84", DATUM["World Geodetic System 1984", ELLIPSOID["WGS 84", 6378137, 298.257223563]], PRIMEM["Greenwich", 0], UNIT["Degree", 0.0174532925199433]]	metre

391 rows

Figure 5.6 Partial information shown for the sys.spatial_reference_systems table for SRID 4326.

The string value in the well_known_text field contains the definition of the spatial reference:

Coordinate System:	GEOGCS	WGS 84
Datum:	DATUM	World Geodetic System 1984
	ELLIPSOID	WGS 84, 6378137, 298.257223563
Prime Meridian:	PRIMEM	"Greenwich", 0 (longitude 0)
Unit of Measurement:	UNIT	"Degree", 0.0174532925199433

In Chapter 4, we saw that data types can serve as *constraints* when data is input into a field. This ensures values being entered are within the limits specified by the design of the field and table. If the values in a field will all belong to one SRID, then we can add a field constraint to enforce this requirement. The T-SQL following code ensures that all values entered in the GeoLoc field have an SRID of 4326.

```
ALTER TABLE dbo.Location
ADD CONSTRAINT [enforce_srid_geographycolumn]
CHECK (GeoLoc.STSrid = 4326)
GO
```

Once completed, verify the constraint has been created by refreshing the JProCo database folder in the Object Explorer and then navigating to the Constraints folder of the Location table as shown in Figure 5.7.

Object Explorer > JProCo > dbo.Location > Constraints > enforce_srid_geographycolumn

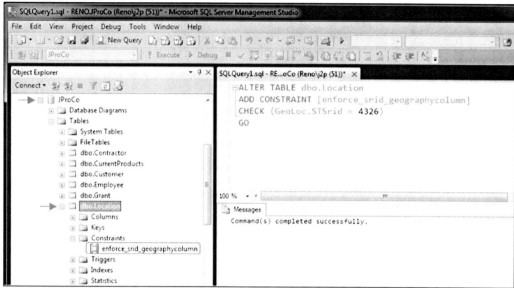

Figure 5.7 Location of the enforce_srid_geographycolumn constraint on the Location table.

GEOGRAPHY Functions

We are now a little familiar with the Point() function. There are other functions (or methods) available for use with the **GEOGRAPHY** data type. The next two functions we will examine in this section, STAsText() and STDistance(), are examples of *GEOGRAPHY instance functions*. References to the term *GEOGRAPHY instance functions,* or the GEOGRAPHY data type, are available from SQL Server 2012 resources (e.g., MSDN, Microsoft SQL Server Books Online 2012).

Previously, we successfully combined latitude and longitude into a single field called GeoLoc. However, since the values in the GeoLoc column are a little tricky to read, it would be nice to convert this data into a more user friendly format. We can accomplish this by creating a variable to convert each city's GeoLoc value into its respective longitude and latitude values.

```
DECLARE @Seattle GEOGRAPHY;
DECLARE @Boston GEOGRAPHY;

SELECT @Seattle = GeoLoc
FROM Location
WHERE LocationID = 1

SELECT @Boston = GeoLoc
FROM Location
WHERE LocationID = 2
```

175

```
SELECT @Seattle.STAsText() AS Seattle,
@Boston.STAsText() AS Boston
```

	Seattle	Boston
1	POINT (-122.231 47.455)	POINT (-71.0298 42.372)

		1 rows

Figure 5.8 STAsText() is one of the Spatial Type functions used with the GEOGRAPHY type.

The STDistance() method calculates the shortest distance (in meters) between two **GEOGRAPHY** data points. To have STDistance() return the distance from Seattle to Boston in kilometers (KM), we divide the result by 1000. Without this additional calculation, the result is over 4 million meters (4,008,321 meters).

```
DECLARE @Seattle GEOGRAPHY;
DECLARE @Boston GEOGRAPHY;

SELECT @Seattle = GeoLoc
FROM Location
WHERE LocationID = 1

SELECT @Boston = GeoLoc
FROM Location
WHERE LocationID = 2

SELECT @Seattle.STDistance(@Boston) AS [Distance in Meters],
@Seattle.STDistance(@Boston)/1000 AS [Distance in KMs]
```

	Distance in Meters	Distance in KMs
1	4008321.24761243	4008.32124761243

		1 rows

Figure 5.9 Results of the Seattle to Boston distance calculation (About 4,008 Kilometers).

Finally, let's change the distance calculation to show the same distance in miles. As there are 1609 meters per mile, the distance from Seattle to Boston is a little over 2491 miles.

```
DECLARE @Seattle GEOGRAPHY;
DECLARE @Boston GEOGRAPHY;

SELECT @Seattle = GeoLoc
FROM Location
WHERE LocationID = 1

SELECT @Boston = GeoLoc
FROM Location
WHERE LocationID = 2
```

```
SELECT
@Seattle.STDistance(@Boston)/1609 AS [Distance in Miles]
```

	Distance in Miles
1	2491.18784811214

	1 rows

Figure 5.10 It is just over 2491 miles from Seattle to Boston.

GEOGRAPHY Polygon

As a young child I just loved it when my mother gave me a workbook full of connect-the-dots games. Starting with the first dot and drawing a line in order, it was fun to see the complete picture when the task was finished. By connecting several points in a row and closing it back up at the end, we can actually make the geography type hold a polygon. This is a great way to represent a landmass, like the United States, instead of just a single point on the map. By connecting enough dots together, it is possible to draw any land mass (Figure 5.11).

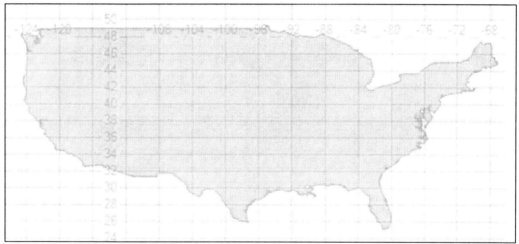

Figure 5.11 The USA polygon is made up from connecting many points together.

So then, what connect-the-dots sequence will draw a rough sketch of the continental United States?

Let's look at this example, which begins where I live (in the northwest corner), which we will designate as the upper left corner. Looking at an atlas, we see it's about 124 degrees west longitude and 49 degrees north latitude (Figure 5.12).

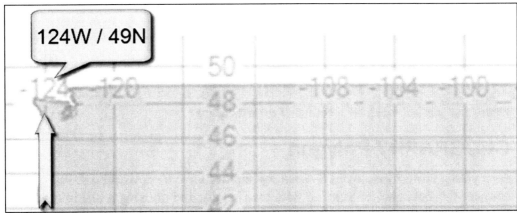

Figure 5.12 The Northwest corner of the USA is located at approximately 124W and 49N.

Looking at the lower right corner of the USA, we see that it is located at 80 degrees west longitude and 25 degrees north latitude (Figure 5.13).

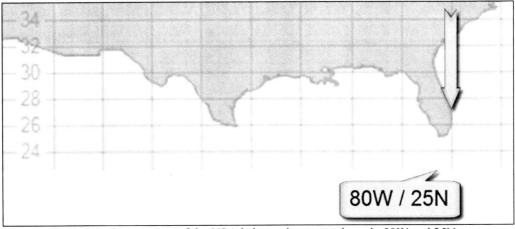

Figure 5.13 The southeast corner of the USA is located at approximately 80W and 25N.

By continuing to draw points that mark the edges of the United States we can produce a very fine version of the United States. By marking several points with known coordinates we can make a rough drawing of the United States. We will then store all these points as a Geograpy type and view the results.

We begin by identifying the 16 points needed to get a rough geographical shape which resembles the map of the continental United States (Figure 5.14).

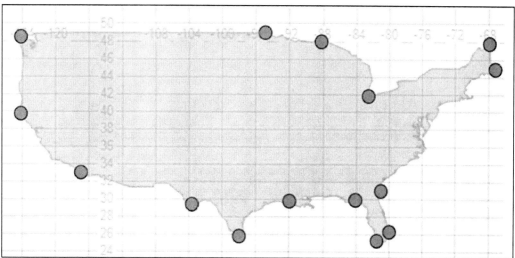

Figure 5.14 We will use these 16 Longitude /Latitude points to make a rough drawing of the USA.

Let's play our game of Connect-the-Dots, where we start and end at the same point, by drawing each point in order and ending at the same point we started at in the upper left corner (Figure 5.15).

READER NOTE: *We could have picked any point as our starting / stopping point.*

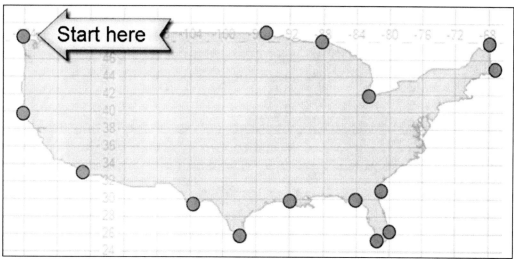

Figure 5.15 GEOGRAPHY polygons must start and stop on the same point.

It is important that we go in a counterclockwise manner as seen in Figure 5.16. Attempting to draw in a clockwise manner, will cause SQL Server to give a rather confusing error message about hemispheres.

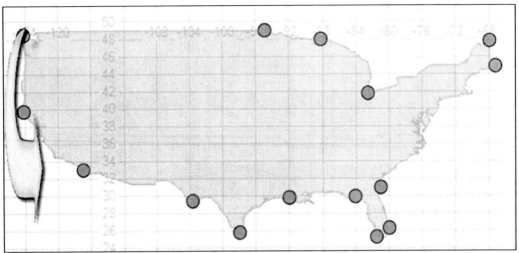

Figure 5.16 These reference points must be drawn in a counterclockwise manner.

READER NOTE: *For these earth-friendly numbers, we can use either the GEOGRAPHY or the GEOMETRY data type to accomplish a rough outline.*

We are now ready to declare a GEOGRAPHY data type and provide the values for the 16 points representing an outline of the United States. These 16 points will be placed inside the parentheses of the STGeomFromText() function. It is important to know that geography data type functions end with a semi-colon.

All 16 points will go inside a set of single quotes as the first parameter to the STGeomFromText() function. The second parameter is an SRID value of 4326. This SRID value is a WSG84 standard, which is one of many standards beyond the scope of this book, so we encourage using this common standard for our example.

Since the continental United States is a single enclosed shape, we only need one set of parentheses inside our first parameter. In order to draw Hawaii or Alaska, multiple parenthesis would be necessary to have additional enclosed shapes.

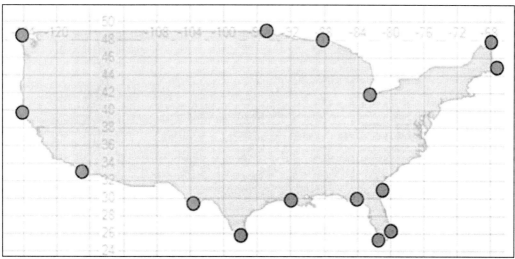

Figure 5.17 These 16 points are used as character parameters in the STGeomFromText() function.

READER NOTE: *To help learn how to place all these points into the function, STGeomFromText(), we will build the query in several steps with important notes along the way. Do not try to execute these samples until instructed to do so, as it would result in an error message.*

We will begin with the basic outline of our SELECT statement. The first parameter is enclosed in a set of single quotes with the keyword Polygon and a set of outer parenthesis that will hold a set of inner parenthesis for each shape in the polygon.

```
DECLARE @RoughUSA GEOGRAPHY;
SET @RoughUSA = GEOGRAPHY::STGeomFromText(
'Polygon ()',4326);
```

Let's draw our first point. Since a west longitude is a negative number, we will enter -124. Since north latitude is a positive number, we will enter 49. These two numbers are separated by a space.

```
DECLARE @RoughUSA GEOGRAPHY;
SET @RoughUSA = GEOGRAPHY::STGeomFromText(
'Polygon ((-124 49))',4326);
```

The next point is at -124 west and 40 degrees north. The second set of numbers is separated from the first set of numbers by a comma.

```
DECLARE @RoughUSA GEOGRAPHY;
SET @RoughUSA = GEOGRAPHY::STGeomFromText(
'Polygon ((-124 49, -124 40))',4326);
```

By continuing to enter numbers all the way to the lower tip of Florida, our results will contain the 9 points shown in the following code and Figure 5.18.

```
DECLARE @RoughUSA GEOGRAPHY;
SET @RoughUSA = GEOGRAPHY::STGeomFromText(
'Polygon ((-124 49, -124 40, -119 33, -104 29, -97 26,
-92 30, -84 30, -82 25, -80 26))',4326);
```

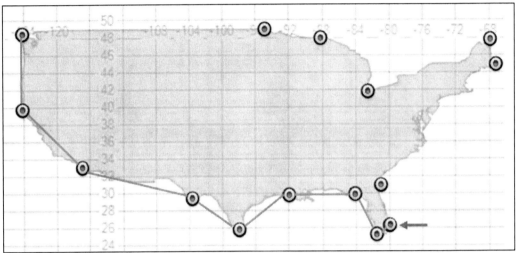

Figure 5.18 After entering 9 of 16 points, our code has 9 sets of numbers separated by 8 commas.

Continue by entering the next 6 points shown in the following code sample. Once this is accomplished, there will be a total of 15 points entered inside of the pair of parenthesis for the Polygon. We are nearly finished with the outline and only need to enter the final point to enclose this shape (Figure 5.19).

```
DECLARE @RoughUSA GEOGRAPHY;
SET @RoughUSA = GEOGRAPHY::STGeomFromText(
'Polygon ((-124 49, -124 40, -119 33, -104 29, -97 26,
-92 30, -84 30, -82 25, -80 26, -81 31, -67 45, -68 48,
-83 42, -88 48, -95 49))',4326);
```

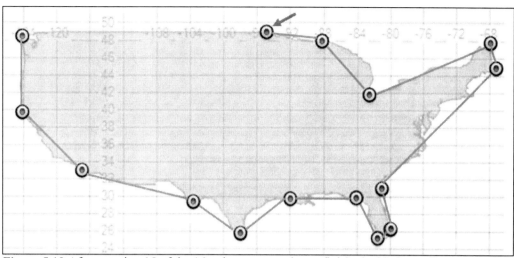

Figure 5.19 After entering 15 of the 16 points, we are almost finished with the outline.

The final step in any good game of Connect-the-Dots is to connect the last dot with the first dot.

READER NOTE: *The following code sample is the last step in this exercise and will run exactly as written to produce a graphical view for a simple polygon that resembles the borders of the continental United States.*

We can now finish writing this query demonstrating how to use the GEOGRAPHY function, STGeomFromText(). We will include a SELECT statement, so when the code is run together it will show a value returned from the function (Figure 5.20).

```
--Run this code to see results for STGeomFromText() function
DECLARE @RoughUSA GEOGRAPHY;
SET @RoughUSA = GEOGRAPHY::STGeomFromText(
'Polygon ((-124 49, -124 40, -119 33, -104 29, -97 26,
-92 30, -84 30, -82 25, -80 26, -81 31, -67 45, -68 48,
-83 42, -88 48, -95 49, -124 49))',4326);

SELECT @RoughUSA AS RoughUSA
```

RoughUSA

```
1  0xE6100000010410000000000000000080484000000000000005FC00000000000004440000000
   0000005FC000000000008040400000000000C05DC00000000000003D40000000000005AC000
   00000000003A40000000000004058C00000000000003E40000000000000057C00000000000003E
   40000000000000055C0000000000000394000000000008054C00000000000003A40000000000000
   0054C00000000000003F4000000000004054C000000000008046400000000000C050C0000000
   000000484000000000000051C0000000000000454000000000000C054C0000000000000484000
   0000000000056C000000000008048400000000000C057C000000000008048400000000000005F
   C00100000002000000000100000FFFFFFFF0000000003
```

1 rows

Figure 5.20 The GEOGRAPHY data type value returned by the STGeomFromText().

Finished! We can also get a graphic view of these data points by clicking on the Spatial Results tab, shown in Figure 5.21.

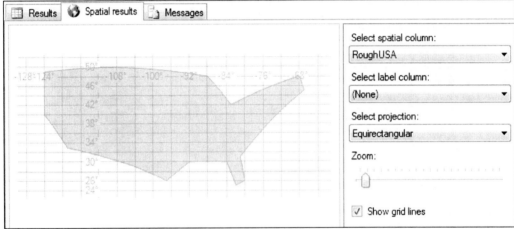

Figure 5.21 The Spatial results table shows the visual representation of the 16 points entered.

Lab 5.1: GEOGRAPHY Data Type

Lab Prep: Each lab has one or more Skill Checks. Start with Skill Check 1 and proceed until reaching the Points to Ponder section.

Before beginning this lab, verify that SQL Server 2012 is properly installed and operating. Before running the lab setup script for resetting the database (SQLQueries2012Vol3Chapter5.1Setup.sql), please make sure to close all query windows within SSMS. An open query window pointing to a database context can lock that database preventing it from updating when the script is executing. A simple way to assure all query windows are closed, is to exit out of SSMS, then open a new instance of SSMS, and lastly run the setup script.

Skill Check 1: Add a sixth location to the JProCo.dbo.Location table using values for each field shown. ***Hint:*** *Use the Point() static function to populate the GeoLoc field during the INSERT statement.*

LocationID	Street	City	State	Latitude	Longitude
6	915 Wallaby Drive	Sydney	Null	-33.876	151.315

Calculate the latitude and longitude values into the GeoLoc field. Once the sixth location is added to the table, run the following SELECT statement. When done the results should resemble Figure 5.22.

```
SELECT LocationID, City, Latitude, Longitude, GeoLoc
FROM Location
```

	LocationID	City	Latitude	Longitude	GeoLoc
1	1	Seattle	47.455	-122.231	0xE61000...B4C88E5EC0
2	2	Boston	42.372	-71.0298	0xE61000...3EE8C151C0
3	3	Chicago	41.953	-87.643	0xE61000...E926E955C0
4	4	Spokane	47.668	-117.529	0xE61000...22DB615DC0
5	5	Philadelphia	39.888	-75.251	0xE61000...6210D052C0
6	6	Sydney	-33.876	151.315	0xE61000...7A14EA6240

6 rows

Figure 5.22 Skill Check 1 adds a sixth record to Location table and calculates its GeoLoc value.

Skill Check 2: In order to perform this Skill Check, it is necessary to have first completed Skill Check 1 (Having six records in the JProCo.dbo.Location table).

Run a SELECT statement to show all fields and records from the Location table. Click on the Spatial Results tab, and then choose the Bonne option from the Select projection dropdown menu.

Each of the six locations will appear as a tiny black dot. Find all six locations and their mouse-over tags by holding the mouse pointer over each dot. Moving the 'Zoom' slider bar incrementally to the right makes it much easier to observe each of the tiny black dots representing the geographical points in the Location table.

(Figure 5.23 has been edited to make all mouse-over tags appear simultaneously, however SQL Server's normal behavior is for only one tag to appear at a time.)

Finally, click anywhere inside the grid and drag the map around. Observe that both the latitude and longitude axis labels adjust dynamically.

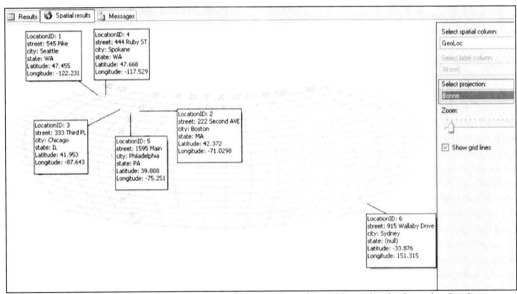

Figure 5.23 Skill Check 1 adds a sixth record to the Location table and calculates its GeoLoc value. The result from Skill Check 2 shows a graphical representation of all points added to the Location table.

READER NOTE: *It is not possible to save or export results from the Spatial Results tab. It is simply meant as a handy tool to view the spatial data.*

Skill Check 3: Cross Join the Location table with itself to find all cities that JProCo is located in and their respective distances from each other. Order the results with the greatest MilesApart values appearing at the top and the least appearing at the bottom of the list. When done, the results should resemble Figure 5.24.

	BeginCity	EndCity	MilesApart
1	Sydney	Boston	10088.9933868984
2	Boston	Sydney	10088.9933868984
3	Sydney	Philadelphia	9861.02737887156
4	Philadelphia	Sydney	9861.02737887156
5	Chicago	Sydney	9237.63404167734
30	Seattle	Spokane	220.37798803349

30 rows

Figure 5.24 A sample of the 30 records returned by Skill Check 3.

Answer Code: The T-SQL code to this lab can be found in the downloadable files in a file named Lab5.1_GeographyDataType.sql.

Points to Ponder - GEOGRAPHY Data Type

1. The **GEOGRAPHY** data type stores round-earth latitude and longitude earth coordinates that represent points, lines, and polygons.

2. Only the **GEOGRAPHY** data type can store GPS data defined by the OGC.

3. A method can calculate the distance between two **GEOGRAPHY** coordinates.

4. STDistance() is an instance method which returns the closest path between two **GEOGRAPHY** points in meters.

5. We know points on the earth can be referenced by latitude and longitude, which are two spatial numbers that intersect at one point. Representing longitude and latitude with two readable numbers, such as -122.57 47.5, is called Well-Known Text (WKT).

6. The SQL Server GEOGRAPHY data type combines both latitude and longitude values into one larger binary number that is not easy for a human to read.

7. It's very easy to get the Well-Known Text from a SQL Server spatial data type by calling the STAsText() method of the GEOGRAPHY data type.

8. WKT stands for **W**ell-**K**nown **T**ext for a position on earth. If a location is 124 degrees west longitude and 40 degrees north latitude, the WKT coordinate would be (-124 40).

9. West longitude numbers = negative, east longitude numbers = positive. North latitude numbers = positive, south latitude numbers = negative.

10. WKT, the most used source for SQL Server GEOGRAPHY types, are input by longitude first and latitude second with a space between them. Example: (-119 30) is 119 west longitude and 30 north latitude.

11. Many of the instance functions which SQL Server 2008 introduced are based on the OGC (Open Geospatial Consortium) standard. In the OGC standard, the ST prefix stands for **S**patial-**T**emporal (space-time).

12. SQL Server follows the ST naming convention for most methods (functions), despite the fact that SQL Server's spatial types don't yet include a time aspect. On the job, SQL Server developers may refer to the ST as denoting a **ST**andard method (e.g., Reduce() and MakeValid() are examples of functions which do not use an ST prefix). Other developers may explain it as standing for Some Type of GEOGRAPHY/GEOMETRY object.

GEOMETRY Data Type

In SQL Server 2008 and 2012, there are two spatial data types, **GEOMETRY** and **GEOGRAPHY**. One is better for measuring surroundings and creating maps, while the other is better for GPS or other types of global measurements.

In the last section, we looked at the **GEOGRAPHY** type, which works with GPS and other types of global measurements that represent points on the earth and tend to work best with a spherical (globe-shaped) map. However, when we need to use a *flat map* to represent land measurements, **GEOMETRY** is the planar spatial data type best suited to measure smaller areas (i.e., those which do not need to factor in the curvature of the earth).

GEOMETRY allows the ability to make custom maps. Perhaps we need to plot out the area included within a property boundry to see where certain items are in relation to everything else (e.g., landmarks, structures, boundaries, etc.), rather than places around the globe. Suppose that we have a small industrial plot measuring 28 meters in length and 21 meters in width. Of course, not all of the land is used for a single building. The plot includes a yard, warehouse, parking lot and a woodpile. We want to break this industrial plot down into one square meter increments, mapping out where everything goes and store it in our database. The **GEOMETRY** data type is a great tool for breaking down sections of a known area, adding a numbered grid and then creating a custom map (Figure 5.25).

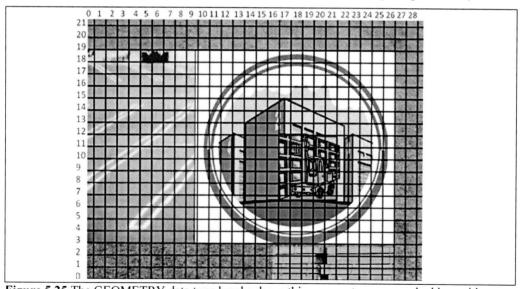

Figure 5.25 The GEOMETRY data type breaks down this new custom map and adds a grid.

Polygons

The term *polygon* refers to a many-sided object. Squares, rectangles, and triangles are all *polygons*. Making a polygon is like connecting the dots.

Our example plot for an industial yard is a perfect rectangle shape, although the yard plot could have been in the shape of a triangle, a hexagon, or a perfect square. Since we will not always know what the shape will be, we're going to call this a polygon, which allows for any enclosed shape.

When drawing out the perimeter of a polygon using the **GEOMETRY** data type, it helps us by filling in all the squares and plotting it out. Our polygon example for a yard begins at (0, 0), goes all the way to (28, 0), then (28, 21), followed by (0, 21), and finally back to (0, 0). Creating a rectangular polygon in code is as simple as connecting these 4 dots together to enclose the shape as shown in Figure 5.26.

```
--code to create a Polygon for the Yard plot
SELECT GEOMETRY::STGeomFromText(
'POLYGON ((0 0, 28 0, 28 21, 0 21, 0 0))',0)
```

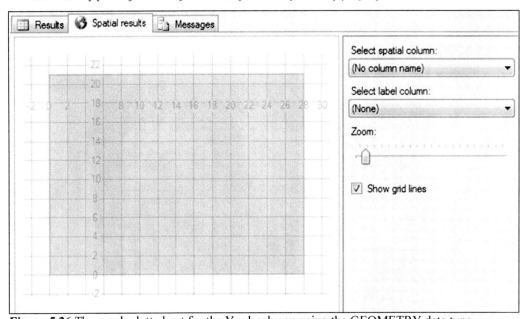

Figure 5.26 The graph plotted out for the Yard polygon using the GEOMETRY data type.

READER NOTE: *Try inserting these polygon coordinates (0 0, 9 0, 0 5, 0 0) to make a right-angle triangle.*

A requirement of working with a polygon is that the first and last coordinates must match (Begin and end in the same place to create an enclosed shape). Another requirement is that each coordinate pair is separated with a space between them and each set of coordinates that helps draw the polygon is separated by a comma.

The next example of a warehouse is also a polygon, whose dots are at (10 3, 26 3, 26 19, 10 19, 10 3). The **GEOMETRY** data type allows for coordinates to be entered in either a clockwise or counterclockwise manner (These examples are entered in counterclockwise). The final example shown is a woodpile, located at (16 0, 26 0, 26 2, 16 2, 16 0).

READER NOTE: *We will be adding a Parking Lot to the Yard in Lab5.2 at the end of this section.*

Let's put all these coordinates together (Yard, Warehouse and Woodpile), to look at the graph plotted out by the GEOMETRY data type in Figure 5.27.

```
SELECT GEOMETRY::STGeomFromText(
'POLYGON ((0 0, 28 0, 28 21, 0 21, 0 0),
(10 3, 26 3, 26 19, 10 19, 10 3),
(16 0, 26 0, 26 2, 16 2, 16 0))',0)
```

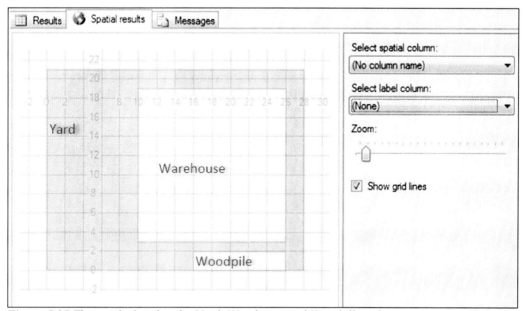

Figure 5.27 The graph showing the Yard, Warehouse and Woodpile polygons.

Looking at the graph, we can easily answer a few questions.

1) Is the Warehouse inside the coordinates of the Yard? result = 1 (yes)

2) Is the Woodpile inside the coordinates of the Yard? result = 1 (yes)
3) Is the Woodpile inside the coordinates of the Warehouse? result = 0 (no)

Creating GEOMETRY as a Field in a Table

Let's take a look at our old familiar HumanResources.RoomChart table (from the JProCo database) and the records it contains. It looks like we have four rooms that are populated. The last record (R_ID 5), is filled with NULLs in every field and is waiting for more data to be entered into it (Figure 5.28).

```
SELECT *
FROM HumanResources.RoomChart
```

	R_ID	R_Code	RoomName	RoomDescription	RoomNotes
1	1	RLT	Renault-Langsford-Tribute	NULL	NULL
2	2	QTX	Quinault-Experience	NULL	NULL
3	3	TQW	TranquilWest	NULL	NULL
4	4	XW	XavierWest	NULL	NULL
5	5	NULL	NULL	NULL	NULL

5 rows

Figure 5.28 The record for R_ID 5 currently has all NULL values and needs more data.

At this time the HumanResources.RoomChart table does not hold any mapping or geography type information. We want to make a map to show where these rooms are located, so we need to add a sixth field, which will be a **GEOMETRY** type.

Run the following code and notice that every record now has the ability to store a RoomLocation with the GEOMETRY data type.

```
ALTER TABLE HumanResources.RoomChart
ADD RoomLocation GEOMETRY NULL
GO

SELECT *
FROM HumanResources.RoomChart
```

	R_ID	R_Code	RoomName	RoomDescription	RoomNotes	RoomLocation
1	1	RLT	Renault-Langsford…	NULL	NULL	NULL
2	2	QTX	Quinault-Experien…	NULL	NULL	NULL
3	3	TQW	TranquilWest	NULL	NULL	NULL
4	4	XW	XavierWest	NULL	NULL	NULL
5	5	NULL	NULL	NULL	NULL	NULL

5 rows

Figure 5.29 Every record now has the ability to store a RoomLocation (Data type GEOMETRY).

The record for R_ID 5 is pretty plain - no room name, no code name, etc. So, let's catch this record up with the other records in the table.

```
UPDATE HumanResources.RoomChart
SET R_Code = 'YRD',
    RoomName = 'Industrial Yard',
    RoomDescription = 'Holds lumber and stocking'
WHERE R_ID = 5
GO

SELECT * FROM HumanResources.RoomChart
```

	R_ID	R_Code	RoomName	RoomDescription	RoomNotes	RoomLocation
1	1	RLT	Renault-Langsford...	NULL	NULL	NULL
2	2	QTX	Quinault-Experien...	NULL	NULL	NULL
3	3	TQW	TranquilWest	NULL	NULL	NULL
4	4	XW	XavierWest	NULL	NULL	NULL
5	5	YRD	Industrial Yard	Holds lumber ...	NULL	NULL

5 rows

Figure 5.30 R_ID 5 has been updated with basic information.

Populating a GEOMETRY Data Type

The STPolyFromText() function is a *GEOMETRY instance method* which creates a **GEOMETRY** object. We will use this function to create **GEOMETRY** objects for use in the HumanResources.RoomChart table by populating some of the RoomLocation fields with usable data.

The first record to be updated is R_ID 5 (The Yard). Inside the parentheses of the STPolyFromText function, we need to specify the polygon coordinates for the first parameter. For the second parameter, we will insert a 0, which is the SRID (**S**patial **R**eference **ID**entifier) for the **GEOMETRY** data type. As we saw when working with the **GEOGRAPHY data** type, the planar **GEOMETRY** data can have many SRIDs to choose from.

We must be specific about choosing the SRID (which in this case is 0), since we might have different spatial areas. Think of the SRID as a map number. Imagine a 3-story building where we may want to compare Map-0 (the main floor) versus Map-1 or Map-2 (The upper floors). Whenever we compare two instances of spatial data, they both must have the same SRID.

```
UPDATE HumanResources.RoomChart
SET RoomLocation = GEOMETRY::STPolyFromText(
'POLYGON ((0 0, 28 0, 28 21, 0 21, 0 0))',0)
WHERE R_ID = 5
GO
```

By looking at the results, we can see that the RoomLocation field has been populated with some sort of **GEOMETRY** type. The first digit (before the X) is the SRID we supplied to the function as the second parameter.

```
SELECT RoomName, RoomLocation
FROM HumanResources.RoomChart
WHERE R_ID = 5
```

	RoomName	RoomLocation
1	Industrial Yard	0x000000…0000000003

1 rows

Figure 5.31 R_ID 5 contains some sort of GEOMETRY type.

If we wanted to buy fencing to put around the Yard, we need to know the total length of the perimeter before purchasing the fencing material. We can get this calculation by using the STLength() function, which determines the total distance in meters for the perimeter of the Yard, aliased as FenceMeters (Figure 5.32).

```
SELECT RoomName, RoomLocation,
RoomLocation.STLength() AS FenceMeters
FROM HumanResources.RoomChart
WHERE R_ID = 5
```

	RoomName	RoomLocation	FenceMeters
1	Industrial Yard	0x000000…0000000003	98

1 rows

Figure 5.32 We need to figure out how big our perimeter is, so we can buy fencing.

What is the area of this industrial yard plot? We can use the STArea() function to calculate the area and alias it as SqMetersArea. We can see from Figure 5.33 that the total area is 588 square meters (28 meters * 21 meters).

```
SELECT RoomName, RoomLocation,
RoomLocation.STLength() AS FenceMeters,
RoomLocation.STArea() AS SqMetersArea
FROM HumanResources.RoomChart
WHERE R_ID = 5
```

	RoomName	RoomLocation	FenceMeters	SqMetersArea
1	Industrial Yard	0x000000...0000000003	98	588

1 rows

Figure 5.33 The area of the industrial yard plot is 588 square meters (28 length * 21 width).

Be aware that many instance method functions, such as STPolyFromText(), are case-sensitive and must be typed in correctly. This is noteworthy, since SQL Server is generally case *insensitive* and does not behave differently whether you input code as upper or lower case. For example, the 'P' in Poly must be capitalized. If by mistake, the function STPolyFromText() is typed with a lower case 'p', then SQL Server will generate the error shown in Figure 5.34.

```
UPDATE HumanResources.RoomChart
SET RoomLocation = GEOMETRY::STPolyFromText(
'POLYGON ((0 0, 28 0, 28 21, 0 21, 0 0))',0)
WHERE R_ID = 5
GO
```

```
Messages
Msg 6506, Level 16, State 10, Line 3
Could not find method 'STpolyFromText' for type
'Microsoft.SqlServer.Types.SqlGeometry' in assembly Microsoft.SqlServer.Types'
```

0 rows

Figure 5.34 This error shows when you use the wrong case with a case-sensitive instance method.

GEOMETRY Functions

We have already learned about the STPolyFromText() function. There are many more, and an entire book could be dedicated to Spatial Data theory and functions. We are going to limit our focus to STLength(), STArea(), and STContains().

The STLength() and STArea() are two of the built-in functions for the **GEOMETRY** data type. Now we're going to add a record for the Warehouse, which sits inside the industrial yard, as the sixth record of the table.

Remember to use an SRID of 0, which indicates the Warehouse is on the same space/plane as the Industrial Yard.

```
INSERT INTO HumanResources.RoomChart VALUES
(6,'WRS','Warehouse','Holds supplies', NULL,
GEOMETRY::STPolyFromText(
'Polygon ((10 3, 26 3, 26 19, 10 19, 10 3))',0))
```

Now we have two records with populated GEOMETRY types in our RoomChart table. Let's repeat the process to add another record for the Lumber Area (the Woodpile) with an R_ID of 7. Continue to use an SRID of 0 as the Lumber Area is included in the same space/plane as the Industrial Yard and Warehouse.

```
INSERT INTO HumanResources.RoomChart VALUES
(7,'WOD','Lumber Area', NULL, NULL,
GEOMETRY::STPolyFromText(
'Polygon ((16 0, 26 0, 26 2, 16 2, 16 0))',0))
```

We now have three different areas occupying a single space/plane:

    1) Industrial Yard   *2) Warehouse*   *3) Lumber Area*

Let's capture all three areas together and then run some built-in comparisons. We can see the values in the table, and although they are not really readable to the human eye, at least we can see the values are there.

```
DECLARE @Yard GEOMETRY
DECLARE @Warehouse GEOMETRY
DECLARE @Lumber GEOMETRY

SELECT @Yard = RoomLocation
FROM HumanResources.RoomChart
WHERE R_ID = 5

SELECT @Warehouse = RoomLocation
FROM HumanResources.RoomChart
WHERE R_ID = 6

SELECT @Lumber = RoomLocation
FROM HumanResources.RoomChart
WHERE R_ID = 7

SELECT @Yard AS Yard, @Warehouse AS Warehouse,
@Lumber AS Lumber
```

	Yard	Warehouse	Lumber
1	0x000000…0000000003	0x000000…0000000003	0x000000…0000000003

1 rows

Figure 5.35 We would like to run some built-in comparisons, but these values aren't user-friendly.

Let's do a more meaningful comparison and ask ourselves the question, *"Does the Yard contain a Warehouse, or a Lumber Area?"* Is there a function for the GEOMETRY data type that can easily answer this question? Yes! The

STContains() function will return a value of either a 1 if the answer is yes, or a 0 if the answer is no.

```
DECLARE @Yard GEOMETRY
DECLARE @Warehouse GEOMETRY
DECLARE @Lumber GEOMETRY

SELECT @Yard = RoomLocation
FROM HumanResources.RoomChart
WHERE R_ID = 5

SELECT @Warehouse = RoomLocation
FROM HumanResources.RoomChart
WHERE R_ID = 6

SELECT @Lumber = RoomLocation
FROM HumanResources.RoomChart
WHERE R_ID = 7

SELECT @Yard.STContains(@Warehouse) AS IsWarehouseInYard,
@Yard.STContains(@Lumber) AS IsLumberInYard
```

	IsWarehouseInYard	IsLumberInYard
1	1	1
		1 rows

Figure 5.36 Yes, the yard contains a Warehouse and a Lumber Area.

Finally, let's ask a question where we are sure the answer is *NO* to make sure the STContains() function is working as expected (Figure 5.37). *"Does the Warehouse contain a Lumber Area?"*

```
DECLARE @Yard GEOMETRY
DECLARE @Warehouse GEOMETRY
DECLARE @Lumber GEOMETRY

SELECT @Yard = RoomLocation
FROM HumanResources.RoomChart
WHERE R_ID = 5

SELECT @Warehouse = RoomLocation
FROM HumanResources.RoomChart
WHERE R_ID = 6

SELECT @Lumber = RoomLocation
FROM HumanResources.RoomChart
WHERE R_ID = 7
```

```
SELECT @Warehouse.STContains(@Lumber) AS IsLumberInWarehouse
```

IsLumberInWarehouse
1 0

1 rows

Figure 5.37 The answer is no, to the question "Does the Warehouse contain a Lumber Area?"

Now, when we query the entire HumanResources.RoomChart table, we can see a graphical representation of the data in the RoomLocation field by clicking on the Spatial Results tab (Figure 5.38). While it is not possible to save or export any results shown in the Spatial Results tab, it is a really handy tool for visualizing our spatial data.

Any of the five fields from the HumanResources.RoomChart table can serve as the label (e.g., R_ID, R_Code, RoomName and RoomDescription), or simply keep the default value of (None) to suppress the displaying of any label(s).

```
SELECT *
FROM HumanResources.RoomChart
```

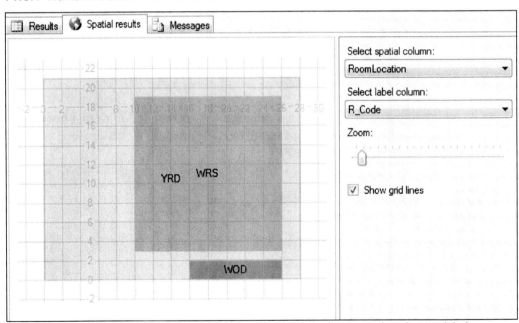

Figure 5.38 The spatial results tab for the RoomChart table using R_Code values as labels.

Lab 5.2: GEOMETRY Data Type

Lab Prep: Each lab has one or more Skill Checks. Start with Skill Check 1 and proceed until reaching the Points to Ponder section.

Before beginning this lab, verify that SQL Server 2012 is properly installed and operating. Before running the lab setup script for resetting the database (SQLQueries2012Vol3Chapter5.2Setup.sql), please make sure to close all query windows within SSMS. An open query window pointing to a database context can lock that database preventing it from updating when the script is executing. A simple way to assure all query windows are closed, is to exit out of SSMS, then open a new instance of SSMS, and lastly run the setup script.

Skill Check 1: Add an eighth record to the HumanResources.RoomChart table to represent the Parking Lot of the Yard Area. Use the following information to populate the R_ID, R_Code, RoomName, RoomDescription and RoomNotes fields.

R_ID	R_Code	RoomName	RoomDescription	RoomNotes
8	PRK	Yard Parking Lot	NULL	NULL

Populate the RoomLocation field with the correct GEOMETRY data type coordinates based on the spatial results of Figure 5.39.

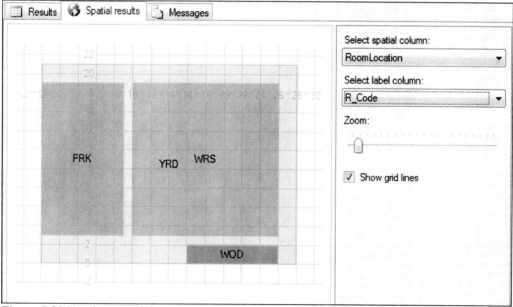

Figure 5.39 Use these spatial results to set the coordinates of the Parking Lot.

When done, the results should resemble those shown in Figure 5.40.

```
SELECT *
FROM HumanResources.RoomChart
```

	R_ID	R_Code	RoomName	RoomDescription	RoomNotes	RoomLocation
5	5	YRD	Yard	Industrial Yard Space	NULL	0x00…0003
6	6	WRS	Warehouse	Company Main Warehouse	NULL	0x00…0003
7	7	WOD	Lumber Area	Lumber Area	NULL	0x00…0003
8	8	PRK	Yard Parking	NULL	NULL	0x00…0003

8 rows

Figure 5.40 The results produced by Skill Check 1.

Skill Check 2: Write a query to determine if either the Yard or the Warehouse contains a Parking Lot space in the HumanResources.RoomChart table. When finished the results should resemble Figure 5.41.

	IsParkLotInYard	IsParkLotInWarehouse
1	1	0

1 rows

Figure 5.41 Result produced by Skill Check 2.

Answer Code: The T-SQL code to this lab can be found in the downloadable files in a file named Lab5.2_GeometryDataType.sql.

Points to Ponder - GEOMETRY Data Type

1. SQL Server 2008 and 2012 have two specific spatial data types **GEOMETRY** and **GEOGRAPHY**.

2. The **GEOMETRY** data type stores flat XY grid coordinates for points, lines, and polygons.

3. The **GEOGRAPHY** data type stores round-earth latitude and longitude earth coordinates that represent points, lines, and polygons.

4. The default SRID (spatial reference identifier) for the **GEOMETRY** type is 0.

5. Some instance method functions work with both **GEOMETRY** and **GEOGRAPHY** data types. For example, the instance method STDistance can calculate the distance between two coordinates, whether they are for **GEOMETRY** or **GEOGRAPHY** data types. However, some instance method functions only work with the GEOMETRY data type (e.g., STTouches(), STOverlaps(), STPointOnSurface(), etc.).

6. Be aware that some instance method functions are case-sensitive (e.g., STPolyFromText). This is noteworthy, since SQL Server is generally *case insensitive* and does not behave differently whether code is input as upper or lower case. Making a mistake of mistyping STPolyFromText in a query will cause SQL Server to generate an error: *Could not find method 'STPolyFromText' for type 'Microsoft.SqlServer.Types.SqlGeometry' in assembly 'Microsoft.SqlServer.Types'.*

7. It is possible to determine whether two spatial objects have overlapping territory by using the STOverlaps() instance method function.

8. Areas of any enclosed shape are called polygons.

9. Many of the instance functions which SQL Server uses are based on functions defined by the OGC (Open Geospatial Consortium) standard. In the OGC standard, the ST prefix stands for **S**patial-**T**emporal (space-time).

10. SQL Server follows the ST naming convention for most functions, despite the fact that SQL Server's spatial types don't yet include a time aspect. On the job, SQL Server developers may encounter those who refer to the ST portion as denoting a **ST**andard method (e.g., Reduce() and MakeValid() are examples of functions which do not use an ST prefix). Other developers may explain it as standing for **S**ome **T**ype of GEOGRAPHY/GEOMETRY object.

Chapter Glossary

GEOGRAPHY: A data type that can store info for areas and points on the earth.

GEOMETRY: The planar spatial data type and the one to measure smaller areas (i.e., do not need to factor in the curvature of the earth).

GEOMETRY instance method: A type of function that creates GEOMETRY objects.

Geospatial data: Latitude and Longitude values used by GEOGRAPHY functions.

OGC: An acronym that stands for Open Geospatial Consortium.

Point-static function: A function used in GEOGRAPHY functions.

Polygon: A many-sided enclosed object.

Spatial data type: GEOMETRY & GEOGRAPHY types are spatial data types.

Spatial reference identifier: Acronym is SRID. This identifies which spatial reference system the coordinates belong to.

Spatial-temporal: The ST prefix in functions stands for **S**patial-**T**emporal.

SRID: A geography value, also known as a **S**patial **R**eference **ID**entifier.

Standard method: Some developers refer to the ST as denoting a **ST**andard method while other developers say it stands for **S**ome **T**ype of GEOMETRY object.

STArea(): One of the two built-in functions of the **GEOMETRY** data type**.**

STContains(): A SQL Server function that determines if the calling instance spatially contains all of the instance passed to it as a parameter. This function works with either the GEOGRAPHY or GEOMETRY data types.

STDistance(): An instance method which returns the closest path between two GEOGRAPHY points in meters.

STGeomFromText(): A SQL function that converts text to spatial points.

STLength(): One of the two built-in functions of the GEOMETRY data type.

STPolyFromText(): An instance method which creates a GEOMETRY object.

WKT: An acronym for the phrase **W**ell-**K**nown **T**ext, which represents the point where a latitude and longitude coordinate meet with two readable numbers, such as 47.5° latitude and -122.57° longitude.

Review Quiz - Chapter Five

1.) You know that SQL Server 2008 introduced two special data types. Which data type has a built in method for determining the distance between two points on the earth in meters?

O a. GEOMETRY

O b. GEOGRAPHY

2.) You know that SQL Server 2008 introduced two special data types. One uses round-earth calculation and the other uses planar grid calculation. Which data type uses round-earth data for determining the distance between two points on the earth in meters?

O a. GEOMETRY

O b. GEOGRAPHY

3.) Which data type is ideal for you to create your own custom maps (e.g., maps of warehouse storage or a sports playing field)?

O a. GEOMETRY

O b. GEOGRAPHY

4.) The STDistance function of the GEOGRAPHY data type calculates the distance between two points in …

O a. Feet

O b. Meters

O c. Kilometers

O d. Miles

O e. Units

5.) The GEOMETRY data type calculates the distance between two points in…

O a. Feet

O b. Meters

O c. Kilometers

O d. Miles

O e. Units

6.)   Your growing company is dividing areas of the country into sales territories. Your database already has every customer's GPS location stored. You plan to set up sales boundaries and set up a process for determining the distance between your customers and your nearest store. What is the best data type for this operation?

O a. GEOMETRY

O b. GEOGRAPHY

O c. XML

7.)   You are creating a table that stores the spatial information of customers and all your store locations. You need to calculate the distance between a customer and the store nearest to them in meters. Which data type should you use?

O a. GEOMETRY

O b. GEOGRAPHY

Answer Key

1.)   The GEOMETRY data type stores flat grid coordinates for points, lines and polygons, but does not have a built in method for determining distance, so (a) is incorrect. The GEOGRAPHY data type has a built in method STDistance()that measures distance. Therefore (b) is the correct answer.

2.)   GEOMETRY is the planar special data type used to measure smaller areas where the curvature of the earth does not need to be factored in, so (a) is incorrect. The GEOGRAPHY data type uses round-earth calculation, so (b) is the correct answer.

3.)   The GEOGRAPHY data type can use GPS data to measure distance but would not allow custom maps to be created, so (b) is incorrect. The GEOMETRY data type will allow for custom maps to be created, so (a) is the correct answer.

4.)   The STDistance() function calculates distance in meters, so (a), (c), and (d) would be incorrect. Additional calculations would need to be done to convert to feet, kilometers, and miles. The GEOMETRY data type calculates distance in units, so (e) is incorrect. Therefore, (b) Meters is the correct answer.

5.)   When using the GEOMETRY data type the distance between points is calculated in units. Therefore (a), (b), (c), (d) are incorrect and (e) is the correct answer.

6.) The GEOMETRY data type is used to make custom maps and does not use GPS data, so (a) is incorrect. XML are text based documents that contains data and metadata but does not use GPS data, so (b) is incorrect. Since the GEOGRAPHY data type is the only type listed that uses GPS data, (b) is the correct answer.

7.) The GEOGRAPHY data type compensates for 'round earth' ellipsoidal calculations and returns the distance in meters, so (b) is the correct answer.

Bug Catcher Game

To play the Bug Catcher game, run the SQLQueries2012Vol3BugCatcher05.pps file from the BugCatcher folder of the companion files. These files can be obtained from the www.Joes2Pros.com website.

[THIS PAGE INTENTIONALLY LEFT BLANK.]

Chapter 6. Spatial Aggregates

In business we often hear the phrase, "We had a good quarter." Immediately, we know this means a three month span where sales and profits have been aggregated together for the company. Take a company like Costco that might have $65 billion in total sales during the 4th quarter (October, November and December). Of course, this total comes not from a single sale of a 65 billon dollar yacht, rather from millions of sales for common items like snacks, drinks, clothes, and light bulbs.

In Volume 2 we learned how to use GROUP BY and SUM to calculate totals and combine similar data. In the case of Costco we group by quarter and then sum on the sales. Although aggregates are commonly used with numbers, they can also be used with land coordinates to assemble them together, much like a jigsaw puzzle.

READER NOTE: *Please run the SQLQueries2012Vol3Chapter6.0Setup.sql script in order to follow along with the examples in the first section of Chapter 6. All scripts mentioned in this chapter may be found at* www.Joes2Pros.com.

Spatial Unions and Collections

My elementary school was right across the street from my home. The playground in back of the school was very large and had 3 full sized football (soccer) fields. Not all of this land belonged to the school. Across from the play fields was the Boys and Girls Club, which is a charity for after school kids' projects for parents that need to work late. Since they are typically not open during school hours, the land they owned was able to be enjoyed during the day by my school. In this case, the land of the school and the club are aggregated to make one giant play and exercise area.

OGC (Open Geospatial Consortium) Functions Recap

In this example of the school and club, we aggregated the land for two owners. This ability became available with SQL Server 2008, although there was no way to aggregate the land for three owners into a single query. Let's recap how SQL Server aggregated spatial results between two shapes with the following examples.

```
SELECT * FROM HumanResources.RoomChart
```

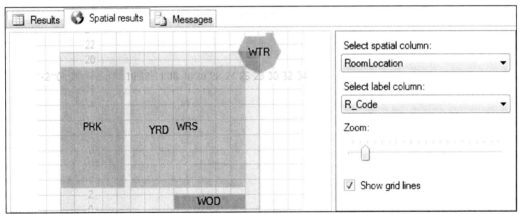

Figure 6.1 Graphic representation of each area located in all or part of the Yard.

By narrowing our focus to look at only the Water Tower and the Yard shapes, we can easily see that the Water Tower is only part way on the property of the Yard owner (Figure 6.2).

```
SELECT *
FROM HumanResources.RoomChart
WHERE R_ID IN (5,9)
```

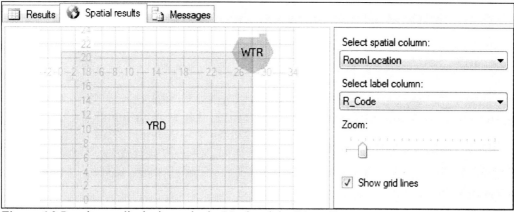

Figure 6.2 Results are displaying only the Yard and the Water Tower.

What happens when an object occupies space in a portion of another object? When we ran the previous code, the results show how the Water Tower is partially in the Yard (Figure 6.2). How will the STContains() function see if the Water Tower is contained within the Yard? Will the answer to this question be YES, or NO? How about the Parking Lot, is it contained in the Yard? The results for the following code sample shown are in Figure 6.3.

```
DECLARE @Yard GEOMETRY
DECLARE @Wtr GEOMETRY
DECLARE @Prk GEOMETRY

SELECT @Yard = RoomLocation
FROM HumanResources.RoomChart
WHERE R_ID = 5

SELECT @Wtr = RoomLocation
FROM HumanResources.RoomChart
WHERE R_ID = 9

SELECT @Prk = RoomLocation
FROM HumanResources.RoomChart
WHERE R_ID = 8

SELECT @Yard.STContains(@Wtr) AS IsTowerInYard,
@Yard.STContains(@Prk) AS IsParkInYard
```

IsTowerInYard	IsParkInYard
1 0	1
	1 rows

Figure 6.3 Does the Yard contain the Water Tower (No), or the Parking Lot (Yes)?

Aggregate Unions and Collections

What if there was a requirement to combine all three of the biggest Scandinavian countries into one trading zone? A graphical representation of this union can be accomplished by aggregating the shapes of Finland and Sweden together, producing a larger shape, then aggregating this larger shape with Norway, and return the new single Scandinavian shape. Likewise, combining all the countries of Northern Africa into a single shape by adding one country at a time can get really tedious and prone to looping errors. Also, overall performance would certainly suffer while attempting to repeatedly store all those shapes in memory at one time.

We can see how to bring two shapes together by using the STUnion() function with the GEOMETRY data stored in the Yard and Water Tower fields. Building the query is identical to how we previously determined if the Park or the Water Tower were contained in the Yard with the STContains() function. All we need to do is replace the STContains() function with the STUnion() function. The graphical view of this code sample is shown in Figure 6.4.

```
DECLARE @Yard GEOMETRY
DECLARE @Wtr GEOMETRY

SELECT @Yard = RoomLocation
FROM HumanResources.RoomChart
WHERE R_ID = 5

SELECT @Wtr = RoomLocation
FROM HumanResources.RoomChart
WHERE R_ID = 9

SELECT GEOMETRY = @Yard.STUnion(@Wtr)
```

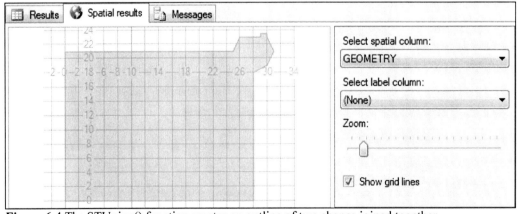

Figure 6.4 The STUnion() function creates an outline of two shapes joined together.

There are other functions available for aggregating shapes together that eliminate the need for declaring and selecting variables.

Let's look at an example of how to use the UnionAggregate() method and look at what the results are by running the following code (Figure 6.5).

```
SELECT GEOMETRY::UnionAggregate(RoomLocation)
FROM HumanResources.RoomChart
WHERE R_ID IN (5,9)
```

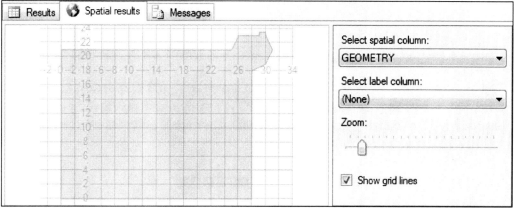

Figure 6.5 The UnionAggregate() method consumes the GEOMETRY field directly to create a shape.

What if we wanted to be able to see the original outline of the smaller shapes as well as the outline of the new larger shape all at the same time? How can we get SQL Server to produce these results? Fortunately there is a CollectionAggregate() method that will do this for us and is simple to use. By simply substituting the name of the method from the previous query, with this new method name, the graphical results will now show the interior and exterior lines of the combined shape of the Yard and Water Tower (Figure 6.6).

```
SELECT GEOMETRY::CollectionAggregate(RoomLocation)
FROM HumanResources.RoomChart
WHERE R_ID IN (5,9)
```

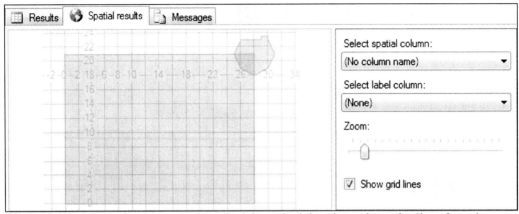

Figure 6.6 The CollectionAggregate() method draws both interior and exterior lines for a shape.

The biggest benefit offered by the **UnionAggregate()** and **CollectionAggregate()** functions, is that they consume a GEOMETRY data type field directly as a parameter. This feature greatly simplifies the amount of code we need to write and makes it much easier to read as well.

Grouping Unions and Collections

In the last example we had to be really smart in our WHERE clause (like knowing that R_ID 5 and R_ID 9 was shape data) and the result was we got one shape. If we wanted one combined shape that represented our Yard and Water Tower for every land owner in our zone we would have to write a new WHERE clause for each owner and then combine them. Fortunately, this can be accomplished in one query without using a WHERE clause to separate the owners. However, we must first understand how an individual piece contributes to the aggregate shape and refresh our understanding of how the GROUP BY clause works with spatial data.

Let's look at examples of some business case uses when working with shapes. We are going to use a special table named SkiAreas that is normally not in the dbBasics database. The data contained in this table will help solidify how we can easily combine shapes together to support different business requirements.

First, we will need to find out what kind of data resides in this table. The next code sample will show all the fields and records of the SkiAreas table.

```
USE dbBasics
GO

SELECT *
FROM SkiAreas
```

	ShapeID	ShapeCode	ShapeName	ShapeParentCode	ShapeOgraphy	ShapeMetry
1	1	ID	Idaho State	US	0xE6100…003	0xE610…003
2	2	MT	Montana State	US	0xE6100…003	0xE610…003
3	3	Kt	Kootenai County	ID	0xE6100…003	0xE610…003
4	4	Sh	Shoshone County	ID	0xE6100…003	0xE610…003
5	5	Cl	Clearwater County	ID	0xE6100…003	0xE610…003
6	6	Ln	Lincoln County	MT	0xE6100…003	0xE610…003
7	7	Sd	Sanders County	MT	0xE6100…003	0xE610…003
8	8	M1	Runt Mountain	**	0xE6100…003	0xE610…003

8 rows

Figure 6.7 All the records in the SkiAreas table of the dbBasics database.

It looks like there are a couple of states (Idaho and Montana), a few counties (Kootenai, Shoshone, Lincoln, etc…) and a place called Runt Mountain.

We can get a little more specific, by looking for just the ShapeName and the ShapeMetry fields. Click on the spatial results tab and in the 'Select label column:' drop-down menu choose the ShapeName field to see the names for the shapes returned by the query.

Try zooming in on the shapes inside the grid, by moving the slider located in the right-hand panel, incrementally side-to-side for a close-up view of the smaller shapes and the labels that go with them. Remember, that it is also possible to pan across the grid shapes by doing a left-click with the mouse and then drag the grid in the spatial results tab. An example of a zoomed in view is shown in Figure 6.8.

```
SELECT ShapeName, ShapeMetry
FROM SkiAreas
```

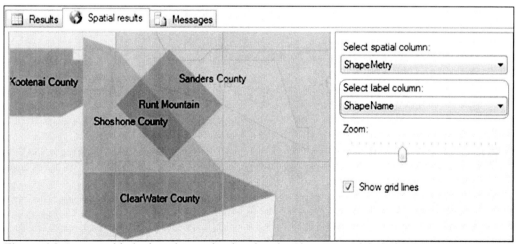

Figure 6.8 A zoomed in look at the results showing the ShapeName labels for the counties.

With five counties in two different states, a travel brochure would normally show three of these counties in Idaho and two counties in Montana. The owners of the ski resorts in these counties are thinking about doing a marketing campaign together and creating a regional economic zone for all of their ski areas. They have asked us to create a graphical view of what this zone would look like.

```
SELECT ShapeName, ShapeMetry FROM SkiAreas
WHERE ShapeName LIKE '%County'
```

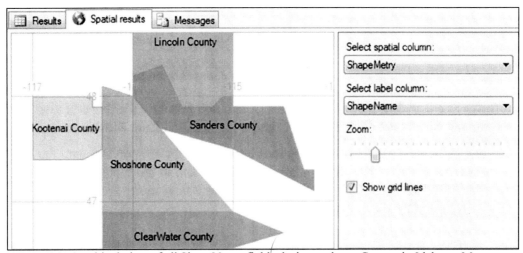

Figure 6.9 Graphical view of all ShapeName fields designated as a County in Idaho or Montana.

Now that we have a working query that displays each county in the SkiAreas table, we can easily convert it to a query using the UnionAggregate() function. This will be used to combine each county into a single shape for this marketing region. That shape of the region will fulfill the request from the group representing the owners of each ski area.

```
SELECT GEOMETRY::UnionAggregate(ShapeMetry)
FROM SkiAreas
WHERE ShapeName LIKE '%County'
```

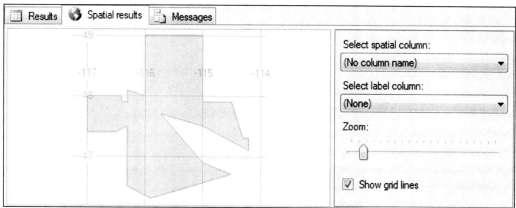

Figure 6.10 Combining all the counties into a single shape with the UnionAggregate() method.

In case the marketing department, or some of the ski area owners still want to visualize how each county fits into this overall shape, let's also perform a query that uses the CollectionAggregate() method, which will preserve the original boundaries of each county inside the larger shape boundary (Figure 6.11).

```
SELECT GEOMETRY::CollectionAggregate(ShapeMetry)
FROM SkiAreas
WHERE ShapeName LIKE '%County'
```

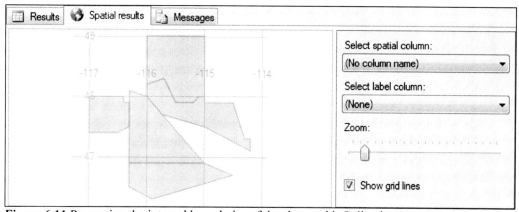

Figure 6.11 Preserving the internal boundaries of the shape with CollectionAggregate() method.

Before we begin our next aggregation example, we need to take a closer look at some of the individual shapes in the SkiAreas table. Being able to look at a visual representation of the individual counties meets the requirements set by the ski area owners. However, some of the key members of the marketing team are unfamiliar with the area and are unable to tell by just looking at the shapes for each county or even the county name, which one is in Idaho, and which one belongs to Montana.

Let's write a query that will show the individual counties, while allowing us to label them with the ShapeParentCode field. This field contains information that will distinguish each county by the State that it is located in. The results for this query are shown in Figure 6.12. Be sure to use the '**Select label column**' drop-down list to select the ShapeParentCode column to label the shapes properly.

```
SELECT ShapeName, ShapeMetry, ShapeParentCode
FROM SkiAreas
WHERE ShapeName LIKE '%County'
```

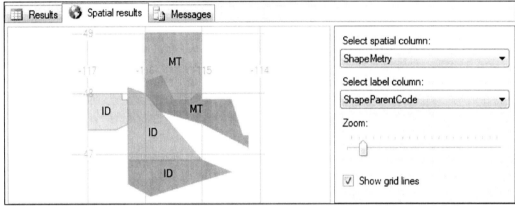

Figure 6.12 Labeling each county by ShapeParentCode field showing which State it belongs to.

What if someone from the marketing team wants to get a 'Ten Thousand foot view' of this newly created economic region that shows the Idaho and Montana counties as a group located inside a larger shape of these two States combined together?

In order to accomplish a request like this, we will need to use a GROUP BY clause in addition to the UnionAggregate() method. Since the ShapeParentCode field contains the least selective metadata we will use it for both the grouping field and the labeling field.

Recall that for every non-aggregated field listed in the SELECT statement, we must list it in the GROUP BY clause in order to see it in our result set, and have the query run without errors. This rule applies the same way when working with spatial data. Let's run the following code and look at the results in Figure 6.13.

```
SELECT ShapeParentCode,
GEOMETRY::UnionAggregate(ShapeMetry)
FROM SkiAreas
GROUP BY ShapeParentCode
```

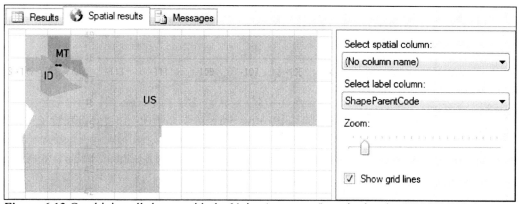

Figure 6.13 Combining all shapes with the UnionAggregate() method and a GROUP BY clause.

We can also use a GROUP BY clause with the CollectionAggregate() method to combine all the shapes in the SkiAreas table together into one large shape, while maintaining all the internal boundaries within each group of shapes.

This is as easy as replacing the UnionAggregate() method name with the CollectionAggregate() method name. The rest of the previous query remains the same, only the results will now distinguish the State boundary between Idaho and Montana to help visualize where they are located within the larger shape with the 'US' label (Figure 6.14).

```
SELECT ShapeParentCode,
GEOMETRY::CollectionAggregate(ShapeMetry)
FROM SkiAreas
GROUP BY ShapeParentCode
```

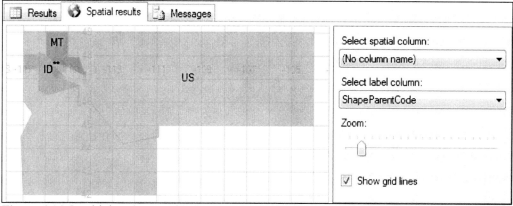

Figure 6.14 Combining shapes with the CollectionAggregate() method and a GROUP BY clause.

Lab 6.1: Spatial Unions and Collections

Lab Prep: Each lab has one or more Skill Checks. Start with Skill Check 1 and proceed until reaching the Points to Ponder section.

Before beginning this lab, verify that SQL Server 2012 is properly installed and operating. Before running the two lab setup scripts for resetting the database (SQLQueries2012Vol3Chapter6.1Setup.sql first and close all query windows and then run SQLQueries2012Vol3Chapter6SpecialSetup.sql), please make sure to close all query windows within SSMS. An open query window pointing to a database context can lock that database preventing it from updating when the script is executing. A simple way to assure all query windows are closed, is to exit out of SSMS, then open a new instance of SSMS, and lastly run the setup script.

Skill Check 1: In the dbBasics database context, aggregate the two shapes shown in Figure 6.15 (created by the following code) into a single shape with the internal borders preserved as seen in Figure 6.16.

```
SELECT *
FROM SkiAreas
WHERE ShapeCode IN ('Sh','M1')
```

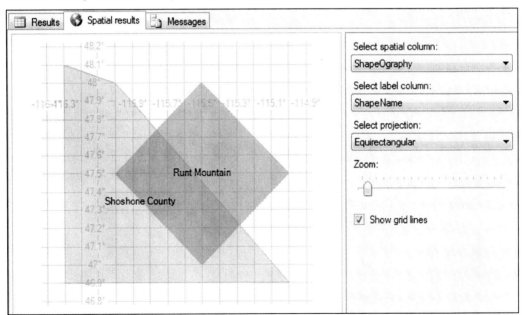

Figure 6.15 Aggregate these two shapes into a single shape while keeping all internal lines.

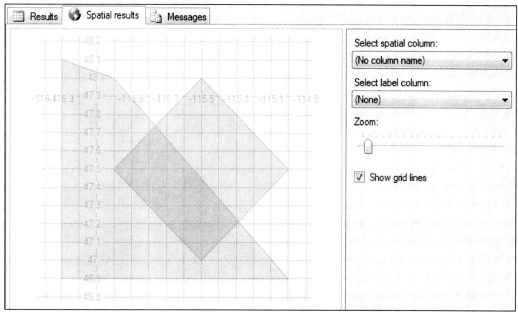

Figure 6.16 The graphical results shown upon the completion of Skill Check 1.

Skill Check 2: Modify the query from Skill Check 1 to display a single polygon without any internal borders. When done, the results will resemble Figure 6.17.

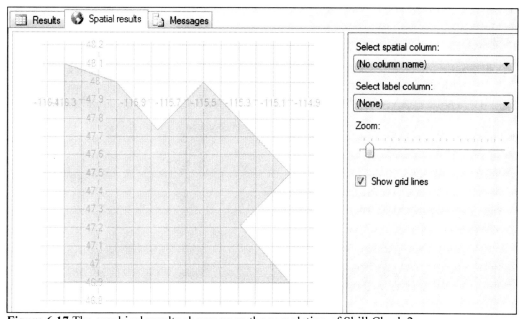

Figure 6.17 The graphical results shown upon the completion of Skill Check 2.

Skill Check 3: In the dbBasics database context, combine all the shapes of the Idaho Counties (Kootenai, Shoshone and Clearwater) in the dbo.SkiAreas table, into a single polygon shape without any internal borders. Use the ShapeMetry field as the parameter for this method. When done, the results will resemble those shown in Figure 6.18.

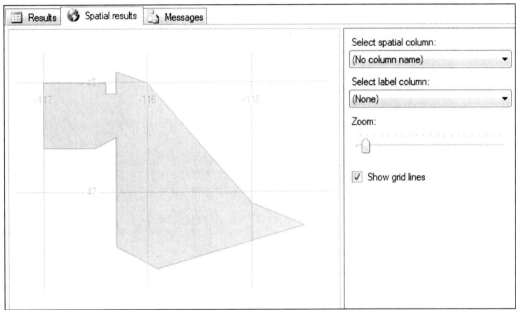

Figure 6.18 The graphical results shown upon the completion of Skill Check 3.

Skill Check 4: In the JProCo database context, aggregate the shapes shown in Figure 6.19 (created by the code below) into a single polygon shape grouped on the RoomNotes field. Use the ShapeMetry field as the parameter for this method. When done, the results will resemble those shown in Figure 6.20.

```
SELECT ShapeMetry
FROM SkiAreas
WHERE ShapeName LIKE '%County'
AND ShapeParentCode = 'ID'
```

READER NOTE: *Since it is not possible to use a GROUP BY clause with an LOB data type, it will be necessary to CAST the RoomNotes field as an NVARCHAR(20) to complete this Skill Check.*

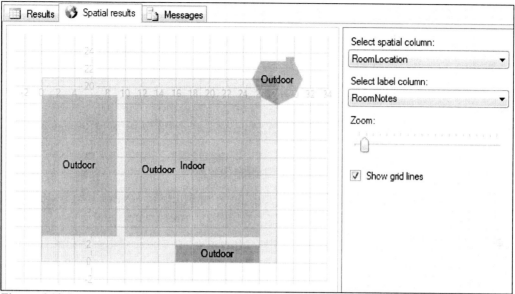

Figure 6.19 Aggregate the Indoor and Outdoor shapes together and show all internal borders.

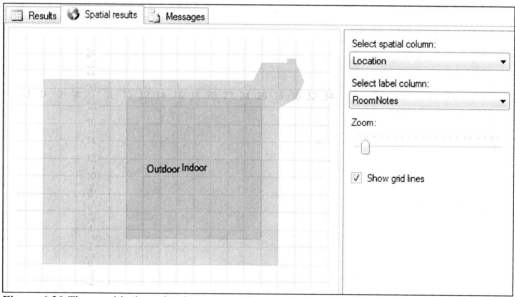

Figure 6.20 The graphical results shown upon the completion of Skill Check 4.

Answer Code: The T-SQL code to this lab can be found from the downloadable files named Lab6.1_SpatialUnionsAndCollections.sql.

Points to Ponder - Spatial Unions and Collections

1. OGC Spatial functions were introduced with SQL Server 2008.

2. STUnion() is an OGC method for Spatial aggregates that can combine two spatial instances, but cannot aggregate an entire collection of instances.

3. The UnionAggregate() and CollectionAggregate() functions are new functions introduced with SQL Server 2012.

4. The UnionAggregate() method combines multiple polygons into a single polygon and often removes any unnecessary interior boundaries.

5. The CollectionAggregate() method combines multiple polygons into a single polygon and preserves any interior boundaries.

6. Spatial aggregates allow for shapes to be combined across a spatial field of multiple rows, the same way that an aggregate function for numeric fields can use a GROUP BY clause with multiple rows.

Spatial Envelope Aggregates

It probably won't take much explanation to understand the concept of an envelope. After all, most of us either use or see one being used in our everyday life. Envelopes are generally needed to mail items, whether it contains a letter, a contract, or even bill payments. We can find many different sizes of envelopes at any office supply store. We can choose from protective envelopes for mailing family photos, manila envelopes for business purposes, and the more common white envelope for personal letters. Whatever is being sent in the mail, we simply need to choose an envelope that is the right size by selecting one that is slightly bigger than the shape of the item being mailed.

SQL Server also uses envelopes with shapes and there are three types available to choose from, depending on the desired results. Examples of these three aggregate envelope shapes are shown in Figure 6.21 using a simple polygon shape for the State of Idaho.

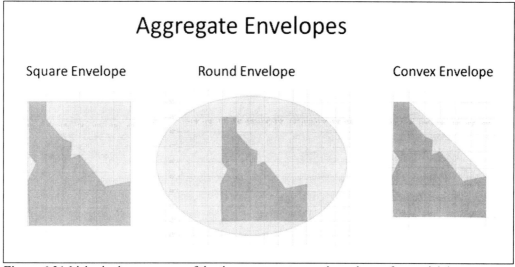

Figure 6.21 Idaho is shown as one of the three aggregate envelope shapes for spatial data.

EnvelopeAggregate() for GEOMETRY

Remember that SQL Server has two unique data types, GEOGRAPHY and GEOMETRY, designed to hold spatial data. These data types both allow the use of envelopes around their shapes, although there are some slight differences in how they work and the results returned by the query. Let's begin by examining how the EnvelopeAggregate() method works with the GEOMETRY data type by using the JProCo database and work with the HumanResources.RoomChart table that we are already familiar with.

Begin by writing the following code to focus on the RoomLocation field and filtering the results for viewing the Water Tower only (Figure 6.22).

```
SELECT RoomLocation
FROM HumanResources.RoomChart
WHERE R_ID IN (9)
```

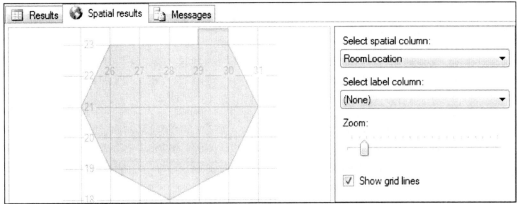

Figure 6.22 Results of a simple query showing the Water Tower shape alone.

We can now make a slight modification to the first query by adding a call to the EnvelopeAggregate() method and moving the RoomLocation field inside the parentheses to be used as the parameter for the method to work on.

It would be natural to think that this method would return both the shape of the object being filtered on and the containing envelope shape. Let's run the following query and see if the results meet our expectations (Figure 6.23).

```
SELECT GEOMETRY::EnvelopeAggregate(RoomLocation)
FROM HumanResources.RoomChart
WHERE R_ID IN (9)
```

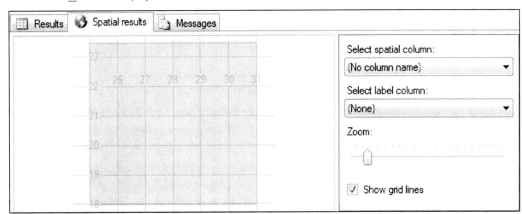

Figure 6.23 The shape result after running our basic EnvelopeAggregate() method query.

It seems that there is something missing from the previous query. Where is the shape of the Water Tower? Is the envelope hiding it? Yes, in effect the EnvelopeAggregate() method draws a square shape around the outside of an object, while contacting only the outermost points necessary to complete the square shape for containing the object. The object inside the container will not be visible.

In order to see the object inside the container created by the EnvelopeAggregate() method, we need to put on our X-Ray glasses by writing a query that can do this. We know that we already have two queries, that when run by themselves produce one of the two shapes that we are looking for. What type of query will allow us to view all results from two queries with the same number of fields and data types?

Of course, a UNION ALL operator can do this for us! Write both queries again, with a UNION ALL placed between them and view the results in Figure 6.24.

```
SELECT GEOMETRY::EnvelopeAggregate(RoomLocation)
FROM HumanResources.RoomChart
WHERE R_ID IN (9)
    UNION ALL
SELECT RoomLocation
FROM HumanResources.RoomChart
WHERE R_ID IN (9)
```

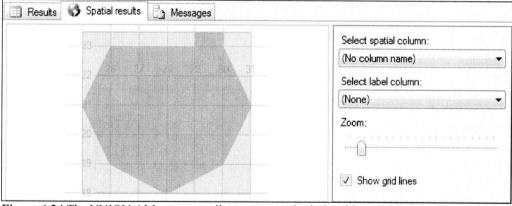

Figure 6.24 The UNION ALL operator allows us to see both the object and the envelope together.

For the remaining examples, we need to change our database context to dbBasics, as we will once again be working with the SkiAreas table. Use the SSMS UI to change the database context from JProCo to dbBasics before attempting to run the code samples in this section.

In this section, we will see how the EnvelopeAggregate() method responds differently to GEOMETRY and GEOGRAPHY data types. We will begin with writing a query to find the ShapeMetry field, which contains the GEOMETRY spatial data for the State of Idaho (Figure 6.25).

```
SELECT ShapeMetry
FROM SkiAreas
WHERE ShapeCode = 'ID'
```

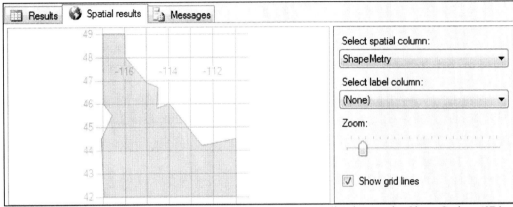

Figure 6.25 The graphical results of a GEOMETRY query predicating on the ShapeCode = 'ID'.

To create the container for holding the Idaho shape as a GEOMETRY object, we will need to use the EnvelopeAggregate() method and pass in the ShapeMetry field as its parameter. We can see the results of this query in Figure 6.26.

```
SELECT GEOMETRY::EnvelopeAggregate(ShapeMetry)
FROM SkiAreas
WHERE ShapeCode = 'ID'
```

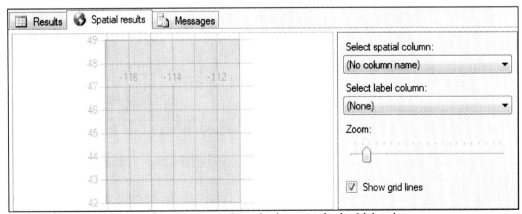

Figure 6.26 Using the EnvelopeAggregate() method to contain the Idaho shape.

By using a UNION ALL operator between the last two queries, we can visualize how the Idaho GEOMETRY object is contained in the square envelope shape created by the EnvelopeAggregate() method (Figure 6.27).

```
SELECT GEOMETRY::EnvelopeAggregate(ShapeMetry)
FROM SkiAreas
WHERE ShapeCode = 'ID'
   UNION ALL
SELECT ShapeMetry
FROM SkiAreas
WHERE ShapeCode = 'ID'
```

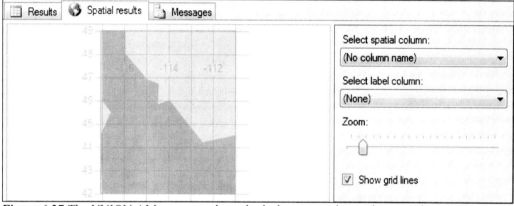

Figure 6.27 The UNION ALL operator shows both shapes together at the same time.

EnvelopeAggregate for GEOGRAPHY

The code for making a GEOGRAPHY envelope shape is much like that of the GEOMETRY envelope shape, although the outcome of the results will be different for these two reasons:

1. The GEOGRAPHY data type stores information that is ellipsoidal to take into account the curvature of the earth for its calculations.

2. The GEOMETRY data type stores information that is planar, so it does not need to take the curvature of the earth into account for its calculations.

The SkiAreas table has two fields which store values forming the shape of Idaho, a GEOGRAPHY data type named ShapeOgraphy and a GEOMETRY data type named ShapeMetry. Our earlier example of combining the Idaho and Montana shapes together, creating a single larger shape, used the values from ShapeOgraphy.

READER NOTE: *Do not mix data types when calling a method using spatial data. Since the information stored in the GEOGRAPHY and GEOMETRY data types are unique, any inconsistency will result in an error (*Figure 6.28*).*

Change the code for the calling data type from GEOMETRY in our previous query to GEOGRAPHY. This change will help us see what the difference is between these two data types when we run the code. Be sure to keep the ShapeMetry field as the parameter for the EnvelopeAggregate() method and as the field used in the lower SELECT statement. View the results in Figure 6.28.

```
SELECT GEOGRAPHY::EnvelopeAggregate(ShapeMetry)
FROM SkiAreas
WHERE ShapeCode = 'ID'
  UNION ALL
SELECT ShapeMetry
FROM SkiAreas
WHERE ShapeCode = 'ID'
```

Messages
Msg 206, Level 16, State 2, Line 1
Operand type clash: geometry is incompatible with geography

0 rows

Figure 6.28 This error message is the result of using a GEOMETRY data type as a parameter in a GEOGRAPHY call to the EnvelopeAggregate() method.

We can see from the error message in Figure 6.28 that it is important to confirm the data type of the field being passed into the EnvelopeAggregate() method is the same as the data type calling the method.

A slight change to our code will fix the error message and produce a graphical result showing both the Idaho shape as a GEOGRAPHY data type and the container drawn by the EnvelopeAggregate() method.

```
SELECT GEOGRAPHY::EnvelopeAggregate(ShapeOgraphy)
FROM SkiAreas
WHERE ShapeCode = 'ID'
  UNION ALL
SELECT ShapeOgraphy
FROM SkiAreas
WHERE ShapeCode = 'ID'
```

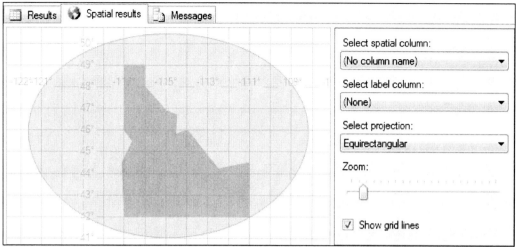

Figure 6.29 The GEOGRAPHY::EnvelopeAggregate() method draws an ellipsoidal container.

When we look at this image, there is something very different about the style of container drawn to hold the Idaho shape. Containers drawn for the GEOGRAPHY data type will be an ellipsoid, since this data type must consider the curvature of the earth when performing its calculations.

Convex Hull Aggregate

An envelope shaped like a square, a rectangle, or even elliptical is a great container for nearly every shape. However, the more complex the shape that is being contained in one of these envelopes, the more 'empty' space there is remaining around the main shape (compare Figure 6.29 to Figure 6.32).

What if we could create an envelope shaped like a hexagon, a decagon, or an even greater number of sides to more closely match the shape of the contained object? Well, we do have another envelope option for doing this exactly!

Before working with the next set of code samples, use the SSMS UI to make sure the database context is set to JProCo. We are going to build the query for using the ConvexHullAggregate() method in the same manner as we have built the queries using the EnvelopeAggregate() method.

The following query of the HumanResources.RoomChart table will produce results to view the shape of the Water Tower alone (Figure 6.30).

```
SELECT RoomLocation
FROM HumanResources.RoomChart
WHERE R_ID IN (9)
```

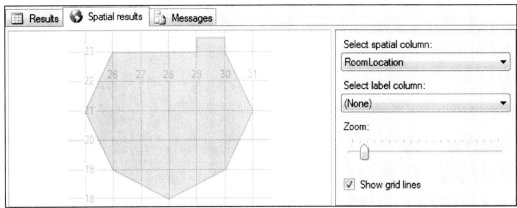

Figure 6.30 Results of a simple query showing the Water Tower shape alone.

We can now write a query that will draw a multi-sided container for the Water Tower by calling the ConvexHullAggregate() method with a GEOMETRY data type and passing in the RoomLocation field as the parameter for the method to perform its calculations on. The results are shown in Figure 6.31.

```
SELECT GEOMETRY::ConvexHullAggregate(RoomLocation)
FROM HumanResources.RoomChart
WHERE R_ID IN (9)
```

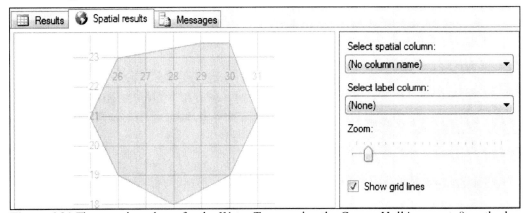

Figure 6.31 The container shape for the Water Tower using the ConvexHullAggregate() method.

Finally, we can bring these two queries together with a UNION ALL operator in order to view the container drawn by the ConvexHullAggregate() method and the Water Tower shapes together, as seen in Figure 6.32.

```
SELECT GEOMETRY::ConvexHullAggregate(RoomLocation)
FROM HumanResources.RoomChart
WHERE R_ID IN (9)
   UNION ALL
SELECT RoomLocation
FROM HumanResources.RoomChart
WHERE R_ID IN (9)
```

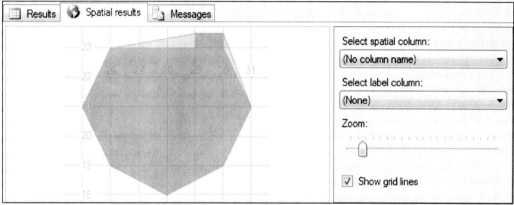

Figure 6.32 The ConvexHullAggregate() method container and Water Tower shape together.

A convex hull is an envelope with lots of corners. The ConvexHullAggregate() method draws a boundary around the shape connecting to each outermost corner, while always turning in the same direction, until it has completed drawing all the way around the shape and enclosing it in a container that most closely matches the original shape.

Lab 6.2: Spatial Envelope Aggregates

Lab Prep: Each lab has one or more Skill Checks. Start with Skill Check 1 and proceed until reaching the Points to Ponder section.

Before beginning this lab, verify that SQL Server 2012 is properly installed and operating. Before running the lab setup script for resetting the database (SQLQueries2012Vol3Chapter6.2Setup.sql), please make sure to close all query windows within SSMS. An open query window pointing to a database context can lock that database preventing it from updating when the script is executing. A simple way to assure all query windows are closed, is to exit out of SSMS, then open a new instance of SSMS, and lastly run the setup script.

Skill Check 1: In the dbBasics database context, use the SkiAreas table to write a query that will draw a round envelope around Montana and show both shapes. When done, the results will resemble those shown in Figure 6.33.

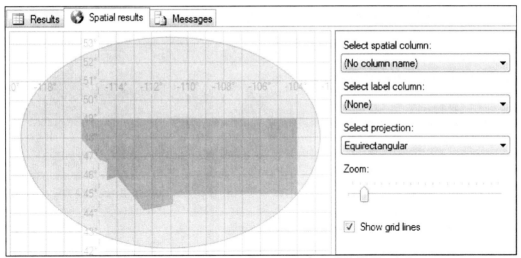

Figure 6.33 The graphical results shown upon the completion of Skill Check 1.

Skill Check 2: In the dbBasics database context, use the SkiAreas table to write a query that will draw a rectangle envelope around Montana and show both shapes. When done, the results will resemble those shown in Figure 6.34.

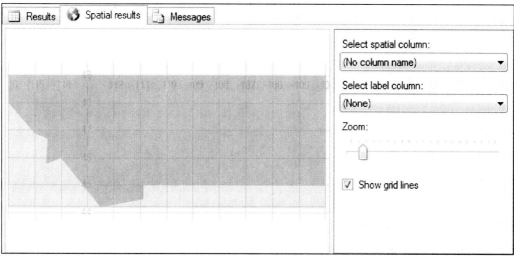

Figure 6.34 The graphical results shown upon the completion of Skill Check 2.

Skill Check 3: In the dbBasics database context, use the SkiAreas table to write a query that will draw a convex hull envelope around both Idaho and Montana, in addition to displaying both shapes. When done, the results will resemble those shown in Figure 6.35.

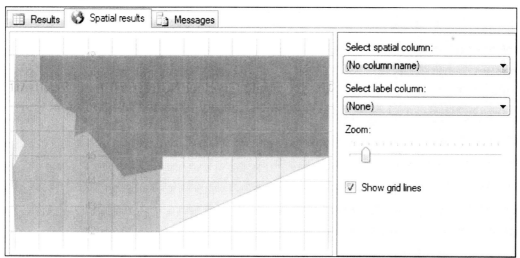

Figure 6.35 The graphical results shown upon the completion of Skill Check 3.

Answer Code: The T-SQL code to this lab can be found in the downloadable file named Lab6.2_SpatialEnvelopeAggregates.sql.

Points to Ponder - Spatial Envelope Aggregates

1. SQL Server 2012 has four new spatial aggregate functions.
   - o UnionAggregate()
   - o EnvelopeAggregate()
   - o CollectionAggregate()
   - o ConvexHullAggregate()

2. All aggregates are implemented as static functions against the name of the data type, as seen in the following examples:
   - o GEOGRAPHY::Aggregate(*GeographyField*).
   - o GEOMETRY::Aggregate(*GeometryField*).
   - o GEOGRAPHY::ConvexHullAggregate(*SpatialLocation*).

3. The ConvexHullAggregate() method draws around the shape connecting to each outside corner while always turning in the same direction until it completes its path all the way around the shape.

4. The EnvelopeAggregate() method places the smallest size box or circle that will contain a shape around it.

5. For the GEOMETRY data type, the EnvelopeAggregate() method returns a rectangular polygon envelope.

6. For the GEOGRAPHY data type, the EnvelopeAggregate() method returns a circular object, that when calculated, loosely binds the selected input objects.

Chapter Glossary

UnionAggregate(): A spatial method that performs a union operation on the shapes passed into the method (must be the same data type as the calling object). The result is a polygon shape that incorporates all the outside boundaries of the individual shapes to form a single polygon shape. It can be used with either the GEOGRAPHY or GEOMETRY data types.

CollectionAggregate(): A spatial method that performs a union operation on the shapes passed into the method (must be the same data type as the calling object). The result is a polygon shape that incorporates all the outside boundaries of the individual shapes to form a single polygon shape, in addition to preserving the internal boundaries of the individual shapes. It also can be used with either the GEOGRAPHY or GEOMETRY data types.

EnvelopeAggregate(): A spatial method that draws a planar container around shape objects with a GEOMETRY data type and an ellipsoidal container around shape objects with a GEOGRAPHY data type.

ConvexHullAggregate(): A spatial method that draws a container around a shape object with a GEOMETRY data type that most closely resembles the shape of the object by connecting all of the outermost points of the object.

UNION ALL: A SQL Server operator that can be used to combine two or more queries sharing the same number of fields and data types. This is the best way to view a container drawn by either an EnvelopeAggregate() method or a ConvexHullAggregate() method along with the shape of the object it contains in a single spatial result set.

Review Quiz - Chapter Six

1.) You have a SQL 2012 database with shapes of all 50 states. You are asked to aggregate California and Oregon into one shape with no internal lines being preserved. What are two ways this can be done?

☐ a. With the STUnion() function.

☐ b. With the STContains() function.

☐ c. With the UnionAggregate() function.

☐ d. With the CollectionAggregate() function.

2.) Which spatial function is not new to SQL Server 2012?

O a. The STUnion() function.

O b. The UnionAggregate() function.

O c. The CollectionAggregate() function.

3.) Which of the following spatial aggregated queries below will not execute?

O a.
```
SELECT ShapeParentCode,
GEOMETRY::UnionAggregate(ShapeMetry) AS Location
FROM dbo.SkiAreas
GROUP BY ShapeParentCode
```

O b.
```
SELECT ShapeParentCode,
GEOMETRY::CollectionAggregate(ShapeMetry) AS Location
FROM dbo.SkiAreas
GROUP BY ShapeParentCode
```

O c.
```
SELECT ShapeParentCode,
GEOMETRY::STUnion(ShapeMetry) AS Location
FROM dbo.SkiAreas
GROUP BY ShapeParentCode
```

O d.
```
SELECT GEOMETRY::UnionAggregate(ShapeMetry) AS Location
FROM dbo.SkiAreas
```

4.) We have a spatial shape of California and want to return an envelope hull container to fit it inside. The new container is an oval. What type of function was used to return this shape?

O a. GEOGRAPHY::EnvelopeAggregate()

O b. GEOMETRY::EnvelopeAggregate()

O c. GEOGRAPHY::ConvexHullAggregate()

5.) We have a spatial shape of India and use an aggregate to create the new shape that will hold the India shape. The new container is wrapped around India and has 6 corners all turning in the same direction. What method did we use?

O a. GEOGRAPHY::EnvelopeAggregate()

O b. GEOMETRY::EnvelopeAggregate()

O c. GEOGRAPHY::ConvexHullAggregate()

Answer Key

1.) The STContains() function does not create a new shape, rather it calculates if a shape is inside another shape, so (b) is wrong. Since the CollectionAggregate() function preserves the internal lines that were required to be eliminated, (d) is incorrect. There are only two shapes to combine with no internal lines, so either (a) or (c) will work.

2.) Spatial aggregate functions are new to SQL Server 2012. The STUnion() function existed in SQL Server 2008 and isn't new, therefore (a) is correct.

3.) Spatial aggregate functions work just fine with a GROUP BY clause, so (a) and (b) are not the problem. STUnion() can NOT be used in a GROUP BY clause, so (c) is the correct answer of the query that won't run.

4.) A ConvexHullAggregate() function will never give back a circle making (c) incorrect. The EnvelopeAggregate() function will create an oval if the calling data type is GEOGRAPHY, so (a) is correct.

5.) An EnvelopeAggregate() function will either return an oval or a four sided polygon, so (a) and (b) are incorrect. The ConvexHullAggregate() function makes 3 or more corners to enclose the shape, so (c) is the correct answer.

Bug Catcher Game

To play the Bug Catcher game, run the SQLQueries2012Vol3BugCatcher06.pps file from the BugCatcher folder of the companion files. These files can be obtained from the www.Joes2Pros.com website.

[THIS PAGE INTENTIONALLY LEFT BLANK.]

Chapter 7.   Creating Indexes

If we were to walk into a giant mall that we had never been to and wanted to find a store called Tech-Shirts, how would we find it? What is the better choice, walking by every store until we see the name, or heading straight to the mall directory map and looking for the name? Either system will eventually result in success. By using the directory at the mall, we can save many steps in reaching our location quickly. The mall has to devote a little extra space to directory kiosks in the middle of a few walkways, but the payoff is huge. Like many things in life which grow large in size, the mall has indexed all its units for our convenience.

This is one example of how indexes work, and the same principle applies to how SQL Server locates information stored in a database. By creating an index based on what is searched for most, we can get big performance gains with a nominal amount of additional storage space for the indexed data.

The reason we employ indexes in our tables and queries is to clear the way for SQL Server to efficiently locate and retrieve the data requested. In previous Chapters, we've looked at the organization of data files and data pages. We know that the ideal placement of data is one that maximizes the amount of data read and returned per disk I/O (input/output) cycle. In other words, one that allows SQL Server to work with the most data in the fewest number of steps.

This is the first of three Chapters we will spend on the topic of indexing in SQL Server. Yet, despite devoting roughly half of this book to indexes, it won't be adequate to cover indexes in an exhaustive or deeply technical fashion. The SQL Server Database Engine is a complex, highly organized and highly powerful system. Our goal will be to engage all readers – from beginners to advanced developers – to impart an understanding of how indexing works, the rules of thumb for applying the right types of indexes to achieve specific goals, and indexing pitfalls to avoid when designing tables and queries.

READER NOTE: *Please run the SQLQueries2012Vol3Chapter7.0Setup.sql script in order to follow along with the examples in the first section of Chapter 7. All scripts mentioned in this chapter may be found at* www.Joes2Pros.com.

The Clustered Index

The store names in a shopping mall are not lined up in alphabetical order. In other words, Zales could be right next to Benetton. These two stores might occupy Units 410 and 411. Thus, the stores in a mall are *clustered* by unit number. The **clustered index** represents the actual physical order of the data. A book is ordered by page numbers. If we locate page 99, then we know exactly where page 100 is. Thus, we could say the pages in a book represent a *clustered index* and they are *clustered* by page number.

Data Storage Terms

Think of a memory page as a carton of 12 eggs and each egg represents a row of data. If we only had two eggs to store, then only one carton would be needed. There are still 10 slots available for when we get more eggs to store. Since all the cartons are the same size and modifying the carton is not allowed, acquiring more and more eggs will eventually require more than one carton. What happens when the 12th and 13th eggs finally arrive? Naturally, we will fill up the first carton with the 12th egg and get another carton for the 13th egg.

Similarly, only so many records will fit into one memory page. If more records come in, then SQL Server will use multiple memory pages for that table.

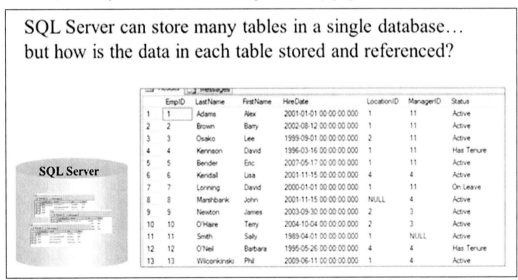

Figure 7.1 How is data in each table stored and referenced by SQL Server?

Records

While a table can have a maximum of just 1024 columns, or fields, it can have trillions of records. What makes a table take up space is the number of records in that table. If a table had no records, then it would take up very little space.

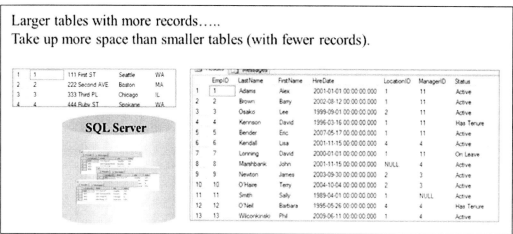

Figure 7.2 Small tables with fewer records take up less space than larger tables.

Memory Pages

So just how many records will fit into a single memory page? When more records come in, how does SQL Server manage multiple memory pages for each table?

A page can hold up to 8K of data. If, for example, each record used 2K of data, then 4 records would fit into a single memory page. If this table had 12 records, then it would fill 3 complete memory pages. When the 13th record arrives, a 4th memory page is needed to accommodate this new record (Figure 7.3, Figure 7.4 and Figure 7.5).

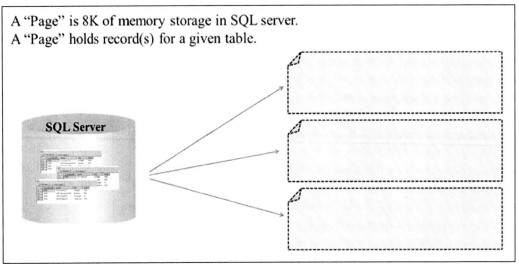

A "Page" is 8K of memory storage in SQL server.
A "Page" holds record(s) for a given table.

SQL Server

Figure 7.3 A Memory Page holds records for a table, depending on how large each record is.

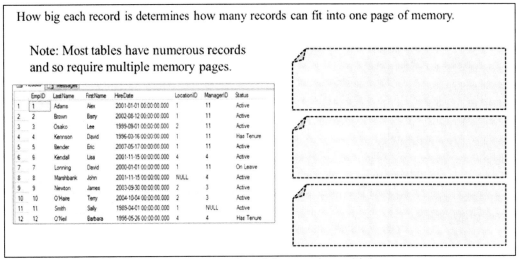

How big each record is determines how many records can fit into one page of memory.

Note: Most tables have numerous records and so require multiple memory pages.

	EmpID	LastName	FirstName	HireDate	LocationID	ManagerID	Status
1	1	Adams	Alex	2001-01-01 00:00:00.000	1	11	Active
2	2	Brown	Barry	2002-08-12 00:00:00.000	1	11	Active
3	3	Osako	Lee	1999-09-01 00:00:00.000	2	11	Active
4	4	Kennson	David	1996-03-16 00:00:00.000	1	11	Has Tenure
5	5	Bender	Eric	2007-05-17 00:00:00.000	1	11	Active
6	6	Kendall	Lisa	2001-11-15 00:00:00.000	4	4	Active
7	7	Lonning	David	2000-01-01 00:00:00.000	1	11	On Leave
8	8	Marshbank	John	2001-11-15 00:00:00.000	NULL	4	Active
9	9	Newton	James	2003-09-30 00:00:00.000	2	3	Active
10	10	O'Haire	Terry	2004-10-04 00:00:00.000	2	3	Active
11	11	Smith	Sally	1989-04-01 00:00:00.000	1	NULL	Active
12	12	O'Neil	Barbara	1996-05-26 00:00:00.000	4	4	Has Tenure

Figure 7.4 Most tables have numerous records and thus require multiple memory pages.

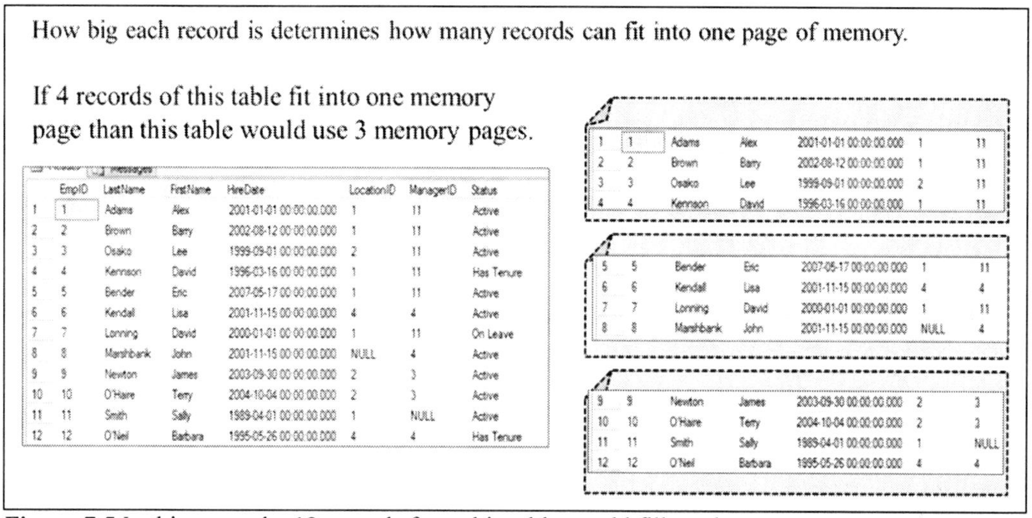

How big each record is determines how many records can fit into one page of memory.

If 4 records of this table fit into one memory page than this table would use 3 memory pages.

Figure 7.5 In this example, 12 records from this table would fill up three memory pages.

Since the physical storage of data impacts the speed and efficiency of queries, we will explore how indexes can impact the physical location of data and the way SQL Server retrieves data.

Clustered Index Data in Memory

In *SQL Queries 2012 Joes 2 Pros Volume 2*, we learned that using an ORDER BY clause allows us to view a table's records in any order we like based on the field chosen and if it will be in an ascending or descending direction. This is true regardless of the order in which the table has physically stored its rows. If we don't use an ORDER BY clause, then we get the table's natural sort order. What is a natural sort order? It is the sequence, from beginning to end, in which each row is physically stored in the table. We can decide to instruct a table how it should store its data or let the table store data in the order as it is entered.

Absent a clustered index or constraints, (e.g., a primary key, a foreign key, etc.), the default order of records is the order in which they were entered into the table. As we read at the opening of the Chapter, the clustered index represents our selection of the actual physical order of the data.

If we decide to add a clustered index to this table based on the SSN field, then regardless of the order in which we insert these records, each record will be stored in order of the SSN field. If we insert SSN 888-88-8888 first and then later add SSN 222-22-2222, then SQL Server would physically reorder the records in storage so they line up by SSN.

Clustered Indexes: This table is sorted in the system by SSN. The clustered index is the placement order of a table's records in memory pages.

Page 1		
222-22-2222	Jonny	Dirt
565-66-6767	Sally	Smith
888-88-8888	Irene	Intern
Empty	Empty	Empty
Page 2		
Empty	Empty	Empty
Empty	Empty	Empty
Empty	Empty	Empty
Empty	Empty	Empty

Figure 7.6 The clustered index is the placement order of a table's records in memory pages.

The **clustered index** is the placement order of a table's records in memory pages. When inserting new records, each record will be inserted into the memory page in the order it belongs.

Since, Rick Morelan's SSN value of 555-55-5555 belongs with the 5's, his record will be physically inserted in memory between Jonny Dirt and Sally Smith (Figure 7.7). Is there enough room in the page to accommodate this record without having to move other record(s) to a new page? Yes there is, and once this record is inserted, the first memory page is full.

Inserting Data Into a Page

New data

555-55-5555	Rick	Morelan

Page 1		
222-22-2222	Jonny	Dirt
565-66-6767	Sally	Smith
888-88-8888	Irene	Intern
Empty	Empty	Empty
Page 2		
Empty	Empty	Empty
Empty	Empty	Empty
Empty	Empty	Empty
Empty	Empty	Empty

Figure 7.7 When inserting a record(s), it is inserted into the memory page in the order it belongs.

Next, we have another new record coming in, Vince Verhoff (Figure 7.8). His record belongs in sequence after Irene Intern, so this record will begin occupying the next page of memory.

Inserting Data Into a New Page

New data

999-99-9999	Vince	Verhoff

Page1

222-22-2222	Jonny	Dirt
555-55-5555	Rick	Morelan
565-66-6767	Sally	Smith
888-88-8888	Irene	Intern

Page2

Empty	Empty	Empty
Empty	Empty	Empty
Empty	Empty	Empty
Empty	Empty	Empty

Figure 7.8 The Vince Verhoff record will begin occupying the next page of memory.

Page Splits

The clustered index is the placement order of a table's records in memory pages. When we insert new records, each record will be inserted into the memory page in the order it belongs. Page splits arise when records from one memory page are moved to another page during changes to the table.

As the next record (Major Disarray) is being inserted, (Figure 7.9) SQL Server discovers that it belongs between Jonny and Rick. Since there is no room remaining in this memory page, some records will need to be shifted around to complete the insert for Major Disarray. When Rick and Sally's records are shifted down to create the space for Major Disarray a page split occurs as Irene's record will need to move to the second page.

Page splits are considered very bad for performance, and there are a number of techniques to reduce, or even eliminate, the risk of page splits.

Inserts With Page Splits

New data

444-44-4444	Major	Disarray

Page1

222-22-2222	Jonny	Dirt
555-55-5555	Rick	Morelan
565-66-6767	Sally	Smith
888-88-8888	Irene	Intern

Page2

999-99-9999	Vince	Verhoff
Empty	Empty	Empty
Empty	Empty	Empty
Empty	Empty	Empty

Page Splits: The moving of data from one page to another during data manipulation.

Figure 7.9 Since there's no room in the first memory page, some records will need to shift around. The page split occurs when Irene's record moves to the second page.

Next we'll see this data entered into the HumanResources.Contractor table, which contains a clustered index on the SSN field using the following code:

```
IF EXISTS(
SELECT * FROM sys.tables
WHERE [name] = 'Contractor')
DROP TABLE HumanResources.Contractor
GO

CREATE TABLE HumanResources.Contractor (
SSN CHAR(11) PRIMARY KEY,
FirstName VARCHAR(25) NOT NULL,
LastName VARCHAR(35) NOT NULL,
Email VARCHAR(50) NOT NULL,
Pay MONEY NULL)
GO
```

Notice SSN is set as a primary key. A primary key is a constraint which ensures non-nullability and uniqueness (i.e., no duplicate values) in a field. *SQL Queries 2012 Volume 4* covers primary keys and constraints in depth.

Only one primary key per table is allowed. When creating a primary key, SQL Server creates two objects: the primary key and an index, which by default is a clustered index. The data in this table will be physically ordered by SSN, as this field is also the primary key.

We are now ready to insert the first three records into this table.

```
INSERT INTO HumanResources.Contractor VALUES
('222-22-2222','Jonny','Dirt','Jdirt@JProCo.com',35000),
('656-66-6767','Sally','Smith','SallyS@JProCo.com',45000),
('888-88-8888','Irene','Intern','I-IreneI@JProCo.com',NULL)
```

For this exercise, we will presume that each page of memory consists of four records. Thus, the three records we just inserted will occupy the same memory page (Figure 7.10).

```
SELECT * FROM HumanResources.Contractor
```

	SSN	FirstName	LastName	Email	Pay
1	222-22-2222	Jonny	Dirt	Jdirt@JProCo.com	35000.00
2	656-66-6767	Sally	Smith	SallyS@JProCo.com	45000.00
3	888-88-8888	Irene	Intern	I-IreneI@JProCo.com	NULL

3 rows

Figure 7.10 Three records reside in the first memory page of HumanResources.Contractor.

This means there is space for another record to be inserted into the first memory page of this table, making a total of four records (Figure 7.11).

```
INSERT INTO HumanResources.Contractor VALUES
('555-55-5555','Rick','Morelan','rmorelan@JProCo.com',25000)
```

```
SELECT * FROM HumanResources.Contractor
```

Memory Page: 1				
222-22-2222	Jonny	Dirt	Jdirt@JProCo.com	35000.00
555-55-5555	Rick	Morelan	rmorelan@JProCo.com	25000.00
656-66-6767	Sally	Smith	SallyS@JProCo.com	45000.00
888-88-8888	Irene	Intern	I-IreneI@JProCo.com	NULL
Memory Page: 2				
empty	Empty	Empty	empty	empty
empty	Empty	Empty	empty	empty
empty	Empty	Empty	empty	empty
empty	Empty	Empty	empty	empty

Figure 7.11 The physical layout of memory page 1 with the fourth record inserted.

In our example, the first memory page is now full, since it contains four records. The second memory page is empty. The layout of the memory page is depicted in Figure 7.11 with the fourth record of Rick Morelan (highlighted) added between

Jonny Dirt and Sally Smith. The last two records, Sally Smith and Irene Intern, have shifted down to make room for the insertion of the Rick Morelan record in proper sequence, according to the clustered index constraint of the primary key (SSN field).

The next insert is for the Vince Verhoff record, which will go directly into the second memory page, this record does not cause a page split, since his SSN value is greater than the highest SSN value in the first memory page.

```
INSERT INTO HumanResources.Contractor VALUES
('999-99-9999','Vince','Verhoff','Viv@JProCo.com',65000)

SELECT * FROM HumanResources.Contractor
```

Memory Page: 1				
222-22-2222	Jonny	Dirt	Jdirt@JProCo.com	35000.00
555-55-5555	Rick	Morelan	rmorelan@JProCo.com	25000.00
656-66-6767	Sally	Smith	SallyS@JProCo.com	45000.00
888-88-8888	Irene	Intern	I-IreneI@JProCo.com	NULL
Memory Page: 2				
999-99-9999	Vince	Verhoff	Viv@JProCo.com	65000.00
empty	Empty	Empty	empty	empty
empty	Empty	Empty	empty	empty
empty	Empty	Empty	empty	empty

Figure 7.12 The insert of Vince's record goes into the 2nd memory page and causes no page split.

By looking at the SSN values in the table, we can see that Vince's SSN value is 999-99-9999 representing the last possible SSN value, as it is the highest possible nine-digit SSN. This means the SSN value for the next record added will tell us whether there will be a page split or not.

Any subsequent INSERT statement with an SSN value range of 888-88-8889 through 999-99-9998 will go into one of the three available rows in the second memory page. Of course, this means that any SSN value below 888-88-8888 will cause a page split.

Since the SSN value for Major Disarray is 444-44-4444 it must be inserted into Memory Page 1 between Jonny and Rick. This will cause a page split, as Irene Intern's record must move be moved to Memory Page 2 (Figure 7.13).

READER NOTE: *It won't take long before almost every insert causes a page split.*

```
INSERT INTO HumanResources.Contractor VALUES
('444-44-4444','Major','Disarray','Majord@JProCo.com',20000)
SELECT * FROM HumanResources.Contractor
```

Memory Page: 1				
222-22-2222	Jonny	Dirt	Jdirt@JProCo.com	35000.00
444-44-4444	Major	Disarray	Majord@JProCo.com	20000.00
555-55-5555	Rick	Morelan	Rmorelan@JProCo.com	25000.00
656-66-6767	Sally	Smith	SallyS@JProCo.com	45000.00
Memory Page: 2				
888-88-8888	Irene	Intern	I-IreneI@JProCo.com	NULL
999-99-9999	Vince	Verhoff	Viv@JProCo.com	65000.00
empty	Empty	Empty	Empty	Empty
empty	Empty	Empty	Empty	Empty

Figure 7.13 Inserting Major Disarray's record forces Irene Intern's record to cause a page split.

Fill Factor

While we won't go into all the behind-the-scenes details for the impact of a page split, we know they are bad for performance and want to be aware of techniques to reduce or eliminate the likelihood of page splits.

The fill factor property was introduced in SQL Server 2000 and helps prevent the need for pages to split. We can tell SQL Server not to fill up every section of every page on the first sweep of data. Recall that a clustered index requires that all records must be stored in physical order.

We can set the fill factor property to instruct SQL Server to leave a specific percentage of space in the memory page empty for later inserts. This helps to minimize how often SQL Server needs to move new data around other existing pieces of data, thus increasing input performance.

To verify, or set this property using the SSMS GUI (Figure 7.14), we need to locate the Options page by navigating to the following path:

Object Explorer > Databases > JProCo > Tables > HumanResources.Contractor > Indexes > right-click on the **Index > Properties > Options**

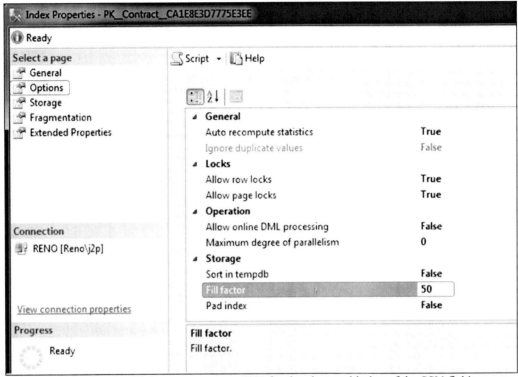

Figure 7.14 Setting the fill factor property to 50% for the clustered index of the SSN field.

Setting a fill factor property with a value of less than 100% will use more space on disk, however the benefit is that it will reduce or eliminate the likelihood of page splits and increase overall input performance.

A fill factor of 50% will leave every other record empty on the initial insert of data into the HumanResources.Contractor table (Figure 7.15).

```
TRUNCATE TABLE HumanResources.Contractor

INSERT INTO HumanResources.Contractor VALUES
('222-22-2222','Jonny','Dirt','Jdirt@JProCo.com',35000),
('656-66-6767','Sally','Smith','SallyS@JProCo.com',45000),
('888-88-8888','Irene','Intern','I-IreneI@JProCo.com',NULL)

SELECT *
FROM HumanResources.Contractor
```

Memory Page: 1				
222-22-2222	Jonny	Dirt	Jdirt@JProCo.com	35000.00
empty	Empty	Empty	Empty	Empty
656-66-6767	Sally	Smith	SallyS@JProCo.com	45000.00
empty	Empty	Empty	Empty	Empty
Memory Page: 2				
888-88-8888	Irene	Intern	I-IreneI@JProCo.com	NULL
empty	Empty	Empty	Empty	Empty
empty	Empty	Empty	Empty	Empty
empty	Empty	Empty	Empty	Empty

Figure 7.15 A fill factor of 50% will leave every other record empty on the initial data insert.

With a fill factor of 75%, the initial insert will immediately fill 75% of the records in the table and leave 25% of the records empty. In other words, every fourth record will be empty. A fill factor of 90% will leave every tenth record empty.

Instead of using the SSMS UI to set the fill factor, we can choose to write T-SQL code to accomplish this task as well. The following code will rebuild all indexes with a fill factor of 75%:

```
ALTER INDEX ALL
ON [HumanResources].[Contractor]
REBUILD WITH (FILLFACTOR = 75)
GO
```

Identity Fields

We've learned that setting the fill factor property to less than 100% will use up additional space in order to help reduce page splits. In our next example, we will examine another approach to eliminate page splits that has the benefit of wasting no space and allows the use of a 100% fill factor property setting.

Let's use an example with the HumanResources.Contractor table, by adding an extra identity field to keep track of each insert. Creating a clustered index based on this identity field we can see that the physical sort for a memory page is based on the new identity field of each record (Figure 7.16).

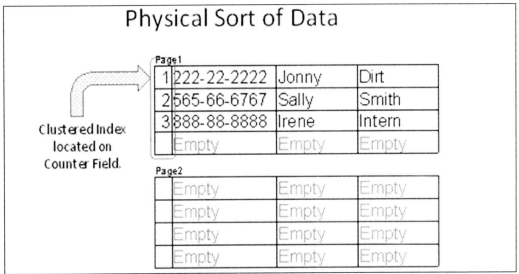

Figure 7.16 The physical sort of memory page after adding a clustered index on an identity field.

Why is this better than adjusting the fill factor property for reducing page splits? The best way to see the difference is to drop the HumanResources.Contractor table, rebuild it to include an identity field with a clustered index, and use the default fill factor of 100%. Finally, we can begin inserting the records causing the page splits in the first two examples and see what happens this time.

```
IF EXISTS(
SELECT * FROM sys.tables
WHERE [name] = 'Contractor')
DROP TABLE HumanResources.Contractor
GO

CREATE TABLE HumanResources.Contractor (
ctrID INT IDENTITY(1,1),
SSN CHAR(11),
FirstName VARCHAR(25) NOT NULL,
LastName VARCHAR(35) NOT NULL)
GO

CREATE CLUSTERED INDEX CI_Contractor_ctrID
ON HumanResources.Contractor(ctrID)
GO
```

```
INSERT INTO HumanResources.Contractor VALUES
('222-22-2222','Jonny','Dirt'),
('656-66-6767','Sally','Smith'),
('888-88-8888','Irene','Intern'),
('555-55-5555','Rick','Morelan'),
('999-99-9999','Vince','Verhoff'),
('444-44-4444','Major','Disarray')
```

Recall from our first example, that when Rick Morelan's record was inserted it caused the Sally Smith and Irene Interns records to be shifted down in the memory page, because the physical sort order was determined by the SSN value. Then, as the Major Disarray record was inserted it caused a page split, since it needed to fit between the Jonny Dirt and Rick Morelan record based on the SSN value.

Now, when Rick Morelan's record is inserted, the identity field (ctrID) is assigned a value of 4. This allows it to fill the last space in the first memory page and avoids the need to shift the Sally Smith and Irene Intern records. The next record to be inserted is Vince Verhoff, and this record immediately fills the first space on the second memory page. When the last record, Major Disarray, is inserted the ctrID identity field assigns it a value of 6. This will place the record immediately after the Vince Verhoff record, completely avoiding a page split! (Figure 7.17)

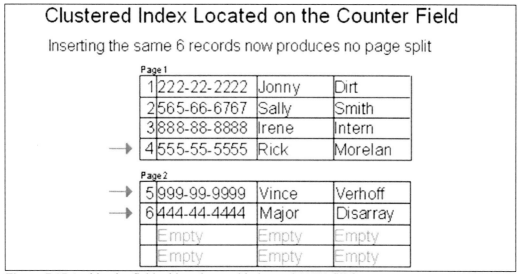

Figure 7.17 An identity field with a clustered index and 100% fill factor prevents page splits.

Lab 7.1: Clustered Indexes

Lab Prep: Each lab has one or more Skill Checks. Start with Skill Check 1 and proceed until reaching the Points to Ponder section.

Before beginning this lab, verify that SQL Server 2012 is properly installed and operating. Before running the lab setup script for resetting the database (SQLQueries2012Vol3Chapter7.1Setup.sql), please make sure to close all query windows within SSMS. An open query window pointing to a database context can lock that database preventing it from updating when the script is executing. A simple way to assure all query windows are closed, is to exit out of SSMS, then open a new instance of SSMS, and lastly run the setup script.

Skill Check 1: In the JProCo database, use the SSMS UI to change the fill factor property of the dbo.Supplier table's only index to 70%.

Skill Check 2: Drop and re-create the HumanResources.Contractor table with the same fields and records as shown immediately after Figure 7.9 in this section. Include an identity field named ctrID that is also the primary key. When finished, the results should resemble Figure 7.18.

```
SELECT * FROM HumanResources.Contractor
```

	ctrID	SSN	FirstName	LastName	Email	Pay
1	1	222-22-2222	Jonny	Dirt	Jdirt@JProCo.com	35000.00
2	2	656-66-6767	Sally	Smith	SallyS@JProCo.com	45000.00
3	3	888-88-8888	Irene	Intern	I-IreneI@JProCo.com	NULL
4	4	555-55-5555	Rick	Morelan	rmorelaN@JProCo.com	25000.00
5	5	999-99-9999	Vince	Verhoff	Viv@JProCo.com	65000.00
6	6	444-44-4444	Major	Disarray	Majord@JProCo.com	20000.00

6 rows

Figure 7.18 Re-create the Contractor table with an identity field which is also the primary key.

Answer Code: The T-SQL code to this lab can be found in the downloadable files in a file named Lab7.1_ClusteredIndex.sql.

Points to Ponder - Clustered Indexes

1. An index is an ordered list of values from a table.

2. An index is used by an RDBMS (like SQL Server) to organize data for frequent searches to improve performance and data access.

3. Indexes can be created when you create the table, or they can be added after the table is created.

4. Columns that change frequently OR are too wide don't make good clustered indexes.

5. Properly designed indexes improve query performance.

6. When you create a primary key on a table, a clustered index is created for you by default.

7. A clustered index determines the physical organization of data in the table.

8. Each table can have only one clustered index.

9. A heap is a table without a clustered index.

10. When creating a primary key or unique constraint SQL Server automatically creates a unique index during the CREATE TABLE or ALTER TABLE statements.

11. If a frequently changed field is contained in a clustered index, then the entire row of data might be moved so the physical sort can remain intact.

12. The adjustment of memory pages is known as a page split.

13. The FILL FACTOR option allows a percentage of free space to be allocated on the leaf level pages to reduce the occurrences of page splits.

14. Leaf level is a term that represents the actual storage location of data.

15. The main purpose of the FILL FACTOR option is to postpone and reduce page splits.

16. The lower the FILL FACTOR percentage, the fewer page splits produced.

17. The lower the FILL FACTOR percentage, the more unused space created.

18. If the primary key is on an IDENTITY field, then there are no page splits, even with a 100% FILL FACTOR.

19. Think of the FILL FACTOR setting as a one-time allocation event. In other words, the FILL FACTOR percentage is applied at the time an index is created, or rebuilt. It does not include ongoing monitoring to make sure *x* **percentage** of empty rows exist in a table.

20. Tables that are clustered based on an IDENTITY column are not subject to page splits and therefore do not benefit from a FILL FACTOR.

21. A field with an IDENTITY property produces system-generated, sequential values that identify each row in the table.

22. An IDENTITY column must use one of the following data types: DECIMAL, INT, NUMERIC, SMALLINT, BIGINT, or TINYINT.

23. Each table can have only one column with an IDENTITY property, and the column cannot allow NULL values or contain a DEFAULT.

24. There are four main ways to obtain information on existing indexes.

    1) SQL Server Management Studio
    2) System Stored Procedures
    3) Catalog Views
    4) System Functions

25. Sometimes heaps are better than clustered indexes.

26. Heaps make better sense for a table with one of these conditions:

    o The data which the index is based upon is volatile (changes often)
    o The table data is very compact (i.e., small)
    o The table contains mostly duplicated rows

27. The term, predicate, describes the filtering of a query with criteria, most often with a WHERE or HAVING clause. To say a query is *predicating* on the InvoiceID field means it is filtering based upon criteria specified for the InvoiceID field. The condition WHERE InvoiceID = 3 is the *predicate* of the following query:

```
SELECT * FROM SalesInvoiceDetail
WHERE InvoiceID = 3
```

Non-Clustered Indexes

Sometimes we look at everything before deciding what to pick and sometimes our options are conveniently narrowed down for us. This can be true of our search patterns when shopping, when looking at a restaurant menu, or when looking at available options for our reports and data.

At a very high level, this is a helpful way to think about the two distinct approaches SQL Server takes toward retrieving query data. Sometimes SQL Server must scan all available data in a database object(s) in order to provide the data requested. At other times, SQL Server is able to use one or more indexes to quickly zero in on the requested data.

Before we tackle our main topic of Non-Clustered indexes, we need to find out exactly what indexes are doing for us when we write a query.

Index Scan

A **scan** is the scenario described above where we look at every possible item before deciding what to pick. This is not always bad, especially with small lists intended to be analyzed thoroughly. When going to a new restaurant, we typically look over all the menu choices before deciding what to eat. This will take longer and longer as the menu gets bigger. However, in a large list where we know what the item is that we are looking for, a scan of every item becomes a big waste of time and we would end up wishing for a list that was better organized.

For example, when visiting my favorite restaurant with a vegetarian colleague, I noticed he immediately went to the lower left corner and picked one of their three vegetarian options. This restaurant chose to *index* the menu by the types of food choices to make them easier to find. However, another restaurant we visited did not do this, but simply placed an asterisk next to each vegetarian item. With the vegetarian options interspersed throughout the menu, my guest had no choice but to scan the entire menu to locate the items which met his criteria.

Index Seek

A **seek** is when the indexes are set up to search with fewer steps than a scan. Being able to quickly find exactly what we need is a wonderful thing. Everyday life is filled with examples of orderly systems to help us locate what we want quickly.

For example, suppose I handed my friend the 400 page *Joes 2 Pros* Programming Book and asked them to turn to page 210. Since the pages are in numbered order, it's easy to eliminate the tedious amount of time caused by doing a scan of each page from the beginning until they find page 210. There is simply no need to begin at page 1 when going straight to the middle of the book and then turn a few pages to the right until locating page 210. *Going straight to the needed page in very few hops is known as a **seek** lookup.*

On the other hand, suppose I had asked my friend to find the page in the *Joes 2 Pros Programming Book* which contains a word with the letter O appearing in it four times. It will likely take them a very long time to find that page, since it would be necessary to scan each page in the entire book in order to find the requested data. Similarly, some queries can cause SQL Server to scan ALL records to find the requested data because they are not selective enough.

Let's imagine the request had been a little more specific, by asking to find the word "onomatopoeia" in a book. Knowing that most books have an index, a search would most likely begin by flipping to the back of the book, check the index, and find the number of the page which contains the term onomatopoeia. Since we now know the precise page number, we could ***seek*** directly to the page containing the desired word. So the fact that the index kept track of the data needed, it quickly pointed us to the location of the data, speeding up the search time considerably.

Clustered Indexes Recap

In the first section of this chapter, we learned that *clustered indexes* arrange records in a physical order according to the column with a clustered index placed on it.

Our last example showed that a book is essentially *clustered* in order by page numbers, and it is indexed by words. In geek speak, we would say a book has a *clustered index* by pages, and it has a *Non-Clustered index* pointing directly to the pages where specific words are located.

Thus, the purpose of indexes in SQL Server is much like that of an index found in the back of a book. The index will take up a little extra space, but it can greatly speed up searching for the data. *Indexes typically reduce query processing time.*

By looking at the Indexes folder of the CurrentProducts table, we can see it has one index. Let's look at the index properties window to see which field it is based on (Figure 7.19).

Object Explorer > Databases > JProCo > Tables > dbo.CurrentProducts > Indexes > right-click on the index (**PK_CurrentP...**) > **Properties > General (page)**

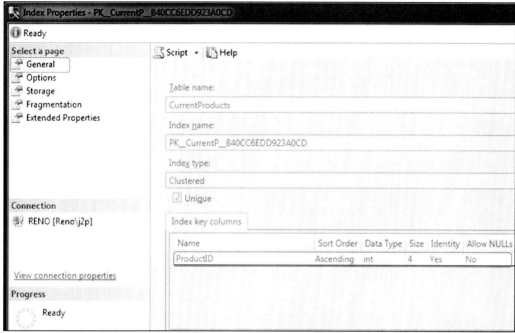

Figure 7.19 The clustered index for the dbo.CurrentProducts table is based on the ProductID field.

Since this clustered index is based on the ProductID field, any query predicating on the ProductID field should run very quickly. We can test this out by running two different queries, one predicating on ProductID with the clustered index and the other predicating on the SupplierID field without an index.

The first query with the clustered index performing a seek lookup, should run much faster than the second query without an index performing a table scan.

```
--Query #1 predicates on a clustered index field
SELECT * FROM CurrentProducts
WHERE ProductID = 5

--Query #2 predicates on a non-indexed field
SELECT * FROM CurrentProducts
WHERE SupplierID = 1
```

Let's take a look at the Execution Plan of the first query. This can be accomplished in one of two ways. Write the code for the first query and then click on the toolbar icon (Display Estimated Execution Plan) shown in Figure 7.20. It will then execute the code while displaying the estimated Execution Plan in the results window. Alternatively, write and execute the code for the first query and then press Ctrl+L to display the estimated Execution Plan in the results window.

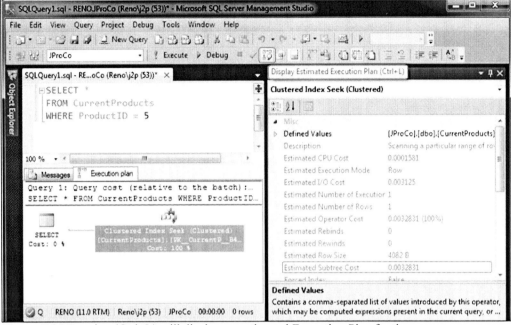

Figure 7.20 Pressing (Ctrl+L) will display an estimated Execution Plan for the query.

To get more detail about what happened during the execution of this query, we can simply hover with the mouse pointer over the Clustered Index Seek icon. However, this information quickly disappears when moving the mouse pointer away from the icon. Another method to view the detailed results for the Execution Plan is to right-click on the Clustered Index Seek icon and click on the Properties selection. This will open the Properties window in the SSMS UI as shown on the right-hand side of Figure 7.20. By observing the results for the "Estimated Subtree Cost", we can see how long the operation takes down to the millisecond.

Next we will look at the Execution Plan for the second query. Since this query is predicated on the SupplierID field, it will not be covered by the clustered index and SQL Server performs a clustered index scan to find the results (Figure 7.21).

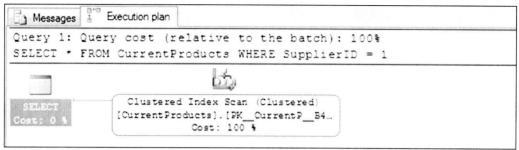

Figure 7.21 The estimated Execution Plan for the second query shows it will perform a scan.

The following next two queries shown return the same record. When running these queries separately, notice the second query takes longer to find the same record.

```
--Query #1 predicates on the ctrID field
SELECT * FROM HumanResources.Contractor
WHERE ctrID = 1

--Query #2 predicates on the SSN value
SELECT * FROM HumanResources.Contractor
WHERE SSN = '222-22-2222'
```

The Execution Plan for the first query shows a clustered index seek (Figure 7.22).

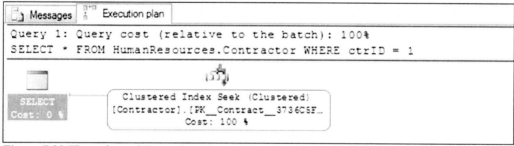

Figure 7.22 The estimated Execution Plan predicated on the ctrID field does a seek lookup.

The Execution Plan for the second query shows it will do a scan (Figure 7.23).

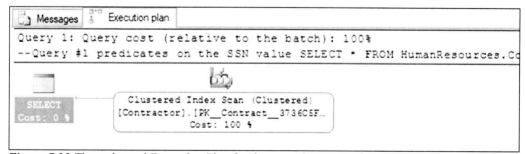

Figure 7.23 The estimated Execution Plan for the second query performs a clustered index scan.

Why does the first query predicated on the ctrID field use a seek lookup, while the second query predicated on the SSN field is only able to do a clustered index scan? Looking in the Indexes folder of the HumanResources.Contractor table, we see the only index is the clustered index based on the ctrID field (Figure 7.24).

Object Explorer > Databases > JProCo > Tables > HumanResources.Contractor > Indexes > right-click on the index (**PK_Contract**...) > **Properties > General (page)**

Figure 7.24 The table's only index is the clustered index based on ctrID.

Is it possible to create a clustered index based on the SSN field in order to speed up a query predicated on this field? No, because the physical order of the records is determined by a clustered index and since there can only be one object determining the physical order per table, there can only be one clustered index. However, a table can have many **Non-Clustered indexes**.

Creating Non-Clustered Indexes

So what are **Non-Clustered indexes** and how do we use them?

Non-Clustered indexes allow us to look at our data from many perspectives. If a clustered index physically orders a table's records, then a **Non-Clustered index** is a way of organizing information in a non-physical manner.

Let's think back to our book example. We know the sequential ordering of the pages is analogous to a clustered index. It's extremely helpful to have the pages in order, but can the page numbers themselves actually tell us anything about the nature of the book? When picking up this book and deciding to learn about the new spatial data types in SQL Server, most people will look in the index and find over a dozen pages listed which include a reference to spatial data types. Do the three digit numbers 159, 164, or 168 give any direct information about the topic? No, but they do provide a method to rapidly find the desired information. This is similar to the way Non-Clustered indexes are often used in conjunction with clustered indexes in speeding up queries.

Recall that with our last two queries on the HumanResources.Contractor table, we discovered the records are physically arranged in order of ctrID. However, if we perform other queries on this table involving fields more important to us, such as pay and name data, then these types of queries will become slower as the table grows larger with contractors being added from locations all over the world.

Our shopping mall directory illustrates how we can have many Non-Clustered indexes in a table, despite having just one clustered index. The mall has chosen to assign a number to each of the stores based on the physical order of their location, much like a clustered index. Most customers are more concerned with the store name rather than the store number. A list which keeps track of the store names in alphabetical order is one possible example of a Non-Clustered index.

Another example of a Non-Clustered index for a shopping mall would be a list that keeps track of the store categories (e.g., Children's, Cosmetics, Electronics, Toys, Kitchenware, Men's Apparel, Women's Shoes, etc.). Yet another possibility for a Non-Clustered index would be a list keeping track of all the restaurants in the mall. Before the winter holidays, some stores remain open an additional two hours for holiday shoppers. A list keeping track of the stores that stay open late would be another example of a Non-Clustered index.

A Non-Clustered index is ordered and points us to the desired location. The shopping mall directory allows customers to quickly locate a store they want by referencing the physical location, such as a store number (Clustered index). Similarly, a Non-Clustered index will order its items by different categories and point to their positions in the clustered index.

Unique Non-Clustered Indexes

Non-Clustered indexes may be used with fields that have either unique or non-unique values.

Years ago at the Tacoma mall there are two T-Mobile stores. One is really a kiosk in the center of the mall. Their directory does not require the two stores to have different names. Therefore, the directory at the mall is a **non-unique Non-Clustered index**.

Take a moment to observe the fields located in the HumanResources.Contractor table and think about which Non-Clustered indexes may be unique versus indexes that are non-unique. Often times the HumanResources personnel need to search for an employee by their SSN. We should make a unique Non-Clustered index on this field because each employee's SSN is a unique value which we query frequently.

Let's add a unique Non-Clustered index to the HumanResources.Contractor table using the SSMS UI, by following the following path shown: (Figure 7.25)

Object Explorer > Databases > JProCo > HumanResources.Contractor >
right-click on **Indexes > New Index > Non-Clustered Index**

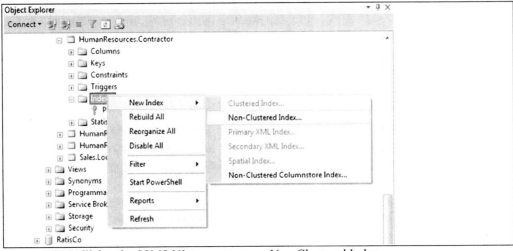

Figure 7.25 Utilizing the SSMS UI to create a new Non-Clustered Index.

When creating a Non-Clustered index, it is good practice to give it a prefix of UNCI, which helps to remind us that it's a **U**nique **N**on-**C**lustered **I**ndex. The name of our index will be UNCI_Contractor_SSN, next, mark the 'Unique' check box, and then click the Add button to add a key column to the index (Figure 7.26).

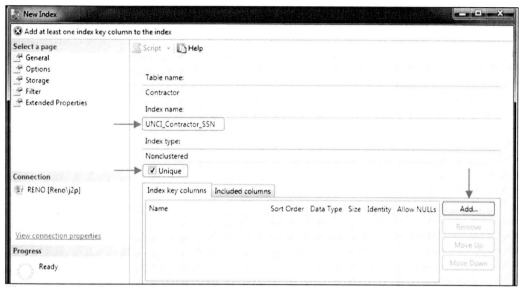

Figure 7.26 The dialog window to create a New Index in the HumanResources.Contractor table.

The next step is to select the SSN column to add to the index and then press the OK button to close the Select Columns dialog window (Figure 7.27). Finally press the OK button to close the New Index dialog window.

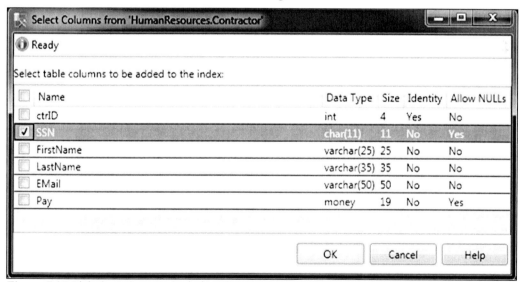

Figure 7.27 Pick the column to be indexed.

We can verify the UNCI_Contractor_SSN unique non-clustered index has been added to the HumanResources.Contractor table by using the Object Explorer.

Object Explorer > Databases > JProCo > HumanResources.Contractor > Indexes

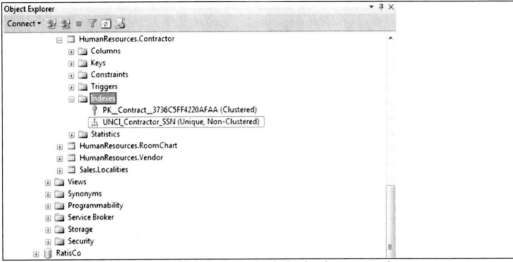

Figure 7.28 Verify that the UNCI_Contractor_SSN index has been created.

Recall that when we started, the first query performed a seek lookup, because it was predicated on the clustered index ctrID field and the second query performed a scan because it was predicated on the non-indexed SSN field. Let's see what happens when we run the second query again after creating the unique non-clustered index for the SSN field.

Success! We can see that the Execution Plan now performs the more efficient Non-Clustered index seek instead of a much slower scan (Figure 7.29).

```
SELECT * FROM HumanResources.Contractor
WHERE SSN = '222-22-2222'
```

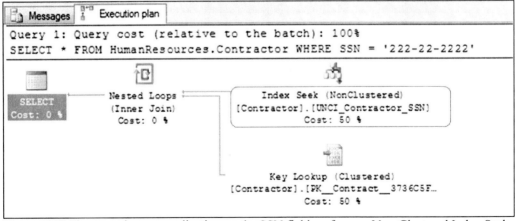

Figure 7.29 The second query predicating on the SSN field performs a Non-Clustered Index Seek.

Lab 7.2: Non-Clustered Indexes

Lab Prep: Each lab has one or more Skill Checks. Start with Skill Check 1 and proceed until reaching the Points to Ponder section.

Before beginning this lab, verify that SQL Server 2012 is properly installed and operating. Before running the lab setup script for resetting the database (SQLQueries2012Vol3Chapter7.2Setup.sql), please make sure to close all query windows within SSMS. An open query window pointing to a database context can lock that database preventing it from updating when the script is executing. A simple way to assure all query windows are closed, is to exit out of SSMS, then open a new instance of SSMS, and lastly run the setup script.

Skill Check 1: One of the department heads has expressed the need for a unique Non-Clustered index for the Email field of the HumanResources.Contractor table be created and named UNCI_Contractor_Email. Create this index using the SSMS UI and show that it has been successfully created by displaying it in the Object Explorer. When done the window should resemble Figure 7.30.

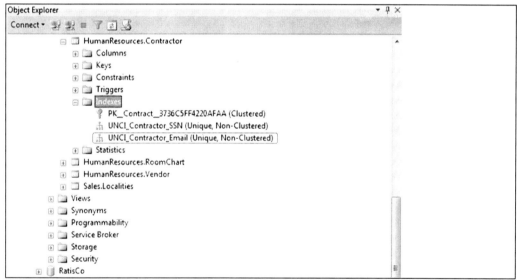

Figure 7.30 Skill Check 1 creates the index UNCI_Contractor_Email.

Answer Code: The answer to this lab can be found in the downloadable files in a file named Lab7.2_NonClusteredIndexes.sql.

Points to Ponder - Non-Clustered Indexes

1. A table that does not have a clustered index is referred to as a heap and a table that has a clustered index is referred to as a clustered table.

2. A Non-Clustered index can be placed on a heap or on a clustered table.

3. In SQL Server 2005, each table was allowed up to 249 Non-Clustered indexes and 1 clustered index. Since SQL Server 2008, each table may have up to 999 Non-Clustered indexes.

4. Non-Clustered indexes are useful when users require multiple ways to search for data.

5. The term "coverage" refers to the number of columns predicated on in a query which are supported by an index.

6. Covered queries reduce disk I/O and improve query performance.

7. Non-Clustered indexes work best when the data selectivity ranges from highly selective to unique.

8. Non-Clustered indexes do not affect the physical location of data. Rather, Non-Clustered indexes create a list of pointers to the rows where the data resides.

9. It's best to create the clustered index before you create Non-Clustered indexes in a table.

10. Non-Clustered indexes are automatically rebuilt when:
    o An existing clustered index on the table is dropped.
    o A clustered index on the table is created.
    o A column covered by the Non-Clustered index changes.

11. Indexes can be created by using the SSMS UI or T-SQL code.

12. A unique index ensures all data in a field is unique and has no duplicates.

13. Columns that are used with a unique index should be set to NOT NULL. A unique index cannot be added to a column containing multiple NULL values because these are considered duplicates when a unique index is created. A unique index will allow at most one NULL value.

Chapter Glossary

Clustered Index: The clustered index represents the actual physical order of data.

Clustered table: A table that has a clustered index.

Coverage: This refers to the number of columns predicated on in a query that are supported by an index.

Execution Plan: An Execution Plan visualizes how a query is executed.

FILL FACTOR: The fill factor setting was introduced in SQL Server 2000 and helps prevent the need for pages to split.

Heap: A table that does not have a clustered index.

Identity Fields: A field with an IDENTITY property produces system-generated sequential values that identify each row in the table.

Index Scan: A low-selective search requires SQL Server to look at every record before returning results.

Index Seek: A highly-selective search allowing SQL Server to look at indexed records only, resulting in far fewer steps, before returning results.

Natural sort order: The sequence, from beginning to end, in which each row is stored in the table.

Non-Clustered Index: This type of index allows searching for data from many perspectives; a Non-Clustered index is a way of organizing information in a non-physical manner.

Non-unique Non-Clustered Index: An index with non-unique or duplicate values.

Page Splits: Page splits arise when records from one memory page are moved to another page during changes to the table.

PRIMARY KEY: A constraint which ensures non-nullability and uniqueness (i.e., no duplicate values) in a field.

Review Quiz - Chapter Seven

1.) A heap has:

O a. No clustered indexes.

O b. One clustered index.

O c. Many clustered indexes.

2.) You want to reserve your table to have 25% free pages and use 75% of the available pages. What should you do?

O a. Use the default fill factor.

O b. Use a fill factor of 25.

O c. Use a fill factor of 75.

O d. Disable the fill factor.

3.) What is true about clustered and Non-Clustered indexes? (Choose two)

☐ a. You can have only one clustered index per table.

☐ b. You can have up to 999 clustered indexes per table.

☐ c. You can have only one Non-Clustered index per table.

☐ d. You can have up to 999 Non-Clustered indexes per table.

4.) You have a table with one clustered index and one Non-Clustered index. Later research shows that another field called 'date' is often queried and would benefit from some type of index. What can you do?

O a. Create another clustered index.

O b. Create another Non-Clustered index.

5.) Your SQL Server 2012 database stores all employees in a table. There are new employees added every day. This table has a clustered index based on the EmployeeID column. You often query by SSN but the query is too slow. How can you support an efficient reporting solution by SSN?

O a. Create another clustered index.

O b. Create another Non-Clustered index.

Answer Key

1.) A table that has a clustered index is referred to as a clustered table, so (b) is incorrect. A table can have only 1 clustered index making (c) incorrect. A table that does not have a clustered index is referred to as a heap, making (a) the correct answer.

2.) When the 'Set fill factor' setting is enabled the fill setting is automatically set to 100%, so (a) is incorrect. A fill factor of 25% would fill 25% of the records and leave 75% empty, so (b) is incorrect. When the 'Set fill factor' is disabled then no fill factor will be set, so (d) is incorrect. With a fill factor of 75%, the initial insert would immediately fill 75% of the records in the table and leave 25% of the records empty, so (c) is the correct answer.

3.) Because there can be only 1 clustered index per table, (b) is incorrect. Because there can be up to 999 Non-Clustered indexes per table, (c) is incorrect. There can be only 1 clustered index per table, however there can be up to 999 Non-Clustered indexes per table, so (a) and (d) are correct.

4.) Because there can only be 1 clustered index per table and the table already has a clustered index, answer (a) is incorrect, making (b) the correct answer.

5.) Because there can only be 1 clustered index per table and the table already has a clustered index, answer (a) is incorrect, making (b) the correct answer.

Bug Catcher Game

To play the Bug Catcher game, run the SQLQueries2012Vol3BugCatcher07.pps file from the BugCatcher folder of the companion files. These files can be obtained from the www.Joes2Pros.com website.

[THIS PAGE INTENTIONALLY LEFT BLANK.]

Chapter 8. Creating Indexes with Code

I knew a SQL Developer who was a whiz at creating indexes that really made the databases and queries he worked on purr like a kitten. His branch manager was so pleased, that he told his superiors at the main office in Toledo about how well everything worked at his branch location compared to theirs. Of course, upper management immediately requested that my friend walk their DBA through all the steps necessary to bring their databases and queries up to speed. However, my friend thought it would be too risky giving someone, even a DBA; a bunch of point-and-click instructions, as missing even one of those steps could break the performance on the entire system. Instead, he offered to create a set of T-SQL code scripts that could be sent to the SQL team in Toledo. The team could then run the scripts and get the same speedy, reliable results his branch experienced every day.

While indexes can be created by clicking through the SSMS User Interface, a best practice is to create them by running reusable code scripts. The Toledo scenario highlights the usefulness of being able to leverage code which has been validated.

This chapter will set up the same types of indexes we saw in the previous chapter by using T-SQL code, instead of the SSMS UI. Writing code for indexes and index options is what this chapter is all about.

READER NOTE: *Please run the SQLQueries2012Vol3Chapter8.0Setup.sql script in order to follow along with the examples in the first section of Chapter 8. All scripts mentioned in this chapter may be found at* www.Joes2Pros.com.

Coding Indexes

We have already practiced creating different types of indexes using the SSMS UI for the HumanResources.Contractor table. When we finished with this table it had three indexes on it, a pre-existing clustered index and the two Non-Clustered indexes that we created in the exercise.

The JProCo database also contains a table called HumanResources.Vendor, which has fields that are nearly the same as the HumanResources.Contractor table. The Vendor table also has a clustered index (Generated by the primary key constraint). We can see the layout of the two tables in Figure 8.1.

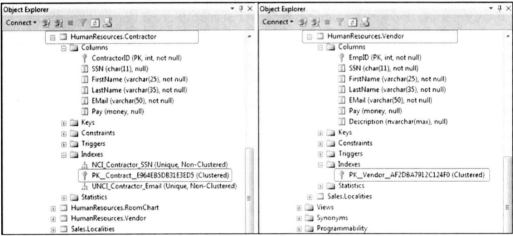

Figure 8.1 The HumanResources.Vendor table is similar to the HumanResources.Contractor table.

Non-unique Option

We will create a Non-Clustered index on SSN and a Non-Clustered index on the Email field, except this time we'll create our indexes using T-SQL code.

Let's start off by creating the NCI_Vendor_SSN Non-Clustered index for the HumanResources.Vendor table. After executing the code and refreshing the indexes folder in the Object Explorer, we will see the newly created index NCI_Vendor_SSN (Right side of Figure 8.2).

```
CREATE NONCLUSTERED INDEX NCI_Vendor_SSN
ON HumanResources.Vendor(SSN)
GO
```

There's a subtle difference between the Non-Clustered index for the SSN field index on the Contractor table (Left side of Figure 8.2) and the SSN field index on the Vendor table (Right side of Figure 8.2). Notice the distinctions between the Non-Clustered indexes for the SSN field of these two tables.

- o Contractor table: UNCI_Contractor_SSN is a *unique* Non-Clustered index.

- o Vendor table: NCI_Vendor_SSN is a *non-unique* Non-Clustered index.

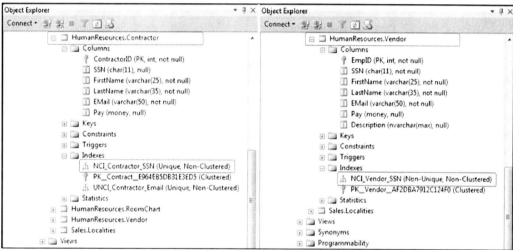

Figure 8.2 The Non-Clustered index we just created on SSN in the Vendor table is non-unique.

Unique Option

We are now going to drop the non-unique Non-Clustered index we just created, and then re-create it as a unique Non-Clustered index.

```
DROP INDEX NCI_Vendor_SSN
ON HumanResources.Vendor
GO
```

In order to create the **NCI_Vendor_SSN** as a unique Non-Clustered index it will require specifying the UNIQUE keyword right after the CREATE command.

```
CREATE UNIQUE NONCLUSTERED INDEX UNCI_Vendor_SSN
ON HumanResources.Vendor(SSN)
GO
```

READER NOTE: *Accidently, or intentionally leaving the UNIQUE keyword out of the CREATE statement will allow duplicate values in the table.*

After executing the code and refreshing the Object Explorer, we will see the UNCI_Vendor_SSN unique Non-Clustered index as shown in Figure 8.3.

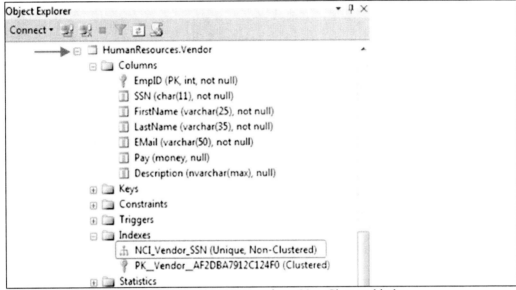

Figure 8.3 UNCI_Vendor_SSN now shows as a unique, Non-Clustered index.

Lab 8.1: Coding Indexes

Lab Prep: Each lab has one or more Skill Checks. Start with Skill Check 1 and proceed until reaching the Points to Ponder section.

Before beginning this lab, verify that SQL Server 2012 is properly installed and operating. Before running the lab setup script for resetting the database (SQLQueries2012Vol3Chapter8.1Setup.sql), please make sure to close all query windows within SSMS. An open query window pointing to a database context can lock that database preventing it from updating when the script is executing. A simple way to assure all query windows are closed, is to exit out of SSMS, then open a new instance of SSMS, and lastly run the setup script.

Skill Check 1: Using T-SQL code, create a unique Non-Clustered index named UNCI_Vendor_Email on the HumanResources.Vendor table. Once this index has been created, verify that it exists by looking in the Object Explorer. When done, the results should resemble Figure 8.4.

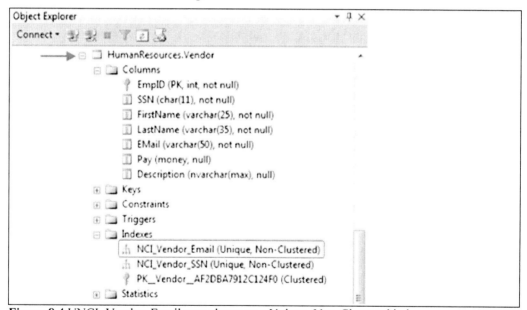

Figure 8.4 UNCI_Vendor_Email now shows as a Unique, Non-Clustered index.

Answer Code: The T-SQL code to this lab can be found in the downloadable files in a file named Lab8.1_CodingIndexes.sql.

Points to Ponder - Coding Indexes

1. There are three indexing options in SQL Server:

   1) Clustered indexes
   2) Non-Clustered indexes
   3) No indexes

2. Non-Clustered indexes can be implemented on heaps.

3. Bonus Feature: When a Primary Key is created for a table, by default, a clustered index is created on this field at the same time, unless the NONCLUSTERED argument is explicitly used.

4. Larger numbers of Non-Clustered indexes in an OLTP (acronym for **On-Line Transaction Processing**) application affect the performance of INSERT, UPDATE, and DELETE statements because all indexes must be updated as changes are made to the table.

5. Indexes can be created by using the SSMS UI or with T-SQL code.

6. The T-SQL command for creating an index is CREATE INDEX.

7. Once indexes are generated, SQL Server will update them automatically. Whenever data changes in an indexed table, the corresponding indexes are updated, as well.

Index Options

In the last section we saw that the same index, on the same table, could have been specified as unique or non-unique. Either way, a Non-Clustered index was created on the table. There are many more options for building indexes, like using multiple fields in one index as well as setting the speed and size of the indexes. This section will explore the common options that can be specified when creating an index.

In an employee table it is quite clear that a given SSN value belongs to a specific employee. For example, if 555-55-5555 belongs to Rick Morelan and he later leaves the company, then no other employee can use that number because it deterministically belongs to Rick. In fact, if Rick also works part time at the local college teaching night classes, then 555-55-5555 would have the same significance in the college's database.

How about a TerritoryID field with a value of 6? What does TerritoryID 6 mean? In one company it might be equivalent to the Central Canada territory and in another company, it could be the Midwestern United States territory.

Suppose these two companies merge, and each company has its own TerritoryID 6. There is a very real danger of duplicate values existing in the TerritoryID field with different meanings in the TerritoryName field, as shown here:

TerritoryID	TerritoryName
6	Central Canada
6	Midwestern United States

Composite Index

In most business cases, we want to avoid having duplicate records in a database. Duplicate records often cause reports for the management team to be inaccurate, which leads to poor decisions being made that can affect the entire company.

Observe that in Figure 8.5, there are six distinct cities listed. Yet, there are three cities that appear twice each (Springfield, Des Moines and Toledo). This is because Springfield, Oregon and Springfield, Michigan are two different cities. The same is true with Toledo (Oregon and Ohio) and Des Moines (Washington and Iowa).

```
SELECT * FROM Sales.Localities
```

	GeoID	State	City	Population
1	1	Oregon	Springfield	35000
2	2	Michigan	Springfield	68000
3	3	Washington	Des Moines	24000
4	4	Iowa	Des Moines	212000
5	5	Oregon	Toledo	6500
6	6	Ohio	Toledo	413000

6 rows

Figure 8.5 Six distinct states are listed, despite some cities appearing twice, in different states.

The Sales.Localities table has a unique clustered index on the GeoID field, preventing two records having a GeoID value of 6. However, this index doesn't enforce having only one combination of a City and State in the table.

We can test this by inserting a record into the Sales.Localities table containing a duplicate City and State combination of Toledo, Ohio.

```
INSERT INTO Sales.Localities VALUES
('Ohio','Toledo',45000)
```

By running a simple query, we can see there are now three records listing Toledo as a City, with GeoID 6 and GeoID 7 (new record) both located in the State of Ohio, causing the duplicate records highlighted in Figure 8.6.

```
SELECT * FROM Sales.Localities
```

	GeoID	State	City	Population
5	5	Oregon	Toledo	6500
6	6	Ohio	Toledo	413000
7	7	Ohio	Toledo	45000

7 rows

Figure 8.6 No rules prevent Toledo, Ohio inserted twice with two different GeoID values.

To undo our previous insert action that created GeoID 7, we will need to run a reset script for this table, **SQLQueries2012Vol3Chapter8SpecialReset.sql** located in the LabSetupFiles folder. Once that's done, the Sales.Localities table will have the same structure and records that we began this exercise with. This table is vulnerable to future City/State duplicate combinations, so we must take steps to ensure that such duplications are prevented in the future.

In order to formulate an indexing plan, we need to first understand the combination of fields in our data which constitute uniqueness. So what is unique about cities in the United States?

Well, a city name may exist only once per state – that is to say, two cities in one state are not permitted to have the same name. It is legal to have a Springfield, Oregon and a Springfield, Michigan, however, it is not possible to have two cities named Springfield within a single state.

Can we prevent the duplicate City/State combinations by creating a unique Non-Clustered index on the City name? No, if we were to create this index based only on the City name, it would not allow the GeoID 2 record of Springfield, Michigan to exist, as GeoID 1 of Springfield, Oregon is already in the table. So, we cannot achieve our goal by simply locking down the City field.

Can we prevent the duplicate City/State combinations by creating a unique Non-Clustered index on the State name? No, if we were to create this index based only on the State name, it would not allow for more than one City to be entered for the same State. In other words, the table would never be able to have more than 50 records, since each State could only appear once in the table. So, we cannot achieve our goal by simply locking down the State field.

It looks like we will need an index combining these two restrictions together.

Coding Unique Composite Index

A **composite index** combines multiple fields together as part of one index. These combined fields will create a constraint where only one combination of the fields is allowed in a table. Subsequent attempts to add duplicate instances of this same combination into the table will be prevented by the index.

Great! We can meet our goal of preventing duplicate records formed by entering the same City/State combination into the table more than once by creating a composite index for the Sales.Localities table. A composite index will give the table data integrity, while also allowing cities with the same name, although in different states, to appear in the Sales.Localities table.

Let's create a unique Non-Clustered index named UNCI_Localities_CityState with the following code. Notice that there are two fields (City, [State]) listed for the Sales.Localities table in the ON clause. By listing multiple fields, we have created a *composite index*.

```
CREATE UNIQUE NONCLUSTERED INDEX UNCI_Localities_CityState
ON Sales.Localities(City,[State])
GO
```

Verify that the new unique Non-Clustered index, UNCI_Localities_CityState, has been created by using the Object Explorer. The results should resemble Figure 8.7.

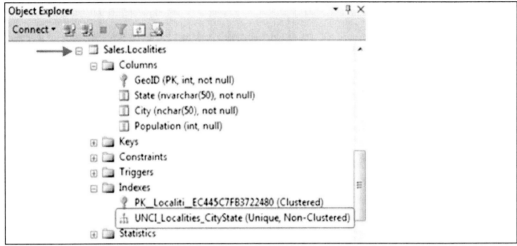

Figure 8.7 Verifying the UNCI_Localities_CityState composite index has been created.

We can test our new composite index by attempting to insert a duplicate record for Toledo, OH into the Sales.Localities table. The error message shown in Figure 8.8 confirms the UNCI_Localities_CityState composite index is working.

```
INSERT INTO Sales.Localities VALUES
('Ohio','Toledo',45000)
```

```
Messages
Msg 2601, Level 14, State 1, Line 1
Cannot insert duplicate key row in object 'Sales.Localities' with unique index
'UNCI_Localities_CityState'. The duplicate key value is (Toledo, Ohio).
                                                                    0 rows
```

Figure 8.8 We are testing our new composite index by attempting to insert a duplicate record.

A composite index uses two or more fields added together as one larger field. This concatenation of fields makes the composite index use more space than an index on a single field, although it does have some performance benefits. For example, the following query is faster, thanks to our composite index UNCI_Localities_CityState.

```
SELECT City, [State]
FROM Sales.Localities
WHERE City = 'Toledo'
```

The query runs faster, because the index helps the WHERE clause find the city named Toledo much easier. This query must display data from the City and State fields, which it can now access directly from the composite index. Since all the data needed for the query is already contained in the index, there is no need for the SELECT statement to look for data in the table. If the query contained one more field, additional I/O would likely cause a need to access the table as well.

Indexes With Included Columns

We've learned that an index will help the efficiency of the WHERE clause, and that the SELECT statement often gets data directly from the index location. If one more field were added to the SELECT statement above, we must re-create the index to include the additional field. However, this can become problematic because the index creation will require more processing time as each combination of fields must be maintained. An **INCLUDE option** can help our dilemma, by allowing us to effectively add more fields (i.e., non-key columns) to a Non-Clustered index while only requiring one of the fields to be part of the actual key calculation.

This strategy works particularly well when the query contains a field used in the Non-Clustered index, and the WHERE clause predicates on this same field. In our last example, we will discover how an INCLUDE option extends the functionality of an index and brings along the other fields named in our SELECT query.

Recall that we added a unique Non-Clustered index on the SSN field of the Contractor table. We found that creating Non-Clustered indexes can help us when querying data and that indexes can also enforce uniqueness of certain fields. In the case of the SSN field, it can do both.

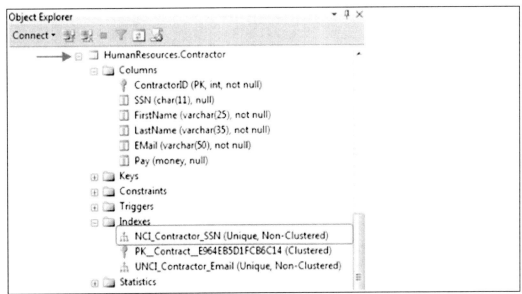

Figure 8.9 Non-Clustered Indexes can aid in queries and enforce uniqueness of certain fields.

In the following query shown, the WHERE clause finds the SSN value in the Non-Clustered index. Since the SELECT list wants only this value, there is no need to look up the corresponding values in the clustered index. When all of the required fields are in the Non-Clustered index, then an Index Seek will be performed, as shown in the Execution Plan (Figure 8.10).

```
SELECT SSN
FROM HumanResources.Contractor
WHERE SSN = '222-22-2222'
```

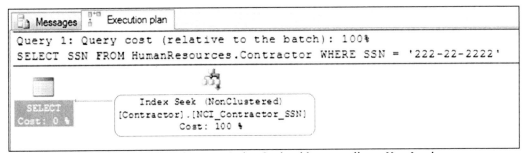

Figure 8.10 The Execution Plan shows an Index Seek without needing a Key Lookup.

The following query will run slower, as not all of the required fields in the SELECT list (FirstName, LastName) are part of the Non-Clustered index. Since the data for the FirstName and LastName fields is found in the same row (they belong to the same contractor), it can be accessed by the Key value from the clustered index and has only a small impact on performance (Figure 8.11).

```
SELECT SSN, FirstName, LastName
FROM HumanResources.Contractor
WHERE SSN = '222-22-2222'
```

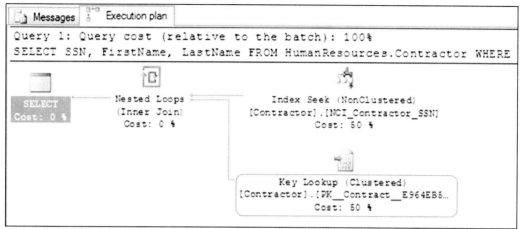

Figure 8.11 This query runs slightly slower, because the SELECT list has fields which are not part of the Non-Clustered index and thus requires a Key Lookup to the clustered index.

What is happening internally with the SQL Server Query Optimizer to have two queries with the same predicate run with different Execution Plans? Let's look at the first two steps of the query Execution Plan from Figure 8.11 to find out how SQL Server searches for records.

When we examine the UNCI_Contractor_SSN unique Non-Clustered index a little closer, we see that it is indexed on the SSN column. When this index is created or modified, it will contain all the data in each row for the SSN column. Since there is also a clustered index (PK_Contract_*identifier*) on this table, it will also contain all the Key values that match each SSN value stored in the index.

Think of a Non-Clustered index as a copy of the table's records but with only a few fields. Look at the sample table (Figure 8.12) to help visualize what data is stored inside the UNCI_Contractor_SSN unique Non-Clustered index when it is created.

| UNCI_Contractor_SSN (unique Non-Clustered index) ||
SSN	ContractorID
222-22-2222	1
444-44-4444	6
555-55-5555	4
656-66-6767	2
888-88-8888	3
999-99-9999	5

Figure 8.12 The UNCI_Contractor_SSN index stores data when it is created.

The index looks like a table with two columns physically ordered by the SSN value (first column) and also contains the Key value (ContractorID) associated with each SSN value along with it (Second column).

We can glimpse into how the SQL Server Query Optimizer performs its search to retrieve the data requested in a query shown in Figure 8.13. Let's follow along...

The first part of the query to be examined is the FROM clause, which tells the Query Optimizer what table to begin looking for data in, as well as any additional configuration metadata that is associated with the table, such as indexes, views, security, etc.

The next part of the query to be examined is the WHERE clause. Here the Query Optimizer finds the search is predicated on the SSN field with a value equal to '555-55-5555'. Since the Query Optimizer already knows UNCI_Contractor_SSN is indexed on the SSN field it immediately moves from the table to the data stored in this index. Finding the value it is looking for in the third row, it checks for the Key value stored in the adjacent column which is ContractorID 4.

Immediately after finding the Key value associated with the SSN, the Query Optimizer shifts its focus to the data stored in the PK_Contractor clustered index. Finding the Key value of 4 in the fourth row of the index, the Query Optimizer can now begin to extract the values for the fields required by the SELECT statement (SSN, FirstName, LastName). In this case, all of the necessary data for the query was stored in the two indexes and the Query Optimizer returns the data it has retrieved to the requesting service.

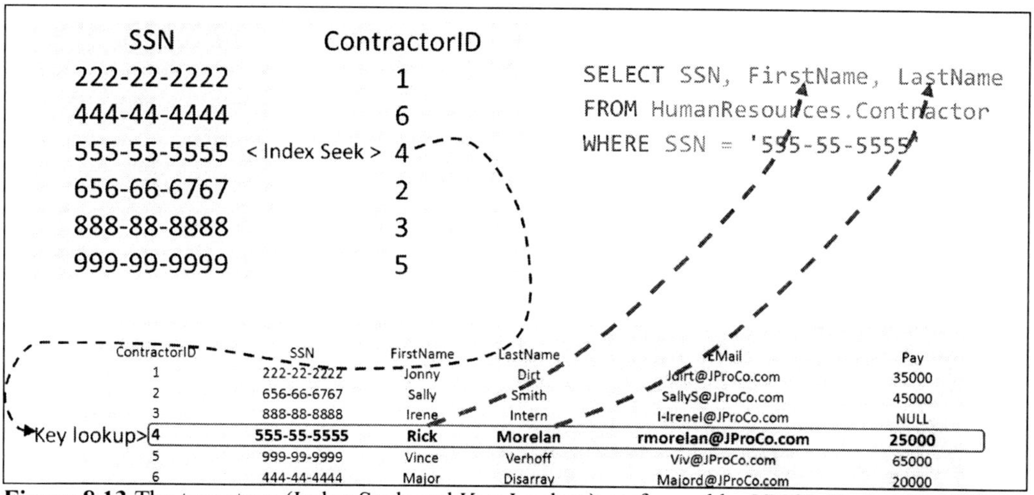

Figure 8.13 The two steps (Index Seek and Key Lookup) performed by UNCI_Contractor_SSN.

The next query example, shown in Figure 8.14 is faster as the Query Optimizer will only need to make one hop to retrieve the data it is searching for. As always, the Query Optimizer begins searching with the FROM clause, to learn what table to look in, plus any indexes associated with the table. The Query Optimizer then looks at the WHERE clause predicate. Since the Query Optimizer already knows UNCI_Contractor_SSN is indexed on the SSN field it immediately moves from the table to the data stored in this index. Finding the value (555-55-5555) it is looking for stored in the third row, it moves on to the last step of retrieving the only field required by the SELECT statement (SSN), passing this to the requesting service.

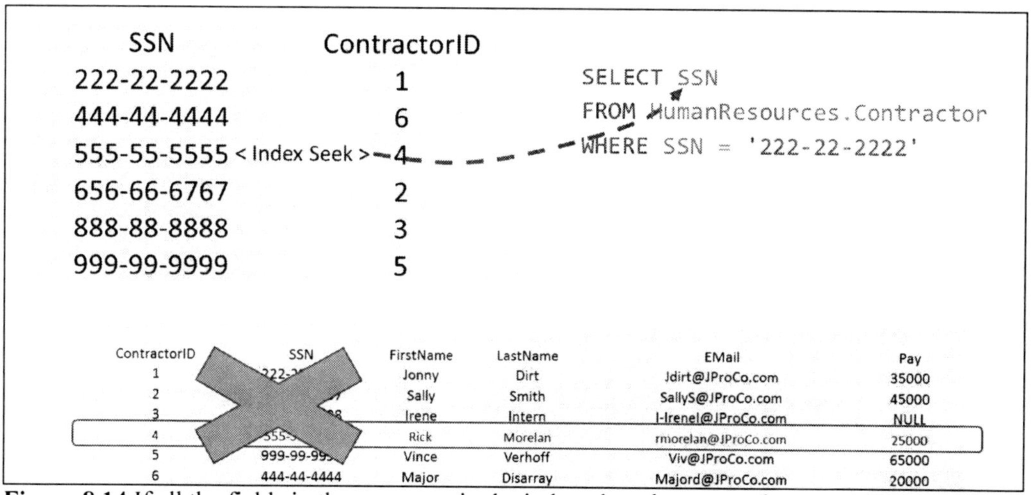

Figure 8.14 If all the fields in the query are in the index, then the query plan runs with one step.

Our last example, illustrated in Figure 8.15, is for a frequently run query with three fields required in the SELECT statement, one of which is not covered by an index (FirstName). It is possible to achieve a gain in performance by placing all three of these fields into a composite index, even though the FirstName field will not add anything more to the uniqueness of the index. Since this breaks one of the fundamental rules for building an index (uniqueness), it will also increase the storage overhead by containing more data than necessary to optimize the query.

Implementing the INCLUDE option offers an even better approach, keeping the storage overhead for the index small, while still having the non-indexed fields perform very rapidly when retrieved during the SELECT statement.

By supplying the FirstName field as the focus of the INCLUDE clause in the CREATE INDEX statement, the UNCI_Contractor_SSN index will have three fields supplied to the covered query, enabling it to avoid performing a Key Lookup.

```
CREATE INDEX UNCI_Employee_SSN
ON HumanResources.Contractor(SSN) INCLUDE(FirstName)
GO
```

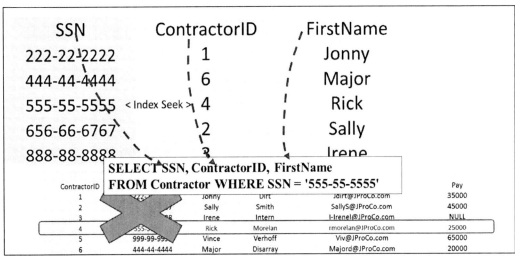

Figure 8.15 Including the FirstName field for the UNCI_Contractor_SSN index gives three fields to supply the covered query without needing to do a Key Lookup.

If the services running the query above began to heavily include the LastName field in the SELECT statement in addition to the original three fields, we can add this as a non-key field along with the FirstName field. To modify a Non-Clustered index, it must be dropped and then re-created with the syntax for INCLUDE:

```
DROP INDEX UNCI_Employee_SSN
ON HumanResources.Contractor
GO
```

We can now run the following code to re-create the Non-Clustered index, which will now include two non-key columns (FirstName, LastName) along with the index (SSN) in order to improve query performance:

```
CREATE UNIQUE INDEX UNCI_Employee_SSN
ON HumanResources.Contractor(SSN)
INCLUDE(FirstName, LastName)
GO
```

Verify the index is created in the Object Explorer and then double-click on the index to open the Index Properties dialog window. Next, we can click on the 'Included columns' tab, to see that the FirstName and LastName columns are now part of the configuration for this index (Figure 8.16). Click 'Ok' to close the Index Properties dialog window to complete this part of the exercise.

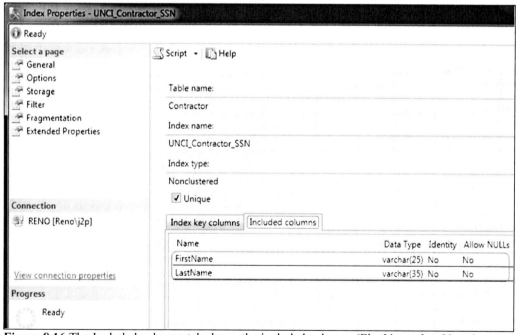

Figure 8.16 The Included columns tab shows the included columns (FirstName, LastName).

ONLINE Option With Indexes

How long it takes to build a new index depends on how much data is in the table at the time it is created. It could take a fraction of a second or sometimes it could take several hours. During that time, the table is offline and not able to handle any requests. At least, that was true for SQL Server 2000 and earlier versions.

Would a business owner be happy if a table is offline while an index is being created and built? If so, that's great, because once the index is built, queries will run much faster.

Beginning with SQL Server 2005 and continuing to the current version, SQL developers now have the option to keep a table online and available to users during index creation. The creation step takes a bit longer to accomplish this flexibility, however, it's a worthwhile tradeoff because the table will have zero downtime.

Creating an index on a table normally brings the table offline while the index is created. In this chapter, the indexes we've built/dropped/re-created have all been on small tables. Thus, these tables were down for only a fraction of a second, which really didn't cause any disruption.

Suppose the HumanResources.Contractor table had a million, or more, records. We're planning some index maintenance or creations, which would bring the table down for a few minutes (If not longer). Suppose this is a table that is used in such a high volume, that we cannot afford to have it unavailable to our customers, not even for a second. The ONLINE = ON option can help keep the table online during the creation process for the index.

Let's drop the current index, and then re-create it with absolutely zero downtime.

```
DROP INDEX UNCI_Contractor_SSN
ON JProCo.HumanResources.Contractor
GO

CREATE UNIQUE INDEX UNCI_Contractor_SSN
ON HumanResources.Contractor(SSN)
INCLUDE(FirstName, LastName)
WITH(ONLINE=ON)
GO
```

We can see the index re-created in Object Explorer and in the Index Properties dialog window. Everything appears identical to our previous creation of this index when we introduced the included columns. The ONLINE option helped to re-create everything and kept the table available, just as we expected.

Covered Query vs. Covering Index

Sometimes the term 'covered query' is used to indicate a query has a 'covering index' on it. 'Covered queries' and 'covering indexes' are closely related concepts, but they are not the same thing. A 'covered query' occurs when every column used in a query is covered by one or more indexes. This includes every column in the SELECT list, as well as every column in the WHERE clause. A 'covering index' is where the needed data is found more quickly through pointers from the Non-Clustered index to the data in the cluster.

Filtered Index

This is a feature introduced with SQL Server 2008 and it is great for those cases when a large number of NULLs appear, and the goal is to only index the actual data (i.e., the non-NULL data).

We know that indexes perform at their best when they're on a field which contains highly selective data. Selectivity is one of the measures SQL Server uses to determine which index to use, or whether it should ignore an index(es).

Is the CompanyName field in the Customer table (Figure 8.17) highly selective?

```
SELECT * FROM dbo.Customer
```

	CustomerID	CustomerType	FirstName	LastName	CompanyName
3	3	Consumer	Patricia	Martin	NULL
4	4	Consumer	Mary	Lopez	NULL
5	5	Business	NULL	NULL	MoreTechnology.com
6	6	Consumer	Ruth	Clark	NULL
7	7	Consumer	Tessa	Wright	NULL

775 rows

Figure 8.17 CompanyName is highly selective on values that are not NULL.

In the CompanyName field, 773 of 775 records are the same – that is to say they are NULLs. So as a whole, having only three different values out of 775 records (i.e., NULL, MoreTechnology.com, and Puma Consulting) is *not selective*. The data in the CustomerType field relates to the data in CompanyName and thus, has low selectivity (i.e., 773 of 775 records have a value of 'Consumer').

An argument could be made that the non-NULL CompanyName values are actually unique and thus highly selective. Since most of the values are NULLs, we don't tend to predicate on CompanyName. We would only predicate on CompanyName when we query the dbo.Customer table for a specific company.

The following code predicates on the CompanyName, searching for a company called MoreTechnology.com (One of the two non-NULL values in this column).

```
SELECT *
FROM dbo.Customer
WHERE CompanyName = 'MoreTechnology.com'
```

	CustomerID	CustomerType	FirstName	LastName	CompanyName
1	5	Business	NULL	NULL	MoreTechnology.com

1 rows

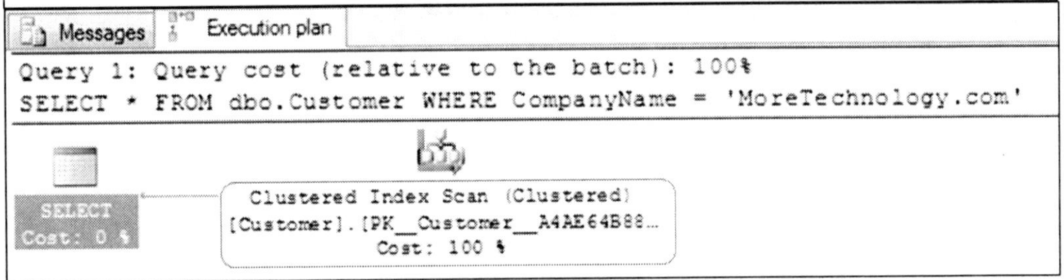

Messages   Execution plan

```
Query 1: Query cost (relative to the batch): 100%
SELECT * FROM dbo.Customer WHERE CompanyName = 'MoreTechnology.com'
```

SELECT
Cost: 0 %

Clustered Index Scan (Clustered)
[Customer].[PK__Customer__A4AE64B88...
Cost: 100 %

Figure 8.18 A query filtering on the CompanyName field looks for 'MoreTechnology.com'.

Look at the Execution Plan of the query again. Notice that the query performs an index scan to locate the row. Ideally, we want to add a Non-Clustered index based on the CompanyName field and instruct the index to only populate its table with data from the field with a value (Ignore NULL values). The benefit of a filtered index is that we can now add criteria during the creation process.

How do we turn a non-selective field like CompanyName into a selective one? We recognize there are very few non-NULL values in the field and create an index filter to remove them. Thus, every record will be unique, which is extremely selective!

```
CREATE NONCLUSTERED INDEX NCI_Customer_CompanyName
ON dbo.Customer(CompanyName)
INCLUDE(CustomerType)
WHERE CompanyName IS NOT NULL
GO
```

Use the Object Explorer to verify that the NCI_Customer_CompanyName index has been created. Then double-click on the index name to open the Index Properties dialog window (Figure 8.19). Once the Index Properties dialog window is open, left-click on Filter in the 'Select a page' pane in the upper left portion of the window. The expression we used for this index is shown here in Figure 8.20.

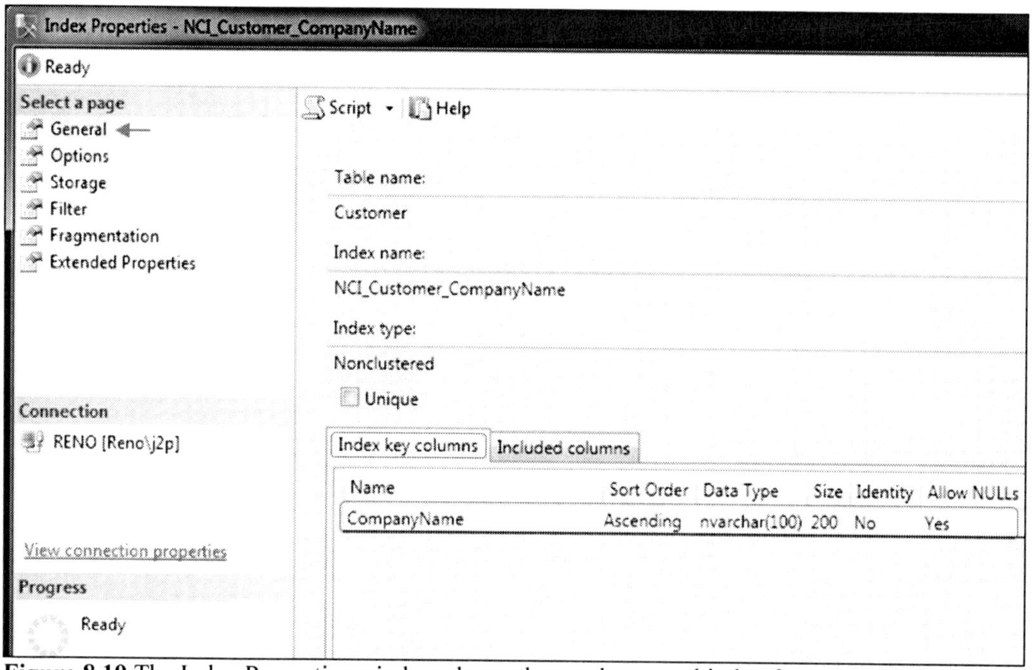

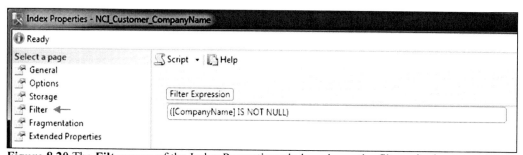

Figure 8.19 The Index Properties window shows the newly created index for CompanyName.

Figure 8.20 The **Filter** page of the Index Properties window shows the filter criteria we specified.

The Execution Plan for the following query is predicating on the CompanyName field and searching for any values equal to MoreTechnology.com. Recall, that before we created the NCI_Customer_CompanyName filtered index, this same query resulted in a slow and tedious Index Scan, (Figure 8.18) having to look at all 775 records to find the one record equal to MoreTechnology.com.

After creating the NCI_Customer_CompanyName filtered index, the Execution Plan shows the query performing a much faster Index Seek, with a Key Lookup (Figure 8.21).

```
SELECT * FROM dbo.Customer
WHERE CompanyName = 'MoreTechnology.com'
```

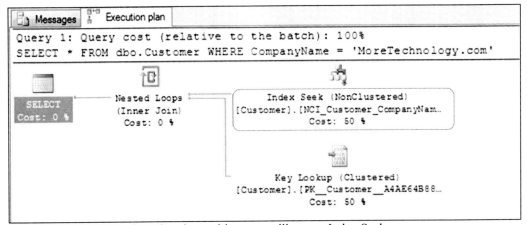

Figure 8.21 The Execution Plan shows this query will use an Index Seek.

Lab 8.2: Index Options

Lab Prep: Each lab has one or more Skill Checks. Start with Skill Check 1 and proceed until reaching the Points to Ponder section.

Before beginning this lab, verify that SQL Server 2012 is properly installed and operating. Before running the lab setup script for resetting the database (SQLQueries2012Vol3Chapter8.2Setup.sql), please make sure to close all query windows within SSMS. An open query window pointing to a database context can lock that database preventing it from updating when the script is executing. A simple way to assure all query windows are closed, is to exit out of SSMS, then open a new instance of SSMS, and lastly run the setup script.

Skill Check 1: In the JProCo database context, create a unique Non-Clustered composite index named UNCI_Employee_FirstNameLastName for the Employee table. This index should enforce a rule that two employees cannot have the same first and last names. Verify the index has been created using the Object Explorer. When done, the results should resemble Figure 8.22.

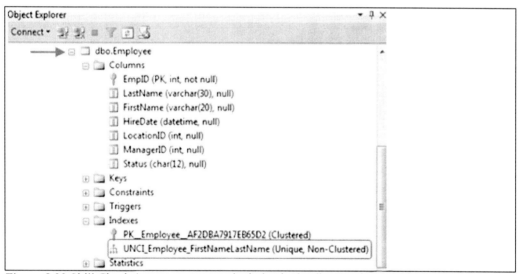

Figure 8.22 Skill Check 1 creates a composite index in the dbo.Employee table.

Skill Check 2: In the JProCo database context, create a unique Non-Clustered composite index named UNCI_Vendor_SSN for the HumanResources.Vendor table. Ensure that the Vendor table is optimized for the type of query shown in the following code (all the data is accessed directly from the index) In addition, the table must remain online while the index is being created.

```
SELECT *
FROM HumanResources.Vendor
WHERE SSN = '321-22-2222'
```

READER NOTE: *Since the UNCI_Vendor_SSN index already exists from an earlier example, it will be necessary to drop the index before re-creating it to meet the requirements for Skill Check 1.*

Verify the index has been created using the Object Explorer. When done, the results should resemble Figure 8.23.

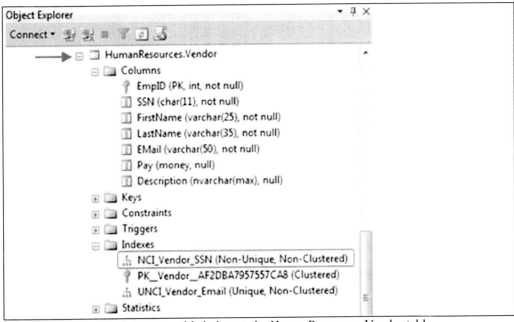

Figure 8.23 Skill Check 2 creates this index on the HumanResources.Vendor table.

Skill Check 3: In the JProCo database context, create a unique Non-Clustered composite index named NCI_SalesInvoiceDetail_UnitDiscount for the dbo.SalesInvoiceDetail table. The UnitDiscount field should not allow any values that are equal to zero. Verify the index has been created using the Object Explorer. When done, the results should resemble Figure 8.24.

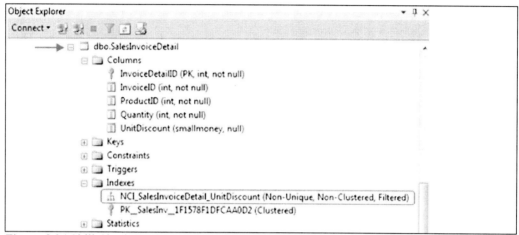

Figure 8.24 Skill Check 3 creates the index shown here in the dbo.SalesInvoiceDetail table.

Answer Code: The T-SQL code to this lab can be found in the downloadable files in a file named Lab8.2_IndexOptions.sql.

Points to Ponder - Index Options

1.   A composite index specifies more than one column as the key value.

2.   Composite index key limitations are:
    - o   Maximum 16 columns.
    - o   Maximum 900 bytes.
    - o   Columns must be in the same table or view.

3.   The order in which a composite key is created matters. For example, if most searches were made on the City field, then a City/State index would help performance whereas a State/City index would not.

4.   When creating a composite index, the first column defined should be the most unique.

5.   An INSERT operation processes many rows at once, and if any of them violates the unique constraint, all are rolled back and no inserts are made.

6.   To make violating inserts fail and the remaining inserts succeed, then set the IGNORE_DUP_KEY to ON in the CREATE INDEX statement.

7.   IGNORE_DUP_KEY causes only the violating rows to fail.

8.   The syntax for IGNORE_DUP_KEY places it in the WITH (options) section of the statement: WITH (IGNORE_DUP_KEY = ON)

9.   When creating a unique index on a table that already contains data, SQL Server will first validate that there are no existing duplicate values.

10.   Introduced with SQL Server 2005, the WITH (ONLINE = ON) is an option of the CREATE INDEX command, working only in the Enterprise edition. When using this option, queries and other indexes can still access the underlying table while the index creation operation is in progress.

11.   The sp_helpindex system stored procedure returns details of the indexes created for the specified table.

```
EXEC sp_helpindex [HumanResources.Vendor]
```

12.   Filtered Indexes allow additional criteria when the index is created.

Chapter Glossary

Coding Indexes: Using code to create an index.

Composite Index: A composite index is where multiple fields are included as part of one index.

Covering Index: A 'covering index' is where the needed data is found more quickly through pointers from the Non-Clustered index to the data in the cluster.

Filtered Index: This is a feature introduced in SQL Server 2008 and it is great if a large number of NULLs appear, yet you only want to index the real data.

IGNORE_DUP_KEY: When you use **WITH (IGNORE_DUP_KEY = ON)** this causes only the violating rows to fail.

INCLUDE: To add more fields to your index while only requiring one of the fields to be part of the index calculation you can use the INCLUDE option.

Included Columns: The additional non-key fields added to your Non-Clustered index through use of the INCLUDE option. Because SQL Server doesn't include these fields in the calculation of the index, included columns can help you bypass the limitation on size and number of columns permitted in an index (900 bytes, 16 columns).

Index Options: There are various options available to enhance performance and functionality of an index, such as using multiple fields in one index, or setting the speed and size of the indexes.

ONLINE Option: Introduced with SQL Server 2005, the WITH (ONLINE = ON) is an option of the CREATE INDEX command, working only in the Enterprise edition. When using this option, queries and other indexes can still access the underlying table while the index creation operation is in progress.

OLAP: Acronym for **O**nline **A**nalytical **P**rocessing. This refers to a system which is geared toward reporting reliable data. This type of system is not updated in real-time (i.e., OLTP), instead it emphasizes efficiency, speed of data retrieval and report building.

OLTP: Acronym for **O**nline **T**ransaction **P**rocessing. This refers to a system which continuously performs numerous transactions. The design and performance of such systems are geared toward accommodating many transactions per second.

Review Quiz - Chapter Eight

1.) You work with a SQL Server 2012 database named FASTDB. Table1 is a very large table that is used frequently. You discover a table scan when looking at the Execution Plan for Table1 and the query contains the following statement:

```
SELECT Col1, Col2
FROM Table1
WHERE Col3 = <value>
```

You need to provide maximum query performance and Table1 must remain available to connections at all times. What should you do?

O a. Implement horizontal partitioning.

O b. Update all statistics on Table1 in FASTDB.

O c. Use the CREATE STATISTICS statement in FASTDB to create missing statistics on Col3 of Table1.

O d. Set the priority boost server option to 1.

O e. Execute the following statement:

```
CREATE INDEX Index1 ON Table1(Col3)
INCLUDE(Col1,Col2) WITH(ONLINE=ON)
```

O f. Execute the following statement:

```
CREATE INDEX Index1 ON Table1(Col3)
```

2.) You work with a database named JProCo on a SQL Server 2012 machine. You discover poor query performance on the Employee table for a selective query that uses the SSN field. A clustered index already exists based on the EmployeeID field. You need to provide maximum query performance and keep the table available to users at all times. What should you do?

O a. Update all statistics on the Employee table.

O b. Use the CREATE STATISTICS statement in your JProCo database.

O c. Set the priority boost server option to 1.

O d. Execute the following statement:

```
CREATE INDEX IX_1 ON Employee(SSN)
```

O e. Execute the following statement:

```
CREATE INDEX IX_1 ON Employee(SSN) WITH(ONLINE=ON)
```

3.) You have a database with a 15GB table named dbo.SalesInvoice. This dbo.SalesInvoice table gets a lot of updates and inserts. You discover that excessive fragmentation is caused by frequent page splits. You have plenty of extra space in your data files if you need it. What code should you run to reduce the page splits?

O a. `ALTER TABLE dbo.SalesInvoice`
`ADD PageComment VARCHAR(50) NULL`

O b. `EXEC sp_helptext dbo.SalesInvoice`

O c. `ALTER INDEX ALL ON dbo.SalesInvoice`
`REBUILD WITH(FILL FACTOR = 50)`

O d. `UPDATE TABLE dbo.SalesInvoice`
`SET FILLFACTOR = 50 WHERE FILLFACTOR = 100`

4.) You have a field in the Employee table named Gender which is either M or F. You have over 1000 records in the employee table, with a clustered index based on EmpID. You often query the Employee table with the following criteria: WHERE Gender = 'M'. What should your index scheme be for the Gender Field?

O a. There should be no index based on this field.

O b. There should be a clustered index based on this field.

O c. There should be a Non-Clustered index based on this field.

O d. There should be a default index based on this field.

O e. There should be a GEOMETRY data type in this field.

5.) You have a field in your Employee table named HireDate which is not NULL. You have over 1000 records in your Employee table and 995 distinct hire dates. The clustered index is based on EmpID. You often query the Employee table with specific criteria like the following:

`WHERE HireDate = '1/1/2005'`

What should your index scheme be for the HireDate field?

O a. There should be no index based on this field.

O b. There should be a clustered index based on this field.

O c. There should be a Non-Clustered index based on this field.

O d. There should be a default index based on this field.

O e. There should be a GEOMETRY data type in this field.

6.) You have a field in your Employee table named HireDate which is not NULL and highly selective, as almost everyone has their own HireDate different from other employees. You have a field called Gender which is not very selective. Your primary key is a composite of FirstName and LastName. You want to optimize the index of the following query:

```
SELECT FirstName, LastName, HireDate, Gender
FROM Employee WHERE HireDate = '1/1/2005'
```

Currently the only index is a clustered index. What index strategy would optimize this query?

O a. Create a Non-Clustered index based on HireDate and INCLUDE (Gender).

O b. Create a Non-Clustered index based on Gender and INCLUDE (HireDate).

7.) Your employee table has 10,000 records. The EmpID field is the field the clustered index is based on. There are no other indexes. The SSN field has no index but all the values for each employee are different. The FirstName and LastName fields have many repeating names. The following query is run very often:

```
SELECT EmpID, SSN, FirstName, LastName
FROM Employee WHERE SSN = '555-55-5555'
```

What code will create a Non-Clustered index to optimize this query.

O a. Create a Non-Clustered index based on FirstName and Include (LastName, SSN).

O b. Create a Non-Clustered index based on LastName and Include (FirstName, SSN).

O c. Create a Non-Clustered index based on SSN and Include (FirstName, LastName).

O d. Create a composite Non-Clustered index based on (FirstName, LastName) and Include (SSN).

8.) You work with a database named JPRO1, which is located on a machine running SQL Server 2012. You discover that a table scan on CustPurchase in JPRO1 causes a slow query. CustPurchase is a very large table that is used frequently. The query contains the following statement:

```
SELECT RepID, CouponCode
FROM CustPurchase
WHERE ShoppingCartID = <value>
```

You need to provide maximum query performance. CustPurchase must remain available to users at all times. What should you do?

O a. Update all statistics on CustPurchase in JPRO1.

O b. Use the CREATE statistics statement in JPRO1 to create missing statistics on ShoppingCartID of CustPurchase.

O c. Set the priority boost server option to 1.

O d. Execute the following statement:

```
CREATE INDEX Index1 ON CustPurchase(ShoppingCartID)
INCLUDE(RepID, CouponCode) WITH(ONLINE=ON) GO
```

O e. Execute the following statement:

```
CREATE INDEX Index1
ON CustPurchase(ShoppingCartID ,CouponCode, RepID)
```

9.) You have an employee table with over 100,000 records. The employee table has the following definition:

```
CREATE TABLE Employee (
EmpID INT PRIMARY KEY CLUSTERED,
LastName VARCHAR(30) NULL,
FirstName VARCHAR(20) NULL,
HireDate DATETIME NULL,
LocationID INT NULL,
Gender CHAR(1) NULL)
GO
```

The following query really needs to be optimized:

```
SELECT EmpID, LocationID, HireDate, Gender
FROM Employee
WHERE HireDate IS NOT NULL
AND LocationID IS NOT NULL
```

What Non-Clustered index scheme will optimize this query while taking a minimum amount of disk space?

O a. `CREATE NONCLUSTERED INDEX NCI_Emp`
   `ON dbo.Employee(Gender) INCLUDE(HireDate, LocationID)`

O b. `CREATE NONCLUSTERED INDEX NCI_Emp`
   `ON dbo.Employee(HireDate, LocationID, Gender)`

O c. `CREATE NONCLUSTERED INDEX NCI_Emp`
   `ON dbo.Employee(HireDate) INCLUDE(LocationID)`

O d. `CREATE NONCLUSTERED INDEX NCI_Emp`
   `ON dbo.Employee(HireDate, LocationID) INCLUDE(Gender)`

10.) You have a SalesInvoice table with the following structure:

```
CREATE TABLE dbo.SalesInvoice (
InvoiceID INT NOT NULL PRIMARY KEY CLUSTERED,
OrderDate DATETIME NOT NULL,
PaidDate DATETIME NOT NULL,
FeedBackDate Date DATETIME NULL,
RepID INT NULL,
CustomerID INT NOT NULL)
GO
```

There are over 100 million records in this table. Most people don't bother to leave feedback, so over 99% of the records have NULL for the FeedBackDate. Orders are done online with the assistance of a representative less than 5% of the time, so 95% of the records have a NULL value for RepID. You want to create a Non-Clustered index to optimize the following query:

```
SELECT InvoiceID, FeedBackDate, RepID
FROM dbo.SalesInvoice
WHERE FeedBackDate IS NOT NULL
AND RepID IS NOT NULL
```

How do you set up the Non-Clustered index?

O a. Update all statistics on Table1.

O b.
```
CREATE NONCLUSTERED INDEX NCI_1
ON dbo.SalesInvoice(FeedBackDate, RepID)
INCLUDE(InvoiceID)
```

O c.
```
CREATE NONCLUSTERED INDEX NCI_1
ON dbo.SalesInvoice(InvoiceID)
INCLUDE(FeedBackDate, RepID)
WHERE RepID IS NOT NULL
```

O d.
```
CREATE NONCLUSTERED INDEX NCI_1
ON dbo.SalesInvoice(FeedBackDate, RepID)
INCLUDE(InvoiceID)
WHERE RepID IS NOT NULL
```

11.) You have a stored procedure that selects the AccountNumber, Country, and StateProvince fields from the dbo.Members table of dbBasics. The sproc accepts a parameter to predicate on the AccountNumber field. You have the following query:

```
SELECT AccountNumber, Country, StateProvince
FROM dbo.Members
WHERE AccountNumber = 5
```

By creating a new index you need to optimize the performance of the stored procedure to create a covered query with all fields included. Which T-SQL statement should you use?

O a. ```
     CREATE CLUSTERED INDEX IX_Customer_AccountNumber
        ON dbo.Customer(AccountNumber);
     ```

O b. ```
     CREATE NONCLUSTERED INDEX IX_Customer_AccountNumber
        ON dbo.Customer(AccountNumber)
        INCLUDE(AccountNumber);
     ```

O c. ```
     CREATE NONCLUSTERED INDEX IX_Customer_AccountNumber
        ON dbo.Customer(AccountNumber)
        INCLUDE(Country, StateProvince);
     ```

# Answer Key

**1.)** The fastest way to get an index to cover a query is to put all the data needed by the query inside the index itself. Both (e) and (f) do this but (f) is wrong because it is only predicating for Col3. Since (e) makes a composite index and uses the ONLINE option it is the correct answer.

**2.)** Creating indexes brings the table down for a short period of time, making (d) incorrect. Using the ONLINE = ON option will take more time to create the index, however, the table will be available to users at all times, so (e) is the correct answer.

**3.)** Changing an existing object will require using the ALTER keyword, so (b) and (d) are incorrect. Since we don't want to add a new field (a) is wrong. The correct answer is (c).

**4.)** Indexes only help performance if the field is selective and unique. Having only 'M' or 'F' in 1000 records means an index cannot help, so (b), (c), and (d) are wrong. It is unnecessary to create a spatial type, so (e) is wrong. There isn't a need to create an index on a field with low selectivity, so (a) is correct.
     ```

5.) Any field with highly selective values will benefit from an index, so (a), (d), and (e) are wrong. Both (b) and (c) sound good but there cannot be two clustered indexes on a table and one already exists, so (b) is wrong. The correct answer is to create a Non-Clustered index, so (c) is correct.

6.) Since we are searching for HireDate we don't want to base the index on Gender, so (b) is wrong. A Non-Clustered index contains the field listed plus the clustered index. Since we want the index on HireDate and the clustered index is on two fields, there will be three fields in this index. The FirstName, LastName, and HireDate fields will be in the index already. The SELECT list also wants gender to be included, so (a) is correct.

7.) Since the WHERE clause is on SSN we need to base it on SSN, so (a), (b), and (d) are incorrect. If we create a Non-Clustered index on SSN and the clustered index is on EmpID, then the Non-Clustered index will have both fields (EmpID and SSN) and it only needs to have FirstName and LastName included. Since (c) includes FirstName and LastName, we get all fields covered, so (c) is the right answer.

8.) Our query is looking for a ShoppingCartID so we need to base the index off of that alone, so (e) is wrong. We can simply include the fields we want, making (d) correct.

9.) We have four fields in our query and if we base the index off of HireDate and LocationID then we will have those two fields plus the cluster of EmpID already in the index. The only field we need to include would be Gender, so (d) is the correct answer.

10.) Since the RepID is almost always a NULL, we need to filter on that, making (a) and (b) wrong since they don't do that at all. The remaining indexes cover the query pretty well, but there is no need for an expensive composite query, so (d) is wrong. The best answer is (c).

11.) Since we need an INCLUDE clause, (a) is wrong. AccountNumber already exists, so (b) is wrong as it does not help us. The best answer is (c) since it covers all the fields in the SELECT statement.

Bug Catcher Game

To play the Bug Catcher game, run the SQLQueries2012Vol3BugCatcher08.pps file from the BugCatcher folder of the companion files. These files can be obtained from the www.Joes2Pros.com website.

[THIS PAGE INTENTIONALLY LEFT BLANK.]

Chapter 9.   Index Analysis

Implementing a good database is a lot like other things in life which we plan and build. We put a lot of planning, care, and effort into building a database much the same way a family would design and build a new home. The Design and Build phases of any project are exciting and important for the success of the project.

Also important to the success of a new structure or system is analysis to confirm that new systems and processes are working as expected. In the Implementation phase of delivering a project, the team often needs to measure actual results versus expected results and make any necessary adjustments.

The same is true when implementing indexes for database tables. Just seeing a database's design is only part of the picture. How the indexes are actually being utilized is the other part. By putting indexes where they will get the most use, you get the most benefit.

This chapter is all about examining the past, current, and future uses of your database in order to ensure you're utilizing the best indexing scheme.

READER NOTE: *Please run the SQLQueries2012Vol3Chapter9.0Setup.sql script in order to follow along with the examples in the first section of Chapter 9. All scripts mentioned in this chapter may be found at* www.Joes2Pros.com.

Query Execution Plans

Just today, as I was coming to my office to work with my technical editor Joel, something happened that caused me to make a decision much the same way SQL Server's Query Optimizer makes a decision. To achieve a productive day, we needed a printer and two laptops, each with a double monitor. Normally I do not store this much gear in my office, so it all travels in a big moving box in the back of my vehicle.

As I removed the box from the vehicle, I looked around and noticed my folding dolly wasn't there. With the dolly, I'm normally able to wheel the large box into the building and upstairs to the office. This box is heavy and difficult to carry. But in the absence of the dolly, my next best choice was to use a little extra brute force, so the goal of getting all this stuff upstairs could be achieved.

Much like the decision making process of SQL Server's Query Optimizer, when I realized my trusted dolly wasn't available I made the decision to complete my task inefficiently rather than not working at all. If my dolly had been in the back of my truck, my decision would have been to use it and make the job easier.

When we add an index where it will really count, the Query Optimizer has the freedom to make a decision which gets the job done without excessive heavy lifting on the part of the SQL Server service.

Covering Indexes

The following code is predicating on the InvoiceID field of the SalesInvoiceDetail table looking for all records matching a value of 5. What would we have to know in order to predict whether this query will be covered or not?

READER NOTE: *Remember, if a query does not have a covering index, then the SQL Server Query Optimizer will perform an index scan of the table.*

```
SELECT *
FROM SalesInvoiceDetail
WHERE InvoiceID = 5
```

	InvoiceDetailID	InvoiceID	ProductID	Quantity	UnitDiscount
1	9	5	16	1	0.00
2	10	5	9	5	0.00
3	11	5	12	3	0.00
4	12	5	11	6	0.00
5	13	5	62	3	0.00
6	14	5	58	4	0.00

6 rows

Figure 9.1 The results returned for InvoiceID 5 of the SalesInvoiceDetail table.

The first thing we need to do is review the indexes for the dbo.SalesInvoiceDetail table. In Figure 9.2 we see it has a clustered index called PK_SalesInv_, which is on the InvoiceDetailID field. This is all we need if the index were predicating on this field in the WHERE clause of the query. However, our query is actually predicating on the InvoiceID field, which is not covered by the InvoiceDetailID field of the PK_SalesInv_ clustered index (Figure 9.2).

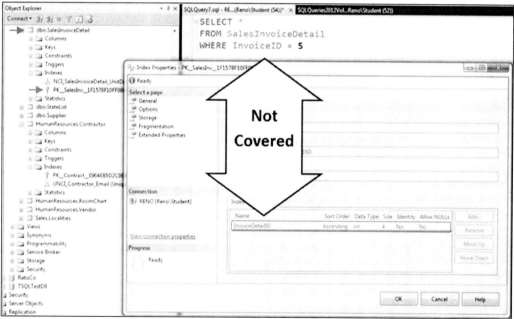

Figure 9.2 The index on SalesInvoiceDetail table does not cover a predicate on InvoiceID field.

Since our query is predicating on a field which doesn't have an index covering it, the Query Optimizer will choose to do a scan, irrespective of whether or not this query is selective. Run this query again and choose to view results from the estimated Execution Plan. We can now see that the Query Optimizer did indeed choose to perform a Clustered Index Scan (Figure 9.3) to return a mere six records from the total of 6960 records in the dbo.SalesInvoiceDetail table.

```
SELECT *
FROM SalesInvoiceDetail
WHERE InvoiceID = 5
```

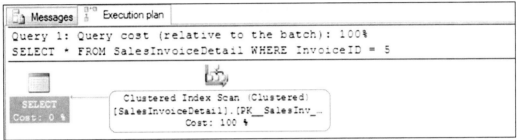

Figure 9.3 Since InvoiceID has no covering index, this query will always result in a scan.

This is not a very efficient search for returning the results of this query. One of our main goals is to find a way to get the Query Optimizer to perform an Index Seek when running this query.

To do this, we will create a Non-Clustered index covering the InvoiceID field. Use the following code to create an index named NCI_SalesInvoiceDetail_InvoiceID based on the InvoiceID field of the dbo.SalesInvoiceDetail table.

```
CREATE NONCLUSTERED INDEX
NCI_SalesInvoiceDetail_InvoiceID
ON SalesInvoiceDetail(InvoiceID)
```

Verify the creation of the index in the Object Explorer by refreshing the folder containing the dbo.SalesInvoiceDetail table. Then open the Indexes folder and double-click on the NCI_SalesInvoiceDetail_InvoiceID index name to open the Index Properties dialog window shown in Figure 9.4. We can now see that this index is based on the InvoiceID column of the SalesInvoiceDetail table.

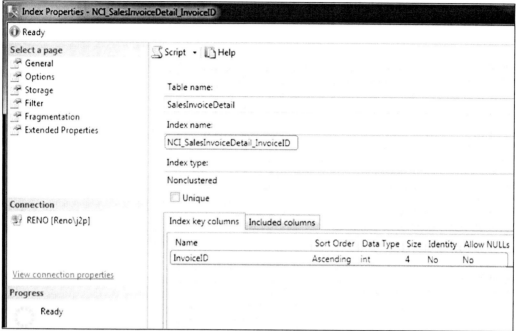

Figure 9.4 The index you created will cover the InvoiceID field of the SalesInvoiceDetail table.

The purpose for creating the NCI_SalesInvoiceDetail_InvoiceID index is to optimize queries that are predicated on the InvoiceID field. When we run the code from the previous query again, we can see from the Execution Plan in Figure 9.5 that the Query Optimizer will now do an index seek based on our Non-Clustered index (NCI_SalesInvoiceDetail_InvoiceID). This is a significant performance gain.

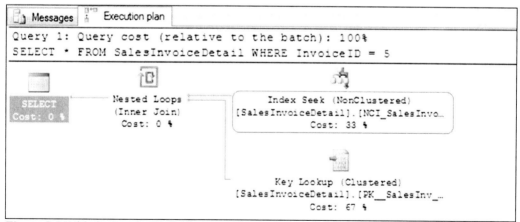

Figure 9.5 With the InvoiceID field covered by the index, Query Optimizer performs a seek.

How Non-Clustered Indexes Work

When turning to the index at the back of any textbook, we can get an idea of how SQL Server processes data when it encounters a Non-Clustered index. For example, the index at the back of the first Joes 2 Pros book, *Beginning SQL Joes 2 Pros* (Figure 9.6). Suppose our class is being given a quiz tomorrow on the REVOKE keyword. We could simply turn to the book's index to find (i.e., *seek*) precisely which pages include the word 'Revoke'. If our book had the index torn out, we would need to *scan* every page to find the two pages with the word 'Revoke'.

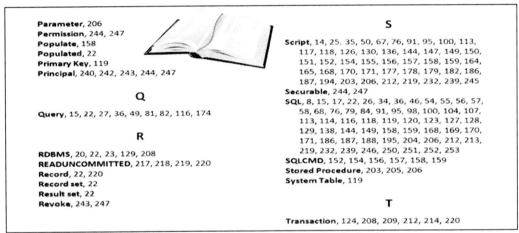

Figure 9.6 An example of what an index looks like in the back of a book.

The sample index from the Beginning SQL Joes 2 Pros book (Figure 9.6) allows us to easily locate the REVOKE keyword. We quickly spot the letter 'R' and then narrow our focus to the words located below it, finding 'Revoke' in the sixth spot. Now that we have found our word, we look to the right of it and find the numbers 243 and 247, representing the page numbers where the REVOKE keyword appears within this book.

This saves a tremendous amount of time versus scanning through the book, page-by-page, word-by-word, until we have searched the entire book to find the two places the REVOKE keyword appears. This is the difference between running a query which is covered by an index (i.e., similar to the book index pointing directly to the page(s) location), versus a query not covered by an index (i.e., the page-by-page, word-by-word scan of the entire book).

The index of a book does not hold the data itself; rather it does point to the exact location of the data pages. Once the location is available, it is a simple matter to turn directly to those two pages and read the information (data) for the REVOKE keyword. As readers of technical books, we can certainly appreciate the value of an index, which makes our research and studying much easier and faster.

Indexes in books typically list their topics from A to Z. If a book were 300 pages, what is the likelihood that the word 'Revoke' would be located around page 200, since R occurs roughly two-thirds of the way into the alphabet? This is unlikely. Only reference materials, like dictionaries and encyclopedias, store their items in alphabetical order. Revoke could easily be on Page 1. Most Non-reference books aren't ordered alphabetically, rather they are ordered by page number.

The main part of this book is ordered *by page number*. The index is ordered *alphabetically by keyword* and the index points to the page numbers. This book is clustered (i.e., physically ordered) by page number, which makes things easy to find once we know what page to look for. The index in the back of the book pointing to the needed page number is similar to a Non-Clustered index in SQL Server. Non-Clustered indexes normally do not contain the needed data, however, they know exactly where it is stored. A Non-Clustered index points to the exact position within a clustered index, so SQL Server can retrieve the data quickly.

When a Query Needs a Covering Index

We've learned quite a bit about the usefulness of indexes and how they help our queries. But at this point, should we just slap an index over every single field of every query's WHERE clause? Maybe this isn't such a good idea. For example: One memorable December 26th, I met a number of developers who believed having indexes to cover every field, was an excellent solution to speed up their queries. A system I was testing had its performance crippled by this solution. After a day of analysis, I recommended removing one such index. Once the offending index was removed, the system benchmarks showed a 77,000% increase in performance. *Yes, Seventy Seven Thousand percent!* A very important, yet lesser understood, process is how indexes work according to the selectivity level of the data.

What was happening? Space and memory were being unnecessarily wasted. It is like paying for something and never using it. Most people try to be conscientious and avoid wasting money by using the things they have paid for. Often these occasions have only a small impact (e.g., wasting 90 cents purchasing a banana that goes uneaten), or they can have more substantial consequences (e.g., paying $100 for a monthly gym membership that is never used).

The same is true in the SQL Server environment. SQL Server needs to spend processing time on anything it is instructed to maintain in addition to its many automatic maintenance tasks. Indexes come at a cost of hard-drive space, memory and CPU time, so they should only be created when they will be beneficial. This section will help to identify what types of Non-Clustered indexes likely are to be used by SQL Server to give a bigger performance benefit than the cost.

If a particular field is being frequently filtered on, then it is a good candidate for building an index. The system I tested that memorable December day had an index on a binary field (e.g., having values 0/1, Y/N, M/F). This binary field was indeed being queried many times per minute all day long. Binary fields by their very nature (on or off) are not very selective. There were about 100,000 records in the table and about 50,000 records had the number 1, while 50,000 were 0. Our query was predicated with a WHERE clause searching for all records with a value of 1. Well, it's faster to scan 100,000 records and filter for what value is required, than it is to individually search 50,000 records with an index. Hence, the Query Optimizer said "Thanks, but no thanks!" to using the index and instead performed a scan each time this query was run. To put it metaphorically, SQL Server was paying for the upkeep of an index it had no intention of ever using in the query.

In the example of the query searching for the number 1, performing a scan was definitely the best option the Query Optimizer had to expedite this query. The real problem however, was the 90 times per second the table received inserted data. Each insert to the table caused an insert into the Non-Clustered index. This meant the index required being recalculated 90 times per second, resulting in a very high processing cost for maintaining an index that was never used by the query.

Selectivity

If a company has 900 employees, how many different Social Security Numbers (SSNs) might there be in the table for their database? We should expect to have 900 distinct values for the SSN. How many different birthdays (including year)? Some will have the same birthday and year, so let's estimate 850 distinct birthdays exist for the 900 employees. How many different genders? Well, there are two genders: Male and Female, so it is likely to be split fairly evenly.

The most selective attribute for this table will be the SSN, where each record has its own unique value, as it is extraordinarily rare for two people to share the same SSN. The least selective characteristic is gender, since there are 900 employees and only two distinct gender values.

READER NOTE: *The higher the selectivity level is for the data in a field, the bigger the performance benefit will be for a given index.*

Data selectivity, such as the unique values for an SSN, is one thing. How a query is written can be just as important. For example, a query written to find employees with an SSN value of 555-55-5555, will find one employee (High selectivity).

```
--Highly selective query
WHERE SSN = '555-55-5555'
```

Conversely, a query written to find every employee that does not have an SSN value of 555-55-5555, will find 899 employees (Very low selectivity).

```
--Low selectivity
WHERE SSN != '555-55-5555'
```

In the back of the *SQL Queries 2012 Joes 2 Pros Volume 1* book, there is an index that shows the word 'Revoke' is very selective, as it appears in only two locations of the entire book. According to this same book index, the word 'SQL' appeared many more times, 58 times to be exact, (Figure 9.6) therefore, we would have to do a lot more seeks just to retrieve all the data. So finding the word 'SQL' in *SQL Queries 2012 Joes 2 Pros Volume 1* wasn't as selective a query as finding the word 'Revoke' in the book. By definition, the less selective the value, the more times it appears. The workload of SQL Server's query engine increases with the number of times a value appears.

How about finding the word 'the'? This is not likely to be a selective query at all. If we were asked to find the word 'the', and presuming 'the' was actually in the index, would looking in the index save us any work? In this case, we are quickly going to agree with the SQL Server Query Optimizer and choose to scan the whole book from beginning to end, since it is much more likely to be faster than using the index. Looking for all pages containing the word 'the' is an example of extremely low selectivity.

A highly selective query is one where the result set will show a small percentage of records from a table. By finding the word 'Revoke' in only two of the 260 pages, or only 1%, of the *SQL Queries 2012 Joes 2 Pros Volume 1* book, we would consider this to be highly selective. When the covering index has a query that is selective enough, then the Query Optimizer chooses to perform an index seek rather than a scan.

What if we were asked to find all pages in *SQL Queries 2012 Joes 2 Pros Volume 1* that do not have the REVOKE keyword? If there are 260 pages in this book and only two contain the word 'Revoke', then there are 258 pages that do not have this word. Performing a search through 100% of the pages (records), which retrieves 99% of the pages (records), is a search with very low selectivity, since so many pages (records) are returned to satisfy the search requirements.

Sometimes, a predicate will actually be on an indexed field but the query being run will actually ignore the covering index and perform a scan. Doing a scan is more efficient than doing so many individual seeks.

Here are the rules of thumb for Scans vs. Seeks:

o   Covered Indexes on queries with a Highly Selective column = Seek

o   Covered Indexes on queries with a Poorly Selective column = Scan

o   Queries without Covered Indexes = Scan

Selective Predicate Operators

Query predicates (i.e., the criteria of our WHERE or HAVING clauses) in SQL Server can make use of operators such as =, !=, >, <, IN, NOT IN and many others. Thanks to our growing understanding of how indexes behave, we can begin to predict which conditions will likely cause a query to seek rather than scan. By running a query from our SalesInvoiceDetail table without any criteria, we find it has nearly 7,000 records (Figure 9.7).

```
SELECT *
FROM SalesInvoiceDetail
```

	InvoiceDetailID	InvoiceID	ProductID	Quantity	UnitDiscount
1	1	1	76	2	0.00
2	2	1	77	3	0.00
3	3	1	78	6	0.00
4	4	1	71	5	0.00
5	5	1	72	4	0.00
6	6	2	73	2	0.00
					6960 rows

Figure 9.7 Querying the SalesInvoiceDetail table without a WHERE clause returns ~7000 rows.

How selective is the following query? With only 6 of the 6960 records related to InvoiceID 5, this is a very selective query and will seek with a covering index.

```
SELECT * FROM SalesInvoiceDetail
WHERE InvoiceID = 5
```

	InvoiceDetailID	InvoiceID	ProductID	Quantity	UnitDiscount
1	9	5	16	1	0.00
2	10	5	9	5	0.00
3	11	5	12	3	0.00
4	12	5	11	6	0.00
5	13	5	62	3	0.00
6	14	5	58	4	0.00

6 rows

Figure 9.8 Predicating on InvoiceID = 5 is a very selective query (Retrieving only 6 rows).

This next query searches for all records which do not have an InvoiceID of 5. This will retrieve over 99% of all the records in the table (6954 of 6960), making this a query with very low selectivity (Figure 9.9).

```
SELECT * FROM SalesInvoiceDetail
WHERE InvoiceID != 5
```

	InvoiceDetailID	InvoiceID	ProductID	Quantity	UnitDiscount
1	1	1	76	2	0.00
2	2	1	77	3	0.00
3	3	1	78	6	0.00
4	4	1	71	5	0.00
5	5	1	72	4	0.00
6	6	2	73	2	0.00

6954 rows

Figure 9.9 Predicating on InvoiceID not being equal to 5 is definitely not selective.

It should be easy to guess what kind of Execution Plan the Query Optimizer will use for this last query. It will definitely choose to scan the table, despite the fact there is a covering index for the predicate, as seen in Figure 9.10.

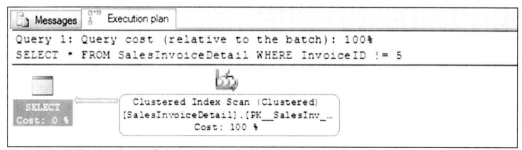

Figure 9.10 The InvoiceID field has a covering index but chooses to scan due to poor selectivity.

This is like our example where flipping through pages of a book (scanning) for the word 'the' was more efficient than using the index of the book by seeking. When selectivity gets too low, there are too many records to seek through and an index becomes less beneficial. In these instances, the SQL Server Query Optimizer recognizes that it is better off scanning all the records.

Optimization Hints

There are two types of hints that will affect whether or not the Query Optimizer decides to use an index in its Execution Plan. One is truly a hint that allows SQL Server to decide whether to seek or scan, and the other is really more of a mandate where our instructions are able to force which index gets used. The **Query Hint** will suggest a way to optimize the query, letting the Query Optimizer pick the index and an **Index Hint** tells the Query Optimizer precisely which index to use.

Index Hint

We have seen several examples of how the SQL Server Query Optimizer is capable of making excellent decisions about how to retrieve data based on the selectivity of the predicated fields. However, we can bypass the decision process of the Query Optimizer by explicitly instructing it to seek based on an index, even though it would normally prefer to scan the entire table.

A slight change to our last query allows us to control how this query will search for the data it is being asked to retrieve. Immediately before the WHERE clause, enter WITH followed by a set of parentheses which contain the keyword INDEX. The keyword INDEX needs its own set of parentheses, which will specify the name of the index we choose to force the Query Optimizer to search with. View the results in Figure 9.11.

```
SELECT * FROM SalesInvoiceDetail
WITH(INDEX (NCI_SalesInvoiceDetail_InvoiceID))
WHERE InvoiceID != 5
```

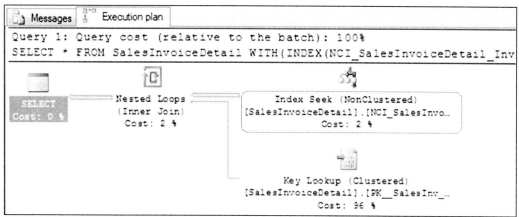

Figure 9.11 This poorly selective query uses a seek based on the index hint provided.

Our ***Index Hint*** instructs the Query Optimizer to seek no matter what it might choose to do on its own. The query Execution Plan (Figure 9.11) confirms that it did seek through every single record, even though a scan would have been faster.

Query Hint

The Query Optimizer looks at an index and the predicated value to decide whether seeking or scanning is more appropriate. Once the value is known, it calculates the selectivity level of the field and determines the best Execution Plan. A highly selective query will likely scan if it's not covered by an index.

The following code is an example of a selective query without a covering index, as there are 775 records in the Customer table and only two of the records have the CustomerType value of 'Business'. The Execution Plan predicating for these two records alone will perform an index scan (Figure 9.12).

```
SELECT *
FROM Customer
WHERE CustomerType = 'Business'
```

```
[Messages]  [Execution plan]
Query 1: Query cost (relative to the batch): 100%
SELECT * FROM Customer WHERE CustomerType = 'Business'

  [   ]              [   ]
 SELECT        Clustered Index Scan (Clustered)
Cost: 0 %      [Customer].[PK__Customer__A4AE64B89...
                        Cost: 100 %
```

Figure 9.12 A selective query with no index will generally perform a scan.

Creating a Non-Clustered index for the Customer table on the CustomerType field will give this query a covering index so that it can perform an index seek. The following code will create a Non-Clustered index named NCI_Customer_CustomerType.

```
CREATE NONCLUSTERED INDEX NCI_Customer_CustomerType
ON Customer(CustomerType)
GO
```

Our query should now be optimized to seek using a covering index. Let's verify the Execution Plan and confirm it will indeed perform an index seek (Figure 9.13).

```
SELECT * FROM Customer
WHERE CustomerType = 'Business'
```

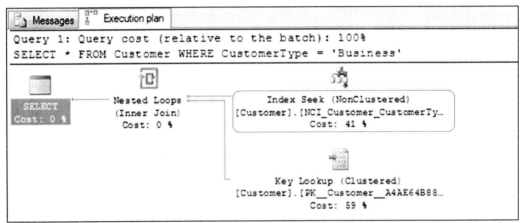

Figure 9.13 After creating the NCI_Customer_CustomerType index, this query now does a seek.

At the beginning of this section on When a Query Hint needs a Covering Index, I gave an example of how not every query covered by an index will seek. Only queries that are selective and have a covering index will seek.

Changing our previous query so the predicate is on a CustomerType with a value of 'Consumer,' will return 773 of the 775 records in the table, which is not very selective. The result is an Execution Plan that will do a scan. Thus, when the query is predicated by the CustomerType 'Business', it will seek. Likewise, when the query is predicated by the CustomerType 'Consumer', it will scan (Figure 9.14).

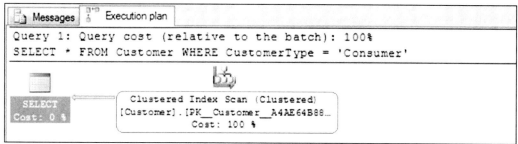

Figure 9.14 NCI_Customer_CustomerType was ignored and the query scans as selectivity is too low.

SQL Server is actually smart enough to take the exact same index and realize, through statistics, which of these criteria is selective and which is not. There is a way to accidentally trick SQL Server into making the wrong decision when using variables in a query. We can take a look at how this happens, by first adding a variable to our current query to show the problem environment, and then we will see how a query hint can help us overcome the problem.

Let's declare a variable named @Type, which is a VARCHAR(50) and set it equal to 'Business'. This variable will be part of the predicate. Running this query will result in two records (Figure 9.15). This is a highly selective query.

```
DECLARE @Type VARCHAR(50)
SET @Type = 'Business'

SELECT *
FROM Customer
WHERE CustomerType = @Type
```

	CustomerID	CustomerType	FirstName	LastName	CompanyName
1	5	Business	NULL	NULL	MoreTechnology.com
2	117	Business	NULL	NULL	Puma Consulting

2 rows

Figure 9.15 Setting the @Type variable to 'Business', makes for a highly selective query.

Changing the @Type variable to 'Consumer' will return 773 records having very low selectivity when the query is run (Figure 9.16).

```
DECLARE @Type VARCHAR(50)
SET @Type = 'Consumer'

SELECT *
FROM Customer
WHERE CustomerType = @Type
```

	CustomerID	CustomerType	FirstName	LastName	CompanyName
1	1	Consumer	Mark	Williams	NULL
2	2	Consumer	Lee	Young	NULL
3	3	Consumer	Patricia	Martin	NULL
4	4	Consumer	Mary	Lopez	NULL
5	6	Consumer	Ruth	Clark	NULL
6	1	Consumer	Mark	Williams	NULL

773 rows

Figure 9.16 Using 'Consumer' for the @Type variable has low selectivity.

The query that predicates on 'Consumer' is better off performing a scan, since it's retrieving nearly all the records from the entire table. The query Execution Plan confirms that a scan was performed to get our result set (Figure 9.17).

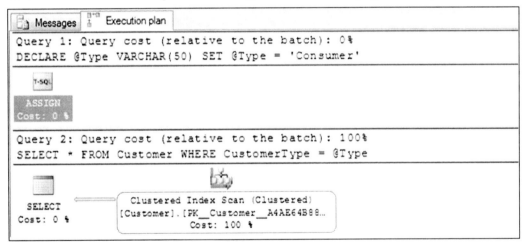

Figure 9.17 Using 'Consumer' for the variable causes a scan.

Let's change our @Type variable back to 'Business'. The Query Optimizer will perform an index scan, as it will not know what value the @Type variable holds until runtime, and is unable to check statistics for a variable before the query runs.

```
DECLARE @Type VARCHAR(50)
SET @Type = 'Business'

SELECT * FROM Customer
WHERE CustomerType = @Type
```

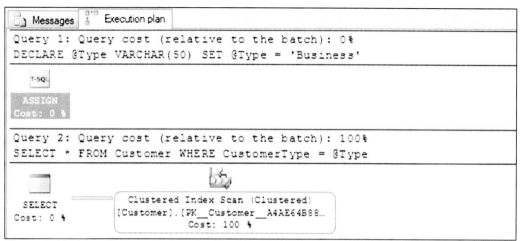

Figure 9.18 Using @Type 'Business' will scan, even with a highly selective predicate and index.

READER NOTE: *When in doubt, the Query Optimizer will always choose an Execution Plan that will perform an index scan.*

When a query predicates on values from variables, it might be necessary to give the query a hint, so the Query Optimizer can access statistics for the table. If our @Type variable is most often set to the value of 'Business', it would be smarter to optimize this query to perform an index seek for this selective CustomerType.

Optimizing this query for a predicate variable anticipating the value being set for 'Business' will require some additional coding. By adding an OPTION clause, containing an OPTIMIZE FOR clause that supplies the 'Business' value to the @Type variable, we can instruct the Query Optimizer to use an Execution Plan that will perform an index seek for our query (Figure 9.19).

```
DECLARE @Type VARCHAR(50)
SET @Type = 'Business'

SELECT *
FROM Customer
WHERE CustomerType = @Type
OPTION(OPTIMIZE FOR (@Type = 'Business'))
```

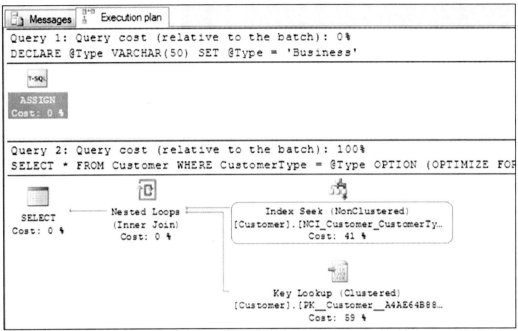

Figure 9.19 Using the Optimize For hint allows a seek on a predicated variable.

Whenever the keyword OPTION appears at the end of the code for a query, it's a signal that a *Query Hint* is being used. In the last example we supplied a hint to the Query Optimizer to optimize the query for the value of 'Business' in the variable. There are more types of query hints available that are quite useful to us.

READER NOTE: *The final coding examples for this section require the use of Microsoft's sample database called **AdventureWorks2012**. Please download this sample database and follow the installation instructions available at Microsoft's CodePlex website http://msftdbprodsamples.codeplex.com/releases/view/55330 prior to running the code shown in these examples.*

Our next example works best with a large number of records, so let's look at the Sales.SalesOrderDetail table of the AdventureWorks2012 database. Some queries can take a while to run, particularly when the result contains a very large record set. In many such cases, we are really not interested in seeing all of the records. A sample of what is in the table is more than enough.

Or, we may want the ability to quickly see a representative sample of the result set while waiting for the rest of the larger record set to be retrieved. Informally, many SQL Developers in this situation will run the query and then stop it after a few seconds to look at the partial results returned by the query. Another common way to accomplish this would be to write a 'Top 50' query which finishes in far less time than trying to retrieve every record available. The disadvantage of both of these shortcuts is that we will never get all the records.

There is a way to query a table, which will run and display the first (*n*) amount of records rapidly. In this case, we will ask for the first 50 records to be returned immediately, while waiting for the query to deliver the rest when it is finished.

The code for writing this **Query Hint** is seen here. Recall that all Query Hints place an OPTION clause with a set of parenthesis at the end of the code for a query. Inside the parenthesis write the keyword FAST followed by the number of records we want returned right away, which is 50. Look at the result window in Figure 9.20 and notice we have records available to review, however the row counter shows zero while the query is still running.

```
SELECT *
FROM Sales.SalesOrderDetail
OPTION(FAST 50)
```

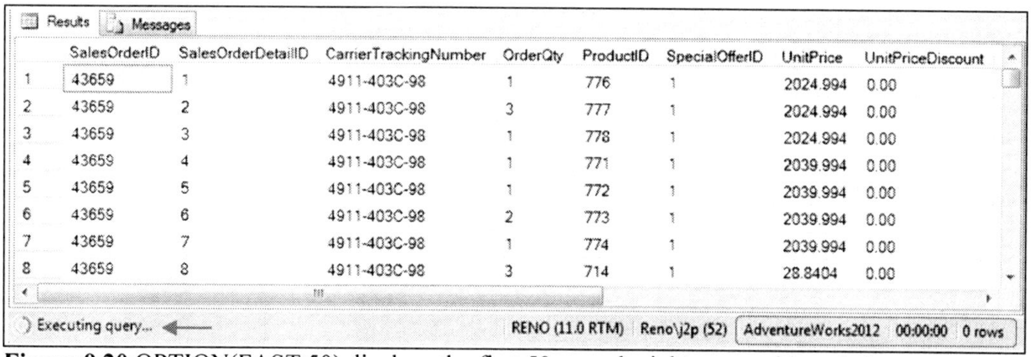

	SalesOrderID	SalesOrderDetailID	CarrierTrackingNumber	OrderQty	ProductID	SpecialOfferID	UnitPrice	UnitPriceDiscount
1	43659	1	4911-403C-98	1	776	1	2024.994	0.00
2	43659	2	4911-403C-98	3	777	1	2024.994	0.00
3	43659	3	4911-403C-98	1	778	1	2024.994	0.00
4	43659	4	4911-403C-98	1	771	1	2039.994	0.00
5	43659	5	4911-403C-98	1	772	1	2039.994	0.00
6	43659	6	4911-403C-98	2	773	1	2039.994	0.00
7	43659	7	4911-403C-98	1	774	1	2039.994	0.00
8	43659	8	4911-403C-98	3	714	1	28.8404	0.00

Executing query...   RENO (11.0 RTM) Reno\j2p (52) AdventureWorks2012 00:00:00 0 rows

Figure 9.20 OPTION(FAST 50) displays the first 50 records right away, although the status indicator shows '0 rows' unil the query is finished.

Our example uses 50 as the number of records requested immediately, although this is really an arbitrary number. We could have easily chosen 5, 25, 60, 150, etc., for the **Query Hint** to return right away, while waiting for the remainder of records to be processed, regardless of how much time it takes.

We can tell when the query is complete because the row counter will finally display the total number of rows retrieved and the query execution clock will stop ticking at the same time. This information is displayed in the lower right-hand corner of the query window (below the results tab) as shown in Figure 9.21.

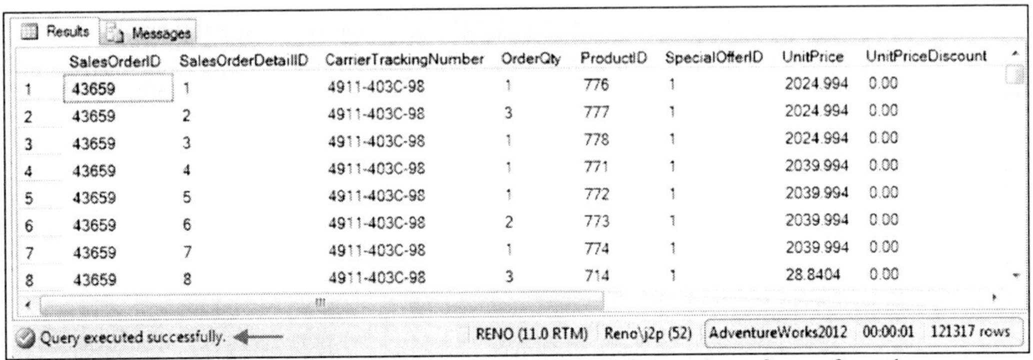

	SalesOrderID	SalesOrderDetailID	CarrierTrackingNumber	OrderQty	ProductID	SpecialOfferID	UnitPrice	UnitPriceDiscount
1	43659	1	4911-403C-98	1	776	1	2024.994	0.00
2	43659	2	4911-403C-98	3	777	1	2024.994	0.00
3	43659	3	4911-403C-98	1	778	1	2024.994	0.00
4	43659	4	4911-403C-98	1	771	1	2039.994	0.00
5	43659	5	4911-403C-98	1	772	1	2039.994	0.00
6	43659	6	4911-403C-98	2	773	1	2039.994	0.00
7	43659	7	4911-403C-98	1	774	1	2039.994	0.00
8	43659	8	4911-403C-98	3	714	1	28.8404	0.00

Query executed successfully. ⟵   RENO (11.0 RTM) Reno\j2p (52) AdventureWorks2012 00:00:01 121317 rows

Figure 9.21 Once the query is done, we see all records and the number of rows from the query.

Lab 9.1: Query Execution Plans

Lab Prep: Each lab has one or more Skill Checks. Start with Skill Check 1 and proceed until reaching the Points to Ponder section.

Before beginning this lab, verify that SQL Server 2012 is properly installed and operating. Before running the lab setup script for resetting the database (SQLQueries2012Vol3Chapter9.1Setup.sql), please make sure to close all query windows within SSMS. An open query window pointing to a database context can lock that database preventing it from updating when the script is executing. A simple way to assure all query windows are closed, is to exit out of SSMS, then open a new instance of SSMS, and lastly run the setup script.

Skill Check 1: Create a Non-Clustered index named NCI_SalesInvoice_CustomerID on the CustomerID field of the SalesInvoice table of the JProCo database. Notice the following query will perform a table scan even though it has a covering index.

READER NOTE: *CustomerID 155 has placed so many orders, that this query is not selective enough to use with the covering index. However, writing a query that predicates on CustomerID 1 will produce a seek lookup using the index.*

```
SELECT *
FROM SalesInvoice
WHERE CustomerID = 155
```

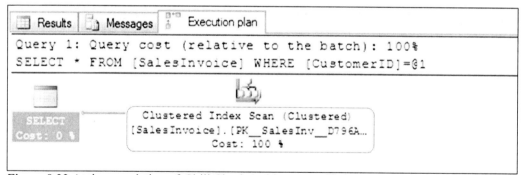

Figure 9.22 At the completion of Skill Check 1, this query still does a scan.

Skill Check 2: Write a query based on the query from Skill Check 1 that will force the SQL Server Query Optimizer to perform a seek lookup by using an index hint on NCI_SalesInvoice_CustomerID.

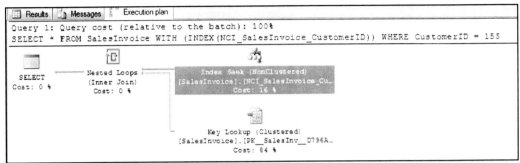

Figure 9.23 By using an Index Hint in Skill Check 2, this query now performs a seek lookup.

Skill Check 3: Management regularly requests reports for CustomerID 1 and is complaining that the query takes too long to complete. Finish the following query so that it is optimized with a query hint when predicated on CustomerID 1.

```
DECLARE @CustID INT
SET @CustID = 1

SELECT * FROM SalesInvoice
WHERE CustomerID = @CustID
--Put "Query Hint" Code here
```

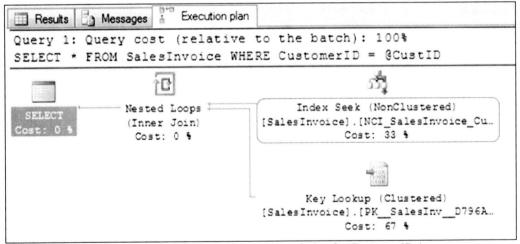

Figure 9.24 A Query Hint is used in Skill Check 3 to optimize for CustomerID 1.

Skill Check 4: SalesInvoiceDetail is the largest table in the JProCo database with almost 7000 records. Write a query that returns all fields and all records of this table, using a query hint that will display the first 10 records right away, while waiting for the remainder of the records to be displayed once the query execution is complete.

Answer Code: The T-SQL code to this lab can be found in the downloadable files in a file named Lab9.1_QueryExecutionPlans.sql.

Points to Ponder - Query Execution Plans

1. An index **seek** is similar to:

   o Turning to the back of this book to look at the index and looking up the required word and then turning directly to the page that contains that word.

2. A index **scan** is similar to:

   o Turning to the first page of this book then searching through all the pages for a word until reaching the end of the book.

3. An index scan is like scanning the entire table row by row. This is a 1 to **n** search, where **n** is the total number of rows in the table. Therefore the scan is efficient if the table is small, or most rows qualify for the predicate.

4. The 'WITH *Index*' hint specifies which index to use. This is very useful to force the query to execute with an index seek, rather than an index scan.

5. The index hint syntax is WITH (INDEX (*IndexName*))

6. An Execution Plan shows how the query is executed. This is useful for seeing if a scan or seek is being performed and for troubleshooting other inefficiencies in a query.

7. If data isn't adequately selective, Query Optimizer may ignore the index and choose to perform a scan on a covered query.

8. The OPTIMIZE FOR query hint will override incorrect SQL parameter sniffing. Parameter sniffing is the default behavior of the Query Optimizer which determines the query Execution Plan at compile time and judges the selectivity of data based on parameter values. A sub-optimal Execution Plan may be stored if the initial run of the query is performed with an atypical data sample.

9. The OPTIMIZE FOR syntax is:

   ```
   OPTION(OPTIMIZE FOR (@Parameter = Value))
   ```

10. A related syntax (OPTIMIZE FOR UNKNOWN) forces the Query Optimizer to look at available statistics before generating the query plan, rather than looking at the parameter values:

    ```
    OPTION(OPTIMIZE FOR (@Parameter = UNKNOWN))
    ```

11. OPTION (FAST **n**) does not make the whole query run any faster; it returns **n** rows to the client as soon as they have been found and then continues with the remaining rows.

Analyzing Indexes

How are the current indexes benefiting us and how can we improve them? While shopping at Costco one day, an employee greeted me after my checkout was done. She said that, based on my buying pattern, the 2% pay back plan has earned me more than the cost of upgrading my membership from Gold to Executive. At first, this was not clear to me so I asked her to explain. My $50 annual membership could be upgraded to a $100 annual membership which would give me 2% back on all purchases. In fact, I had already earned $65 before the end of the year. She offered to give me $15 in pocket to upgrade my membership and consider the upgrade paid in full. The cost of an extra $50 per year for my executive level membership was a worthwhile idea because of my usage patterns at Costco.

For people who sign up for the Executive level membership, then rarely shop at Costco, the opposite is true. Some might be paying an extra $50 per year and only getting $10 back. When something is utilized frequently, a greater return on investment is realized. The same idea is true for indexes. If an index is created that is never used by the Query Optimizer then the extra cost of maintaining the index is wasted. If the index is used frequently then it is worthwhile.

How many times in the last hour, or last day, has SQL Server performed an index seek, rather than a scan, for the queries we have run? Knowing this will help us know how well our indexes are being utilized.

Seek vs. Scan Recap

If the SalesInvoice table did not have a Non-Clustered index on the InvoiceID, then all of the following queries would do a scan:

```
--Scan
SELECT * FROM SalesInvoiceDetail

--Seek if covered.
SELECT * FROM SalesInvoiceDetail
WHERE InvoiceID = 5

--Seek if covered.
SELECT * FROM SalesInvoiceDetail
WHERE InvoiceID IN (5, 10, 60)

--Scan
SELECT * FROM SalesInvoiceDetail
WHERE InvoiceID != 5
```

By placing indexes on fields when querying them selectively, we can increase their performance by having more seeks versus scans on the table.

We know these queries are potentially using the indexes of the SalesInvoiceDetail table. The total number of seeks and scans for this table will grow each time it is queried. Let's get a report on how the SalesInvoiceDetail table's indexes are working for our queries.

Historical Index Metadata

How often are seeks being done on a covering index? That fateful December 26th day I alluded to in the last section happened when someone put an index on a field called Completed. The possible values for the Completed field were either a zero or a one. After doing a little research, we found out that in the last 24 hours we did 4.7 million scans and 0 seeks. Imagine paying for a Costco membership and shopping 4.7 million times at various stores but never once at Costco!

These results clearly showed the overhead to maintain this index was wasted. That silenced all arguments about the benefit of this index. How can we show someone the metadata on index usage? It's a common question that has been addressed by Microsoft through some cool new ways to look at metadata.

Before we can begin, we need to know some items like the *database_id* and the *object_id* of the table we wish to analyze. The name of our database is JProCo, but what is the *database_id* of JProCo? The DB_ID() function returns the *database_id* and the OBJECT_ID() function will return the *object_id* of our table (Figure 9.25).

```
SELECT DB_ID('JProCo') AS database_id,
OBJECT_ID('SalesInvoiceDetail') AS object_id
```

	Database_id	Object_id
1	7	581577110

1 rows

Figure 9.25 The database_id and object_id can be discovered through system-supplied functions.

For this next demonstration, the number 7 will be the *database_id* of the JProCo database and the *object_id* for the SalesInvoiceDetail table is 581577110. We want to see how many seeks and scans have been performed on the SalesInvoiceDetail table, which is the 581577110 object in database 7.

We can query the **sys.dm_db_index_usage_stats** dynamic management view to determine exactly how many seeks and scans have been performed by predicating on the JProCo *database_id* and the SalesInvoiceDetail *object_id*. So far, ten queries have been run on the SalesInvoiceDetail table and the results of running our following code shows we have three seeks and seven scans (Figure 9.26).

```
SELECT * FROM sys.dm_db_index_usage_stats
WHERE [database_id] = 7
AND [object_id] =' 581577110
```

database_id	object_id	index_id	user_seeks	user_scans
1 7	581577110	1	0	7
2 7	581577110	3	3	0
				2 rows

Figure 9.26 Three seeks and seven scans have been run on the SalesInvoiceDetail table.

What happens if we write a query predicating on the InvoiceID field, which has a covering index called NCI_SalesInvoiceDetail_InvoiceID? Since this query is not very selective, the Query Optimizer will most likely perform a table scan and update the *sys.dm_db_index_usage_stats* with this information. Run the following code to find out if this is the case (Figure 9.27).

```
SELECT * FROM SalesInvoiceDetail
WHERE InvoiceID != 5
```

InvoiceDetailID	InvoiceID	ProductID	Quantity	UnitDiscount
1 1	1	76	2	0.00
2 2	1	77	3	0.00
3 3	1	78	6	0.00
4 4	1	71	5	0.00
5 5	1	72	4	0.00
6 6	2	73	2	0.00
				6954 rows

Figure 9.27 This non-selective query should perform another scan.

Run the *sys.dm_db_index_usage_stats* query again to verify the *user_scans* field has changed from 7 to 8 when looking at the results in Figure 9.28.

```
SELECT * FROM sys.dm_db_index_usage_stats
WHERE [database_id] = 7
AND [object_id] = 581577110
```

database_id	object_id	index_id	user_seeks	user_scans
1 7	581577110	1	0	8
2 7	581577110	3	3	0
				2 rows

Figure 9.28 The sys.dm_db_index_usage_stats view verifies one more scan has been run.

To cause another seek to take place, we can run a highly selective query covered by the index. The dynamic management view, ***dm_db_index_usage_stats***, keeps track of each table and its indexes and how many seeks and scans were performed against that table.

SQL Statistics

We are not surprised to see warm ski jackets appearing on display shelves starting in September. It's not cold yet, but we know that winter time is a few months away based on our own recollection of the weather, observed in previous seasons and years. Our own memory of temperature and weather patterns is a knowledge store we informally draw upon when planning for steps we will take before the cold weather arrives (e.g., get boots, mittens, scarves, and heavy jacket out of storage after Halloween; winterize the vehicle prior to November by flushing the car radiator and checking the condition of our snow tires; if it snows before U.S. Thanksgiving (The fourth Thursday of November), then we know it is likely to be a harsh winter; etc.). By sampling existing data, we can make reasonable decisions about things which have not yet happened.

This is precisely what SQL Server does when it comes to statistics. Similar to how we might look or step outdoors to sample the temperature, SQL Server observes data to understand how selective certain values are within a field. With these statistics collected, SQL Server's Query Optimizer can make good seek and scan decisions on fields with covering indexes.

Statistics Sampling

SQL Server looks at the data in its tables long before the first SELECT statement is run on a table. Because it's already done this, SQL Server knows how to best run a query when the time comes. Sampling of this data is stored in statistics, so the Query Optimizer can make the right decisions.

Sampling to save time is something we do in our daily lives. How long do we think it will take to drive to work in the morning? We already have a good estimate, based on doing this many times before. We frequently need to predict how long it will take to do some combination of errands we have never done before. Suppose, for example, our first appointment with a new dentist is this morning and it is necessary to pick up the dog from the poodle parlor afterwards. Based on sampling of the general area, such as knowledge of traffic patterns, weather, and the time of day, we estimate how long it will take and the best way to go. SQL Server takes data samples, as a fraction of the real data in a table, so the Query Optimizer can decide the best way to run a query. These small samplings of data from a table are known as *Statistics*.

The following code will find the first 12 records of the SalesInvoiceDetail table, as shown in Figure 9.29. By visually inspecting this figure, we can sample our way to a few conclusions.

- o The values in the InvoiceDetailID and ProductID fields are unique, which means these values are *highly selective*.

- o The InvoiceID field looks fairly selective with just 5 distinct values.

- o The values in the Quantity field appear less selective.

With this very small amount of data, it is difficult to be certain of our findings. We should probably sample more data to know which fields are selective enough to benefit from an index seek. Statistics are used by the Query Optimizer to know for certain how selective the query results will be based on their given criteria.

```
SELECT TOP (12) *
FROM SalesInvoiceDetail
```

	InvoiceDetailID	InvoiceID	ProductID	Quantity	UnitDiscount
1	1	1	76	2	0.00
2	2	1	77	3	0.00
3	3	1	78	6	0.00
4	4	1	71	5	0.00
5	5	1	72	4	0.00
6	6	2	73	2	0.00
7	7	3	74	3	0.00
8	8	4	14	3	0.00
9	9	5	16	1	0.00
10	10	5	9	5	0.00
11	11	5	12	3	0.00
12	12	5	11	6	0.00

12 rows

Figure 9.29 The SalesInvoiceDetail table has selective and non -selective fields.

If there is a table with millions of records and there are only five records with an InvoiceID of 1, then a query predicating on this field and value is highly selective. A query that has a covering index on the InvoiceID field will benefit during execution by performing an index seek. In order to know exactly how selective the values are within each field, SQL Server needs to first scan the entire table with its millions of records. Scanning the table and then generating statistics is slower than scanning the table when a query is run. Because of the statistics which SQL Server has collected, the Query Optimizer will know how selective each value of each field is without needing to re-scan the entire table when a query is run.

Sometimes, statistics are gathered by scanning the entire table and other times, statistics are gathered by scanning a sample of the table. Right now, the JProCo database reflects a retail operation with small scale customers whose invoices contain just a few products, at most. If JProCo later shifted its focus to a wholesale operation, having invoices with thousands of products on each bulk order, then the same InvoiceID value will be repeated for each line item of a single order. Currently, InvoiceID is a selective field, however, it could slowly become less and less selective as time goes on. Statistics need to constantly be updated to know the most recent selectivity information for an index. A field without an index has no pressing need to retain statistics and any query which predicates on this field will always use a scan instead of an index seek.

The bigger the table, the more statistics there will be for each index on the table. To easily see how statistics are created for a table, let's analyze a small table in the JProCo database with only eight records (HumanResources.RoomChart). Looking closer at these records, we see the R_ID field is unique, which is very selective. The R_Code field is also unique, as is the RoomName field. None of these first three fields contains a duplicate value, meaning each field has 8 different values. However, the RoomNotes and RoomLocation fields each have a NULL value duplicated several times in these eight records (Figure 9.30).

```
SELECT *
FROM HumanResources.RoomChart
```

	R_ID	R_Code	RoomName	RoomDescription	RoomNotes	RoomLocation
1	1	RLT	Renault...	This room is designed...	NULL	NULL
2	2	QTX	Quinault...	Parties and Moral...	NULL	NULL
3	3	TQW	TranquilWest	Misc	NULL	NULL
4	4	XW	XavierWest	NULL	NULL	NULL
5	5	YRD	Yard	Industrial Yard...	Outdoor	0x000...000003
6	6	WRS	Warehouse	Company Main...	Indoor	0x000...000003
7	7	WOD	Wood Pile	Lumber Area	Outdoor	0x000...000003
	8	PRK	Parking Lot	Yard Parking Lot	Outdoor	0x000...000003
8	9	WTR	Water Tower	Shared Space for...	Outdoor	0x000...000003

8 rows

Figure 9.30 The HumanResources.RoomChart is a small table with eight records.

Statistics Metadata

SQL Server has a handy system stored procedure (sproc) called ***sp_helpstats*** for showing which statistics are available for a given table. This sproc requires the name of an object to be passed in as a parameter inside a set of single quotes. Let's execute this sproc by supplying it with the HumanResources.RoomChart table (object name) and look at the results shown in Figure 9.31.

```
EXEC sp_helpstats 'HumanResources.RoomChart'
```

	statistics_name	statistics_keys
1	_WA_Sys_00000001_37A5467C	R_ID

1 rows

Figure 9.31 A list of statistics given for a table by running the ***sp_helpstats*** sproc.

Notice this statistic (_WA_Sys_00000001_37A5467C) is on the R_ID field of the HumanResources.RoomChart table. It is also the only statistic currently being tracked for this table, since SQL Server recognizes that none of the other fields have an index on this table.

To look at details of the statistics stored for the HumanResources.RoomChart table, we can use a **Data****B****ase** **C****onsole** **C****ommand** statement called SHOW_STATISTICS. This statement takes two parameters enclosed inside a pair of parenthesis. The first parameter is the table name, or indexed view enclosed in single quotes. The second parameter is either a statistics index or column name available for the first parameter. Recall, this table has R_ID values 1 thru 8, all of which are unique. The results for the following query are shown in Figure 9.32

```
DBCC SHOW_STATISTICS (
'HumanResources.RoomChart',_WA_Sys_00000001_37A5467C)
```

	Name	Updated	Rows	Rows Sampled	Steps	Density	Average
1	_WA_Sys_00000001_37A5467C	Aug 20 2012 5:22PM	5	5	3	1	4

	All density	Average Length	Columns
1	0.2	4	R_ID

	RANGE_HI_KEY	RANGE_ROWS	EQ_ROWS	DISTINCT_RANGE_ROWS	AVG_RANGE_ROWS
1	1	0	1	0	1
2	3	1	1	1	1
3	5	1	1	1	1

Figure 9.32 The histogram for the only statistic on the HumanResources.RoomChart table.

Histogram

In the second result set of Figure 9.32, we see the R_ID column has an Average Length value of 4 bytes because this field is an integer. The third result set in Figure 9.32 is known as a *histogram*. A histogram displays the spread of values for a field from high to low, and how many values are repeated for that field. For example, R_ID 1, R_ID 3, R_ID 5 records are each listed one time. Notice that not all of the R_IDs are listed in the histogram, only a sampling is provided.

In this histogram we see records with a small number of rows for each value. In fact the *EQ_ROWS* value is 1 for each R_ID record, which signifies that this data is selective. However, if we saw very few large values in the *EQ_ROWS* field, then this would indicate low selectivity.

Creating Statistics

Creating Statistics is usually done automatically. In fact, during the creation process for an index, SQL Server has to sample all the values in the field. SQL Server preserves the data-gathering work performed at the time of index creation by loading a data histogram into the statistics. As data continues to be inserted, deleted and modified in the table, the statistics need to be updated to ensure the best performance for the index. This can be done manually at any time with the Update Statistics statement, or setting the index to auto-update when it is created.

We have statistics on the R_ID field. However, no statistics were kept for the RoomName field because there's no index using that field. Normally, there is no reason to store statistics on a field which has no index. We can force SQL Server to keep statistics on a field that has no index by running a CREATE STATISTICS statement, shown in the following code sample.

```
CREATE STATISTICS RoomChart_RoomName
ON HumanResources.RoomChart(RoomName)
```

Messages
Command(s) completed successfully.

Figure 9.33 Create statistics on a field in a table without having to first create an index.

READER NOTE: *It's considered good practice to name a statistic after the table and field name combination that it represents.*

A new statistic has now been created for the RoomName field of the HumanResources.RoomChart table. Let's see what statistics are shown when we execute the *sp_helpstats* sproc. Notice this table now has two statistic values, with the new RoomChart_RoomName statistic in the second row (Figure 9.34).

```
EXEC sp_helpstats 'HumanResources.RoomChart'
```

	statistics_name	statistics_keys
1	_WA_Sys_00000001_37A5467C	R_ID
2	RoomChart_RoomName	RoomName
		2 rows

Figure 9.34 We see the HumanResources.RoomChart table now has two statistics.

We can find statistics generated by the Query Optimizer for our newly created statistic by running the DBCC SHOW_STATISTICS statement again. Only this time, change the second parameter to the RoomChart_RoomName statistics name and observe the results shown in Figure 9.35.

```
DBCC SHOW_STATISTICS ('HumanResources.RoomChart',
RoomChart_RoomName)
```

Results | Messages

	Name	Updated	Rows	Rows Sampled	Steps	Density	Average key
1	RoomChart_RoomName	Aug 20 2012 7:41PM	9	9	9	0	24.44444

	All density	Average Length	Columns
1	0.1111111	24.44444	RoomName

	RANGE_HI_KEY	RANGE_ROWS	EQ_ROWS	DISTINCT_RANGE_ROWS	AVG_RANGE_ROWS
1	Parking Lot	0	1	0	1
2	Quinault-Experience	0	1	0	1
3	Renault-Langsford-Tribute	0	1	0	1

Figure 9.35 The histogram for the newly created statistic is shown here.

What do these results tell us? Look at the *EQ_ROWS* field in the histogram. We can see that the RoomName field values of Parking Lot, Quinault-Experience, and Renault-Langsford-Tribute each appear only once, so this field is highly selective.

Updating Statistics

As new data gets added to a table, the histogram record values can get out of date. SQL Server will update statistics as necessary to keep the histogram up to date with the data in the table that it represents. The auto-update statistics option is less than perfect, so there is an option of updating it at a specific moment. One way to get better statistics is to manually update them using the UPDATE STATISTICS command. The following example will update all the statistics for the Customer table:

```
UPDATE STATISTICS Customer
```

A table might have many indexes, and just as many statistics. If the table is very large, then updating these statistics may take too much processing time. If only one index was critical for performance, then it would be unnecessary to update every statistic. This next code example will update the statistics for a single index in the Customer table.

```
UPDATE STATISTICS Customer NCI_Customer_CustomerType
```

Lab 9.2: Index Statistics

Lab Prep: Each lab has one or more Skill Checks. Start with Skill Check 1 and proceed until reaching the Points to Ponder section.

Before beginning this lab, verify that SQL Server 2012 is properly installed and operating. Before running the lab setup script for resetting the database (SQLQueries2012Vol3Chapter9.2Setup.sql), please make sure to close all query windows within SSMS. An open query window pointing to a database context can lock that database preventing it from updating when the script is executing. A simple way to assure all query windows are closed, is to exit out of SSMS, then open a new instance of SSMS, and lastly run the setup script.

Skill Check 1: Create a statistic on the dbo.SalesInvoiceDetail table called SalesInvoiceDetail_Quantity. Execute the sp_helpstats system stored procedure to show this statistic is present. When done the results will resemble Figure 9.36.

	statistics_name	statistics_keys
1	SalesInvoiceDetail_Quantity	Quantity

1 rows

Figure 9.36 Observing the results of the sp_helpstats system stored procedure for Skill Check1.

Skill Check 2: Update the SalesInvoiceDetail_Quantity statistic that was created during Skill Check 1.

Skill Check 3: Show the histogram for the SalesInvoiceDetail_Quantity statistic.

	Name	Updated	Rows	Rows Sampled	Steps	Density	Average key
1	SalesInvoiceDetail_Quantity	Aug 20 2012 8:30PM	6960	6960	6	0	4

	All density	Average Length	Columns
1	0.1666667	4	Quantity

	RANGE_HI_KEY	RANGE_ROWS	EQ_ROWS	DISTINCT_RANGE_ROWS	AVG_RANGE_ROWS
1	1	0	680	0	1
2	2	0	1363	0	1
3	3	0	1412	0	1

Figure 9.37 The histogram results for the Sales_InvoiceDetail_Quantity statistic in Skill Check 3.

Answer Code: The T-SQL code to this lab can be found in the downloadable files in a file named Lab9.2_IndexStatistics.sql.

Points to Ponder - Index Statistics

1. When creating a new clustered or Non-Clustered index, the Query Optimizer samples the data to see how selective it is. If the data is in a primary key or unique field, then it will be highly selective, In fact, it will be unique.

2. The Query Optimizer uses statistics to choose the best query Execution Plan by estimating the cost of using an index for a given query.

3. Statistics for indexes which are highly selective are more likely to get used for an index seek (a.k.a., a table seek) during query runtime.

4. If the statistics are sampling a field, like status, which is either a 0 or a 1 with many duplicated records, then the Query Optimizer will call the statistic and probably decide to ignore the index and perform a table scan.

5. By having statistics on hand, the Query Optimizer knows a lot about a field's selectivity without having to look at all the records. The data sample which the statistic saves is called a Histogram.

6. Statistics are saved for reuse when needed at a later time.

7. When creating a new index, the Query Optimizer stores statistical information about the field which has just been indexed.

8. When the AUTO_CREATE_STATISTICS database option is set to ON, the Database Engine creates statistics for columns in the WHERE clause even if they don't have indexes on them.

9. As the data in a table is updated via INSERT, UPDATE and DELETE statements, the statistics can become obsolete and cause the Query Optimizer to make less informed decisions. Therefore, statistics need to be updated.

10. When the AUTO_UPDATE_STATISTICS database option is ON, statistical information is periodically updated as the table changes.

11. By default, SQL Server databases automatically create and update statistics.

12. SQL Server maintains statistics on indexes and key columns of all tables.

13. Each query must be executed at least once in order to generate a statistic.

14. The information that gets stored in a statistic includes:

    o The number of rows and pages occupied by a table's data.
    o The time that statistics were last updated.
    o The average length of keys in a column.
    o Histograms showing the distribution of data in a column.
    o String summaries which are used when performing LIKE queries on character data.

15. The amount of data to be sampled by a statistic can be chosen by using the SAMPLE and FULLSCAN clauses of UPDATE STATISTICS.

Chapter Glossary

FULLSCAN: The amount of data to be sampled by a statistic can be chosen with this clause along with the UPDATE STATISTICS clause.

Histogram: Histograms show the distribution of data in a column.

SAMPLE: The amount of data to be sampled can be chosen with this clause along with the UPDATE STATISTICS clause.

SQL Statistics: SQL does sampling of the data in its tables long before a SELECT statement is run. This data sample is stored in statistics, so the Query Optimizer can make the right decisions.

UPDATE STATISTICS: This command allows you to update statistics on a specific schedule, instead of an automatic schedule.

Dynamic Management View: A view of the runtime settings metadata.

Index Hint: 'WITH *Index*' hint specifies which index the Query Optimizer uses.

OPTION: When the word OPTION appears after any query, it means a query hint is being used for a specific purpose.

OPTIMIZE FOR: The OPTIMIZE FOR hint allows a seek on a predicated variable.

Query Execution Plans: A visual representation of how the query is executed.

Query Hint: The Query Hint will suggest a way to optimize the query and let SQL Server pick the right index to use.

Query Optimizer: The SQL Server Query Optimizer determines the best way to run a query (Using an index seek or a scan).

Selectivity: A highly selective query is one where your result set will show a small percentage of the records from your table.

Review Quiz - Chapter Nine

1.) What are SQL Server Statistics?

O a. Information collected about data in columns and indexes.

O b. Information about the upper limits of how many rows each table can hold.

O c. Information about all transactions contained in the log file.

2.) What are two ways existing statistics get updated?

☐ a. Each time you restart the SQL service.

☐ b. When you issue the UPDATE STATISTICS command.

☐ c. Automatically by the database during DML changes.

☐ d. When you run a query covered by an index.

☐ e. When you create a new index.

3.) What are two ways statistics get created?

☐ a. Each time you restart the SQL service.

☐ b. When you issue the CREATE STATISTICS command.

☐ c. Automatically by the database during DML changes.

☐ d. When you run a query covered by an index.

☐ e. When you create a new index.

4.) You work for Vandalane Inc. Users report that query execution is slow. You investigate and discover that some queries do not use optimal Execution Plans. You also notice that some optimizer statistics are missing and others are out of date. You need to correct the problem so that reports execute more quickly. Which two T-SQL statements should you use?

☐ a. DBCC CHECKTABLE

☐ b. ALTER INDEX REORGANIZE

☐ c. UPDATE STATISTICS

☐ d. CREATE STATISTICS

☐ e. DBCC SHOW_STATISTICS

☐ f. DBCC UPDATE_USAGE

5.) You have the following query:

```
SELECT SalesInvoiceDetailID, SalesInvoiceID, Amount
FROM SalesInvoiceDetail
WHERE SalesInvoiceID = 1500
```

You have a Clustered index on SalesInvoiceDetailID called PK_SIDetail_SalesInvDetID and a Non-Clustered index on SalesInvoiceID called IX_SIDetail_SalesInvID. You want to force the query to use a query Execution Plan that uses an index seek rather than a scan. Which query hint should you use?

O a. HINT(1)

O b. INDEX(1)

O c. WITH(INDEX (PK_SIDetail_SalesInvDetID))

O d. WITH(INDEX (IX_SIDetail_SalesInvID))

O e. WITH(INDEX (PK_SIDetail_SalesInvDetID, IX_SIDetail_SalesInvID))

6.) You have the following query:

```
SELECT *
FROM CurrentProducts
WHERE ShortName = 'Yoga Trip'
```

You have a Non-Clustered index on the ShortName field and the query runs an efficient index seek. You change your query to use a variable for ShortName and now you are using a slow index scan. What query hint can you use to get the same execution time as before?

O a. NOLOCK

O b. LOCK

O c. FAST

O d. OPTIMIZE FOR

O e. MAXDOP

O f. READONLY

7.) Which two types of queries are most likely to perform an Index Scan?

☐ a. Uncovered query

☐ b. Covered query with high selectivity

☐ c. Covered query with low selectivity

8.) You have 15 million rows returned in one query of your SalesInvoiceDetail table and wish to run the entire query. It takes a while to run. You want to return the first 40 records right away. What code will achieve this result?

O a. `SELECT * FROM SalesInvoiceDetail`
    `OPTION(FAST 40)`

O b. `SELECT TOP 40 * FROM SalesInvoiceDetail`

O c. `SELECT * FROM SalesInvoiceDetail`
    `OPTION(OPTIMIZE TOP = 40)`

O d. `SELECT * FROM SalesInvoiceDetail`
    `OPTION(FIRST 40 ONLY)`

9.) You notice that for different parameters the following query sometimes executes quickly but most of the time very slowly.

```
SELECT AddressID, AddressLine1, City, PostalCode
FROM Person.Address
WHERE City = @city_name
AND PostalCode = @postal_code
```

You need to use a query hint for a specific set of parameter values. Which query hint should you use?

O a. FAST

O b. MAXDOP

O c. OPTIMIZE FOR

O d. PARAMETERIZATION FORCED

Answer Key

1.) Because SQL Server maintains statistics on indexed and key columns of all tables, the answers (b) and (c) are incorrect. Therefore (a) is correct.

2.) Restarting the SQL service will delete all statistics, so (a) is incorrect. Creating a new index will store statistical information about the field the index was created on, but it will not update, so (e) is incorrect. Statistics get updated when you run the statement or when SQL notices DML changes have taken place to the table. Therefore (b) and (c) are correct.

3.) If the SQL service was restarted it would wipe out all statistics, so (a) is incorrect. When DML changes are made, statistics are updated but not created, so (c) is incorrect. A query covered by an index will just choose to run an index seek, but not update statistics, so (d) is incorrect. Running a CREATE STATISTICS statement will force SQL SERVER to create statistics on a field. When an index is created SQL SERVER loads the data histogram into the statistics, making (b) and (e) correct.

4.) DBCC CHECKTABLE checks the integrity of pages and structures that make up the table or indexed view, so (a) is not correct. ALTER INDEX REORGANIZE will update the index, but not the statistics, so (b) is not correct. DBCC SHOW_STATISTICS will show what the statistics are, but will not update them, so (e) is not correct. There is not a command DBCC UPDATE_USAGE, so (f) is incorrect. If your optimizer is not getting the right statistics it either means there are none or they are out of date, making (c) and (d) correct.

5.) SQL Server can be forced to use an index using WITH (INDEX... hint), therefore (a) and (b) are incorrect. Since the WHERE clause is on SalesInvoiceID we need to use the index that is on that field. The index PK_SIDetail_SalesInvDetID is on SalesInvoiceDetailID that makes (c) and (e) wrong. The IX_SIDetail_SalesInvID index is on SalesInvoiceID, so (d) is the correct answer.

6.) NOLOCK is a table hint that has no effect on seeks and scans therefore (a) is incorrect. FAST does not change the plan but runs the first records faster, so (c) is wrong. OPTIMIZE FOR is used when a variable is predicated on with a covering index, so (d) is the correct answer.

7.) Only a query with a covering index that has high selectivity will do an index seek. All other plans will do a scan. Therefore (a) and (c) are correct.

8.) You want all records, so TOP will not work, making (b) wrong. You need to use OPTION (FAST n), making (a) correct.

9.) FAST does not change the plan but runs the first records faster, so (a) is wrong. OPTIMIZE FOR is used when a variable is predicated on with a covering index, so (c) is the correct answer.

Bug Catcher Game

To play the Bug Catcher game, run the SQLQueries2012Vol3BugCatcher09.pps file from the BugCatcher folder of the companion files. These files can be obtained from the www.Joes2Pros.com website.

[THIS PAGE INTENTIONALLY LEFT BLANK.]

Chapter 10. The GUID Data Type

I wish I could tell you I am the only "Rick Morelan" in the USA. Although there can be other people with my exact name, we can be identified as two different people since we have two different Social Security Numbers or Social Insurance Numbers. The intention is that in my country each person is to have their own unique number. It's possible that someone in Canada has my exact number. The scope of uniqueness for these numbers is not global, but set country by country. In that case, there may be many people across the world with my exact number but for their country. Currently there is no globally unique number for worldwide identification but the need, sometime in the future to establish this, may exist.

READER NOTE: *Please run the SQLQueries2012Vol3Chapter10.0Setup.sql script in order to follow along with the examples in the first section of Chapter 10. All scripts mentioned in this chapter may be found at* <u>www.Joes2Pros.com</u>.

Introduction to GUIDs

Numbers make great ID fields and for the longest time the integer was the king of fulfilling this requirement. We saw how this worked in Volume 2 by using the identity property with an integer field. We often start counting from one when populating data in a table. If we buy one of our competitors sometime in the future, we might want to place their data into the database at our headquarters. If the company that we purchased also started their tables with the number one, how can we merge our tables together and maintain uniqueness?

In hindsight, it would have been nice if the company we purchased had even numbered identity fields and we had all odd numbered identity fields. Well, that might work for two businesses merging. What if a third company was purchased and we needed to add their database to ours as well? There is no telling how big any new project will scale over the next 10 or 20 years.

Here comes the GUID data type to save the day! If our ID field is using the GUID data type and another table we want to merge into a data warehouse is also using this data type, it is guaranteed they will all be unique from as many computers as we are gathering data from.

GUID is an acronym for **G**lobal **U**nique **ID**(entifier) and is a unique 16 byte number. The term GUID and UNIQUEIDENTIFIER are often interchangeable within the SQL Server community.

Recap of Identity Integers

The UNIQUEIDENTIFIER data type was new to SQL Server 7.0 and often is used with auto generated fields similar to the use of an INT in an IDENTITY column.

The IDENTITY property is going to insert values in an incremental order, unlike the random order produced by a UNIQUEIDENTIFIER data type using the NEWID() function.

Attempting to merge two tables generated by an IDENTITY column into a single table is very likely to end up with gaps, or conflicting values (Duplicates). Let's create a very simple table and insert five rows of test data into the table to review how this works. The results are shown in Figure 10.1.

```
CREATE TABLE TestInt (
IntID INT IDENTITY(1,1),
IntName VARCHAR(25))
GO

INSERT INTO TestInt VALUES
('One'), ('Two'), ('Three'), ('Four'), ('Five')

SELECT * FROM TestInt
```

	IntID	IntName
1	1	One
2	2	Two
3	3	Three
4	4	Four
5	5	Five

5 rows

Figure 10.1 Recap of working with an INT IDENTITY column in a table.

Introduction of UNIQUEIDENTIFIER Data Type

Like an integer, the GUID is a number. However, instead of being a base 10 number like the integer, it is a hexadecimal number (Base 16). All GUIDs have a format of *8hex-4hex-4hex-4hex-12hex* as shown here: B8DC0F5E-E4EF-4EA4-BC39-40721AFE680D

A big advantage of the GUID data type over an IDENTITY column of INT, is they are unique across all tables, databases, and computers, over any foreseeable time period (Hundreds of years or more). This is very useful when combining records from multiple SQL Servers into a single data warehouse, as it will certainly avoid any conflicting entries based on this field.

We can quickly see exactly what a GUID looks like and how to easily generate this unique hexadecimal number by using the following code sample. When viewing the results shown in Figure 10.2, notice how the same code generates a different value each time the NEWID() function is called.

READER NOTE: *Whenever the NEWID() function is called, it will return a value of the UNIQUEIDENTIFIER data type (e.g., a GUID).*

```
SELECT NEWID() AS 'GUID-A'
SELECT NEWID() AS 'GUID-B'
SELECT NEWID() AS 'GUID-C'
```

	GUID-A
1	E005915A-6A34-45E9-A57A-DF638BED1A18

	GUID-B
1	952E6FD0-6B14-48BE-BA2B-685B7CDDC5E2

	GUID-C
1	4B73C91D-AE84-41B2-97D2-233860A78032

3 rows

Figure 10.2 Calling the NEWID() function creates a UNIQUEIDENTIFIER data type (GUID).

Now let's create another simple table using a UNIQUEIDENTIFIER (GUID) instead of an IDENTITY column, and then insert the same VARCHAR() values in each of the five rows of test data that we used for the TestInt table. It is important to remember that GUIDs are not generated automatically by SQL Server and it is recommended to use the DEFAULT keyword both when creating and inserting data into the table. The results are shown in Figure 10.3.

```
CREATE TABLE TestGuid (
GuidID UNIQUEIDENTIFIER DEFAULT NEWID(),
IntName VARCHAR(25))
GO

INSERT INTO TestGuid VALUES
(DEFAULT, 'One'), (DEFAULT, 'Two'), (DEFAULT, 'Three'),
(DEFAULT, 'Four'), (DEFAULT, 'Five')

SELECT * FROM TestGuid
```

	GuidID	IntName
1	6F6EAB2C-FF82-4057-BF9F-ECC3BA62CF6C	One
2	BBC1B87E-0E0B-4D55-ABB9-0D585653CA7F	Two
3	CB8379E0-AB76-4AC4-B5E0-24DE9C3DFD1F	Three
4	B97F7594-3E3E-42B7-B268-A0CAD0F30914	Four
5	8DD0310C-7844-4C08-9B0D-A266F3F3A11F	Five

5 rows

Figure 10.3 Simple table using a UNIQUEIDENTIFIER column (GUID).

When comparing the results of the TestInt table values (Figure 10.1) to the TestGuid table values, (Figure 10.3) we can see that the first column in both tables contain unique values, they share a common field name for the second column, in addition to having duplicate values for each respective row in the table.

READER NOTE: *You will get a different GUID in your example so please vary the new few figures with your results.*

Comparison Operators on GUIDs

Is it possible to use any or all of the comparison operators that we have become so fond of using in our queries? Will we have to use special functions to perform this simple task?

At first glance, a GUID with its long, multi-part, hexadecimal numbers appear to be cumbersome and difficult to work with. When working with an IDENTITY column, we know that using comparison operators on an integer is a very effective way of filtering records to find only the records we are searching for. This code sample is a very familiar method of finding a specific employee record.

```
SELECT * FROM Employee
WHERE EmpID = 5
```

Let's find out how comparison operators work with GUIDs in a few simple steps. We can begin by copying the value of the GUID from the first record of the TestGuid table (shown in Figure 10.3) into the predicate value for the GuidID field in the following query. We can see by the results that the = operator does work with a GUID and returns the desired record for the first row (Figure 10.4).

```
SELECT * FROM TestGuid
WHERE GuidID = '6F6EAB2C-FF82-4057-BF9F-ECC3BA62CF6C'
```

	GuidID	IntName
1	6F6EAB2C-FF82-4057-BF9F-ECC3BA62CF6C	One
		1 rows

Figure 10.4 The equals '=' comparison operator works with the GUID data type.

We can test several other comparison operators and view their results by using the following code samples:

```
SELECT * FROM TestGuid
WHERE GuidID != '6F6EAB2C-FF82-4057-BF9F-ECC3BA62CF6C'
```

	GuidID	IntName
1	BBC1B87E-0E0B-4D55-ABB9-0D585653CA7F	Two
2	CB8379E0-AB76-4AC4-B5E0-24DE9C3DFD1F	Three
3	B97F7594-3E3E-42B7-B268-A0CAD0F30914	Four
4	8DD0310C-7844-4C08-9B0D-A266F3F3A11F	Five
		4 rows

Figure 10.5 The not equals '!=' comparison operator works with the GUID data type.

```
SELECT * FROM TestGuid
WHERE GuidID > '6F6EAB2C-FF82-4057-BF9F-ECC3BA62CF6C'
```

GuidID	IntName
	0 rows

Figure 10.6 The greater than '>' comparison operator works with the GUID data type.

```
SELECT * FROM TestGuid
WHERE GuidID < '6F6EAB2C-FF82-4057-BF9F-ECC3BA62CF6C'
```

	GuidID	IntName
1	BBC1B87E-0E0B-4D55-ABB9-0D585653CA7F	Two
2	CB8379E0-AB76-4AC4-B5E0-24DE9C3DFD1F	Three
3	B97F7594-3E3E-42B7-B268-A0CAD0F30914	Four
4	8DD0310C-7844-4C08-9B0D-A266F3F3A11F	Five
		4 rows

Figure 10.7 The less than '<' comparison operator works with the GUID data type.

```
SELECT * FROM TestGuid
WHERE GuidID LIKE '%E%'
```

	GuidID	IntName
1	6F6EAB2C-FF82-4057-BF9F-ECC3BA62CF6C	One
2	BBC1B87E-0E0B-4D55-ABB9-0D585653CA7F	Two
3	CB8379E0-AB76-4AC4-B5E0-24DE9C3DFD1F	Three
4	B97F7594-3E3E-42B7-B268-A0CAD0F30914	Four
		4 rows

Figure 10.8 The LIKE comparison operator works with the GUID data type.

```
SELECT * FROM TestGuid
WHERE GuidID BETWEEN '6F6EAB2C-FF82-4057-BF9F-ECC3BA62CF6C'
AND '6F6EAB2C-FF82-4057-BF9F-ECC3BA62CF6C'
```

	GuidID	IntName
1	6F6EAB2C-FF82-4057-BF9F-ECC3BA62CF6C	One
		1 rows

Figure 10.9 The BETWEEN comparison operator works with the GUID data type.

It appears that the GUID data type does not pose any problems when writing simple queries using comparison operators. Other than the length and complexity of typing the value for a GUID, we can just as easily use it as a predicate value, or any other typical use for a comparison operator, with a distinct exception. There is a problem using a GUID in combination with non-comparison operators.

Non-Comparison Operators on GUIDs

Ok, we can definitely use comparison operators such as =, !=, <, >, LIKE and BETWEEN with GUIDs in a query. What about working with the common non-comparison operators like +, -, *, / in addition to those that are used for more scientific purposes. Can we add two GUIDs together and retrieve the sum of their two values as a new single GUID? How about simply adding a GUID value to an integer value, such as incrementing a GUID by 1?

These are very good questions, because as we progress on our path to becoming a professional SQL Developer, we will be using non-comparison operators quite frequently in our code to satisfy the needs of our clients and superiors. Let's begin answering the question by finding a GUID with the number 2 somewhere in its hexadecimal value.

```
SELECT * FROM TestGuid
WHERE GuidID LIKE '%2%'
```

	GuidID	IntName
1	6F6EAB2C-FF82-4057-BF9F-ECC3BA62CF6C	One
2	CB8379E0-AB76-4AC4-B5E0-24DE9C3DFD1F	Three
3	B97F7594-3E3E-42B7-B268-A0CAD0F30914	Four
4	8DD0310C-7844-4C08-9B0D-A266F3F3A11F	Five
		4 rows

Figure 10.10 All records in the TestGuid table, having GuidID values with number 2 in them.

If we were to write some code that queries the TestInt table on the integer field we have some options. We can find a record that when adding the number 1 to the IntID value equals an IntID of 2. In doing so we would expect the first record to be returned (1 + 1 = 2). We can see this is the case, by looking at the query results shown in Figure 10.11.

```
SELECT * FROM TestInt
WHERE IntID + 1 LIKE '%2%'
```

	IntID	IntName
1	1	One
		1 rows

Figure 10.11 The record containing IntID 1 is returned based on the predicate of this query.

This query works because IntID is an INT (Integer) data type and the physical number 1 being added to it is recognized by SQL Server as an integer as well.

What happens when we try to perform this same operation in a query that substitutes the TestInt table with the TestGuid table and swaps the IntID field in the predicate with the GuidID field storing a UNIQUEIDENTIFIER data type?

Will SQL Server find a way to interpret these different values, or will it cause a conflict in the calculation? We can run the following code and observe the results shown in Figure 10.12.

```
SELECT * FROM TestGuid
WHERE GuidID + 1 LIKE '%2%'
```

```
Messages
Msg 206, Level 16, State 2, Line 1
Operand type clash: uniqueidentifier is incompatible with int
                                                        0 rows
```

Figure 10.12 Error message from attempting to add a GUID and an Integer together.

OK, it appears that we cannot use non-comparison operators with a GUID as they are not compatible with integers when SQL Server attempts to perform the calculation. The result is the error message shown from the last query we ran. After a little thought, this makes a lot of sense, because a hexadecimal value is alpha-numeric (e.g., a mix of letters and numbers to form a single value). We learned a lesson when we were children that letters and numbers cannot be added, subtracted, multiplied, or divided with each other and SQL Server enforces these same rules.

Two Ways to Generate GUIDs

What do we do when our team lead tells us that they have just been informed that one of our tables will need to start accepting GUIDs from the front-end application that it is serving? Fortunately, there is a simple way to generate or assign GUID values within our table whenever they are needed by using T-SQL code.

A UNIQUEIDENTIFIER data type local variable can be set in these ways:

o   By using the SET @InvoiceGUID = NEWID() function.

o   Converting from a string. Example: Use the following string as the second parameter of a CONVERT() function with a UNIQUEIDENTIFIER data type (`'12345678-AAAA-BBBB-CCCC-123456789FED'`).

By now, we are already familiar with the NEWID() function and have used it several times in our code throughout this section of the Chapter. However, the second option of creating a GUID with the CONVERT() function looks new… so let's try a couple of coding examples to find out how this can work for us.

Anytime we need to use the CONVERT() function, it is important to remember that it takes in two parameters to perform its calculations. Inside a set of parentheses, the first parameter is the data type that the second parameter will be converted into. In our example this is a UNIQUEIDENTIFIER. The second parameter is the expression value that will be converted. In our example this is a string value enclosed in single quotes that is in the format of a GUID.

We are now ready to put this new information into action. Our first code sample will create a UNIQUEIDENTIFIER, also known as a GUID, from a string value that we supply to the second parameter of the CONVERT() function. The results for this code sample are shown in Figure 10.13.

READER NOTE: *It is necessary to write the string value in the same format as a GUID data type, or SQL Server will fail to perform the string conversion and produce an error message.*

```
SELECT CONVERT(UNIQUEIDENTIFIER,
'12345678-AAAA-BBBB-CCCC-123456789FED') AS StringToGUID
```

StringToGUID
1 12345678-AAAA-BBBB-CCCC-123456789FED

1 rows

Figure 10.13 Using the CONVERT() function to create a GUID from a string.

Testing to see what happens when a string that is either too short or too long for the GUID format requirement is a good idea. We will definitely want to know what will happen if the front-end application happens to supply a string value with an unexpected length of characters to our table.

Our first code sample will test the output from SQL Server when a string that is too short is supplied to our table. Will SQL Server randomly generate the additional characters necessary to create a valid GUID, or will this code result in an error? Run the code and check the results in Figure 10.14.

```
SELECT CONVERT(UNIQUEIDENTIFIER,
'12345678-AAAA') AS ShortStringToGUID
```

Messages
Msg 8169, Level 16, State 2, Line 4
Conversion failed when converting from a character string to uniqueidentifier.
0 rows

Figure 10.14 The string to GUID conversion fails if too few characters are supplied in the string.

It looks like the first test has failed because there were not enough characters supplied to the CONVERT() function in the string value and it did not meet the formatting standard for a GUID data type.

Our last test will determine what happens if we provide too many characters in the last segment of the string when passing it into the CONVERT() function. Let's run the code sample shown here and look at the results shown in Figure 10.15.

```
DECLARE @InvoiceGUID UNIQUEIDENTIFIER;

SET @InvoiceGUID = CONVERT(UNIQUEIDENTIFIER,
'12345678-AAAA-BBBB-CCCC-123456789FED TOO MUCH DATA')

SELECT @InvoiceGUID AS LongStringToGUID
```

LongStringToGUID
1   12345678-AAAA-BBBB-CCCC-123456789FED
1 rows

Figure 10.15 Too many characters in the string to GUID conversion will truncate the string.

The CONVERT() function will truncate the string to fit the GUID data type formatting rules when too many characters are provided in the last section of the GUID by the string parameter.

In other words, as long as the string parameter meets the minimum requirements of the GUID formatting rules, it will succeed.

READER NOTE: *If too few, or too many characters are provided in the first four sections of the GUID then the operation will fail. Additionally, if too few characters are supplied in the fifth (last) section of the GUID then the operation will fail. The only time the operation will succeed if too many characters are supplied, is when they are in the last section of the GUID.*

Lab 10.1: Introduction to GUIDs

Lab Prep: Each lab has one or more Skill Checks. Start with Skill Check 1 and proceed until reaching the Points to Ponder section.

Before beginning this lab, verify that SQL Server 2012 is properly installed and operating. Before running the lab setup script for resetting the database (SQLQueries2012Vol3Chapter10.1Setup.sql), please make sure to close all query windows within SSMS. An open query window pointing to a database context can lock that database preventing it from updating when the script is executing. A simple way to assure all query windows are closed, is to exit out of SSMS, then open a new instance of SSMS, and lastly run the setup script.

Skill Check 1: Create a table named Skill10 in the JProCo database having two fields SkillID and SkillName. The SkillID field will be a UNIQUEIDENTIFIER data type that defaults to the NEWID() function. The SkillName field will be a VARHCHAR(20) data type.

Populate the Skill10 table with two records with the first SkillName entered as 'One' and the second SkillName entered as 'Two'. Finally, query all the records in the Skill10 table and the results should resemble those shown in Figure 10.16.

```
SELECT *
FROM Skill10
```

	SkillID	SkillName
1	E4C88CDD-2B0A-4E86-9447-C3BC4F979199	One
2	634878EE-904D-4596-8B1F-2319D1084012	Two
		2 rows

Figure 10.16 Create a Skill10 table with the SkillID field using the NEWID() function.

Skill Check 2: Alter the Contractor table in the JProCo database to contain a field called ctrGuid. Update the table with the ctrGuid field populated by the NEWID() function. Finally, query all the records in the Contractor table and the results should resemble those shown in Figure 10.17.

```
SELECT *
FROM Contractor
```

	ctrID	LastName	FirstName	HireDate	ctrGuid
1	1	Barker	Bill	2006-01-07	DBE222C4-BE5B-4CE4-85E4-60AD47CDB88A
2	2	Ogburn	Maurice	2006-10-27	3FE904A8-9B4E-416A-B39D-72159FDC5A49
3	3	Fortner	Linda	2009-11-22	11E27207-1233-4C59-9393-712E62FECA62
4	4	Johnson	Davey	2009-03-07	EFCB8572-B026-4CCE-86DD-563FA30CFC73

4 rows

Figure 10.17 Add a ctrGuid field using the NEWID() function to the Contractor table.

Answer Code: The T-SQL code to this lab can be found from the downloadable files named Lab10.1_IntroductionToGUIDs.sql.

Points to Ponder - Introduction to GUIDs

1. GUID is an acronym for **G**lobal **U**nique **ID**(entifier).

2. A GUID is a unique 16 byte number.

3. UNIQUEIDENTIFIERs in SQL Server are also called GUIDs.

4. In SQL Server every column or variable has a data type.

5. The UNIQUEIDENTIFIER data type was new to SQL Server 7.0 and often is used in auto generating values similar to the use of an INT in an IDENTITY column.

6. The IDENTITY property is going to insert the values in an incremental order. A UNIQUEIDENTIFIER using the NEWID() function will create GUIDs in a random order.

7. If we were to take two tables generated by an identity column and merge them into a single table it is very likely to end up with gaps.

8. A UNIQUEIDENTIFIER data type local variable can be set in two ways:
    o   Using the SET @InvoiceGUID = NEWID() function.
    o   Converting from a string.
        Example: `SELECT CONVERT(UNIQUEIDENTIFIER,'12345678-AAAA-BBBB-CCCC-123456789FED')`

9. Using too many characters for a GUID with the CONVERT() function will truncate the data to the correct size of a GUID data type. For example:

    ```
    SET @InvoiceGUID = CONVERT(UNIQUEIDENTIFIER, '12345678-AAAA-BBBB-CCCC-123456789FED TOO MUCH DATA')
    ```

    Will return: 12345678-AAAA-BBBB-CCCC-123456789FED

Advantages / Disadvantages of GUIDs

If we go shopping for a new car, we know what the advantages are to getting the GT (Grant Touring) version. We get the cool sound system, deluxe GPS, A/C, and leather interior. In this case, why doesn't everyone get the GT version? Answer: It costs more. So, if GUIDs are so much better than INTs, the reason we might not choose them is their size. Let's take the time to really know the advantages and disadvantages of GUIDs versus their smaller Integer counterparts for ID fields.

Advantages of Using a GUID

A big advantage of the GUID over an INT IDENTITY column is that they are unique across all tables, databases, and computers, over any time period. This can be very useful when combining records from multiple SQL Servers into a single data warehouse. Let's look at how Data Warehousing works with Integers versus GUIDs.

Warehousing IDENTITY Field Records

Let's explore data warehousing two regular tables into a single table when they are both sourced from IDENTITY fields. We can start by creating two tables in the JProCo database (ServerA and ServerB), each having the same configuration, with an IDENTITY field called IntID and a VARCHAR(20) field.

```
USE JProCo
GO

CREATE TABLE ServerA (
G_ID INT IDENTITY(1,1),
G_Name VARCHAR(20))
GO

CREATE TABLE ServerB (
G_ID INT IDENTITY(1,1),
G_Name VARCHAR(20))
GO
```

We are now ready to populate these two tables with some basic data. In order to make it easy to identify each table, we will populate each with distinct values.

- o   ServerA with values *One thru Five*
- o   ServerB with values *Six thru Ten*

```
INSERT INTO ServerA VALUES
('One'), ('Two'), ('Three'), ('Four'), ('Five')

INSERT INTO ServerB VALUES
('Six'), ('Seven'), ('Eight'), ('Nine'), ('Ten')
```

Verify that these inserts worked correctly with a query that displays all fields and records from both tables with the following code:

```
SELECT * FROM ServerA

SELECT * FROM ServerB
```

	G_ID	G_Name
1	1	One
2	2	Two
3	3	Three
4	4	Four
5	5	Five

5 rows

Figure 10.18 All fields and records for the ServerA table.

	G_ID	G_Name
1	1	Six
2	2	Seven
3	3	Eight
4	4	Nine
5	5	Ten

5 rows

Figure 10.19 All fields and records for the ServerB table.

Now that we know our two tables simulating a data stream from two different servers is working, we can create a table that will simulate a central data warehouse that stores all of the data from multiple servers in a single location. We will call this new table DataWarehouse and it will consist of a field called IntID with an INT data type that is a PRIMARY KEY and a VARCHAR(20) data type field called IntName.

```
USE JProCo
GO

CREATE TABLE DataWarehouse (
G_ID INT PRIMARY KEY,
G_Name VARCHAR(20))
GO
```

Once the DataWarehouse table is created, we can begin to populate it with all the data from the ServerA and ServerB tables. This is easy to accomplish with a simple INSERT INTO statement as shown here:

```
INSERT INTO DataWarehouse
SELECT * FROM ServerA
```

Messages
(5 row(s) affected)
0 rows

Figure 10.20 Populating the DataWarehouse table with data from ServerA works correctly.

```
INSERT INTO DataWarehouse
SELECT * FROM ServerB
```

Messages
Msg 2627, Level 14, State 1, Line 1
Violation of PRIMARY KEY constraint 'PK__DataWare__9E5447965E46C7B3'.
Cannot insert duplicate key in object 'dbo.DataWarehouse'.
The duplicate key value is (1).
The statement has been terminated.
0 rows

Figure 10.21 Error message given while populating the DataWarehouse with data from ServerB.

The error message shown in Figure 10.21 indicates that the insert of data from ServerB failed due to a violation of the PRIMARY KEY constraint. This exercise has exposed the main problem encountered when merging multiple tables with an IDENTITY field into a field with a PRIMARY KEY, since it is impossible to ensure that each value being inserted will be unique.

Warehousing UNIQUEIDENTIFIER Field Records

OK, in order to successfully merge data from multiple tables into a single table, we must make sure that each record being inserted into the central table has a field that we know is unique.

Before we can do this, let's drop all three tables and start fresh with a new plan.

```
DROP TABLE ServerA
GO

DROP TABLE ServerB
GO

DROP TABLE DataWarehouse
GO
```

This next example of data warehousing two regular tables into a single table will use a UNIQUEIDENTIFIER field from both tables. We can accomplish this by creating two tables in the JProCo database (ServerA and ServerB). Each table will have a field with a UNIQUEIDENTIFIER data type generated by the NEWID() function as a DEFAULT value.

```
USE JProCo
GO

CREATE TABLE ServerA (
G_ID UNIQUEIDENTIFIER DEFAULT NEWID(),
G_Name VARCHAR(20))
GO

CREATE TABLE ServerB (
G_ID UNIQUEIDENTIFIER DEFAULT NEWID(),
G_Name VARCHAR(20))
GO
```

We are now ready to populate these two tables with some basic data. In order to make it easy to identify each table, we will populate each with distinct values.

- o   ServerA with a *DEFAULT* value and then values *One through Five*
- o   ServerB with a *DEFAULT* value and then values *Six through Ten*

```
INSERT INTO ServerA VALUES
(DEFAULT, 'One'), (DEFAULT, 'Two'),
(DEFAULT, 'Three'), (DEFAULT, 'Four'), (DEFAULT, 'Five')

INSERT INTO ServerB VALUES
(DEFAULT, 'Six'), (DEFAULT, 'Seven'),
(DEFAULT, 'Eight'), (DEFAULT, 'Nine'), (DEFAULT, 'Ten')
```

Verify that these inserts worked correctly with a query that displays all fields and records from both tables with the following code:

```
SELECT *
FROM ServerA

SELECT *
FROM ServerB
```

	G_ID	G_Name
1	AC3AC0A8-870D-419E-BD4B-A66EFCFD5A33	One
2	F2F9DF0C-DAF6-4DA0-9951-20BDA7F71493	Two
3	B77828D0-4418-4321-AC0A-9611CC081F32	Three
4	E3164689-EAC0-4D97-B2C4-B27D3E8D8757	Four
5	FCD830C5-19B9-4B3E-9EC2-CF1FCEF58C97	Five
		5 rows

Figure 10.22 All fields and records from the ServerA table with a UNIQUEIDENTIFIER.

	G_ID	G_Name
1	F278C9D7-9335-45C7-BFF8-3E552D5E5E92	Six
2	70940344-7370-4BF1-B675-FBF70560F99F	Seven
3	65AB8483-EAC3-4371-8E60-5592C87DC46D	Eight
4	F730D9CA-0698-41E0-B50B-FC784B9F6CE4	Nine
5	3B623BEE-8061-4AFA-B9B0-085234875CA5	Ten
		5 rows

Figure 10.23 All fields and records from the ServerB table with a UNIQUEIDENTIFIER.

Great! Our two tables are now simulating a data stream from two different servers. So we can now create a table that will simulate a central data warehouse to store all of the data from these servers in a single location. Let's call this new table DataWarehouse and define a field called G_ID with a UNIQUEIDENTIFIER data type and a VARCHAR(20) data type field called G_Name.

```
USE JProCo
GO
CREATE TABLE DataWarehouse (
G_ID UNIQUEIDENTIFIER PRIMARY KEY,
G_Name VARCHAR(20))
GO
```

With the DataWarehouse table created, we can populate it with data from the ServerA and ServerB tables by using an INSERT INTO statement as shown here:

```
INSERT INTO DataWarehouse
SELECT * FROM ServerA
```

Messages
(5 row(s) affected)
0 rows

Figure 10.24 Populating the DataWarehouse table with data from ServerA works correctly.

```
INSERT INTO DataWarehouse
SELECT * FROM ServerB
```

Messages
(5 row(s) affected)
0 rows

Figure 10.25 Populating the DataWarehouse table with data from ServerB works correctly.

Verify that populating the DataWarehouse table was successful by displaying all the fields and records (Figure 10.26) with a query using the code shown here:

```
SELECT * FROM DataWarehouse
```

	G_ID	G_Name
1	3B623BEE-8061-4AFA-B9B0-085234875CA5	Ten
2	F2F9DF0C-DAF6-4DA0-9951-20BDA7F71493	Two
3	F278C9D7-9335-45C7-BFF8-3E552D5E5E92	Six
4	65AB8483-EAC3-4371-8E60-5592C87DC46D	Eight
5	B77828D0-4418-4321-AC0A-9611CC081F32	Three
6	AC3AC0A8-870D-419E-BD4B-A66EFCFD5A33	One
7	E3164689-EAC0-4D97-B2C4-B27D3E8D8757	Four
8	FCD830C5-19B9-4B3E-9EC2-CF1FCEF58C97	Five
9	70940344-7370-4BF1-B675-FBF70560F99F	Seven
10	F730D9CA-0698-41E0-B50B-FC784B9F6CE4	Nine
		10 rows

Figure 10.26 The DataWarehouse table contains all the data from ServerA and ServerB.

We can see that merging data from multiple tables with a UNIQUIDENTIFIER field into a field with a PRIMARY KEY constraint will work, since we can be certain that every record being inserted into the table has a unique identity. Notice that the natural sort order of the DataWarehouse table is on the G_ID field because of the PRIMARY KEY constraint on this field.

Disadvantages of Using a GUID

One significant drawback to using GUIDs is their size. Since a GUID is four times larger than an INT, any index that is built on them is much slower than an index built on a column using an IDENTITY INT data type.

Another drawback is the possibility of page splits caused by any GUID generated using the NEWID() function. The nature of this function is to produce random values, which is a virtual guarantee the table will have page splits. The odds of this are further increased, as the GUID is 16 bytes and an INT is 4 bytes.

Let's create a query that uses a loop to insert a total of 25,000 records into the TestInt table. We will use a variable with an INT data type named *@LoopNumber* and set it to an initial value of 6, as there are already five records in the TestInt table. Inside the loop, we increment the value of the *@LoopNumber* variable by 1 after inserting each record.

Run the code sample shown here in a new query window:

```
USE JProCo
GO

DECLARE @LoopNumber INT = 6
WHILE @LoopNumber <= 25000
BEGIN
    INSERT INTO TestInt VALUES (@LoopNumber)
    SET @LoopNumber = @LoopNumber + 1
END
```

Verify that populating the TestInt table was successful by displaying all the fields

When the query is complete, we will be able to see how long it takes by looking at the lower right-hand corner of the results window (Figure 10.27).

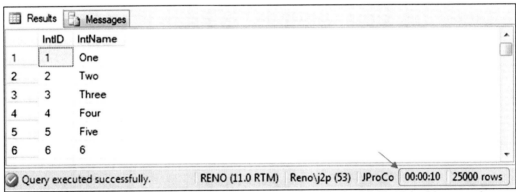

Figure 10.27 Inserting 25000 records into the TestInt table will take 00:00:10 in this example.

Veritfy the records with a query using the code shown here:

```
SELECT * FROM TestInt
```

Our next task is to use a similar loop to insert a total of 25,000 records into the TestGuid table. We only need to make two changes to the structure of the loop for it to begin inserting values into the TestGuid table.

1) Change the name of the table from TestInt to TestGuid.
2) Add a *DEFAULT* value separated by a comma from *@LoopNumber*.

```
DECLARE @LoopNumber INT = 6
WHILE @LoopNumber <= 25000
BEGIN
  INSERT INTO TestGuid VALUES (DEFAULT, @LoopNumber)
  SET @LoopNumber = @LoopNumber + 1
END
```

When the query is complete, we will be able to see how long it takes by looking at the lower right-hand corner of the results window (Figure 10.28).

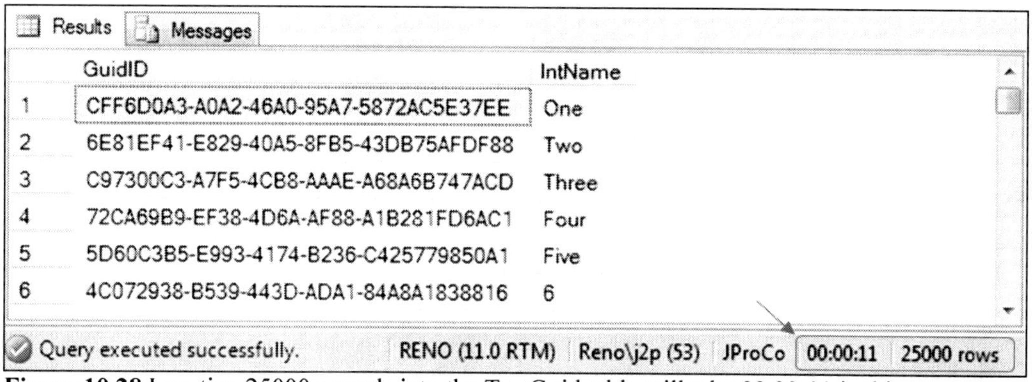

Figure 10.28 Inserting 25000 records into the TestGuid table will take 00:00:11 in this example.

Verify that populating the TestGuid table was successful by displaying all the fields and records with a query using the code shown here:

```
SELECT * FROM TestGuid
```

The results after inserting a total of 25,000 records into both the TestInt and TestGuid tables show that the TestInt query loop performed faster (10 seconds) than the TestGuid query loop (11 seconds).

READER NOTE: *The length of time it takes to run these two queries can vary a great deal depending on the configuration of the machine that they are executed on, in addition to the processes and services that are running behind the scenes at the same time. It is possible for both queries (loops) to take the same amount of time to run, or even to have the TestInt loop run slower than the TestGuid loop.*

Lab 10.2: Advantages/Disadvantages of GUIDs

Lab Prep: Each lab has one or more Skill Checks. Start with Skill Check 1 and proceed until reaching the Points to Ponder section.

Before beginning this lab, verify that SQL Server 2012 is properly installed and operating. Before running the lab setup script for resetting the database (SQLQueries2012Vol3Chapter10.2Setup.sql), please make sure to close all query windows within SSMS (An open query window pointing to a database context can lock that database preventing it from updating when the script is executing). A simple way to assure all query windows are closed, is to exit out of SSMS, then open a new instance of SSMS, and lastly run the setup script.

Skill Check 1: Create a table named ServerC with the same structure as the ServerB table created earlier in this section. Next, INSERT five records with values for the IntName field: 'Eleven', 'Twelve', 'Thirteen', 'Fourteen' and 'Fifteen' into the ServerC table.

Finally, run the query shown in the following code:

```
SELECT *
FROM ServerC
```

When done, the results should resemble those shown in Figure 10.29.

	G_ID	G_Name
1	0732FC69-0BE5-41D9-AA94-56749692BA0C	Eleven
2	852611ED-662F-450E-BD1D-03E62F1458CA	Twelve
3	847F601C-CFBE-40A4-B2F4-6C12449CE9F3	Thirteen
4	5B7AED54-334B-4599-B50B-B8FEA306F6AA	Fourteen
5	6BF51A3D-E97C-4676-ADB8-8D91BAB1E8C0	Fifteen

5 rows

Figure 10.29 Create a ServerC table (with ServerB structure) and then populate the table.

Skill Check 2: Insert the records from the ServerC table created in Skill Check 1 into the DataWarehouse table. After inserting the records, run the query shown with the following code:

```
SELECT *
FROM DataWarehouse
```

When done, the results should resemble those shown in Figure 10.30.

	G_ID	G_Name
1	852611ED-662F-450E-BD1D-03E62F1458CA	Twelve
2	3B623BEE-8061-4AFA-B9B0-085234875CA5	Ten
3	F2F9DF0C-DAF6-4DA0-9951-20BDA7F71493	Two
4	F278C9D7-9335-45C7-BFF8-3E552D5E5E92	Six
5	65AB8483-EAC3-4371-8E60-5592C87DC46D	Eight
6	0732FC69-0BE5-41D9-AA94-56749692BA0C	Eleven
7	847F601C-CFBE-40A4-B2F4-6C12449CE9F3	Thirteen
8	6BF51A3D-E97C-4676-ADB8-8D91BAB1E8C0	Fifteen
9	B77828D0-4418-4321-AC0A-9611CC081F32	Three

15 rows

Figure 10.30 Insert data from the ServerC table into the DataWarehouse table for Skill Check 2.

Answer Code: The SQL code to this lab can be found in the downloadable file named Lab10.2_AdvantagesDisadvantagesOfGUIDs.

Points to Ponder - Advantages/Disadvantages of GUIDs

1. A big advantage of the GUID over an IDENTITY column is that they are unique across all tables, databases, and computers, over any time period. This is very useful when combining records from multiple SQL Servers into one data warehouse.

2. The drawback to using GUIDs is size, so indexes built on them are slower than indexes built on IDENTITY INT Columns.

3. Another drawback to GUIDs using the NEWID() function is the random nature of the inserts can cause page splits.

4. Only comparison operators can be used with a UNIQUEIDENTIFIER, such as '=', '!=', '<', '>', '<=', '>=', 'IS NULL', 'IS NOT NULL', 'IN', 'NOT IN', 'LIKE', 'NOT LIKE' and 'BETWEEN'.

GUID Performance

We know GUIDs are new and cool, however, it is important for us to do everything we can to make sure they perform the best they possibly can. How we generate a GUID and how we implement them will require making the right plan to use them.

GUID Functions

SQL Server already has a function named NEWID() that can generate a GUID value for a field in a table. So, why was the NEWSEQUENTIALID() function created when it appears to do the same thing? Let's compare these two functions used to generate UNIQUEIDENTIFIERs to see what the actual differences are.

Let's begin by looking at the output value (Figure 10.31) generated by these two functions by running the following code:

```
SELECT NEWID() AS 'NEWID() Value'
```

NEWID() Value
1   E13D4342-4112-4048-BFB6-718CF424C7F1

1 rows

Figure 10.31 GUID value generated by calling the NEWID() function with a SELECT statement.

```
SELECT NEWSEQUENTIALID() AS 'NEWSEQUENTIALID() Value'
```

Messages
Msg 302, Level 16, State 0, Line 1 The newsequentialid() built-in function can only be used in a DEFAULT expression for a column of type 'uniqueidentifier' in a CREATE TABLE or ALTER TABLE statement. It cannot be combined with other operators to form a complex scalar expression.

0 rows

Figure 10.32 Calling the NEWSEQUENTIALID() function with a SELECT statement results in an error message from SQL Server.

We can immediately recognize that there is a difference between these two functions, since the NEWID() function worked as expected, while the NEWSEQUENTIALID() function produced an error message (Figure 10.32) instead of the new GUID value that we were expecting it to deliver.

When we read the error message, we find that SQL Server only allows the NEWSEQUENTIALID() function to be called at the time a new field is created and it **must** also be used in conjunction with a DEFAULT constraint.

Using NEWSEQUENTIALID() for Fields

Starting with SQL Server 2005, the NEWSEQUENTIALID() function was added to allow the creation of sequentially increasing GUID values. This benefits SQL Server performance by reducing page splits and making inserts quicker.

By their very nature, both the NEWSEQUENTIALID() and the NEWID() functions create a unique value of the UNIQUEIDENTIFIER data type.

Let's create a table with the same basic structure as the TestGuid table we created earlier in this chapter. The code sample shown here was originally used to create the TestGuid table:

```
CREATE TABLE TestGuid (
GuidID UNIQUEIDENTIFIER DEFAULT NEWID(),
IntName VARCHAR(25))
GO
```

We only need to change the name of the table to TestSeq and then replace the NEWID() function with the NEWSEQUENTIALID() function to begin using our new table and observe the values generated when each new record is inserted.

```
USE JProCo
GO

CREATE TABLE TestSeq (
GuidID UNIQUEIDENTIFIER DEFAULT NEWSEQUENTIALID(),
IntName VARCHAR(25))
GO
```

We are now ready to populate the TestSeq table with some basic data. Once again, we need to use the DEFAULT keyword as the first value for each record and for the second value in each record use the values '1', '2', '3', '4' and '5'.

```
INSERT INTO TestSeq VALUES
(DEFAULT,'1'), (DEFAULT,'2'),
(DEFAULT,'3'), (DEFAULT,'4'), (DEFAULT,'5')
```

Verify that populating the TestSeq table was successful by displaying all the fields and records (Figure 10.33) with a query using the code shown here:

```
SELECT * FROM TestSeq
```

	GuidID	IntName
1	C95756F8-2209-E211-B9C6-00190E02C264	1
2	CA5756F8-2209-E211-B9C6-00190E02C264	2
3	CB5756F8-2209-E211-B9C6-00190E02C264	3
4	CC5756F8-2209-E211-B9C6-00190E02C264	4
5	CD5756F8-2209-E211-B9C6-00190E02C264	5

5 rows

Figure 10.33 TestSeq table with values generated by the NEWSEQUENTIALID() function.

Verify that all of the GuidID values are in sequential order, by observing that the first three characters are unique and they increment sequentially. The example in Figure 10.33 confirms this as shown here:

- o C95...
- o CA5...
- o CB5...
- o CC5...
- o CD5...

READER NOTE: Whenever we are required to have GUIDs in sequential order, we need to implement the NEWSEQUENTIALID() function and the DEFAULT constraint with a UNIQUEIDENTIFIER data type in the field definition.

NEWSEQUENTIALID() Performance

In our previous performance test using a loop to insert a total of 25,000 records into the TestInt and TestGuid tables, we found that the TestInt query loop performed faster than the TestGuid query loop. This is mainly attributed to the fact that an INT data type takes up four times less memory space than a GUID.

Does this mean that a GUID generated by the NEWID() function will perform the same as a GUID generated by a NEWSEQUENTIALID() function? The best way to find out is to use the same loop structure used by the TestGuid table.

The only change necessary is renaming the table name from TestGuid to TestSeq, as shown in the following code sample:

```
DECLARE @LoopNumber INT = 6
WHILE @LoopNumber <= 25000 --00:12 Seconds
BEGIN
  INSERT INTO TestSeq VALUES (DEFAULT, @LoopNumber)
  SET @LoopNumber = @LoopNumber + 1
END
```

When the query is complete, we will be able to see how long it takes by looking at the lower right-hand corner of the results window (Figure 10.34).

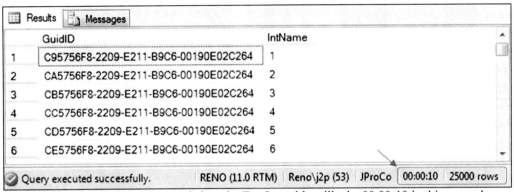

Figure 10.34 Inserting 25000 records into the TestSeq table will take 00:00:10 in this example.

Verify that populating the TestSeq table was successful by displaying all the fields and records with a query using the code shown here:

```
SELECT * FROM TestSeq
```

Just like before, the results after inserting a total of 25,000 records into both the TestGuid and TestSeq tables show that the TestSeq query loop performed faster (10 seconds) than the TestGuid query loop (11 seconds).

READER NOTE: *The length of time it takes to run these two queries can vary a great deal depending on the configuration of the machine that they are executed on, in addition to the processes and services that are running behind the scenes at the same time. It is possible for both queries (loops) to take the same amount of time to run, or even to have the TestSeq loop run slower than the TestGuid loop.*

Lab 10.3: GUID Performance

Lab Prep: Each lab has one or more Skill Checks. Start with Skill Check 1 and proceed until reaching the Points to Ponder section.

Before beginning this lab, verify that SQL Server 2012 is properly installed and operating. Before running the lab setup script for resetting the database (SQLQueries2012Vol3Chapter10.3Setup.sql), please make sure to close all query windows within SSMS. An open query window pointing to a database context can lock that database preventing it from updating when the script is executing. A simple way to assure all query windows are closed, is to exit out of SSMS, then open a new instance of SSMS, and lastly run the setup script.

Skill Check 1: Alter the Contractor table in the JProCo database to contain a field called ctrSeq. Make this a UNIQUEIDENTIFIER data type that is non-nullable and defaults to use the NEWSEQUENTIALID() function. Finally, query all the records in the Contractor table and the results should resemble Figure 10.35.

```
SELECT * FROM Contractor
```

	ctrID	LastName	FirstName	HireDate	ctrSeq
1	1	Barker	Bill	2006-01-07...	4C461750-DAE2-E111-819D-00190E02C264
2	2	Ogburn	Maurice	2006-10-27...	4D461750-DAE2-E111-819D-00190E02C264
3	3	Fortner	Linda	2009-11-22...	4E461750-DAE2-E111-819D-00190E02C264
4	4	Johnson	Davey	2009-03-07...	4F461750-DAE2-E111-819D-00190E02C264

4 rows

Figure 10.35 Skill Check 1 adds a ctrSeq field using the NEWSEQUENTIALID() function.

Answer Code: The T-SQL code to this lab can be found in the downloadable file named Lab10.3_GUIDPerformance.sql.

Points to Ponder - GUID Performance

1. Starting with SQL Server 2005, the NEWSEQUENTIALID() function creates sequentially increasing GUIDs to increase performance.

2. Both the NEWSEQUENTIALID() function and the NEWID() function create a unique value of the UNIQUEIDENTIFIER data type (GUID).

3. Using a NEWSEQUENTIALID() function can be faster than the NEWID() function because the NEWID() function generates its value randomly from the entire GUID range, rather than caching from where it left off.

4. Even if SQL Server starts again, the new low starting point of the next GUID will continue to be Globally Unique.

5. The NEWSEQUENTIALID() function can only be used with a DEFAULT constraint on a UNIQUEIDENTIFIER column when defining a new field.

6. The NEWSEQUENTIALID() function cannot be used in queries.

7. The NEWSEQUENTIALID() function creates an incrementally higher GUID each time it is called on a specified computer, since the time the current instance of SQL Server was started.

8. The impact on database performance from a NEWID() function versus the NEWSEQUENTIALID() function for UNIQUEIDENTIFIER columns should be weighed out on how they benefit a particular database design.

9. The NEWSEQUENTIALID() function generates a value faster, because it is less random and it is easier to insert because the sequential nature will produce fewer page splits.

10. Rebooting SQL Server may cause the NEWSEQUENTIALID() function to begin generating values with a lower number than the last value generated before rebooting the server. Sequential inserts are only good for as long as SQL Server remains up and running.

Chapter Glossary

GUID: A common name used for the UNIQUEIDENTIFIER data type. It is an acronym for **G**lobal **U**nique **ID**entifier.

NEWID(): A function that generates a random GUID at the time that it is called. It can be used in DML and DDL statements.

NEWSEQUENTIALID(): A function that generates a sequential GUID at the time that it is called. Each GUID will increment by one from the previous GUID on the current instance of SQL Server. If SQL Server is restarted for any reason the sequential values will begin at a different value (Lower or higher). This function can only be used when defining a field with a UNIQUEIDENTIFIER data type and must include a DEFAULT constraint.

UNIQUEIDENTIFIER: This data type is 16 bytes in size and virtually guarantees a unique value across all platforms, databases and tables when it is generated by either the NEWID() or NEWSEQUENTIALID() function. The specific format of a UNIQUEIDENTIFIER is: *8hex-4hex-4hex-4hex-12hex*

Review Quiz - Chapter Ten

1.) How many bytes are in a GUID?

   O a. 2 bytes

   O b. 4 bytes

   O c. 8 bytes

   O d. 16 bytes

   O e. It ranges from 8 – 24 bytes.

   O f. It is a LOB and gets a 16 byte pointer.

2.) Which query will NOT throw an error?

   O a. `SELECT NEWID()`

   O b. `SELECT NEWSEQUENTIALID()`

   O c. `SELECT NEWID() + 1`

3.) Which query will NOT throw an error?

   O a. `SELECT NEWID() + NEWID()`

   O b. `SELECT CONVERT(UNIQUEIDENTIFIER, '12345678-AAAA-BBBB')`

   O c. `SELECT CONVERT(UNIQUEIDENTIFIER, '12345678-AAAA-BBBB-CCCC-123456789FED TOO MUCH DATA')`

4.) What is the advantage of using a UNIQUEIDENTIFIER data type versus using an integer with an identity field?

   O a. The UNIQUEIDENTIFIER is smaller.

   O b. The UNIQUEIDENTIFIER is faster.

   O c. The UNIQUEIDENTIFIER has been around longer.

   O d. The UNIQUEIDENTIFIER can guarantee uniqueness across ID fields from multiple sources.

5.) What is true about the NEWSEQUENTIALID() function? Choose three.

   ☐ a. GUIDs are generated in Random order.

   ☐ b. GUIDs are generated in Sequential order.

   ☐ c. It often performs faster than the NEWID() function.

   ☐ d. It will cause more page splits than the NEWID() function.

   ☐ e. It will cause fewer page splits than the NEWID() function.

   ☐ f. It was created in SQL Server 2012.

6.) You want to have GUIDs automatically generated for the QuizID field of your table and also plan to make the QuizID field unique and clustered. To cut down on page splits you want the GUID number to be sequential. Which DDL code will achieve this result?

O a.
```
CREATE TABLE Quiz (
   QuizID UNIQUEIDENTIFIER PRIMARY KEY DEFAULT NEWID(),
   QuizName VARCHAR(20))
GO
```

O b.
```
CREATE TABLE Quiz (
   QuizID UNIQUEIDENTIFIER PRIMARY KEY DEFAULT
   NEWSEQUENTIALID(), QuizName VARCHAR(20))
GO
```

O c.
```
CREATE TABLE Quiz (
   QuizID UNIQUEIDENTIFIER DEFAULT NEWID(),
   QuizName VARCHAR(20))
GO
```

O d.
```
CREATE TABLE Quiz (
   QuizID UNIQUEIDENTIFIER DEFAULT NEWSEQUENTIALID(),
   QuizName VARCHAR(20))
GO
```

Answer Key

1.) A GUID is a UNIQUEIDENTIFIER data type, which is always 16 bytes, making (d) the right answer.

2.) Arithmetic (non-comparison) operators cannot be used on a GUID, so (c) is wrong. The NEWSEQUENTIALID() function can only be used with a DEFAULT value when a field is created and cannot be used as part of a query, so (b) is incorrect. The SELECT NEWID() query will work, making (a) the correct answer.

3.) Arithmetic (non-comparison) operators cannot be used on a GUID, so (a) is wrong. Too little data in the CONVERT() function will fail, so (b) is incorrect. Placing too much data into the last section of the CONVERT() function will work, as it will truncate the excess data, so (c) is correct.

4.) An integer is smaller and faster, making (a) and (b) incorrect. The GUID is much newer than the integer, making (c) wrong. The global uniqueness of the GUID makes (d) the correct answer.

5.) The NEWSEQUENTIALID() function was released with SQL Server 2005, making (f) incorrect. The order of generated GUIDs is sequential and not random, making (a) wrong. Sequential inserts cause fewer page splits, so (d) is wrong. The correct answers are (b), (c) and (e).

6.) To generate sequential GUIDs requires using the NEWSEQUENTIALID() function, making (a) and (c) incorrect. Since the QuizID field must also be unique and clustered, it is necessary to specify an index or PRIMARY KEY, therefore (b) is the correct answer.

Bug Catcher Game

To play the Bug Catcher game, run the SQLQueries2012Vol3BugCatcher10.pps file from the BugCatcher folder of the companion files. These files can be obtained from the www.Joes2Pros.com website.

[THIS PAGE INTENTIONALLY LEFT BLANK.]

Chapter 11. Transactions and Locking

When we host a dinner, we are in control of when it's time for the guests to eat and what will be served. While preparing dinner and placing food on the plates, our guests have to wait to eat. As soon as we are done cooking and serving the plates to our guests, they can begin eating. Because of this process, we have exclusive access to the food and our guests will gladly wait until the dinner is served for them to eat.

Many of the guests don't need exclusive access to the plates. For example I remember a dinner where my friend Sita had his one year old son on his lap and they both ate from the same plate. For a more scaled example think of a party food platter with 4 people all choosing their snacks at the same time.

We typically know which objects in our daily life can be shared simultaneously with others and when it makes more sense to have exclusive access to a resource. SQL Server knows when to share and when to exclusively lock its resources too. This chapter is about how SQL Server uses transactions and locking to keep the resources it controls safe.

READER NOTE: *Please run the SQLQueries2012Vol3Chapter11.0Setup.sql script in order to follow along with the examples in the first section of Chapter 11. All scripts mentioned in this chapter may be found at* www.Joes2Pros.com.

SQL Locking

I saw a piece of clipart where someone is sitting on a tree branch while trying to saw it off. The problem is if the character is successful it will cause him to fall down. The saw will allow him to cut this branch, or any other as he chooses. SQL Server is a bit smarter than this. For example, we have found that it is impossible to drop a database while we are using the same database. How does SQL Server manage to be smart and protective enough to put in these safety locks for us? The answer is it uses a process called *locking*.

We think of locks as something that does not let anyone else in. This type of lock is called an exclusive lock. A shared lock is different. Think of a punch bowl at a party. Anyone is allowed to use it and in fact three people can be standing around this bowl and serving themselves at the same time. The only time we could not use the bowl is if the host says, "Stand back everyone, while I refill or change the punch bowl!" At that moment, the host puts an exclusive lock on the punch bowl and nobody can use it. The times when the host is not changing the punch bowl, everyone has a shared lock on (access to) the bowl.

It could be argued that nobody has any lock on the bowl, as they are just using it. Well, if the host wanted to refill the bowl while a guest was using it she would probably wait until the guest finished using it, and then take the bowl. A shared lock is able to finish the current use of the object, without getting kicked out in the middle of the process.

Sometimes SQL Server exercises safety features that cause DML statements like DELETE or SELECT to fail when they would otherwise succeed. For example, even a user with *sysadmin* privileges to SQL Server is unable to delete a database while that database is in use. This safety mechanism is a SQL Server process known as a *lock*. In this next lab we will explore how locks are put in place and how to monitor existing locks.

Activity Monitor

So just who is using what resources and at what level? There are many ways to find out. Because we will be attempting to delete an entire database and its tables, we will make sure to test against our dbMovie sample database for the examples used during this exercise.

READER NOTE: *Before starting this next exercise close all open query windows. During the following exercises DO NOT CLOSE any query windows until reaching Lab 11.1 and then close all query windows prior to doing the lab.*

Open a new query window in SSMS and run the code shown here:

```
USE JProCo
GO

DROP DATABASE dbMovie
GO
```

Messages
Command(s) completed successfully.
0 rows

Figure 11.1 Dropping the dbMovie database from the JProCo context is allowed.

Keep the JProCo database context and change the DROP DATABASE statement to focus on JProCo instead of the dbMovie database which is now gone. Take note of the SPID (Service Profile Identifier) number of the query window being used and run the code shown here.

```
USE JProCo
GO

DROP DATABASE JProCo
GO
```

Figure 11.2 Dropping the JProCo database from the JProCo context is not allowed.

As expected, dropping the JProCo database while we are in the JProCo context is prevented by SQL Server, because it is locked while we are using its resources.

In Figure 11.2 we see that the code to DROP the JProCo database is being run with the SPID connection number of 52. SQL decides the SPID when you open the query window so your number may be different. Remember how to locate the SPID number in the upper right-hand corner of the query window tab, as we will need to know the SPID number for the remaining exercises and the lab in this section.

While keeping the current connection open (SPID 52 in this example), open a new query window (this will automatically create a new connection with a new SPID number) and write the T-SQL code to use the master database context followed by the code for dropping the JProCo database.

```
USE master
GO

DROP DATABASE JProCo
GO
```

Figure 11.3 Dropping the JProCo database from the master database context (SPID 55) is being prevented by SQL Server because it is locked while in use by SPID 52.

We know that dropping the JProCo database from the master database context is normally allowed. So why did SQL Server issue an error message stating that JProCo is currently in use? SPID #55 shown in Figure 11.3 is the query window connection that we used to DROP the JProCo database from the master database context, which means that it is definitely not using any of the JProCo resources.

So the problem must exist with the only other connection currently open, which is SPID #52. That's right! SQL Server knows that SPID #52 has its database context set to JProCo, which allows it to run any code against this database as long as the connection remains open, or until the database context is changed.

Even though the SPID #52 connection does not have any code being executed and is effectively inactive, SQL Server has issued a lock that will prevent the JProCo database or any of its objects from being dropped until the connection is closed, or the context focus has been changed to a different database.

Notice that it took several seconds (20 seconds in this example), while SQL Server waited for SPID #52 to either close, or change its database context before officially issuing the error message that the JProCo database is currently in use and cannot be dropped (Figure 11.3).

There is a tool provided with SQL Server to help us easily visualize what connections are open, which connections are being blocked and the connections they are being blocked by. This tool is called the Activity Monitor and it can either be accessed from the SSMS toolbar by clicking on the icon in the 'Standard' SQL tools toolbar, (arrow in Figure 11.4) or by using the keyboard shortcut and typing 'CTRL' + 'ALT' + 'A' keys at the same time.

Figure 11.4 Accessing the Activity Monitor with the SSMS toolbar icon (See arrow).

Here is a look at what the Activity Monitor looks like (Figure 11.5).

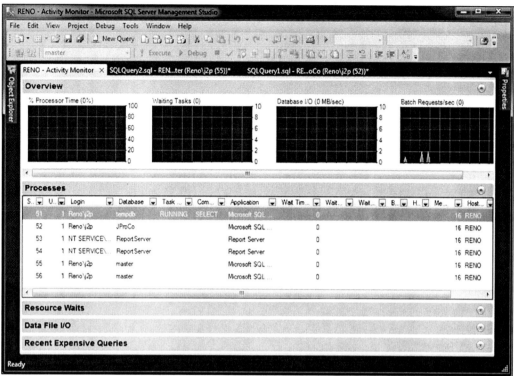

Figure 11.5 A screenshot of the SQL Server Activity Monitor.

By expanding the '*Processes*' tab (closed by default), we can view all the connections currently open in this instance of SQL Server. Some of these connections are being used by SQL Server directly (System) and in the example shown here, SPID #52 and SPID #55 are the only two connections that are being used by the User.

Notice that in Figure 11.5 neither of our two SPID connections is showing any activity. Let's switch to the query window that is using the master database context to DROP the JProCo database (SPID #55 in this example).

Click on the '! Execute' button to run this code and then switch back to the Activity Monitor tab to watch what happens while this code is running. The Activity Monitor results shown in Figure 11.6 allow us to see that the DROP DATABASE command for SPID #55 is in a SUSPENDED state because it is being Blocked By SPID #52.

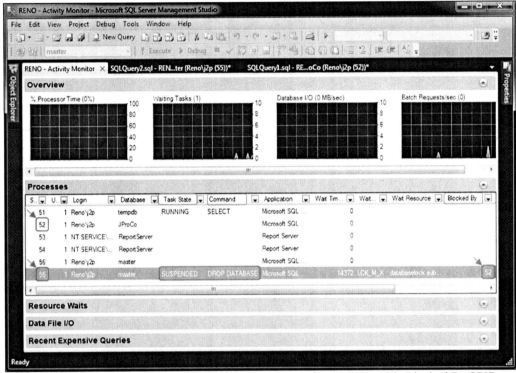

Figure 11.6 The Activity Monitor shows that the code running in SPID 55 is Blocked By SPID 52.

sp_who and sp_who2

Activity Monitor is a great way to visually look at the processes running on our system. It allows us to get a result set of activity for consumption while it is happening. In other words, we want a table showing results of what is happening.

sys.dm_exec_requests

There are two great system stored procedures, sp_who and sp_who2, that produce a tabular result of all the connections running on SQL Server at the time the sproc is executed. These connections are formally known as the Server Process ID, or more commonly by its acronym SPID. We often find that only a fraction of the SPIDs (connections) shown in the result set are actually waiting for a request.

Let's open another query window connection and execute the sp_who system stored procedure after first clicking on the '! Execute' button of the window using the master database context that is dropping the JProCo database (Figure 11.7).

```
EXEC sp_who
```

	spid	ecid	status	logina...	hostname	blk	dbname	cmd	request_id
34	36	0	background	sa		0	master	FT FULL PASS	0
35	39	0	background	sa		0	NULL	UNKNOWN TOKEN	0
36	51	0	sleeping	Reno\...	RENO	0	tempdb	AWAITING COMMAND	0
37	52	0	sleeping	Reno\...	RENO	0	JProCo	AWAITING COMMAND	0
38	53	0	sleeping	Reno\...	RENO	0	master	AWAITING COMMAND	0
39	54	0	sleeping	NT S...	RENO	0	Repor...	AWAITING COMMAND	0
40	55	0	suspended	Reno\...	RENO	52	master	DROP DATABASE	0
41	56	0	runnable	Reno\...	RENO	0	master	SELECT	0

Query executed successfully.   RENO (11.0 RTM)

Figure 11.7 Results from executing the sp_who sproc while the code in SPID #55 is running.

The sp_who2 system stored procedure offers a little more information in its result set, such as the last column shown in Figure 11.8 labeled CPUTime.

```
EXEC sp_who2
```

	SPID	Status	Login	HostName	BlkBy	DBName	Command	CPUTime
27	35	BACKGROUND	sa	.	.	master	FT FULL PASS	0
28	39	BACKGROUND	sa	.	.	NULL	UNKNOWN TOKEN	0
29	51	sleeping	NT S...	RENO	.	Report...	AWAITING COMMAND	0
30	52	sleeping	Reno\...	RENO	.	JProCo	AWAITING COMMAND	16
31	53	sleeping	NT S...	RENO	.	Report...	AWAITING COMMAND	0
32	55	SUSPENDED	Reno\...	RENO	52	master	DROP DATABASE	0
33	56	RUNNABLE	Reno\...	RENO	.	master	SELECT INTO	16

Query executed successfully.   RENO (11.0 RTM) Re

Figure 11.8 Results from executing the sp_who2 sproc while the code in SPID #55 is running.

Another way to view the connections running on our instance of SQL Server is with the sys.dm_exec_requests Dynamic Management View. Once again, we will need to run the code that is using the master database and dropping the JProCo database (SPID #55 in our example) and then switch to a new query window connection to execute this DMV with the code shown here.

```
SELECT *
FROM sys.dm_exec_requests
```

	session_id	request_id	start_time	status	command	sql_handle
30	31	0	2012-09-28 10:36:41.907	background	BRKR TASK	NULL
31	32	0	2012-09-28 10:36:41.907	background	BRKR TASK	NULL
32	33	0	2012-09-28 14:38:46.260	background	FT CRAWL MON	NULL
33	34	0	2012-09-28 10:36:41.910	background	BRKR TASK	NULL
34	39	0	2012-09-28 10:36:45.740	background	UNKNOWN TOKEN	NULL
35	55	0	2012-09-28 14:39:31.287	suspended	DROP DATABASE	0x01000...
36	56	0	2012-09-28 14:39:33.910	running	SELECT	0x02000...

Query executed successfully.   RENO (11.0 RTM) Ren

Figure 11.9 Result set from sys.dm_exec_requests DMV while the code in SPID #55 is running.

You may have more or fewer background processes running on your system. Figure 11.9 shows 36 but your results may show a different number of records.

One of the biggest differences between a result set given by the System Stored Procedures *sp_who / sp_who2* and the DMV *sys.dm_exec_requests,* is which SPID connections are listed.

For example, only the connections that are actively running or are being blocked by another connection will be shown in the result set of the *sys.dm_exec_requests* Dynamic Management View. Notice in Figure 11.9 that SPID #52 is not shown in the results, even though we know there is a query window open in our instance of SQL Server with this SPID number.

If we look at Figure 11.7 and Figure 11.8, which show the result set for executing the *sp_who* and *sp_who2* system stored procedures, we find that each of the SPIDs that are listed in the *cmd* column with the 'AWAITING COMMAND' value are not shown in the result set for Figure 11.9 (*sys.dm_exec_requests*). This is because these three SPID connections are not actively running any requests (code) on the server.

Killing Transactions

Sometimes we need to perform a command immediately and cannot wait for a blocking transaction to finish. There are techniques available that allow us to eliminate, or kill, the SPID associated with blocking a priority transaction.

When a SPID connection is removed in such a severe manner, SQL Server will make an attempt to protect the integrity of the data by immediately rolling back the blocking transaction to its initial state, which allows the SPID containing the priority transaction to run without waiting.

It is possible to immediately kill a SPID connection by using either the SSMS UI, or via T-SQL code. This exercise will demonstrate how to accomplish this task by using a coding example.

We must first open a new query window connection to the JProCo database context and then write a long running query that will block any other connection from trying to access the Location table. An easy way to make this happen is to write a simple UPDATE statement for the Location table inside a transaction block that has a BEGIN TRAN statement without a COMMIT TRAN statement.

The code shown here will create a long running query of the Location table:

```
USE JProCo
GO

BEGIN TRAN
  UPDATE Location
  SET City = 'Vancouver'
  WHERE LocationID = 1
```

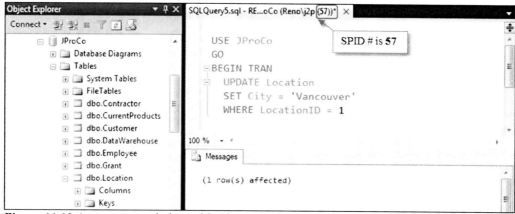

Figure 11.10 A new query window with a long running transaction (SPID #57).

READER NOTE: *Even though it says '(1 row(s) affected)' this does not mean the record is committed. It just means the transaction has completed that step. In this case the record is just affected in the intermediate state.*

Take note of the SPID number of this connection (#57 in our example) and then open another query window connection (new SPID), to write a query that will display all fields and records from the JProCo.dbo.Location table.

```
SELECT *
FROM JProCo.dbo.Location
```

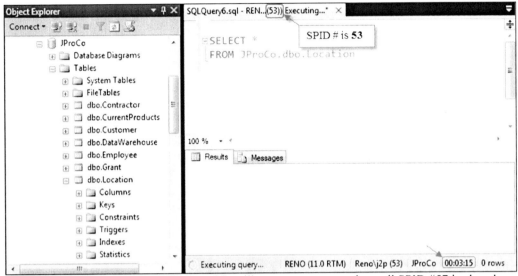

Figure 11.11 A query on the Location table will not return any results until SPID #57 is closed.

Notice that this query will not return the expected result set right away. Instead it continues to run for a very long time (3:15 and still running). In fact, because the connection with the transaction updating the Location table (SPID #57) does not have a COMMIT TRAN or a ROLLBACK TRAN statement, it will continue to run until this connection is closed either manually (closing the query window), or by a KILL command.

Using the KILL command is a very simple process. All we need to know is the SPID number of the connection that is blocking our priority SPID number and then place the blocking SPID number after the KILL command. We have already learned that we can get this information in one of three ways:

1) Execute the *sp_who* System Stored Procedure.

2) Execute the *sp_who2* System Stored Procedure.

3) Query the *sys.dm_exec_requests* Dynamic Management View (DMV).

The example shown in this exercise shows the SPID blocking our priority code connection is SPID #57. So, to stop this offending connection, immediately open a new query window and to allow our priority code to run, use the code shown here:

```
KILL 57
```

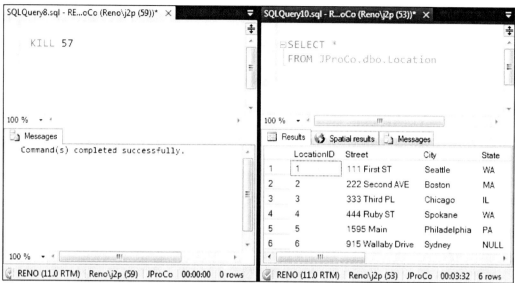

Figure 11.12 After executing the KILL 57 command, the SPID #53 query is able to finish.

Great! In Figure 11.12 we can see that the command to KILL 57 executed successfully and our query of the Location table in SPID #53 was able to return results immediately after SPID #57 closed.

Lab 11.1: SQL Locking

Lab Prep: Each lab has one or more Skill Checks. Start with Skill Check 1 and proceed until reaching the Points to Ponder section.

Before beginning this lab, verify that SQL Server 2012 is properly installed and operating. Before running the lab setup script for resetting the database (SQLQueries2012Vol3Chapter11.1Setup.sql), please make sure to close all query windows within SSMS. An open query window pointing to a database context can lock that database preventing it from updating when the script is executing. A simple way to assure all query windows are closed, is to exit out of SSMS, then open a new instance of SSMS, and lastly run the setup script.

Skill Check 1: This Skill Check will require having three query windows opened sequentially according to the following steps.

READER NOTE: *The query window you used to run the reset script should be closed before you start. DO NOT close any of the query windows you open in Skill Check 1 until after the Skill Check has been completed!*

Step One: Open the first query window and write a T-SQL statement to use the RatisCo database context. Execute this query.

Step Two: Open the second query window and write a T-SQL statement to use the master database context. Continue by writing a DROP statement for the RatisCo database. Execute this query.

Step Three: Open the third query window and write a T-SQL statement that executes the correct system stored procedure that shows which SPID (Step One) is blocking the other SPID (Step Two). When done, the results for this step should resemble the following figure.

	SPID	Status	Login	HostName	BlkBy	DBName	Command	CPUTime	DiskIO	LastBatch	ProgramName	SPID	RI
33	51	sleeping	Re...	RENO	.	master	AWAITING COMMAND	529	256	05/11 07:38:11	Microsoft SQ...	51	0
34	52	sleeping	Re...	RENO	.	JProCo	AWAITING COMMAND	8563	5442	05/11 10:43:08	Microsoft SQ...	52	0
35	53	sleeping	Re...	RENO	.	RatisCo	AWAITING COMMAND	0	0	05/11 11:23:32	Microsoft SQ...	53	0
36	54	SUSPENDED	Re...	RENO	53	master	DROP DATABASE	0	0	05/11 11:23:40	Microsoft SQ...	54	0
37	55	RUNNABLE	Re...	RENO	.	master	SELECT INTO	78	23	05/11 11:23:47	Microsoft SQ...	55	0

Query executed successfully.　　　　　RENO (11.0 RTM)　Reno\Student (55)　master　00:00:00　37 rows

Figure 11.13 Results from executing the correct system stored procedure for Skill Check 1.

Answer Code: The T-SQL code to this lab can be found from the downloadable files named Lab11.1_Locking.sql.

Points to Ponder - SQL Locking

1. At any time, SQL Server can have multiple connections, each accessing different portions of the same database.

2. SQL Server assigns every connection a unique value known as a SPID.

3. SPID is an acronym for **Server Process ID**(entifier).

4. Activity Monitor is a graphical tool that displays information about ANY SQL Server connections that are currently open, whether they are active, inactive (sleeping), running, or suspended.

5. A Dynamic Management View (DMV) gives the current status of dynamic activity for SQL Server in its result set.

6. A System Dynamic Management View (DMV) for any type of object will have a prefix of '***sys.dm_***' and can be found with the path shown here:
    Object Explorer > *DatabaseName* **> Views > System Views**

7. Use a standard SELECT statement to query DMVs.

8. Exclusive locks prevent modifications by any SPID other than the one assigned to the code issuing the lock.

Transactions

A transaction is generally considered to be a sequence of operations performed as a single logical unit of work. Ideally, every transaction exhibits the four key properties known by the acronym ACID (**A**tomic **C**onsistent **I**solated **D**urability). A brief definition of these four properties is shown here:

- o **Atomicity:** A transaction is an atomic unit of work and executes exactly once; either all the work is done or none of it is.

- o **Consistency:** A transaction preserves the consistency of data, transforming one consistent state of data into another consistent state of data. Data bound by a transaction must be semantically preserved.

- o **Isolation:** A transaction is a unit of isolation and each occurs separately and independently of concurrent transactions. A transaction should never see the intermediate stages of another transaction.

- o **Durability:** A transaction is a unit of recovery. If a transaction succeeds, its' updates persist, even if the system crashes or is shut down. If a transaction fails, the system remains in the state previous to committing the transaction.

Every DML statement will run as a transaction in SQL Server. This is why it is unnecessary for a DML statement to use the keyword GO, unlike every DDL statement, which must run as a batch ending with the keyword GO.

The simplest way to describe the steps of a transaction is to use an example of updating an existing record in a table. The goal of the UPDATE statement in our example is to replace the current value of the ***Street*** field for ***LocationID*** 4.

Take a few moments to study the upcoming images in Figure 11.14, Figure 11.15 and Figure 11.16 to better understand the basics of how a SQL Server transaction works behind the scenes.

Our *DML Data Journey* begins with Figure 11.14 when the code for this UPDATE statement runs. Since our code will be changing data in an existing record, the first step SQL Server takes is to retrieve the old record from storage (typically a hard drive), and then load this data into the computer's memory (RAM) and **C**entral **P**rocessing **U**nit (CPU).

In other words, the old record now exists in two places:

1) Persisted storage on a physical device (hard drive) as a database file.
2) Temporary storage in the computer's memory (RAM) as a virtual record.

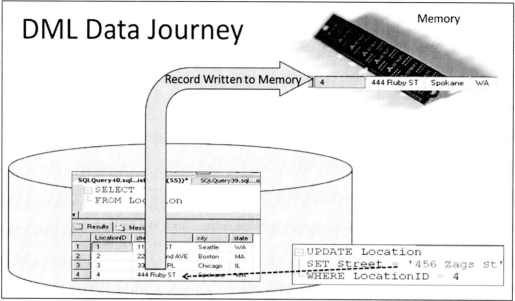

Figure 11.14 When changing data, the first step of the transaction is to retrieve the old record from storage and then load this data into memory.

Once the data for the old record is loaded into memory (RAM), the next step of our *DML Data Journey* takes place. The old record located temporarily in the computer's memory is now modified to reflect the new value for the **Street** field.

To clarify this important point, the old value for the **Street** field (444 Ruby ST) is modified while it is temporarily located in the computer's memory to now contain the new value for the **Street** field (456 Zags St), as shown in Figure 11.15.

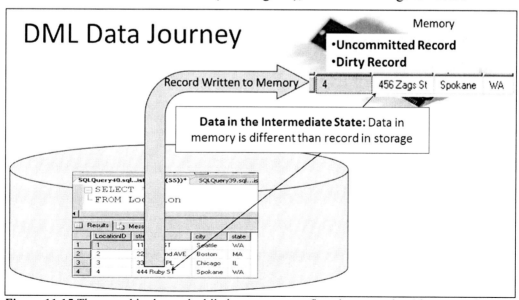

Figure 11.15 The record is changed while in memory to reflect the new value (*dirty record*).

By taking a closer look at Figure 11.15 we are able to visualize how the physical location (hard drive) holds the value for the old record and the temporary location (computer's memory or RAM) now holds the new value for this same record.

Since the new value for the record is being held in a temporary location and has not yet been written to physical storage for the database file, it is considered to be in an *Intermediate State*. Any record located in an *Intermediate State* is known as either an *uncommitted record* or as a *dirty record,* and these two terms can be used interchangeably to describe this condition.

We can see in Figure 11.16 that our *DML Data Journey* is nearly finished. The last step will place the record held in the computer's memory, otherwise known as the *Intermediate State,* back into physical storage. Once the record with the new value has been written to physical storage for the database file, it is considered to be in a *Persistent State*. Any record in a *Persistent State* is called a *committed record*. When the new value officially becomes a *committed record,* SQL Server sends a message confirming how many rows were affected.

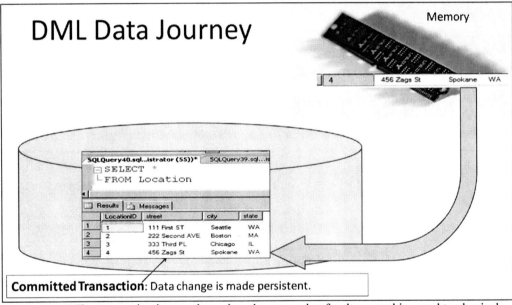

Figure 11.16 The transaction is complete when the new value for the record is saved to physical storage (*Persistent State*) and becomes a *committed record.*

Now that the committed record is in a Persistent State, it only exists in a single physical location (hard drive) and the record located in the computer's memory will be eliminated, since it is no longer needed by SQL Server.

The data for the record held in the computer's memory (*Intermediate State*) can be eliminated or discarded under several conditions. Three of these are listed here:

1) If the transaction completes and the new value for the record is written to the physical storage location and officially becomes a committed record.

2) If for some reason during the transaction process a record in the Intermediate State cannot be written to the physical storage location and the new value for the record is not committed.

3) If for any reason during the transaction process the transaction is rolled back and the new value for the record is not committed.

The steps shown during our *DML Data Journey* are an oversimplification of the real checks and steps that happen under the hood for each transaction. However, these steps do represent the basic principles upon which all transactions are built.

In summary, until the change being made to the record is saved to the physical storage location, the transaction is considered incomplete (Uncommitted). When a record has been changed in the computer's memory, but not yet committed to the physical storage location, it is known as a *dirty record*. While making a change to a record, no other connection can access that record until it becomes a committed record and placed in physical storage.

In this next example, the first UPDATE statement changing the Street field for LocationID 1, places a lock on this record, while the next UPDATE statement waits for the transaction to complete and release the lock. This usually happens in fractions of a second.

In other words, these two UPDATE statements will not run at the same time.

```
UPDATE Location
SET Street = '123 First Ave'
WHERE LocationID = 1

UPDATE Location
SET Street = '199 First Blvd'
WHERE LocationID = 1
```

READER NOTE: *You don't need to run the above code since it is just an example.*

By default every DML statement is a transaction, which makes the previous UPDATE statements their own transactions that have been committed automatically.

Auto Commit Transactions

In that last example we did not have to instruct SQL Server to commit the UPDATE statement. At the end of each statement the transaction process committed each of these records for us. Let's practice this one more time.

READER NOTE: *Before starting this next exercise close all open query windows. During this exercise DO NOT CLOSE any query windows until reaching the next section ~ Explicit Transactions.*

Open a new query window using the dbMovie database context to display all fields and records of the Movie table with the following code:

```
USE dbMovie
GO

SELECT *
FROM Movie
```

	m_ID	m_Title	m_Runtime	m_Rating	m_Teaser
1	1	A-List Explorers	96	PG-13	Description Coming Soon
2	2	Bonker Bonzo	75	G	Description Coming Soon
3	3	Chumps to Champs	75	PG-13	Description Coming Soon
4	4	Dare or Die	110	R	Description Coming Soon
5	5	EeeeGhads	88	G	Description Coming Soon
6	6	Farewell Yeti	92	R	Ice and Terror find...
					7 rows

Figure 11.17 Displaying the result set for querying the dbMovie table.

Open a second query window using the dbMovie database context and write the code shown here for updating the m_Runtime field of all records found in the Movie table:

```
USE dbMovie
GO

UPDATE Movie
SET m_Runtime = m_Runtime + 1
```

Messages
(7 row(s) affected)
0 rows

Figure 11.18 Updating the m_Runtime field for all records in the dbMovie table.

Open a third query window to display all fields and records of the Movie table in the dbMovie database. Compare the results of this third query with the results shown in the first query.

```
SELECT *
FROM dbMovie.dbo.Movie
```

	m_ID	m_Title	m_Runtime	m_Rating	m_Teaser
1	1	A-List Explorers	97	PG-13	Description Coming Soon
2	2	Bonker Bonzo	76	G	Description Coming Soon
3	3	Chumps to Champs	76	PG-13	Description Coming Soon
4	4	Dare or Die	111	R	Description Coming Soon
5	5	EeeeGhads	89	G	Description Coming Soon
6	6	Farewell Yeti	93	R	Ice and Terror find…

7 rows

Figure 11.19 Verify that m_Runtime values in this figure are 1 minute higher than Figure 11.17.

Verify that the m_Runtime field value is one minute greater for the result set in this last query (Figure 11.19) than in the first query (Figure 11.17).

Explicit Transactions

Explicit transactions are something we experience every day. When we are at a gas station and go to pay the cashier before putting fuel into our car, we are completing an explicit transaction. This process involves two main steps which must be completed for an explicit transaction to occur:

1) We pay for the fuel.
2) We fill the gas tank with fuel.

An explicit transaction is one where all events of the transaction either happen together, or they don't take place at all. In the previous example, if we don't pay money upfront, we will not receive any fuel. If our credit card is approved, we get fuel and can continue to drive our car.

When we transfer money from savings to checking accounts, we are performing another explicit transaction. A transfer from savings to checking is actually two separate events. If we transfer $500 to checking, we expect to see a $500 withdrawal from savings and a $500 deposit to checking. Our bank would not call us the next day to say they successfully withdrew $500 from savings, but did not manage to credit our checking account.

Would we say one out of two is not bad? No, because either the money was transferred or not. The following code is vulnerable to failure during a transfer from savings to checking:

```
UPDATE SavAccount
SET Balance = Balance - 500
WHERE CustomerID = 18568

UPDATE CkAccount
SET Balance = Balance + 500
WHERE CustomerID = 18568
```

READER NOTE: *This above code is just a sample and not to be run in the database.*

If SQL Server fails after the first update, but before the second one, we would have a loss of data. We need to specify that both statements above will either succeed or fail as a single unit. The problem is that each UPDATE statement is, by default, an individual transaction.

The example of a checking account transfer is a very simplified version of a transaction. Naturally a bank would have more code in place than just what is seen here. For example, they might have a condition to check for a negative balance and purposefully abort the transaction if there are any negative numbers. This type of logic can be found in the *SQL Queries 2012 Volume 4* book. We can place many DML statements into one transaction if they need to run together. To make sure the two statements above run as a single explicit transaction, we can use the following code:

```
BEGIN TRAN
  UPDATE SavAccount
  SET Balance = Balance - 500
  WHERE CustomerID = 18568

  UPDATE CkAccount
  SET Balance = Balance + 500
  WHERE CustomerID = 18568
COMMIT TRAN
```

A failure taking place before the COMMIT TRAN statement means that the records never get committed to permanent storage. The TRAN keyword is short for transaction.

This simplified example is great to start understanding what is happening during an explicit transaction. Let's try this one more time using the dbMovie database and adding in what we learned from our earlier lessons with SQL Locking.

READER NOTE: *Before starting this next exercise close all open query windows. During this exercise DO NOT CLOSE any query windows until reaching the first Skill Check of Lab 11.2 Transactions.*

Open a new query window using the dbMovie database context. Write the code shown here to begin a new transaction with an UPDATE statement that will subtract a minute from the m_Runtime values for all records in the Movie table.

```
USE dbMovie
GO

BEGIN TRANSACTION
  UPDATE Movie
  SET m_Runtime = m_Runtime - 1
```

Messages
(7 row(s) affected)
0 rows

Figure 11.20 An explicit transaction updating the m_Runtime field by subtracting one minute.

Open a second query window using the dbMovie database context to display all the fields and records of the Movie table. We can see in Figure 11.21 that the query in SPID #54 has been running for 00:02:05 and has still not returned any results.

```
USE dbMovie
GO

SELECT * FROM Movie
```

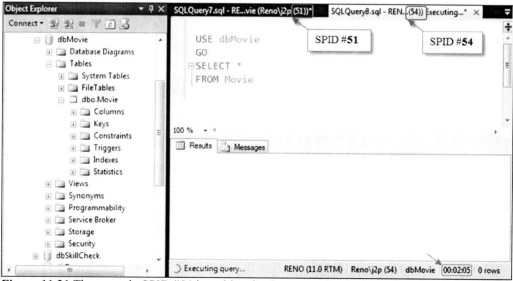

Figure 11.21 The query in SPID #54 is waiting for the transaction in SPID #51 to be committed.

Open the Activity Monitor by accessing it from either the SSMS toolbar by clicking on the icon in the 'Standard' SQL tools toolbar, or by using the keyboard shortcut and typing the 'CTRL' + 'ALT' + 'A' keys at the same time.

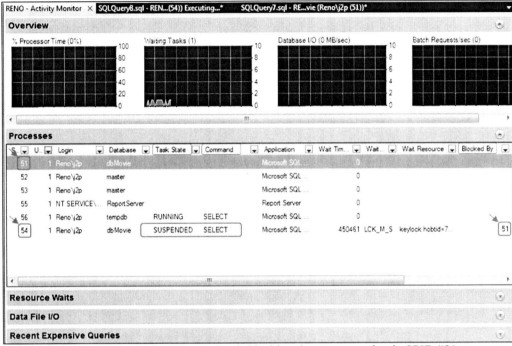

Figure 11.22 Verifying which SPID number is blocking the query running in SPID #54.

Open a third query window and a write a query using the *sys.dm_exec_requests* DMV to locate the SPID number that is blocking the query running in SPID #54.

```
SELECT session_id, [status], command, blocking_session_id
FROM sys.dm_exec_requests
WHERE session_id > 50
```

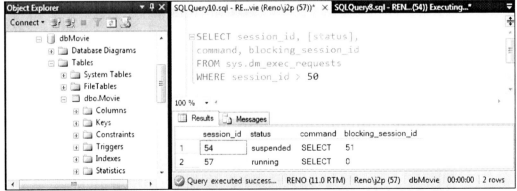

Figure 11.23 Identifying the SPID blocking our query of the Movie table in SPID #54.

Go back to the first query window with the long-running explicit transaction (SPID #51 in this example) and add a COMMIT TRANSACTION statement to the end of the code block, so it looks like the code shown here:

```
BEGIN TRANSACTION
  UPDATE Movie
  SET m_Runtime = m_Runtime - 1
COMMIT TRANSACTION
```

Now it is time to highlight and execute just the COMMIT TRANSACTION statement.

After executing the COMMIT TRANSACTION statement by itself, SQL Server will release the lock held on the Movie table and allow the query in SPID #54 to complete successfully.

We can verify this by querying the sys.dm_exec_requests DMV and then return to the query in SPID #54 to see that the query has finished running and the result set of all fields and records from the Movie table is displayed (Figure 11.24).

```
SELECT session_id, [status], command, blocking_session_id
FROM sys.dm_exec_requests
WHERE session_id > 50
```

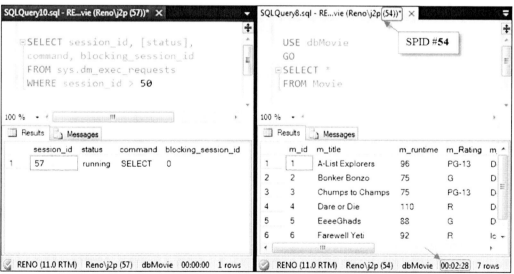

Figure 11.24 The lock has been released on SPID #51 and it is no longer blocking SPID #54.

The Keyword TRAN is interchangeable with the Keyword TRANSACTION. This means that we can save ourselves some typing by using the shorter version of this word after the BEGIN, COMMIT or ROLLBACK commands. An example of this is shown in the following code sample:

```
BEGIN TRAN
  UPDATE Movie
  SET m_Runtime = m_Runtime - 1
ROLLBACK TRAN
```

SQL Server prevents *dirty reads* from taking place. It is possible to temporarily bypass this and access the dirty read data held in the Intermediate State by adding a NOLOCK table hint. The following query is looking for all records from our Movie table even if some records are in the intermediate state.

```
USE dbMovie
GO

SELECT *
FROM Movie (NOLOCK)
```

Exactly how NOLOCK works with Isolation Levels will be covered in the next Chapter.

Lab 11.2: Transactions

Lab Prep: Each lab has one or more Skill Checks. Start with Skill Check 1 and proceed until reaching the Points to Ponder section.

Before beginning this lab, verify that SQL Server 2012 is properly installed and operating. Before running the lab setup script for resetting the database (SQLQueries2012Vol3Chapter11.2Setup.sql), please make sure to close all query windows within SSMS. An open query window pointing to a database context can lock that database preventing it from updating when the script is executing. A simple way to assure all query windows are closed, is to exit out of SSMS, then open a new instance of SSMS, and lastly run the setup script.

Skill Check 1: This Skill Check will require having three query windows opened sequentially according to the following steps.

READER NOTE: *The query window you used to run the reset script should be closed before you start. DO NOT close any of the query windows you open in Skill Check 1 until after the Skill Check has been completed!*

Step One: Open the first query window and write a T-SQL statement to use the JProCo database context. Below the BEGIN TRAN statement, write an UPDATE statement changing the HireDate field value to 1/1/2000 for all records in the Employee table. Execute this query.

Step Two: Open the second query window and write a T-SQL statement to use the JProCo database context. Continue by writing a simple query that selects all records and all fields of the Employee table. Execute this query.

Step Three: Open the third query window and write a T-SQL statement that selects the correct system DMV that shows which SPID (Step One) is blocking the other SPID (Step Two). When done, the results for this step should resemble the following figure (SPID numbers might be different).

	session_id	request_id	start_time	status	command	sql_handle	statement_start_...	state...	plan_h...	database_id	user_id	connectio...	blocking_session_id
1	53	0	2012-05-1...	suspended	SELECT	0x0200000016...	0	-1	0x060...	8	1	8A643B1...	52
2	54	0	2012-05-1...	running	SELECT	0x020000000E...	0	-1	0x060...	8	1	5855BE1...	0

Query executed successfully. RENO (11.0 RTM) | Reno\Student (54) | JProCo | 00:00:00 | 2 rows

Figure 11.25 Results from choosing the correct system DMV to complete Skill Check 1.

Skill Check 2: Modify the query from Step Two, of Skill Check 1, to force the intermediate (dirty) records to be displayed. When done the results will resemble Figure 11.26.

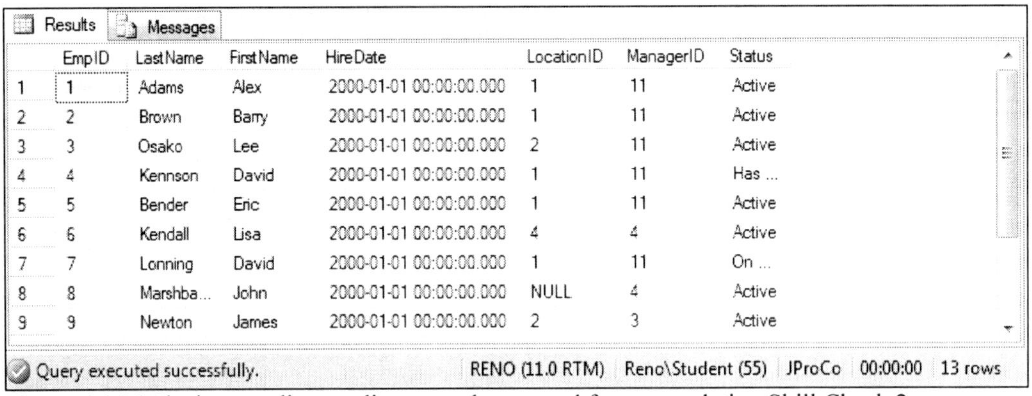

	EmpID	LastName	FirstName	HireDate	LocationID	ManagerID	Status
1	1	Adams	Alex	2000-01-01 00:00:00.000	1	11	Active
2	2	Brown	Barry	2000-01-01 00:00:00.000	1	11	Active
3	3	Osako	Lee	2000-01-01 00:00:00.000	2	11	Active
4	4	Kennson	David	2000-01-01 00:00:00.000	1	11	Has ...
5	5	Bender	Eric	2000-01-01 00:00:00.000	1	11	Active
6	6	Kendall	Lisa	2000-01-01 00:00:00.000	4	4	Active
7	7	Lonning	David	2000-01-01 00:00:00.000	1	11	On ...
8	8	Marshba...	John	2000-01-01 00:00:00.000	NULL	4	Active
9	9	Newton	James	2000-01-01 00:00:00.000	2	3	Active

Query executed successfully.   RENO (11.0 RTM)   Reno\Student (55)   JProCo   00:00:00   13 rows

Figure 11.26 The intermediate or dirty records returned from completing Skill Check 2.

Skill Check 3: Modify the query from Step One, of Skill Check 1, to finalize the open transaction with a ROLLBACK TRAN statement.

Answer Code: The T-SQL code to this lab can be found in the downloadable file named Lab11.2_Transactions.sql.

Points to Ponder - Transactions

1. A transaction is a group of actions treated as a single unit. Transactions ensure data integrity.

2. Transactions are executed on an all-or-nothing basis. If one statement fails, the transaction is rolled back and the previously executed statements are reversed.

3. Use the BEGIN TRANSACTION statement to indicate the beginning of a group of statements that are to be handled together. The COMMIT TRANSACTION statement ends the transaction and saves the changes.

4. Locking is used to coordinate changes in a RDBMS to support multiple transactions on a single database.

5. 'X' stands for Exclusive lock. 'S' stands for Shared lock.

6. Shared locks are used for operations that do not change or update data, such as a SELECT statement.

7. Exclusive locks are used for the data modification operations, such as UPDATE, INSERT, or DELETE.

8. Shared locks are compatible with other shared locks and allow more than one process to use the locked resource at any time.

9. Exclusive locks are not compatible with other locks and don't allow other processes to use the same object.

10. If a query is being blocked, the blocking SPID can be viewed in the Blocked-by Column for the session in the Activity Monitor.

11. With a giant table, an exclusive lock on it could be locking multiple pages and keys.

Deadlocks

Did you ever see the Dr. Seuss cartoon of the north going Zax and the south going Zax? Basically the north going Zax walks north only to pause if something is in his way. Once out of his way he keeps walking north. The south going Zax walks south in the same manner. Eventually, they bump into each other and each states to the other something like, "I will not back up or stand aside, but will wait for you to move... So get out of my way, now, and let me go forth out of the way". They stand there with arms crossed. As summer changes to winter, both become covered with snow and as the years pass neither one can make any headway since they are waiting for the other to yield.

Imagine if SPID #52 says it can't complete its work until SPID #55 is done and conversely, SPID #55 can't complete its work until SPID #52 is done. A situation like this makes it impossible for both transactions to complete successfully and a condition known as a *deadlock* is created. Sometimes locks need to wait for other locks to be released before they finish. Sometimes those locks are being held by several other transactions. A *deadlock* exists when a maze of locks causes eternal waiting for each transaction. This section will demonstrate what some of the possible causes of a *deadlock* are and what can be done to resolve the situation.

Identifying Open Transactions

Let's begin our lesson on deadlocks by reviewing a little bit of what we have learned already to help us visualize open and blocking transactions before we create a deadlock condition.

READER NOTE: *Before starting this next exercise close all open query windows. During this exercise DO NOT CLOSE any query windows until reaching the next section ~ Creating a Deadlock.*

Our first step is to open a new query window using the JProCo database context with the beginnings of an explicit transaction that will be updating the value for the Street field for LocationID 1 in the Location table.

Since we will need to know what the SPID number is for this connection for the remainder of the exercise, let's try out another method for easily obtaining this information in a query. Simply type the following query into the query window that we need to know what the SPID number is and run the code block:

```
USE JProCo
GO

SELECT @@SPID AS SPID_number

BEGIN TRAN
  UPDATE Location
  SET Street = '101 Pike'
  WHERE LocationID = 1
```

SPID_number
51
1 rows

Messages
(1 row(s) affected)
0 rows

Figure 11.27 This query and transaction tell us the SPID number for this connection is 51 and the Street field for LocationID 1 has successfully been changed in the Location table.

By now, we have enough experience with the structure to see a simple query that ran for a long time. There is a chance our system has long running transactions blocking other transactions.

There is a special command that we can use to get some detailed information about the oldest active transaction in our instance of SQL Server. Let's open a second query window and run the code shown here.

```
DBCC OPENTRAN
```

Messages
Transaction information for database 'JProCo'.
Oldest active transaction:
SPID (server process ID): 51
UID (user ID) : -1
Name   : user_transaction
LSN   : (108:81:1)
Start time   : Sep 28 2012 6:25:02:830AM
SID   : 0x0105000000000005150000013ae30f9cfb779f0e82c42ace8030000
0 rows

Figure 11.28 The output produced by running the DBCC OPENTRAN command.

Open a third query window, once again using the JProCo database context to query the Location table for all fields and records.

```
USE JProCo
GO

SELECT * FROM Location
```

As expected, this query will continue to wait for SPID #51 to reach either a ROLLBACK TRAN or COMMIT TRAN statement to close the connection and release the lock it has on the Location table.

We can do this manually by selecting the query window containing the long running transaction (SPID #51 in our example) and finish writing the code for the transaction with a ROLLBACK TRAN statement, as shown in this code sample. Highlight and execute this final statement by itself to release the lock on the table.

```
BEGIN TRAN
  UPDATE Location
  SET Street = '101 Pike'
  WHERE LocationID = 1
ROLLBACK TRAN
```

Messages
Command(s) completed successfully.
0 rows

Figure 11.29 Executing the ROLLBACK TRAN command will release the lock on the table.

Let's take a look at the second and third query windows containing the SELECT statement and the DBCC OPENTRAN command (Figure 11.30).

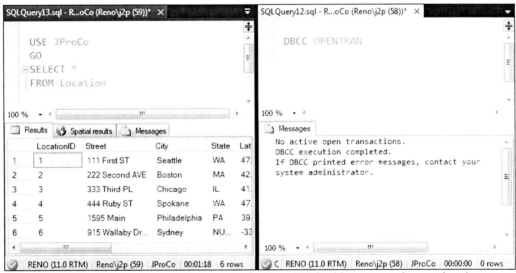

Figure 11.30 With the lock released, the query in SPID #59 is able to run and executing the DBCC OPENTRAN command tells us there are no active transactions.

Great! Our query for all the fields and records of the Location table in SPID #59 is finally able to run after we executed the ROLLBACK TRAN statement on the long running transaction in SPID #51, which released its lock on the table. We were also able to verify that there are no more active transactions by executing the DBCC OPENTRAN command in SPID #58.

Creating a Deadlock

So far, we have become quite familiar with long running, or open transactions that can cause another transaction to wait until the previous transaction releases its exclusive lock on the table. There is another situation that can arise every now and then that is slightly different from what we have learned so far. Even though, at first glance, it can look nearly identical. A deadlock occurs when two or more transactions permanently block each other. These transactions do this by already having an exclusive lock on a resource or object which the other transaction is attempting to lock for itself at the same time.

READER NOTE: *Before starting this next exercise close all open query windows. During this exercise DO NOT CLOSE any query windows until reaching the first Skill Check in Lab11.3: Deadlocks.*

Our first step is to open a new query window using the JProCo database context and writing the beginnings of a long running transaction that is updating the Street value for LocationID 1. Run this code:

```
USE JProCo
GO

BEGIN TRAN
  UPDATE Location
  SET street = '101 Pike'
  WHERE LocationID = 1
```

We will also need to open a second query window using the JProCo database context and writing the beginnings of a long running transaction that is updating the Street value for LocationID 2. Run this code:

```
USE JProCo
GO

BEGIN TRAN
  UPDATE Location
  SET Street = 'Corner Ln'
  WHERE LocationID = 2
```

Notice that we are doing something slightly different with the code in the second query window than we have previously practiced in this chapter. In all of our earlier examples of transactions and locking, we have used a SELECT statement in the second query window connection to query the table used by the UPDATE statement in the first query window.

In this example we are writing an UPDATE statement in the second query window that will issue an exclusive lock on any records with a LocationID of 2, while at nearly the same time the first query window has an UPDATE statement that has issued an exclusive lock on any records with a LocationID of 1. There is a difference between a SELECT statement in a transaction and an UPDATE statement in a transaction. The SELECT statement merely needs access to the data once it becomes available and an UPDATE statement requires an exclusive lock on the data until it is either rolled back or committed.

Our next step is to modify each of these two queries slightly to include a SELECT statement that will attempt to access the exact record that the other transaction has an exclusive lock assigned to it. This is what causes the deadlock condition, as both transactions have an exclusive lock on the very resource that the other transaction is trying to access. Let's put this in place and see what happens!

READER NOTE: *Read the remaining information in this section, examine the sample output in the figures provided and write the code as instructed in the next two paragraphs before proceeding. It is suggested to execute the finished code samples within a few seconds of each other and then compare the results with those shown in the following figures.*

In the first query window modify the current code in the transaction to include a SELECT statement below the existing UPDATE statement that looks for all fields and records in the Location table predicated on a LocationID value of 2. Complete the transaction block by ending it with a COMMIT TRAN statement. Run just the SELECT statement and the COMMIT TRAN statements (highlighted code):

```
USE JProCo
GO

BEGIN TRAN
  UPDATE Location
  SET Street = '101 Pike'
  WHERE LocationID = 1

  SELECT * FROM Location
  WHERE LocationID = 2
COMMIT TRAN
```

Immediately switch to the second query window and modify the current code in the transaction to include a SELECT statement below the existing UPDATE statement that looks for all fields and records in the Location table predicated on a LocationID value of 1 (record being updated in the first query window). Complete the transaction block by ending it with a COMMIT TRAN statement. Run just the SELECT statement and the COMMIT TRAN statements (highlighted code):

```
USE JProCo
GO

BEGIN TRAN
  UPDATE Location
  SET Street = 'Corner Ln'
  WHERE LocationID = 2

  SELECT * FROM Location
  WHERE LocationID = 1
COMMIT TRAN
```

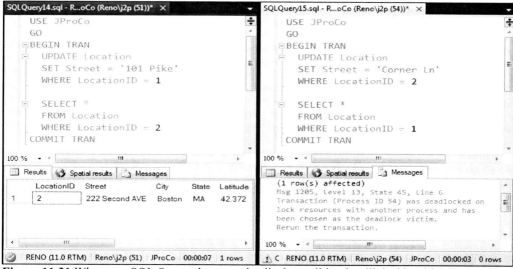

Figure 11.31 Whenever SQL Server detects a deadlock condition it will decide which transaction to terminate. The transaction being terminated is called a deadlock victim.

In case it is difficult to read the error message shown on the right-hand side of Figure 11.31, it is displayed again in a larger format in Figure 11.32.

```
Messages
(1 row(s) affected)
Msg 1205, Level 13, State 45, Line 6
Transaction (Process ID 54) was deadlocked on
lock resources with another process and has been chosen as the deadlock
victim. Rerun the transaction.
                                                    0 rows
```

Figure 11.32 The error message from the right-hand side of Figure 11.3 (Enlarged).

Lab 11.3: Deadlocks

Lab Prep: Each lab has one or more Skill Checks. Start with Skill Check 1 and proceed until reaching the Points to Ponder section.

Before beginning this lab, verify that SQL Server 2012 is properly installed and operating. Before running the lab setup script for resetting the database (SQLQueries2012Vol3Chapter11.3Setup.sql), please make sure to close all query windows within SSMS. An open query window pointing to a database context can lock that database preventing it from updating when the script is executing. A simple way to assure all query windows are closed, is to exit out of SSMS, then open a new instance of SSMS, and lastly run the setup script.

Skill Check 1: This Skill Check will require having two query windows opened sequentially according to the following steps.

READER NOTE: *The query window you used to run the reset script should be closed before you start. DO NOT close any of the query windows you open in Skill Check 1 until after the Skill Check has been completed!*

Step One: Open the first query window and write a T-SQL statement to use the JProCo database context. Below the BEGIN TRAN statement, write an UPDATE statement changing the HireDate field value to 1/1/2000 for EmpID 1 in the Employee table. Execute this query.

Step Two: Open the second query window and write a T-SQL statement to use the JProCo database context. Below the BEGIN TRAN statement, write an UPDATE statement changing the HireDate field value to 1/1/2000 for EmpID 2 in the Employee table. Execute this query.

Skill Check 2: This Skill Check consists of two steps that must be completed in order to achieve the desired results.

Step One: Modify the query from Step One, of Skill Check 1, by adding the following code to the original UPDATE statement. Execute this statement:

```
SELECT * FROM Employee
COMMIT TRAN
```

Step Two: Modify the query from Step Two, of Skill Check 1, by adding the following code to the original UPDATE statement. Execute this statement:

```
SELECT * FROM Employee
COMMIT TRAN
```

After a short period of time, one of the query windows will complete the transaction and the other will display a message shown in the following figure.

```
Messages
Msg 1205, Level 13, State 51, Line 4
Transaction (Process ID 56) was deadlocked on lock resources with another
process and has been chosen as the deadlock victim. Rerun the transaction.
                                                                    0 rows
```

Figure 11.33 The error message resulting from the deadlock created by Skill Check 1 and 2.

Answer Code: The T-SQL code to this lab can be found in the downloadable file named Lab11.3_Deadlocks.sql.

Points to Ponder - Deadlocks

1. Locking prevents multiple users from changing the same piece of data at the same time.

2. Locking allows only one session at a time to make changes to a table or row, although in many cases we will still be able to see it while it is locked.

3. DBCC OPENTRAN displays information about the oldest active transaction only.

4. Activity Monitor and Dynamic Management Views can display all open transactions.

5. A deadlock occurs when two SPIDs are waiting for a resource and neither process can advance because the other process is preventing it from gaining access to the resource.

6. To end a blocking session, locate the SPID and KILL the session.

7. Issue a KILL Process command for a specific session from the Processes tab of the Activity Monitor, or with T-SQL code with the corresponding SPID number.

Chapter Glossary

ACID: An acronym for the four properties every transaction should exhibit, **A**tomic **C**onsistent **I**solated **D**urability. A brief definition is shown here:

- o **Atomicity:** A transaction is an atomic unit of work and executes exactly once; either all the work is done or none of it is.

- o **Consistency:** A transaction preserves the consistency of data, transforming one consistent state of data into another consistent state of data. Data bound by a transaction must be semantically preserved.

- o **Isolation:** A transaction is a unit of isolation and each occurs separately and independently of concurrent transactions. A transaction should never see the intermediate stages of another transaction.

- o **Durability:** A transaction is a unit of recovery. If a transaction succeeds, its' updates persist, even if the system crashes or is shut down. If a transaction fails, the system remains in the state previous to committing the transaction.

Activity Monitor: A tool provided with SQL Server Management Studio that provides information about connections to the Database Engine and the locks that they hold. This tool can be used when troubleshooting database locking issues, and to terminate a deadlocked or otherwise unresponsive process. It has four expandable/collapsible panes to further filter the information shown:

- o **Processes:** Displays info about each active connection to the instance.
- o **Resource Waits:** Displays info about waits for resources.
- o **Data File I/O:** Displays info about throughput for each file connection.
- o **Recent Expensive Queries:** Displays info about the most expensive queries run during the past 30 seconds. Includes current queries and queries that have finished during this time period.

Auto Commit Transaction: The default transaction management mode of the SQL Server Database Engine. Every T-SQL statement is committed or rolled back when it completes. If a statement completes successfully, it is committed; if it encounters any error, it is rolled back.

BEGIN TRAN: A T-SQL statement marking the beginning of an explicit transaction. Each code block following BEGIN TRAN must be logically terminated with a COMMIT TRAN (success) or ROLLBACK TRAN (failure) statement to maintain data consistency and release any resource locks. When SQL Server encounters a BEGIN TRAN statement the @@TRANCOUNT variable is incremented by 1.

COMMIT TRAN: A T-SQL statement marking the ending of a successful implicit or explicit transaction. All data modifications performed since the start of the previous BEGIN TRAN statement are then committed to permanent storage for the database. When SQL Server encounters a COMMIT TRAN statement the @@TRANCOUNT variable is decremented by 1. In the case of nested transactions, any resource locks will remain in place until the outermost COMMIT TRAN or ROLLBACK TRAN statement is reached, signified by an @@TRANCOUNT value equal to 1.

DBCC OPENTRAN: Displays information about the oldest active transaction and the oldest distributed and non-distributed replicated transactions, if any, within the specified database.

Deadlock: A deadlock occurs when two or more transactions permanently block each other, as each transaction has a lock on one or more resources which the other transaction is trying to access at the same time.

DMV: An acronym for **D**ynamic **M**anagement **V**iew.

Dynamic Management View: Views and functions used by SQL Server to return server state information that can be used for monitoring the health of a server instance, diagnosing problems, and tuning performance. DMVs cannot be referenced in T-SQL statements by using single-part names. There are two types:

- o Server scoped: requires VIEW SERVER STATE permission on the server.
- o Database scoped: requires VIEW DATABASE STATE permission on the specific database.

Explicit Transaction: T-SQL code that explicitly defines both the start and end of the transaction. All explicit transactions start with a BEGIN TRAN statement and complete with either a COMMIT TRAN statement (indicating success) or a ROLLBACK TRAN statement (indicating failure).

Lock: An action taken by SQL Server to ensure stability and consistency of data while a transaction is utilizing different types of resources. Locks can be applied at a variety of granularity levels. Small granularity locks (i.e. rows) increase concurrency at the cost of higher overhead, as more locks must be maintained on the resources. Large granularity locks (i.e. tables) decrease concurrency at a greatly reduced cost of overhead, as fewer locks need to be maintained. There are six types of locks (Shared, Update, Exclusive, Intent, Schema and Bulk Update).

KILL: A T-SQL command used to terminate a session (SPID). If there is a lot of work to undo, particularly a long transaction, it may take some time for this action to be completed.

ROLLBACK TRAN: Rolls back an explicit or implicit transaction to the beginning of the transaction, or to a savepoint inside the transaction. This statement can be used to erase all data modifications made since the start of the transaction or to a savepoint. When SQL Server encounters this T-SQL statement all resource locks held by the transaction will be released and @@TRANCOUNT will be reset to a value of 0 unless used with a savepoint (No action taken).

Server Process ID: Each time an application connects to SQL Server, it is assigned a unique new SPID value (SMALLINT data type). This connection will have a defined scope and memory space and cannot interact with other SPIDs. The terms connection, or session are synonymous with SPID.

SPID: An acronym for **Server Process ID**.

sp_who: A system stored procedure (sproc) that provides information about current users, sessions, and processes in the instance of the SQL Server Database Engine (SPID, ecid, status, loginame, hostname, blk, dbname, cmd, request_id).

sp_who2: A system stored procedure (sproc) that provides more information than sp_who about current users, sessions, and processes in the instance of the SQL Server Database Engine (SPID, Status, Login, HostName, BlkBy, DBName, Command, CPUTime, DiskIO, LastBatch, ProgramName, SPID, REQUESTID).

sys.dm_exec_requests: A Dynamic Management View that returns a broad range of information about each session request executing on a SQL Server instance. A common use of this DMV is to extract one or more pieces of information to be passed in as a parameter to a system function for obtaining more specific details.

Review Quiz - Chapter Eleven

1.) What does SPID stand for?

O a. System Process ID

O b. Server Process ID

O c. Server Performance ID

2.) You think there might be a long running uncommitted transaction and you want to investigate. You need to identify both the SPID and the Start time of the oldest active transaction in JProCo. What can you do?

O a. Connect to the JProCo database. Execute DBCC OPENTRAN. View the value in the SPID row and then find the value in the Start time row.

O b. Connect to the master database. Execute DBCC OPENTRAN. View the value in the SPID row and then find the value in the Start time row.

O c. In SSMS, open the Activity Monitor. Select the Processes tab and apply the following filter settings:
Database = JProCo
Open Transactions = Yes
View the ProcessID and Last Batch columns.

3.) You discover that an order application is connected to SQL Server with SPID 55 and it is being Blocked By a wayward process. You investigate and find the blocking SPID is 101. You need to solve this blocking situation quickly, so the user can continue using the application without losing any work. What are two different ways to achieve this goal?
(Each answer is its own complete solution)

☐ a. In SSMS, open a new query window and execute the following statement: Kill 55.

☐ b. In SSMS, open a new query window and execute the following statement: Kill 101.

☐ c. In SSMS, open the Activity Monitor and expand the Processes tab to locate SPID 55, then right-click on it and choose the Kill Process option.

☐ d. In SSMS, open the Activity Monitor and expand the Processes tab to locate SPID 101, then right-click on it and choose the Kill Process option.

☐ e. In SQL Server Configuration Manager, stop and then restart the SQL Server (MSSQLServer) service to kill both sessions.

Answer Key

1.) A System Process ID, more commonly known by its acronym PID, is used by the operating system kernel to provide a temporary unique identifier to a process running on the system, so (a) is incorrect. There is no such thing as a Server Performance ID, which means (c) is incorrect. Server Process ID is the officially recognized name for the acronym SPID, so (b) is correct.

2.) To find the SPID and Start time with the DBCC OPENTRAN command, it must be in the same database context as the open transaction, so (b) is incorrect. Since the DBCC OPENTRAN command is being run in the JProCo context, (a) is the correct answer.

3.) Issuing a KILL 55 statement would close the user connection that needs to stay open, so (a) is incorrect. Likewise, using the Activity Monitor to locate and then use the KILL option with SPID 55 would close the user connection that needs to stay open, so (c) is also incorrect. While using the SQL Server Configuration Manager to start and restart the MSSQLSERVER service would close the blocking SPID 101, it would also close SPID 55 which needs to remain open for the user application, so (e) is incorrect. Since it is necessary to close the blocking SPID 101 with a KILL command, both (b) and (d) would be the correct answer.

Bug Catcher Game

To play the Bug Catcher game, run the SQLQueries2012Vol3BugCatcher11.pps file from the BugCatcher folder of the companion files. These files can be obtained from the www.Joes2Pros.com website.

[THIS PAGE INTENTIONALLY LEFT BLANK]

Chapter 12. Isolation Levels and Concurrency

Most people who have attended school, or work in an office environment can relate to this next story describing how concurrency and isolation affect our everyday lives. I was teaching a Saturday class that was to end on July 15th. The school shortened each class from 6 hours a day to 5 hours per day but kept the total time for the class at 30 hours. Had they not done this the class would have ended on July 7th.

As it turns out, not everyone was notified of the change. This included the department in control of the school website, as it still showed this class would be ending on July 7th. My attendance sheet was correct and the tri fold was updated too. However, this one inconsistency with the ending date shown on the website was still remaining. The students pointed this out to me and insisted my sheet was wrong and the website was correct.

To settle this discrepancy, we all agreed to ask the administration office to please clarify the actual ending date for everyone. One week later the administration office replied that the website showed the correct ending date of July 15th and they don't understand our confusion on this issue. It appears that the information on the website had been updated during the past week, giving the students no chance for finishing class a week early.

READER NOTE: *Please run the SQLQueries2012Vol3Chapter12.0Setup.sql script in order to follow along with the examples in the first section of Chapter 12. All scripts mentioned in this chapter may be found at* www.Joes2Pros.com.

Concurrency Problems

We often seek a doctor's help when we are sick because we want to be healthy. To put it another way, when you are feeling unhealthy you want a solution that will get you healthy again. The words healthy and unhealthy are very similar words with different meanings.

In the medical world they say the poison and the antidotes look almost the same. In SQL there are potential problems and possible cures and they have very similar names. For example a Non-repeatable read is a potential concurrency problem that can be fixed by choosing an Isolation Level called REPEATABLE READ. So Non-repeatable read is the problem and the REPEATABLE READ is the cure.

First we will list the four concurrency problems (Dirty Read, Lost Update, Non-repeatable read, and the Phantom Read). After that we will explore the Isolation levels that can deal with these potential problems.

Pessimistic Concurrency

An artist will probably not sell you their painting while they are still making changes. In fact they probably will not even let you look at it until it's done. They also will not let you grab your own brush and make some updates to the canvas they are working on. Is it pessimistic for the artist to lock their work for only their exclusive access until the updates are done?

To keep the integrity of the artwork in tact the artist has an exclusive lock on the painting until all changes have been made. SQL Server uses locking to ensure transactional integrity and database consistency. Locking prevents the reading of data that is being changed by other users. It also prevents multiple users from changing the same data at the same time.

Usually when we see the word "pessimistic" used in conjunction with any other word or phrase, we associate it with a negative or bad thing. However, in the realm of SQL Server, the term *pessimistic concurrency* is a positive thing from the standpoint of protecting data during a transaction.

This is because any transaction using *pessimistic concurrency* will control all locks to any resources for as long as they are required, for the duration of the transaction until it is either committed or rolled back. In other words, to achieve a high transaction *Isolation Level*, SQL Server places a lock on all records and resources used by the transaction, even if there are no other processes or applications requesting access to them.

Imagine a table with many updates and inserts being performed, but never has a SELECT query run against it. For this type of table, it is a very good strategy to use pessimistic *concurrency*, as it will lock these records each time the updates or inserts are being applied and unlock them when the action is completed.

Dirty Reads

When we are updating or inserting data into a table, an exclusive lock must be granted for this operation to succeed. Once a lock is issued on this table or key, no other locks can be issued until our transaction completes, which prevents any unintentional *dirty reads* of data from occurring.

When our task is to simply read data with a SELECT statement, SQL Server will issue a shared lock on the required resource, which does not need to be exclusive. This feature allows for multiple connections running similar SELECT statements from the same table at once (real time), because there can be many shared locks on that table.

The only time we cannot obtain a shared lock for a given table or other resource is when a previous transaction has already been given an exclusive lock to the data.

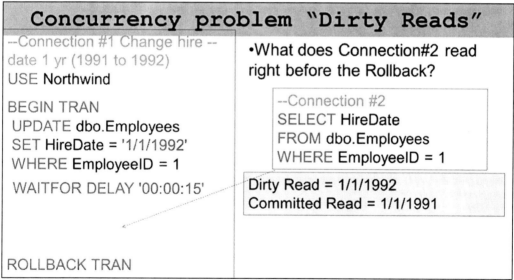

Figure 12.1 A dirty read is when the data being read is in the *Intermediate State* and has not yet been committed to physical storage in a *Persistent State*.

In Chapter eleven, we learned that for every data change to a table there is a brief moment where the data is held in temporary memory (RAM) while the change is being made (*Intermediate State*), but is not yet committed. During this time, any other DML statement needing this data must wait until the lock is released. This is a safety feature to ensure that SQL Server only evaluates official data.

We also learned that some transactions take time and then roll back. In other words, the changes never become official data and in essence never took place. It is possible for a great deal of data to be changed while in the *Intermediate State*, even though it never ends up getting committed.

A *lock* prevents other processes from reading, modifying, or making decisions based on the *dirty data* that exists while in the *Intermediate State*. The result of locking this data is that only committed data is used, which effectively isolates a transaction from any other activity. The drawback to this high degree of isolation is that some processes and applications that could otherwise run instantly, such as a SELECT statement, must now wait to access this resource.

The locks issued by SQL Server reduce the level of *concurrency* for the table or other resource that the lock is applied to. In other words, the ability for multiple processes and applications to access a given SQL Server resource at the exact same time is prevented until the lock is released.

READER NOTE: *Read the remaining information in this section and examine the sample code with output in the figures provided before proceeding. It is suggested to execute the finished code samples within a few seconds of each other and compare the results with those shown in the following figures.*

Before starting this exercise, close all open query windows. During the following examples DO NOT CLOSE any query windows until reaching the next section ~ Non-repeatable reads.

To begin this exercise, open a query window and set the database context to JProCo. Write a transaction that will UPDATE the HireDate field of the Employee table for EmpID 1 with a new value of 1/1/2002. Since we will need this transaction to hold a lock while practicing the remaining steps, we must add a WAITFOR DELAY statement of 1 minute and 30 seconds. Make sure to place these two statements inside an explicit transaction that will be rolled back when it is completed. Run the code sample shown here.

```
BEGIN TRAN
  UPDATE dbo.Employee
  SET HireDate = '1/1/2002'
  WHERE EmpID = 1

  WAITFOR DELAY '00:01:30'
ROLLBACK TRAN
```

The next step is to open a second query window and write a query that looks for all records and fields in the Employee table equal to EmpID 1. An example is provided with the code shown here: (Figure 12.2)

```
SELECT *
FROM Employee
WHERE EmpID = 1
```

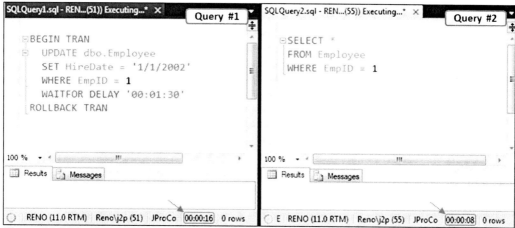

Figure 12.2 The SELECT query must wait for the UPDATE transaction to release its lock.

As expected, the SELECT statement in the second query window (shown on the right-hand side of Figure 12.2 as SPID #55) must wait for the UPDATE transaction in the first query window (left-hand side of Figure 12.2 as SPID #51) to release its lock in order to *read* the table and return the required result set.

This is because the default Isolation Level setting for SQL Server is always READ COMMITTED, which prevents *dirty reads* from taking place. It is possible to temporarily bypass this Isolation Level and access the dirty read data held in the Intermediate State by adding a NOLOCK table hint to our query looking for the record for EmpID 1.

Open a third query window and enter the following code sample. Double check to make sure the UPDATE transaction in the first query window is still running before clicking on the '! **Execute**' button in the toolbar to run this query. If the UPDATE transaction has already finished running, it will be necessary to run this code again and then wait for several seconds before switching to and running the SELECT statement in the third query window (NOLOCK table hint).

```
SELECT *
FROM Employee (NOLOCK)
WHERE EmpID = 1
```

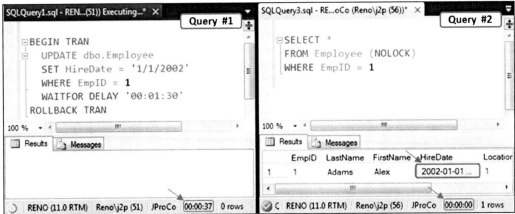

Figure 12.3 The SELECT query is able to access the dirty read data with a NOLOCK table hint.

Notice that the query on the right-hand side of Figure 12.3 runs immediately and returns the *dirty read* data held in the *Intermediate State* .(Hire Date = 1/1/2002)

It is also possible to instruct SQL Server to always allow for dirty reads without the need for a query to be written with the NOLOCK table hint. This can be accomplished by explicitly changing the Isolation Level setting using code. Let's return to the second query window and add the following code before the original SELECT statement block. When complete, the code in the query window should resemble this sample.

Once again, make sure the UPDATE transaction in the first query window is still running before clicking on the '**!** **Execute**' button in the toolbar to run this query. If the UPDATE transaction has already finished running, it will be necessary to run this code again and then wait for several seconds before switching to and running the SELECT statement we just modified.

```
SET TRANSACTION ISOLATION LEVEL
   READ UNCOMMITTED

SELECT *
FROM Employee
WHERE EmpID = 1
```

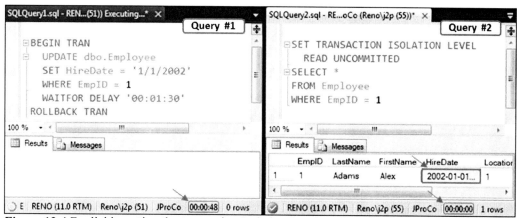

Figure 12.4 Explicitly setting the transaction Isolation Level to allow for dirty reads.

Notice that the query on the right-hand side of Figure 12.4 runs immediately and returns the *dirty read* data held in the *Intermediate State* (Hire Date = 1/1/2002).

Modify the previous command to change the Isolation Level back to the SQL Server default behavior of preventing dirty reads with the following code.

Make sure the UPDATE transaction in the first query window is still running before clicking on the '! **Execute**' button in the toolbar to run this query. If the UPDATE transaction has already finished running, it will be necessary to run this code again and then wait for several seconds before switching to and running the SELECT statement we just modified.

```
SET TRANSACTION ISOLATION LEVEL
   READ COMMITTED

SELECT *
FROM Employee
WHERE EmpID = 1
```

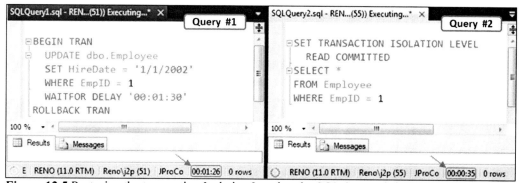

Figure 12.5 Restoring the transaction Isolation Level to the SQL Server default setting.

By observing the SELECT statement on the right-hand side of Figure 12.5, we can see that it must wait for the UPDATE transaction on the left-hand side to release its lock in order to *read* the table and return the required result set.

If we are patient, we can wait for the remainder of the one minute and thirty second delay to confirm our SELECT statement query will indeed read the correct data for the HireDate (1/1/2001) as soon as the lock is released (Figure 12.6).

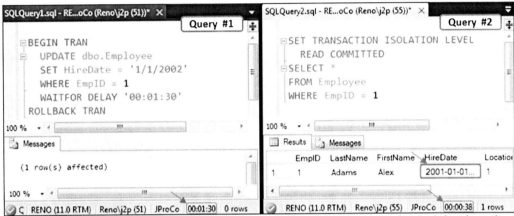

Figure 12.6 The SELECT query displays results after the UPDATE transaction lock is released.

To remember how SQL Server responds to dirty reads, we can reference the information summarized in Table 12.1.

Table 12.1 Summary of which Isolation Level will allow a dirty read.

Isolation Level	Allow Dirty Reads
READ UNCOMMITTED	Yes
READ COMMITTED	No

Non-repeatable reads

At the beginning of this chapter, I recalled a story about how my students had discovered the school website was displaying the incorrect class ending date. By the time the administrative office responded to the student's observation, the web department had already updated the information on the website. Reading from the same data source and row of data on two different occasions and receiving two different result sets is an example of a Non-repeatable read.

There are potential concurrency problems that can be addressed by using the appropriate Isolation Level. If a dirty read is a problem for you, these can be eliminated by using the read uncommitted Isolation Level.

In SQL Server there are potential problems and possible cures that have very similar names as well. For example: A *Non-repeatable read* is a potential concurrency problem that can be cured by choosing an *Isolation Level* called REPEATABLE READ.

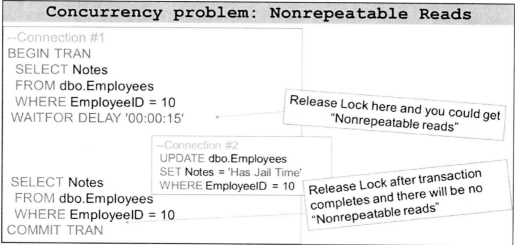

Figure 12.7 An illustration of how a *Non-repeatable read* is created during a transaction.

READER NOTE: *Read the remaining information in this section and examine the sample code with output in the figures provided before proceeding. It is suggested to execute the finished code samples within a few seconds of each other and compare the results with those shown in the following figures.*

Before starting this exercise, close all open query windows. During the following examples DO NOT CLOSE any query windows until reaching the next section ~ Lab 12.1: Pessimistic Concurrency.

Let's begin this exercise by opening a new query window in the JProCo database context. Before doing anything else, we need to determine what the current Isolation Level is for the database. This can easily be accomplished with a DBCC command named USEROPTIONS. Run this code and look at the value returned for the Isolation Level row (READ COMMITTED).

```
DBCC USEROPTIONS
```

	Set Option	Value
9	ansi_warnings	SET
10	ansi_padding	SET
11	ansi_nulls	SET
12	concat_null_yields_null	SET
13	isolation level	READ COMMITTED

13 rows

Figure 12.8 Using the DBCC USEROPTIONS command to determine the current Isolation Level.

Having already learned that the default Isolation Level setting is READ COMMITTED, we are happy to see this value is confirmed in the unmodified JProCo database.

Our next step is to open a second query window in the JProCo database context and write an explicit transaction that will contain two queries that will both return all fields in the Employee table that are equal to EmpID 1 and 2. Separate the two queries with a WAITFOR DELAY of 30 seconds. Make sure the transaction is committed when it completes. Use the code shown here as an example.

```
BEGIN TRAN
   SELECT * FROM Employee
   WHERE EmpID IN (1, 2)

   WAITFOR DELAY '00:00:30'

   SELECT * FROM Employee
   WHERE EmpID IN (1, 2)
COMMIT TRAN
```

Once this code is written we will need to open a third query window to the JProCo database context that updates the HireDate field to 1/1/2011 for EmpID 1 in the Employee table. Use the code shown here as an example.

```
UPDATE dbo.Employee
SET HireDate = '1/1/2011'
WHERE EmpID = 1
```

Run the explicit transaction from the second query window and after a few seconds run the UPDATE statement in the third query window. Return to the SPID with the explicit transaction and wait the remainder of the 30 seconds for the result set to be returned. What will the result set show?

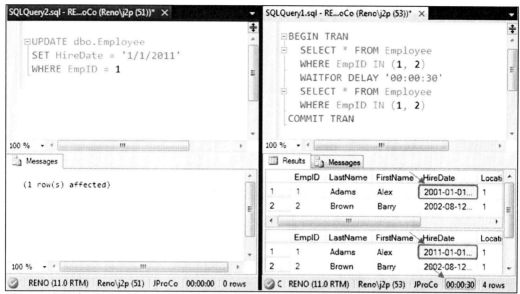

Figure 12.9 The transaction has produced a Non-repeatable read because the UPDATE statement was given access to the Employee table while the transaction was running.

Notice that the even though both SELECT statements are placed in the same explicit transaction and are querying the Employee table for the exact same records, the value for the HireDate for EmpID 1 is different! (Figure 12.9)

This is an example of how *Non-repeatable reads* are created. Since the explicit transaction is not modifying any data, SQL Server issues a shared lock on its resources (Employee table). This allows other transactions that need to modify data in the Employee table to have access to it. So, when the UPDATE statement in the third SPID ran during the 30 second delay of the second SPID, it was issued an exclusive lock in order to make its modifications. The exclusive lock of the UPDATE statement was released long before the explicit transaction completed, thus two different results for the same query were returned in the result set.

In other words, the second SELECT statement in the explicit transaction was unable to repeat the results of the first SELECT statement, resulting in what is known as a Non-repeatable read.

What if we do not want to allow Non-repeatable reads? Is there a way to prevent them from happening in the first place? Yes. Recall that at the beginning of this section, we learned that if a Non-repeatable read is the problem, then the cure is the REPEATABLE READ Isolation Level setting.

Let's open a new query window connection to the JProCo database context and set the Isolation Level to REPEATABLE READ before using the same explicit transaction from our previous test. Use the code shown here to make this change.

```
SET TRANSACTION ISOLATION LEVEL
  REPEATABLE READ
GO

BEGIN TRAN
  SELECT * FROM Employee
  WHERE EmpID IN (1, 2)

  WAITFOR DELAY '00:00:30'

  SELECT * FROM Employee
  WHERE EmpID IN (1, 2)
COMMIT TRAN
```

There is one more change required before testing whether or not setting the Isolation Level to REPEATABLE READ will prevent a *Non-repeatable read* from occurring in the first place.

We know from the result set of the transaction that the HireDate field for EmpID 1 was updated to 1/1/2011, which means we need to change this value again in the SPID with the UPDATE statement. So, for this test we will SET the value of the HireDate field to 1/1/2012 for EmpID 1. Use the code shown here as an example.

```
UPDATE dbo.Employee
SET HireDate = '1/1/2012'
WHERE EmpID = 1
```

OK, run the explicit transaction from the second query window and after a few seconds run the UPDATE statement in the third query window. Return to the SPID with the explicit transaction and wait the remainder of the 30 seconds for the result set to be returned. What will the result set be this time?

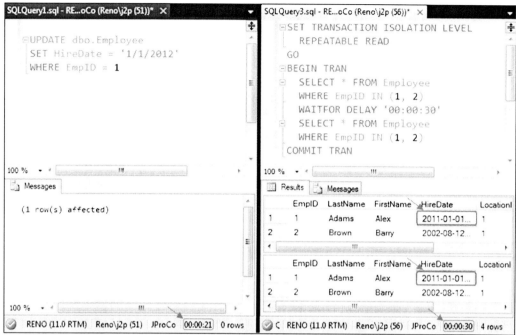

Figure 12.10 Proof that the REPEATABLE READ Isolation Level prevents Non-repeatable reads.

It worked! The result set for the explicit transaction shown on the right-hand side of Figure 12.10 produced a repeatable read for the HireDate field of EmpID 1.

In this test, SQL Server placed an exclusive lock on the explicit transaction, even though it is not modifying any data in the Employee table. This is because the REPEATABLE READ Isolation Level must lock the entire table to prevent a *Non-repeatable read* from happening. Notice that the UPDATE statement on the left-hand side of Figure 12.10 had to wait until the transaction completed before the updating process was able to modify the Employee table.

We can confidently prevent Non-repeatable reads by simply modifying the Isolation Level to the more restrictive REPEATABLE READ setting.

Lab 12.1: Pessimistic Concurrency

Lab Prep: Each lab has one or more Skill Checks. Start with Skill Check 1 and proceed until reaching the Points to Ponder section.

Before beginning this lab, verify that SQL Server 2012 is properly installed and operating. Before running the lab setup script for resetting the database (SQLQueries2012Vol3Chapter12.1Setup.sql), please make sure to close all query windows within SSMS. An open query window pointing to a database context can lock that database preventing it from updating when the script is executing. A simple way to assure all query windows are closed, is to exit out of SSMS, then open a new instance of SSMS, and lastly run the setup script.

Skill Check 1: Instruct SQL Server to set the ISOLATION LEVEL so that an intermediate, or 'dirty read' is not allowed, but Non-repeatable reads are allowed.

Answer Code: The T-SQL code to this lab can be found from the downloadable files named Lab12.1_PessimisticConcurrency.sql.

Points to Ponder - Pessimistic Concurrency

1. SQL Server allows many connections to the database engine at once. This is known as concurrency.

2. The READ UNCOMMITTED Isolation Level allows both dirty reads and Non-repeatable reads.

3. The READ COMMITTED Isolation Level does not allow dirty reads yet does allow Non-repeatable reads.

4. The REPEATABLE READ Isolation Level does not allow dirty reads or Non-repeatable reads.

5. The greater the Isolation Level, the fewer concurrency issues in a database.

6. Greater Isolation Levels like SERIALIZABLE & REPEATABLE READ, have less overhead because they hold locks for longer periods of time.

7. Holding locks for longer periods of time reduces the speed and quantity at which SQL Server can accept concurrent connections.

8. Lower Isolation Levels allow for rapid scaling of concurrent connections.

9. The default Isolation Level for SQL Server is READ COMMITTED.

10. SQL Server locks are held and released for each insert and update even if no conflicting connections appear.

11. Pessimistic concurrency places locks on all transactions, even if there are no conflicting transactions trying to access the same resources.

12. When setting the Isolation Level of a transaction, SQL Server ensures the resources used by the transaction are not accessed by any other transactions.

Optimistic Concurrency

Compare restaurants that take only reservations to restaurants that have a drop in only policy. A seafood restaurant on the waterfront using a reservation system, is willing to perform the extra work required to hold tables aside (lock) for the reserved party, even if a table is held for an hour and the patrons only take 25 minutes to eat their meal. The non-use of this table by anyone else is a smaller consequence than the potential embarrassment of having two important guests believing they have rights to the same table at the same time. Since it is only possible to obtain a table at the waterfront seafood restaurant with a reservation, we know they are using *pessimistic concurrency* to service their clients.

Conversely, a drop in style restaurant, like McDonalds, believes they can do high volume while rarely needing to turn people away because of over capacity. On the rare occasion there is no room for us when we arrive at the door we simply turn around (rollback) and go back home. Since it is not possible to make a dinner reservation (lock) with a drop in style restaurant we can determine they are using *optimistic concurrency* to service their clients.

Concurrency Recap

Before proceeding to learn about optimistic concurrency, let's do a quick review of the lessons we have covered so far, with what concurrency is and how transactions are affected by using pessimistic concurrency.

The ability for SQL Server to have multiple connections to the same database and tables at the same time is called *concurrency*. When we are told: "The Customer table needs a high level of concurrency to satisfy our client's application", it means that the Transaction Isolation Level needs to be set sufficiently low enough to allow as many connections as possible at the same time, even if this means there is a possibility for inconsistent information.

How much inconsistent information is allowed can be determined by whether or not *Non-repeatable reads* and/or *dirty reads* are acceptable to the client. If a table is going to have a high level of inserts and updates performed, it is probably not a good candidate for a high level of concurrency. This is because the input and output of data (throughput) decreases proportionately to higher concurrency, due to the very nature of SQL Server needing to maintain more locks (albeit for a shorter amount of time) with this configuration.

Likewise, lower levels of concurrency are the direct result of higher settings to the Transaction Isolation Level. Tables with high levels of inserts and updates are great candidates for *pessimistic concurrency*, as SQL Server needs to maintain fewer lock on resources (albeit for longer periods of time).

The best candidate for *optimistic concurrency,* are tables that primarily or even exclusively do not modify data (i.e. use SELECT statement queries). These types of objects can easily accept lower Transaction Isolation Level settings such as READ UNCOMMITTED to allow for high concurrency levels with very little risk of encountering *Non-repeatable reads* or *dirty reads* in their queries.

Optimistic SNAPSHOT

A common practice in many work environments is for the Human Resources staff to maintain a master version of all the employees' contact information. To make it easier for managers and their staff to have this same information, a copy is made for them each time the master version is updated. Although the information in the copy is merely a snapshot in time of the master version, it protects the data source from being changed accidently, while making the most recent information available to everyone who needs it.

In our electronic world, the master version is the actual Employee table in the company's database and the copy is a *snapshot* of all the records in this table. This high level of optimistic concurrency, called row versioning, can be obtained since the records in the table don't need exclusive locks, as SQL Server will only check the row if any changes have taken place since the transaction started.

Our next exercise will take a brief look at how to initiate row versioning, better known as Snapshot Isolation, in a transaction.

READER NOTE: *Read the remaining information in this section and examine the sample code with output in the figures provided before proceeding. It is suggested to execute the finished code samples within a few seconds of each other and compare the results with those shown in the following figures.*

Before starting this exercise, close all open query windows. During the following examples DO NOT CLOSE any query windows until reaching the next section ~ Lab 12.2: Optimistic Concurrency.

Let's begin this exercise by opening a new query window in the JProCo database context. Before doing anything else, we need to determine what the current Isolation Level is for the database. This can easily be accomplished with a DBCC command named USEROPTIONS. Run this code and look at the value returned for the Isolation Level row (READ COMMITTED).

```
DBCC USEROPTIONS
```

	Set Option	Value
9	ansi_warnings	SET
10	ansi_padding	SET
11	ansi_nulls	SET
12	concat_null_yields_null	SET
13	isolation level	READ COMMITTED

13 rows

Figure 12.11 The DBCC USEROPTIONS command can display the current Isolation Level.

Having already learned that the default Isolation Level setting is 'READ COMMITTED', we are happy to see this value is confirmed in the unmodified JProCo database.

Our next step is to open a second query window in the JProCo database context and write an explicit transaction that will contain a query that will return all fields in the Employee table that are equal to EmpID 3. Include an UPDATE statement to SET the value of 'Tran' to the LastName field for EmpID 3. Separate the query and the UPDATE statement with a WAITFOR DELAY of 15 seconds. Make sure the transaction is committed when it completes. Use this code as an example.

```
BEGIN TRAN
  SELECT * FROM Employee
  WHERE EmpID = 3

  WAITFOR DELAY '00:00:15'

  UPDATE dbo.Employee
  SET LastName = 'Tran'
  WHERE EmpID = 3
COMMIT TRAN
```

Once this code is written we will need to open a third query window to the JProCo database context that updates the LastName field to 'Update' for EmpID 3 in the Employee table. Use the code shown here as an example.

```
UPDATE dbo.Employee
SET LastName = 'Update'
WHERE EmpID = 3
```

Run the explicit transaction from the second query window and after a few seconds run the UPDATE statement in the third query window. Return to the SPID with the explicit transaction and wait the remainder of the 15 seconds for the result set to be returned. Which UPDATE statement will be committed?

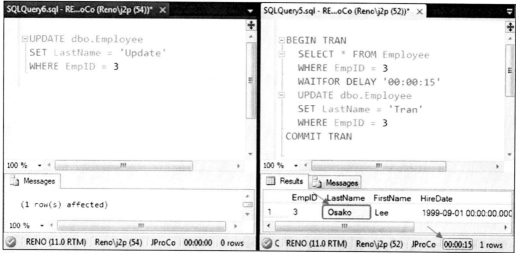

Figure 12.12 Which UPDATE statement committed? LastName = Tran or Update?

The new value for the LastName field will be 'Tran'. Here is a brief outline for how SQL Server managed the explicit and the auto commit transactions.

- The explicit transaction starts.
- SQL Server encounters the SELECT statement and issues a shared lock.
- 8 seconds later, the auto commit transaction starts and is assigned an exclusive lock on the Employee table and the data is committed.
- After 15 seconds the UPDATE statement in the explicit transaction runs and is given an exclusive lock on the Employee table and the data is committed to storage at the end of the transaction.

It is always a good idea to verify what we believed to have happened in a transaction, so let's run a query to show all the fields for EmpID 3 in the Employee table. Since this already exists in the explicit transaction, we can comment out all the code surrounding our query and then run it (Figure 12.13).

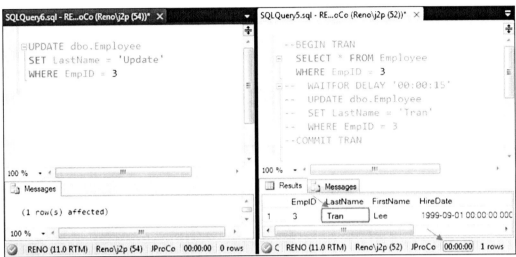

Figure 12.13 Verifying the new value for the LastName field is 'Tran'.

As expected, the value committed for the LastName field for EmpID 3 is 'Tran'.

The previous example behaved as if it was using pessimistic concurrency, because the Isolation Level is still set to READ COMMITTED. We can open a fourth query window to set the Isolation Level to SNAPSHOT followed by the same explicit transaction we used in the second query window of this exercise.

```
SET TRANSACTION ISOLATION LEVEL
    SNAPSHOT
GO

BEGIN TRAN
    SELECT * FROM Employee
    WHERE EmpID = 3
    WAITFOR DELAY '00:00:15'

    UPDATE dbo.Employee
    SET LastName = 'Tran'
    WHERE EmpID = 3
COMMIT TRAN
```

Run the code in the fourth query window and then wait a few seconds before running the UPDATE statement in the third query window. What will the result set be after these two transactions complete? To find out, look at Figure 12.14.

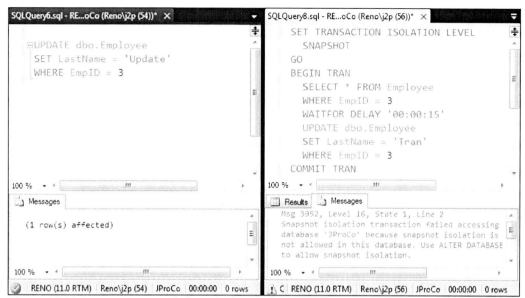

Figure 12.14 An error message is issued when setting the Isolation Level to SNAPSHOT.

If it is difficult to read the error message shown in Figure 12.14, please take a look at Figure 12.15 for an enlarged version of the same message.

```
Messages
Msg 3952, Level 16, State 1, Line 2
Snapshot isolation transaction failed accessing database 'JProCo' because
snapshot isolation is not allowed in this database.
Use ALTER DATABASE to allow snapshot isolation.
                                                              0 rows
```

Figure 12.15 Error message from Figure 12.14 is enlarged to make it easier to read.

Why did we get an error message for this transaction? By reading the message carefully, we can see that the last line states it is necessary to use an ALTER DATABASE command to allow (enable) snapshot isolation.

Before we can enable this option, it will be necessary to either close all the open query windows, or change their database context to master before running the ALTER DATABASE command shown here in a new query window.

```
ALTER DATABASE JProCo
SET ALLOW_SNAPSHOT_ISOLATION ON
GO
```

Either reset the database context in each of the query windows to JProCo, or if the windows have been closed, rewrite the code instructions for the third and fourth query windows shown above (set the database context to JProCo).

Now run the code for the explicit transaction, followed a few seconds later by the auto commit transaction. Will both transactions execute and commit correctly, or will we receive another error?

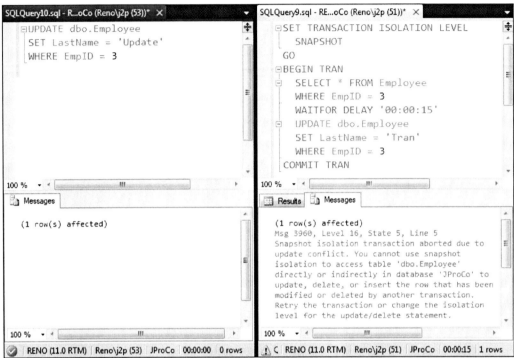

Figure 12.16 An error message appears when trying to UPDATE the same record twice with SNAPSHOT ISOLATION property set to ON.

If it is difficult to read the error message shown in Figure 12.16, please take a look at Figure 12.17 for an enlarged version of the same message.

```
Messages
(1 row(s) affected)
Msg 3960, Level 16, State 5, Line 5
Snapshot isolation transaction aborted due to update conflict. You cannot use
snapshot isolation to access table 'dbo.Employee' directly or indirectly in
database 'JProCo' to update, delete, or insert the row that has been modified
or deleted by another transaction.
Retry the transaction or change the isolation level for the
update/delete statement.
                                                                        0 rows
```

Figure 12.17 Enlarged version of the error message shown in Figure 12.16.

In Figure 12.16 we see a different error message than the one in Figure 12.14. So what caused this newest error message? Is one of our settings incorrect? No. This error is produced because when the Transaction Snapshot Level is set to SNAPSHOT, it is using optimistic concurrency.

A SNAPSHOT reflects the fact that all queries in the transaction see the same version, or snapshot, of the database, based on the state of the database at the moment in time the transaction begins. No locks are acquired on the underlying data rows or data pages in a snapshot transaction. This will permit other transactions to execute without being blocked by a prior uncompleted transaction.

Transactions that modify data do not block transactions that read data, and transactions that read data do not block transactions that write data, as is the case with the READ COMMITTED Isolation Level. This non-blocking behavior also significantly reduces the likelihood of deadlocks for complex transactions.

However, the SNAPSHOT Isolation Level uses an optimistic concurrency model. If a snapshot transaction attempts to commit modifications to data that has changed since the transaction began, the transaction will roll back and an error message will be issued by SQL Server. This is what happened in our exercise.

Notice that the error message was not reached until after the WAITFOR DELAY time of 15 seconds had expired. This means that the auto commit UPDATE transaction setting the LastName field value for EmpID 3 to 'Update' was committed after the explicit transaction utilizing the SNAPSHOT Isolation Level had started. So, when the UPDATE statement in the explicit transaction was encountered, SQL Server recognized that this row had already been modified and immediately rolled back the transaction and issued an error message.

Remember, when using the SNAPSHOT optimistic concurrency model, it is designed to allow read and write transactions from interfering with each other, thus preventing most deadlocks. Whenever two write statements try to modify the same row after the transaction with the SNAPSHOT Isolation Level has started, SQL Server will immediately rollback the transaction and issue an error message.

Lab 12.2: Optimistic Concurrency

Lab Prep: Each lab has one or more Skill Checks. Start with Skill Check 1 and proceed until reaching the Points to Ponder section.

Before beginning this lab, verify that SQL Server 2012 is properly installed and operating. Before running the lab setup script for resetting the database (SQLQueries2012Vol3Chapter12.2Setup.sql), please make sure to close all query windows within SSMS. A simple way to assure all query windows are closed, is to exit out of SSMS, then open a new instance of SSMS, and lastly run the setup script.

Skill Check 1: Write a T-SQL statement that will use the dbBasics database context and then write the code that will instruct this database to use Optimistic Concurrency. Run the following code to display the results of this change. When complete, the results will resemble those in the following figure.

```
DBCC USEROPTIONS
```

	Set Option	Value
1	textsize	2147483647
2	language	us_english
3	dateformat	Mdy
4	datefirst	7
5	lock_timeout	-1
6	quoted_identifier	SET
7	arithabort	SET
8	ansi_null_dflt_on	SET
9	ansi_warnings	SET
10	ansi_padding	SET
11	ansi_nulls	SET
12	concat_null_yields_null	SET
13	isolation level	Snapshot

13 rows

Figure 12.18 Results of the dbBasics database being set to Optimistic Concurrency.

Answer Code: The T-SQL code to this lab can be found in the downloadable file named Lab12.2_OptimisticConcurrency.sql.

Points to Ponder - Optimistic Concurrency

1. DBCC USEROPTIONS will show the Isolation Level of a SPID.

2. Both optimistic and pessimistic concurrency control were introduced with SQL Server 2000 and have been available with each version thereafter.

3. SQL Server 2005 introduced a new SNAPSHOT Isolation Level that can be used for optimistic concurrency (also known as row versioning).

4. Pessimistic concurrency control locks resources for the entire duration of a transaction until it is committed, rolled back, or killed.

5. Optimistic concurrency control (OCC) allows transactions to run without placing an exclusive lock on any resources.

6. OCC decreases the possibility of blocking transactions.

7. In OCC, if the check reveals a conflicting modification then it rolls back, or tries to restart the transaction.

8. OCC is ideal for environments where transaction throughput needs are high and contention for data conflicts are very rare.

9. Having a high contention in OCC can hurt performance since repeatedly restarting transactions is more costly to overhead than a pessimistic lock.

10. There are three stages to an OCC transaction:

    1) **Begin** - A Timestamp is recorded so we know how current this change is. Every transaction gets a timestamp and sequence number.

    2) **Modify** - Reads the database values, makes the modification, and saves the change.

    3) **Validate** - If a change by another connection was made after it began, but before the Modify was done then this change needs to be rolled back or started from scratch.

11. Issuing a SET TRANSACTION ISOLATION LEVEL statement in a stored procedure for the object returns control to the original level.

12. Enabling snapshot isolation is a two-step process.

READ_COMMITTED_SNAPSHOT

It is important to not confuse SET READ_COMMITTED_SNAPSHOT ON with a transactional Isolation Level, as it creates a snapshot or read-only version of the actual database it is applied to. This means all the data and results from previous queries are stored in a temporary database maintained by SQL Server and kept separate from the live version of the database.

This can be very helpful because the data source for queries that only need to read (SELECT statements) is different from the data source used by transactions that need to write data (INSERT, UPDATE, DELETE, MERGE), as shown in Figure 12.19.

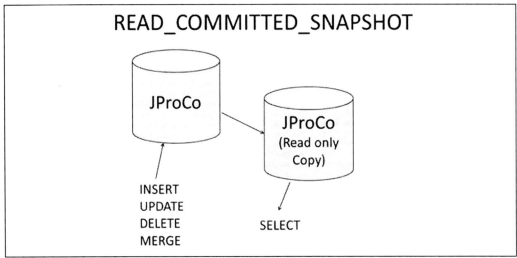

Figure 12.19 An illustration showing how the READ_COMMITTED_SNAPSHOT option behaves when its property is set to ON.

Here are two tests to identify whether or not a particular command that affects concurrency is actually a transactional Isolation Level or not. Each test determines how the command is implemented.

o   If it begins with the SET TRANSACTION ISOLATION LEVEL command then it is definitely a transactional Isolation Level setting.

o   If it begins with an ALTER DATABASE command then it is an option that is being applied to the entire database and not to an individual transaction. *These settings can only be applied when no other connections are open to the database it is being run against.*

Even though SNAPSHOT is an Isolation Level, it requires having the specific property set with an ALTER DATABASE command implementing the optimistic concurrency model it will use during the transaction.

Setting READ_COMMITTED_SNAPSHOT

Whenever we set a property for the SNAPSHOT Isolation Level, it is important to remember that all connections to the database that the ALTER DATABASE command is run against must be closed prior to setting the property. This is necessary for SQL Server to ensure that all resources are available while it is taking a snapshot of the database and its objects.

With this in mind, we simply plan to set the READ_COMMITTED_SNAPSHOT property, by first closing all connections to the database we need a snapshot of and then use the ALTER DATABASE command to implement the property. After the property has been set, we simply set the transactional Isolation Level to SNAPSHOT for our explicit transaction and everything will work fine.

Before we run everything the right way, suppose we intentionally reverse these two steps and test how SQL Server responds. Make sure to review the following READER NOTE before proceeding with the exercise.

READER NOTE: *Read the remaining information in this section and examine the sample code with output in the figures provided before proceeding. It is suggested to execute the finished code samples within a few seconds of each other and compare the results with those shown in the following figures.*

Before starting this exercise, close all open query windows. During the following examples DO NOT CLOSE any query windows until reaching the next section ~ Lab 12.3: READ_COMMITTED_SNAPSHOT.

Let's begin this exercise by opening a new query window in the JProCo database context. Before doing anything else, we need to make sure the Isolation Level is set to READ COMMITTED. Run this code to make sure it is set correctly.

```
SET TRANSACTION ISOLATION LEVEL
   READ COMMITTED
GO

DBCC USEROPTIONS
```

	Set Option	Value
9	ansi_warnings	SET
10	ansi_padding	SET
11	ansi_nulls	SET
12	concat_null_yields_null	SET
13	isolation level	READ COMMITTED
	13 rows	

Figure 12.20 The DBCC USEROPTIONS command can display the current Isolation Level.

Our next step is to open a second query window and write the code necessary to set the database context to JProCo. Execute the code shown here immediately.

```
USE JProCo
GO
```

Once this code is written we will need to open a third query window to set the READ_COMMITTED_SNAPSHOT property to ON for the JProCo database. Go ahead and execute this code immediately.

```
ALTER DATABASE JProCo
SET READ_COMMITTED_SNAPSHOT ON
```

Notice that this ALTER DATABASE command for the JProCo database appears to run for an excessively long time, especially since this database is relatively small (only a few thousand records in total). SQL Server does not issue any error messages to inform us that something is wrong, so what are we to do? The first thing we should do whenever an ALTER DATABASE command does not seem to be executing in a timely manner is use the Activity Monitor or a system stored procedure, such as sp_who, to determine what SPID number is blocking our connection from succeeding.

Once we have located all of the blocking SPIDs, all we need to do is open another query window to issue a KILL command with the appropriate blocking SPID number(s) as the target (Figure 12.21).

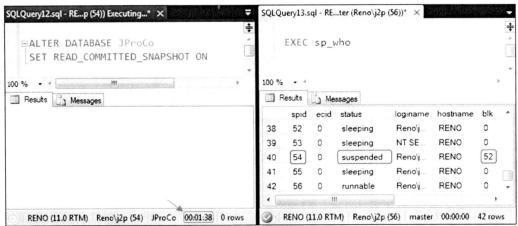

Figure 12.21 Using the sp_who system sproc to find the SPID blocking the ALTER DATABASE command from successfully completing.

When all the blocking SPIDs have been closed we can return to the second query window and observe that the ALTER DATABASE command (Figure 12.22) has now run successfully!

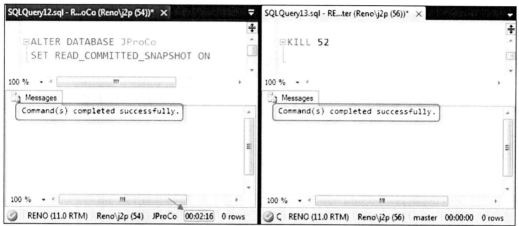

Figure 12.22 After issuing the KILL 52 command the ALTER DATABASE command in SPID #54 can be successfully completed.

Summary: Transaction Isolation Level

Many students have asked if there is a way to quickly reference the different types of Transaction Isolation Levels and how they affect *dirty reads*, *Non-repeatable reads* and *phantom reads*. To satisfy their question, I have put together the following table that quickly and easily summarizes the five Isolation Levels.

Table 12.2 Summary of the effects for implementing all five Isolation Levels used by SQL Server.

Isolation Level	Dirty Read	Non-repeatable read	Phantom Read
READ UNCOMMITTED	Yes	Yes	Yes
READ COMMITTED	No	Yes	Yes
REPEATABLE READ	No	No	Yes
SNAPSHOT	No	No	No
SERIALIZABLE	No	No	No

Lab 12.3: READ_COMMITTED_SNAPSHOT

Lab Prep: Each lab has one or more Skill Checks. Start with Skill Check 1 and proceed until reaching the Points to Ponder section.

Before beginning this lab, verify that SQL Server 2012 is properly installed and operating. Before running the lab setup script for resetting the database (SQLQueries2012Vol3Chapter12.3Setup.sql), please make sure to close all query windows within SSMS. An open query window pointing to a database context can lock that database preventing it from updating when the script is executing. A simple way to assure all query windows are closed, is to exit out of SSMS, then open a new instance of SSMS, and lastly run the setup script.

Skill Check 1: Write the T-SQL code to ALTER the dbBasics database to turn on the READ_COMMITTED_SNAPSHOT property.

Answer Code: The T-SQL code to this lab can be found in the downloadable file named Lab12.3_READ_COMMITTED_SNAPSHOT.sql.

Points to Ponder - READ_COMMITTED_SNAPSHOT

1. SET READ_COMMITTED_SNAPSHOT ON is not a transactional Isolation Level, as it creates a snapshot or read-only database of the current results and is separate from a live database.

2. With READ_COMMITTED_SNAPSHOT, when running a SELECT query, it reads from a read-only copy of the database, but when updating the database, the changes go to the live database and the change is copied back to the read-only database.

3. When setting the READ_COMMITTED_SNAPSHOT there must be no other connections to the database.

4. The following code needs exclusive access to the database in order to run:

    ALTER DATABASE *DBName* SET
    READ_COMMITTED_SNAPSHOT ON;

5. To force this exclusive action, one of the following steps might be necessary:

    o ALTER DATABASE myDB
       SET SINGLE_USER WITH ROLLBACK IMMEDIATE;

    o ALTER DATABASE myDB
       SET READ_COMMITTED_SNAPSHOT ON;

    o ALTER DATABASE myDB
       SET MULTI_USER;

Chapter Glossary

ALLOW_SNAPSHOT_ISOLATION: This enables the ability for storing row versions for optimistic concurrency.

Concurrency: Allows multiple operations to take place at the same time to the same object or database.

Dirty Read: The visibility of a query to a record in the intermediate state that has not been, or may not be committed.

Non-repeatable read: A potential concurrency problem where a record is retrieved twice in a transaction and the values within are different between reads.

Optimistic Concurrency: A concurrency control system that believes most transactions do not interfere with each other and does not use locking. It instead detects conflicts with versioning. Conflicts are detected instead of blocked by locking.

Pessimistic Concurrency: A concurrency control system that locks all transactions even if there is no chance of another transaction interfering. All transactions are locked at some level.

REPEATABLE READ: A pessimistic Isolation Level that deals with the concurrency problem of a Non-repeatable read.

READ COMMITTED: A pessimistic Isolation level that makes sure you do not get any uncommitted reads. This is the default Isolation Level for SQL Server.

READ_COMMITTED_SNAPSHOT: This creates a read-only copy of the database to provide to separate read transactions from write transactions.

READ UNCOMMITTED: The lowest level of pessimistic Isolation level that allows the reading of uncommitted data or dirty reads.

SERIALIZABLE: The highest level of pessimistic Isolation Level that prevents all forms of concurrency problems but does the greatest amount of locking.

SNAPSHOT: Optimistic Isolation level for SQL Server that uses row versioning to improve performance by eliminating the need for blocking scenarios created by locks. Enable this to use an optimistic concurrency level.

Review Quiz - Chapter Twelve

1.) When you read a record in the Intermediate State it is called what?

O a. An early read.

O b. A late read.

O c. A dirty read.

O d. A clean read.

2.) If you increase the Isolation Level, what effect does it have on concurrency?

O a. Greater Isolation Level allows greater concurrency.

O b. Greater Isolation Level allows less concurrency.

O c. Greater Isolation Level has no effect on concurrency.

3.) What is the default Isolation Level for SQL Server?

O a. READ COMMITTED

O b. READ UNCOMMITTED

O c. REPEATABLE READ

O d. SNAPSHOT

4.) If your Isolation Level is set to READ COMMITTED what concurrency problem does that not prevent?

O a. Dirty reads.

O b. Non-repeatable reads.

5.) What is the lowest Isolation Level for Pessimistic concurrency?

O a. READ COMMITTED

O b. READ UNCOMMITTED

O c. REPEATABLE READ

O d. SNAPSHOT

6.) Which type of concurrency does not use locks?

O a. Optimistic

O b. Pessimistic

7.) Which is true about the best time to use optimistic versus pessimistic concurrency? (choose two)

    ☐ a. Use pessimistic for environments where transaction throughput is high but data contention conflicts are very rare.

    ☐ b. Use optimistic for environments where transaction throughput is high but data contention conflicts are very rare.

    ☐ c. Use pessimistic for environments where data contention conflicts from heavy updates are frequent.

    ☐ d. Use optimistic for environments where data contention conflicts from heavy updates are frequent.

8.) Which of the following Isolation Levels is using optimistic concurrency?

    O a. READ COMMITTED

    O b. READ UNCOMMITTED

    O c. REPEATABLE READ

    O d. SNAPSHOT

9.) How do you check your current Isolation Level for your SPID in SQL Server?

    O a. DBCC USEROPTIONS

    O b. DBCC OPENTRAN

10.) You have a staging table named dbo.refunds. 90% of the DML statements run against this table are UPDATE statements and the remaining activity is INSERT statements. A nightly job updates all records older than 30 days into the data warehouse. What type of concurrency would be best for this table?

    O a. Optimistic

    O b. Pessimistic

11.) Which of the following is not an Isolation Level?

    O a. READ UNCOMMITTED

    O b. REPEATABLE READ

    O c. READ_COMMITTED_SNAPSHOT

    O d. SNAPSHOT

Answer Key

1.) There is no such thing as an early, clean or late read, making (a), (b) and (d) all incorrect. Any data that is being read while in the Intermediate State is called a dirty read, so (c) is the right answer.

2.) A higher (greater) Isolation Level will always reduce concurrency as SQL Server is ensuring the data inside the transaction is protected and consistent. This means fewer transactions can have access to the resources at the same time, making both (a) and (c) the wrong answers. Since a higher Isolation Level always reduces concurrency, (b) is the correct answer.

3.) The READ UNCOMMITTED, REPEATABLE READ and SNAPSHOT Isolation Levels must all be manually set to run with a specific transaction, so (b), (c) and (d) are incorrect answers. The default Isolation Level setting for a database is READ COMMITTED, making (a) the correct answer.

4.) The default Isolation Level for SQL Server (READ COMMITTED) will prevent dirty reads, so (a) is incorrect. The READ COMMITTED Isolation Level will allow Non-repeatable and phantom reads, so (b) is correct.

5.) SNAPSHOT is an optimistic concurrency Isolation Level, so (d) is wrong. REPEATABLE READ is a pessimistic concurrency Isolation Level, but it only allows phantom reads, so (c) is wrong. READ COMMITTED is a pessimistic concurrency Isolation Level, but it allows both Non-repeatable reads and phantom reads, making (a) incorrect. Since the pessimistic concurrency Isolation Level READ UNCOMMITTED allows all three types of reads (dirty, Non-repeatable, phantom), (b) is the correct answer.

6.) Pessimistic concurrency is able to maintain data in a stable and secure manner by placing exclusive locks on any transaction that is modifying a resource, which makes (b) the wrong answer. Optimistic concurrency does not have any exclusive locks on transaction resources, so (a) is correct.

7.) Pessimistic concurrency is best in environments where throughput does not need to be high and data contention conflicts are very likely, making (a) the wrong answer. Since optimistic concurrency does not issue any exclusive locks on a transaction, this model should be avoided in situations where heavy updates or modifications to a resource are imminent, making (d) an incorrect choice. Since optimistic concurrency is ideally suited in environments that demand high throughput with very rare occurrences of data contention and pessimistic concurrency is very well suited to environments that have very high levels of updates and modifications to resources, both (b) and (c) are the correct answer.

8.) READ COMMITTED, READ UNCOMMITTED and REPEATABLE READ are pessimistic concurrency Isolation Levels, making (a), (b) and (c) incorrect answers. SNAPSHOT is an optimistic concurrency Isolation Level, so (d) would be the correct answer.

9.) DBCC OPENTRAN lists many data points, although the Isolation Level is not one of them, making (b) the wrong answer. DBCC USEROPTIONS lists many specific settings including the current transaction Isolation Level, so (a) would be the correct answer.

10.) The environment described in this question is made entirely of transactions that are modifying the resources it uses making (a) optimistic concurrency an exceptionally bad answer. Pessimistic concurrency is ideally suited to environments that are primarily made up of transactions that modify resources, so (b) is definitely the correct answer.

11.) READ UNCOMMITTED and REPEATABLE READ are examples of pessimistic concurrency Isolation Levels and SNAPSHOT is an example of an optimistic concurrency Isolation Level, making (a), (b) and (d) incorrect answers. READ_COMMITTED_SNAPSHOT is a command used to set a property to ON or OFF for the optimistic concurrency Isolation Level, SNAPSHOT, and can only be issued with an ALTER DATABASE command for the target database, making (c) the correct answer

Bug Catcher Game

To play the Bug Catcher game, run the SQLQueries2012Vol3BugCatcher12.pps file from the BugCatcher folder of the companion files. These files can be obtained from the www.Joes2Pros.com website.

[THIS PAGE INTENTIONALLY LEFT BLANK]

Chapter 13. Summary SQL Queries Volume 3

Have you ever seen one of the car racing movies where the sports cars have nitrous oxide boost? What do these nitrous boosters do? Without getting too technical, the nitrous oxide boost is used by the driver when the car's performance needs to be taken to the next level. When racing on a straight stretch of road the nitrogen boost can be initiated for a quick burst of speed and power. With ten cars on the track approaching the final stretch and the fourth driver realizes there are six cars behind and only three up ahead what is he going to do? He ignites the nitrous oxide boost launching him and his car past the competitors to win the race.

However, if nitrous oxide is such a magical thing, why not keep it on at all times? Nitrous can only be injected in short bursts and not continuously. There is not only a limited amount of nitrous available running the engine at that level for an extended period of time, but it can also cause the engine to fail! Even if we assume however, there is an unlimited supply of nitrous oxide and the engine is fail-proof, there is another issue. Every race car driver knows that you have to back off the power and slow down into the turns to keep from crashing the car. The boost is only good for going fast in a straight line. It is better to enter the turn at the proper angle, direction, and speed or the car will be thrown off the road and the racer disqualified.

What we covered

Nitrous boost in a movie reminds me of creative tuning. Creative tuning is very similar if you think about it. When I see people doing creative tuning I see them making indexes and thinking that everything is better. Others get faster hardware and think their problems are over. Or maybe with the correct maintenance along the way, performance will be optimal. Performance tuning tips and tricks are all like the nitrogen boost. We need to understand when, how and what context to use them. Many of these things do help, but not for every single scenario.

Here is an example: What happens when there is a lot of NULL data in a column? When you query the data, are you going to get optimal performance? Or if there is an empty value in the column are you going to get optimal performance? Both of these scenarios have different outcomes. Certain kinds of indexes work in some situations but sometimes not so well at other times. It will help to understand the best solution even if there is no right or wrong answer. To get there we need to understand the whole situation: query pattern, what's in other columns, and business needs. When we understand the background then we can do proper tuning.

In this book we taught proper tuning – given the right and optimal data schemas available, and the various data table actions that we should be familiar with. It is as if we have nitrous boost, but didn't know if the car's engine is up to using it. With performance tuning, straight is not always the goal. There are various data types such as XML, special data types, and spatial data. Using indexes is like a nitrous boost. Because of this we have to thoroughly analyze it first. We have to know where it can and can't be applied. This is exactly what we have learned in this book.

Here is a good thing to consider: a friend once told me he placed second in a race so I congratulated him. He then told me there were only two people racing. In performance tuning we face the same thing. We need to know how many queries are running and returning data, is the server busy or not busy, or you may need to know what kind of Isolation Levels there are. From this chapter, we understand the right way to write queries, and the most efficient way to tune them. Up next: with all these tools in hand, how do we do things right? Now it is time to understand the car properly to see if it is ready for the nitrous oxide.

What's Next

SQL Queries 2012 Joes 2 Pros Volume 4 will switch gears and talk about very important concepts about objects in SQL Server. It goes beyond tables, indexes, and procedures. There are other objects with their own ways to contribute to the database. We will learn about constraints, triggers, functions, and views. Stored procedures are another topic which we will go into greater depth. There will be a lot of new 2012 improvements to learn with new time functions and new logical functions.

Combining the knowledge so far of tuning queries with what we just learned about, we will be able to build a robust application which will provide a variety of features and optimal performance. We will be learning about how to avoid cursors and use set theory, as well as dynamic SQL and when to avoid it. The book will familiarize readers with common mistakes and errors to avoid. After book #4, we will be able to confidently build an application.

INDEX

1

CPSIA information can be obtained at www.ICGtesting.com
Printed in the USA
BVOW02s2018170315

392101BV00011B/49/P